THEORY AND INTERPRETATION OF NARRATIVE
James Phelan, Peter J. Rabinowitz, and Robyn Warhol, Series Editors

NARRATIVE PATHS
African Travel in Modern Fiction and Nonfiction

KAI MIKKONEN

THE OHIO STATE UNIVERSITY PRESS · COLUMBUS

Copyright © 2015 by The Ohio State University.
All rights reserved.

Library of Congress Cataloging-in-Publication Data
Mikkonen, Kai.
　Narrative paths : African travel in modern fiction and nonfiction / Kai Mikkonen.
　　pages cm. — (Theory and interpretation of narrative) Includes bibliographical references and index.
　ISBN 978-0-8142-1274-5 (hardback) — ISBN 978-0-8142-9379-9 (cd-rom)
　1. Travelers' writings, European—History and criticism. 2. European fiction—History and criticism. 3. Narration (Rhetoric) 4. Postcolonialism in literature. 5. Africa—In literature. I. Title.
　PN56.T7M55 2015
　809'.93355—dc23
　　　　　　　　　　　　　　2014033910

ISBN 978-0-8142-5202-4
Cover design by Laurence J. Nozik
Text design by Juliet Williams
Type set in Adobe Minion Pro

9 8 7 6 5 4 3 2 1

CONTENTS

List of Illustrations ... vii

Acknowledgments ... ix

INTRODUCTION   Factual Places and Fictional Routes ... 1

PART I • NARRATING AND DESCRIBING WEST AFRICA

1 The Enchanted Arrival: Passage into West Africa in the Travel Writings of Blaise Cendrars, André Gide, and Graham Greene ... 41

2 The Rhetoric of the Mad African Forest in Joseph Conrad, Louis-Ferdinand Céline, and Graham Greene ... 69

3 Travel Narrative between Spatial Sequence and Open Consequence in Graham Greene's *Journey Without Maps* ... 88

PART II • TRAVEL WRITING AND THE NOVEL

4 The Immediacy of Reading: André Gide's Travel Fact and Travel Fictions ... 113

5 The Incongruous Worlds of Evelyn Waugh's Ethiopia ... 147

6 A Critique of the African Picturesque in Georges Simenon's Travel Reportages and Novels ... 183

PART III • INVENTIONS OF LIFE NARRATIVE

7 Virtual Genres in Pierre Loti's and Joseph Conrad's African Travel
   Diaries and Fiction   221

8 Out of Europe: The African Palimpsest in Michel Leiris's *L'Afrique fantôme* 240

9 Africanist Paradoxes of Storytelling in Karen Blixen's *Out of Africa*   266

IN CONCLUSION   Fiction, Colonial Travel Narrative, and the Allegorist   292

References   305
Index   317

LIST OF ILLUSTRATIONS

FIGURE 1   Map of Ubangi-Shari and Chad, showing André Gide's route
            between August 1925 and May 1926   52

FIGURE 2   Map of Liberia, showing Graham Greene's route in the
            spring of 1935   94

FIGURE 3   Map of East Africa, showing the places that Evelyn Waugh
            visited between October 1930 and March 1931   158–59

FIGURE 4   Fictional map from *Black Mischief* by Evelyn Waugh   164

FIGURE 5   Map of Georges Simenon's travel through Africa in the
            summer of 1932   184

FIGURE 6   Map of the River Congo from Norman Sherry's *Conrad's
            Western World,* showing Conrad's route from Boma to
            Stanley Falls and back between June and December 1890   230

FIGURE 7   Map of Mission Dakar-Djibouti (May 1931–February 1933)   243

FIGURE 8   The stork figure in the story "The Roads of Life" in Karen
            Blixen's *Out of Africa*   269

ACKNOWLEDGMENTS

THE IDEA for this book originated in the fall of 2002 when I had the opportunity to spend a month at the Finnish-African Cultural Centre Villa Karo in Grand-Popo, Benin. The many signs of the colonial era that I took note of in Benin and Togo inspired me to explore the ways in which the European travel writers perceived sub-Saharan Africa in the heyday of colonialism. I am grateful to the managers and the staff of Villa Karo, and the many local people, who made this eye-opening visit possible, as well as to my wife Alma for her company during our many memorable excursions in this region.

Without the three years I spent at the Helsinki Collegium for Advanced Studies in 2003–2006, this book would not have been written. It was a great privilege to focus on research for this time and benefit from discussions with stellar scholars from various fields in the humanities and other fields.

Many people have read parts of the book in the course of its development. In the early stages of the work, discussions with David Scott in Helsinki and Dublin, and David's insightful reactions to my work, encouraged me to pursue the project. I also owe debts of gratitude to a number of friends and colleagues in English Philology at the University of Helsinki. I must particularly acknowledge John Calton's helpful readings of earlier drafts of this work, his ideas about a possible title for the book, and his genuine interest in my research during the last years of the writing process. I am also thankful to Howard Sklar, Mark Shackleton, and Laurel Bush, a specialist of travel writing, from the same unit, for reading parts of the work and for their encouragement. Furthermore, I would like to express gratitude for the help that I have received from the University of Helsinki Language Centre while preparing conference papers or articles on this topic over the years. The Centre's hawkeyed proofreaders have included–with apologies to anybody I may have omitted–Glenda Dawn Goss, Nancy Seidel, and Marlene Broemer. I also wish to thank Alan Prohm for his stylistic comments in the beginning of this project. The many conferences where I have presented parts of this work are too numerous to mention, but I must acknowledge the tremendous importance of my colleagues' feedback on these occasions. In particular, I need to thank Françoise Lavocat for her co-operation in organizing the workshop "Transworld Travel" at the ICLA XIXth World Congress, Seoul, South Korea, in August 2010. The book has also greatly benefited from two courses on travel literature that I have given in comparative literature at the University of Helsinki in 2007 and 2012. I owe a great debt to my students whose questions, essays, and course diaries helped me to clarify my ideas.

I offer the most heartfelt thanks to the editors of the TIN series of The Ohio State University Press, Peter J. Rabinowitz and Robyn Warhol, and the two anonymous readers of this series, whose feedback has been the most helpful, generous, and encouraging that I have received in my academic career thus far. I also wish to express my gratitude to the editors of the OSU Press, Sandy Crooms, Lindsay Martin, Katie Gucer, and Tara Cyphers, for their invaluable assistance. Special thanks also to Brian Richardson for his encouragement and interest in my work.

Portions or earlier versions of Chapters 1, 2, 3, and 7 first appeared in the journals *Narrative* 15.3 (2007), *Comparative Critical Studies* 5.2–3 (2008), *Studies in Travel Writing* 15.1 (2011), and *Neohelicon* 40.2 (2013). I would like to express my gratitude to the publishers of these journals for their permission to reproduce this material here. I am also very grateful to the editors, Jim Phelan, Robert K. Weninger, and Tim Youngs, as well as Peter Hajdu and the anonymous peer-reviewers, for their precious feedback, stimulus, and support.

INTRODUCTION

Factual Places and Fictional Routes

> To speak of "literary traveling" is almost a tautology, so intimately are literature and travel implicated with each other. Any child senses this, and any adult recalling his childhood remembers moments when reading was revealed to be traveling.
> —Paul Fussell, *Abroad*

THE AMORPHOUS body of writing that is called "travel literature" has traditionally set up conflicting expectations of empirical objectivity and subjective experience. In other words, the travel account reveals not only the facts of some geographical place but also the personal significance of the travel experience. There is an inherent potential in travel writing to be thought of both in terms of a concrete spatial configuration and as happening to someone here and now, something that is unified in the traveller's personal experience and recounting. Some of the tension between the demands for empirical observation and the requirement that the travelogue capture the reader's attention through the personality of the writer's voice or the marvels in the description may also be reflected in the deep formal ties that have existed between travel literature and the modern novel. One of the most prominent members of the Russian formalist school of literary theory, Roman Jakobson, argued in his influential essay "The Dominant" (1935) that travelogues, as a kind of transitional genre and one form of intimate literature, served an important function in the development of modern fiction: "In certain periods such genres are evaluated as extraliterary and extrapoetical, while in other periods they may fulfil an important literary function because they comprise those elements which are about to be emphasised by belles lettres, whereas the canonical forms are deprived of these elements" (Jakobson 1987, 45). Jakobson's argument is based on the observation that the travelogue contributed in certain essential ways to the development of the Russian novel in the early nineteenth century. Among these contributions was, in particular, the intimate point of view of an individual who lives and travels in the contemporary world and makes subjective observations about that world.

Typically, travel writing conceptualizes space in terms of perpetual movement, while it organizes events and experiences around the temporal structure of the journey mediated through the traveller's consciousness. The same basic structure is common in various forms of modern fiction, such as the adventure or the realist novel, which is structured around a journey plot. Much of the narrative potential of travel lies in the fact that we recognize in it temporal and spatial structures that call for narration. The different stages of travel—departure, voyage, and return—provide the narrative with basic temporal structures that make the reader expect certain things to happen.[1] Furthermore, in the history of the modern novel, travel writing, and especially the accounts of travels to distant lands, has helped to shape the genre in terms of a credible foreign milieu and the description of foreign cultures.[2] In his *Travel Literature and the Evolution of the Novel* (1983), Percy G. Adams has demonstrated how such central characteristics and expectations of travel writing as realist *décor*, foreign settings, and minutely detailed description, were exported to fiction in the seventeenth and eighteenth century, thus making a central contribution to the origins of the modern novel. At this time, moreover, novels started mixing realist description with personal reflection in ways similar to travel literature (Adams 1983, 108–109; Chupeau 1977, 548; Bradburn 2011, 145–50).[3] The description of foreign places and exotic forms of life in travel literature thus helped, on the one hand, to authenticate the

---

1. In narrative and literary studies, it is a kind of commonplace to suggest, with Michel de Certeau, that "every story is a travel story—a spatial practice" (1984, 115). For instance, the chronotope of the road, and the metaphor of "the path of life" that it realizes, is a central feature in Mikhail Bakhtin's history of novelistic plot patterns and is especially important for what Bakhtin calls the adventure novel of everyday life (1981, 120). On the uses of the travel metaphor in narrative theory, and the implications of the conceptual metaphor of NARRATIVE IS TRAVEL, see Mikkonen 2007a. On the same conceptual metaphor, see also Bradburn 2011.

2. We have to keep in mind, however, that perhaps the most prototypical form of travel writing is not a narrative in itself but a travel journal and, furthermore, that travel writing often prioritizes description instead of narration.

3. For Adams, both the literary travel story and the modern novel are based on an "imaginative reshaping of reality" (1983, 134), by which he means that the two genres are produced through "a conflict and an alliance between realism and romance," or between truth claims and imagination (1983, 108–9).

emerging genre of the modern realist novel while, on the other hand, the distant and little known regions that were described in travel literature inspired the novelists to create more credible fictional foreign worlds or invent new worlds more freely (Adams 1983, 147). We can, for instance, think of *Robinson Crusoe* (1719), in which Daniel Defoe used Alexander Selkirk's true story and other actual travel accounts as his source material; Tobias Smollett's *The Expedition of Humphry Clinker* (1771) where the author's own travel experiences in Scotland, France, and Italy provide much of the novel's plot; or, as an example of travel writing that is heavily indebted to the novel, Laurence Sterne's *A Sentimental Journey* (1768), famous for its episodic descriptions of places and encounters on the road, based on the author's travels through France and Italy. Furthermore, Swift's *Gulliver's Travels* (1726, 1735), by parodying the descriptions and reports issued by travellers, explores the similarity between the travel story and the modern novel, both based on an "imaginative reshaping of reality" (Adams 1983, 134).[4]

When fiction and travel writing were collated and juxtaposed in eighteenth-century European writing, their mutual influence revealed something of the nature of the forces—such as the conflicting requirements of objectivity and subjectivity, truthfulness and personality, and the shared interest in creating a sense of a world and telling a good story—that have given rise to the continuous conversions and transformations discernible between the two genres.

In the early twentieth-century context of French and English literatures, which will be our focus in this study, travel writing and the novel again exerted an influence on each other to an extent that deserves the attention of historians of both the modern novel and travel writing. This book will investigate the interaction between travel writing, journal keeping, and fiction in the works of a group of late nineteenth-century and early twentieth-century European writers, who visited, travelled, or lived in sub-Saharan Africa. They include the French writers Pierre Loti, Louis-Ferdinand Céline, André Gide, Michel Leiris, and Georges Simenon, the Swiss writer Blaise Cendrars, and four authors writing in English: Joseph Conrad, Graham Greene, Evelyn Waugh, and Karen Blixen, also known in the English-speaking world by her pseudonym Isak Dinesen. Besides the works of Loti and Conrad, and some of the later works by Greene, Waugh, and Blixen, this book will concentrate

---

4. Historically speaking, the category of a "literary travel narrative" has accommodated many types of writing. Damrosch, for instance, has pointed out that a literary travel narrative can be a poetic record of an actual voyage, a semifictional account loosely based on the author's direct experience, a fictionalization of other people's travel books, or pure fiction disguised as a real-life travelogue, such as *Gulliver's Travels* (Damrosch 2009, 95–96).

on works that were published in the period between the First and the Second World War. The relationship between travel writing and fiction in this particular context has not received much serious critical attention to date. As we shall see in the course of this study, the interaction between travel writing, autobiographical narrative and journal keeping, and fiction (in particular the novel) raises a number of important questions about generic expectations and classification, referentiality, narrative authority and form, and modernist poetics, all questions that are relevant in terms of these authors' entire oeuvres.

The cross-generic exchanges and borrowings in this body of work—sometimes explicitly acknowledged, sometimes not—make it relevant to ask what happens when the boundary between travel writing and fiction is crossed, perhaps even more so when the general distinction between fiction and nonfiction seems to remain intact. Drawing on the findings of this research, this question can be divided into two parts: First, does the cross-generic borrowing affect the distinctiveness of the text's genre? Second, what happens to the autobiographical elements, or the expectation of truthfulness to a lived experience in a travel journal, when the text borrows some of its devices from fiction? Or what happens to the comfortable distinction between fact and fiction when a travel writer authenticates his observations by reference to fiction?[5]

As to the first question, the evidence of this study and its early twentieth-century modernist corpus strongly suggest that the effect of cross-generic borrowing is minimal in terms of a given work's general classification as either fiction or nonfiction. Once a travel narrative has been written, labeled, published, and read as nonfiction, and its referential nature has been established (i.e., it is based on some real-life journey), it remains in the general category of nonfiction regardless of any amount of borrowing of fictional techniques and conventions. As to the second part of the question, by contrast, the evidence of this study strongly suggests that there are myriad ways in which, on the one hand, fiction functions as an important frame in nonfiction travel writing and, on the other hand, nonfiction travel narrative plays an important role in fiction. The cross-generic borrowings from fiction in nonfiction highlight, for instance, how so much in modern travel and autobiographical writing falls outside the realm of what is verifiable, such as the author's thoughts, emotions, memories, attitudes, and evaluations, or the meaning that

---

5. In his application of possible-worlds semantics to literary studies, Lubomir Doležel has formulated the question of the interpenetration between fiction and history in a way that is relevant here: "what happens to the historical when it penetrates into fictional worlds and what happens to the fictional when it intrudes into historical worlds" (1999, 264).

the author gives to the events, places, and experiences of travel. As we shall see, fictional models and worlds serve as an important means for giving form to the traveller's thoughts, emotions, attitudes, and meanings.

In order to be able to make more justified claims about the forms of interaction between travel writing and fiction in early twentieth-century European literatures, we need to proceed by way of the particular, focusing on individual texts and their manipulation of generic conventions and expectations. Before moving to detailed case studies, however, I would like to summarize some of the general findings of this study concerning the main modes of interpenetration between nonfiction travel writing and fiction at this time.

These dimensions of interpenetration include, first of all, the situation of enunciation, by which I mean the importance of the traveller's (or a character's) mediating mind. The research shows that the centrality of the traveller's mediating consciousness, and the experiential frame of the journey, lends itself to comparison with typical devices of narrative fiction such as the use of the first-person narrative voice or the character's internal point of view. In certain of these cases, travel writing may also appropriate narrative devices from fiction so as to portray ambiguity of voice and perspective, for instance to create an impression of a travelling persona or to project a hypothetical audience, one of whose number is the actual reader.

Second, the research shows the importance of description and direct observation in early twentieth-century travel writing and fiction set in Africa. The authors often also foreground the language of their description as a problem, in that way drawing the reader's attention to the difficulty of closing the gap between the means of writing and the world described (i.e., how to relate to the foreign object of description).

Third, the research makes evident the ways in which knowledge of the mediation, which interpose between reality (the object of description, whenever it is not the traveller's own mind) and description in every corner of sub-Saharan Africa, highlights the bookish memory of voyage, especially when a modern writer travels expressly in order to write about the travel experience. This knowledge of mediation, the circulation of cultural givens concerning sub-Saharan Africa, and the traveller's sense of belatedness with regard to the places that he or she visits, is communicated equally in these writers' fiction and nonfiction. The various citations and references to or interpretations of fiction that are embedded in their travel writing perform a great variety of important functions, from affirming the reality of one's experience (possibly in contrast with the external reality) to undermining someone else's impressions, to blotting out uncomfortable aspects of the travel experience (or even accentuating some aspects of it), to creating a sense of contiguity between actual and fictional worlds. The emphasis on the bookish nature of the journey, which is also reflected in the frequent description of acts of reading during the journey, reveals in many of these examples the impact of earlier descriptions, either factual or fictional, that must be dealt with.

Fourth, the issue of "narrativisation," that is, the question of how to give narrative form to the travel experience, emerges particularly strongly in Graham Greene's travelogue and Karen Blixen's African memoir, both as a thematic and compositional consideration.[6] Greene examines, in his *Journey Without Maps* (1936), the difference between the shape of his experience and the shape of narrative. In Blixen's African memoir, the form of her book reflects the central theme of how to find a narrative shape in one's life. Specifically, the story "The Roads of Life" (1937) suggests that stories might reveal a pattern in life (or destiny) but that this pattern can only be expressed indirectly through suggestion. In Michel Leiris's African travelogue (1934), likewise, the problem of how to turn the travel experience into a narrative, or how to analyze the self through writing and journal-keeping, is highly relevant. Leiris's, as well as Gide's and Greene's, interest in *Heart of Darkness* (1902) may also be partly explained by way of Conrad's focus on narrative order and shape in his novella, due to the text's layered and self-conscious narrative structure. The scene of found books and "unreadable" signs in the jungle in *Heart of Darkness* also raises the question how to give narrative form to such signs of life. The crucial features of narrative form—a temporal sequencing of events, causal connection, and the experiential frame or experientiality—will be discussed at greater length in Chapter 3. Beyond recognizing such traits as being characteristic of narratives, however, the concept of narrativisation emphasizes the act of reading and interpreting some text *qua* narrative, be it a fiction or nonfiction, literary or nonliterary narrative.

Fifth, and finally, my analysis of Loti's and Conrad's travel journals and African fictions highlights the importance of the notion of virtual genres. This notion involves a little-studied but essential problem of genre relations pertaining to all elements of fiction that designate that the text has potential relevance as nonfiction or, conversely, everything in nonfiction narratives that implies that the story could have been told, or the description could have been written, as fiction. The analyses show, more precisely, how certain narrative and rhetorical strategies in Loti's and Conrad's fictions raise the (speculative) question of the generic classification of these texts as fiction, and suggest that alternatives may be possible. A given text's virtual but unrealized genre is, in

---

6. "Narrativisation" is Monika Fludernik's redefinition of Jonathan Culler's strategy of naturalization: "the reading of texts as narrative, as constituting narrativity in the reading process" or the "act of imposing narrativity" to a text (Fludernik 1996, 20, 34).

these cases, emphasized by the way in which the travel journal is appropriated in fiction as a kind of laboratory for potential fictions. Equally, fiction may serve not only as an authority or a source of information for travel writing, but also as its potential and unrealized genre, and even a kind of conceptual model. Gide's reading of *Heart of Darkness* as an accurate description of African reality; Leiris's idea of a Conradian story in his travel journal; Blixen's use of fictional stories in her memoir and description of fictional characters coming alive at her farm; Waugh's depiction of Ethiopia as a unique space of potentiality and possible worlds; Greene's literary portraits and caricatures in his travelogue; and Simenon's ironic projection of a narrative audience all point to the potential in the genre of travel writing to be something else, that is, fiction. More precisely, what is involved in these cases, is the potential in fiction to reveal the experiential reality to the reader and, consequently, the potential in nonfiction travel writing and life writing to be as powerful as any fiction, for instance, in creating and evoking a sense of a personal voice, a private experience, or a foreign world, or fusing observations of the African realities with imagination.

The Porous but Insistent Frontier between Fiction and Nonfiction

Despite the many intergeneric borrowings, and boundary crossings in these works, it is important to note that these neither deny nor conflate the general distinction between nonfiction travel writing and fiction. They do not include any straightforward attempts at challenging this boundary. We might recall other more unusual examples of classification and more ambivalent cases on the boundary between fiction and nonfiction, for instance some more recent literary travel books that focus on storytelling and transform real-life experiences into (partly fictional) anecdotes, such as Elias Canetti's *The Voices of Marrakesh* (1967), Bruce Chatwin's *In Patagonia* (1977), or V. S. Naipaul's *The Enigma of Arrival: A Novel in Five Sections* (1987).[7]

---

7. Alan Pryce-Jones's *People in the South* (1932), which combines a travel book and a collection of fictional stories set in South America, might also offer more unusual difficulties of classification in this respect (see Fussell 1980, 176). In addition, we may think of partly fictional travel accounts from the eighteenth century that Charles Batten discusses (1978, 21–24, 56–81), although Batten also claims that any sophisticated eighteenth-century reader of such works (Tobias Smollett's *The Expedition of Humphry Clinker*, for instance) could have intuited whether they were fiction or nonfiction (1978, 24); or literary hoaxes relating to Percy Adams's category of a "travel lie." As evidence of the latter, Adams has referred to cases of seventeenth- and eighteenth-century travel writing that led the (ordinary) reader to believe that the book was a true travel account despite the fictional or borrowed contents (1962, 1–18).

However, many of the examples included here do defy classification within the broad category of nonfiction, undermining for instance the distinction between an intimate journal and a travel book (*Voyage au Congo*, *Waugh in Abyssinia*), a collection of autobiographical poetry and a travel journal (*Feuilles de route*), a memoir and a travelogue (*Journey Without Maps*), ethnographic writing, travel journal and a self-analysis (*L'Afrique fantôme*), a journal and a notebook for fiction-writing (Loti's *Journal*), or a memoir and a collection of colonial (fictional and nonfictional) stories (*Out of Africa*). A further complication in generic classification is that Greene's published travelogue makes it clear that the text is the result of a writing process, where the original travel notes and journal are worked up into a narrative.

One reason for the relative stability of the distinction is that the relationship between fiction and nonfiction travel writing is never purely formal but is dependent on semantic and pragmatic oppositions and contextual criteria that have remained relatively constant at least since the eighteenth century. Suzanne Gearhart has argued, in reference to French Enlightenment classics such as Montesquieu and Diderot, that generic boundaries between fiction and nonfiction, in this case literature and historiography, can be porous but at the same time relatively stable. Her finding is consistent, in a general sense, with the types of generic interaction that concern us here. Gearhart argues, more precisely, that the relationship between literature and history in eighteenth-century France was one in which

> the two terms are seen as formally similar because each borrows from the other and each refuses to acknowledge the borrowing. And yet for the same reasons that history and fiction are not sovereign, they never completely merge. (1984, 28)

In the early twentieth-century context of European literature, cross-generic borrowings and interpenetration between travel writing and fiction became particularly common and self-conscious whenever the authors travelled with the intention of writing about their travels. The sub-Saharan experience was for many of these writers also a means of finding material for fiction. In this way, then, their fictions were contiguous with their nonfiction writing.

However, when these writers' travel writing and fiction refer to the same geographical places, and fiction and nonfiction seem to freely draw on each other's descriptions and conventions, they still continue to project worlds with a different reality status and truth value.[8] A partial explanation for this would

---

8. Speaking of Graham Greene, who hardly mentions his travel companion cousin Barbara in *Journey Without Maps*, Paul Fussell argues that "sometimes suppressions, or virtual sup-

be the semantic argument about the distinctiveness of fiction, namely, that in fiction references to existing realities are not bound to accuracy since nonfiction is referential and fiction is not.[9] In fiction, furthermore, gaps in information are created by the very act of world-making, and they are determined and manipulated by the narrative act itself, in contrast to the epistemological and verifiable gaps in historical worlds (Doležel 1988, 490–491; Doležel 1999, 258; Harshaw 1984, 232). The omissions in travel writing may be checked, evaluated and perhaps filled, at least in principle, against what we know about reality from existing historical documents. The relative independence from referentiality in fiction, or the freedom to be inaccurate, does not imply, however, that fiction would not have any referential properties or that it is not worth investigating the relation between the fictional world and the actual world.[10] In this study I will examine precisely this variety of distances between the actual world of travel writing, or other forms of autobiographical writing, and the fictional world that is created in a novel, a novella, or a short story.

Meanwhile, the contemporary pragmatic-contextual theories of fiction hold that a distinction between fictional and referential discourse cannot be made on the basis of semantic criteria or textual indices alone. Instead, these theories explain that this distinction is founded on our interpretation of the given text's context, including for instance the purpose for which the work is written (i.e., typically the author's intention), the generic operations of the work's means of representation, the generic expectations of its truth value, and the reader's knowledge of other relevant extratextual information.

With regard to nonfiction travel literature, for instance, the relation that a particular work has with other representations of the same geographical places and historical realities can be highly important in evaluating the accuracy of its descriptions. The travel writers often emphasize how their descriptions and experiences of a place are consistent with, complementary, or contrary to existing descriptions of the same travel destinations. In my case studies, the importance of generic expectations is also reflected in the reactions of certain

---

pression, are required less for social or political than for purely artistic reasons" (1980, 175–76). Tim Butcher has pointed out, however, how, in an early draft of Greene's travelogue, not only was Barbara Greene left out but Greene did not make any mention of himself either, preferring to use an alter ego called Trench (Butcher 2010a).

9. See, for instance, Cohn 1999, 15. Cohn defines what she calls the nonreferentiality of fiction as the principle according to which fiction *can* refer to the real world outside the text, "but it *need* not refer to it" (1999, 15). Furthermore, the nonreferentiality of fiction indicates that "references to the world outside the text are not bound to accuracy" and that fiction "does not refer *exclusively* to the real world outside the text" (ibid.).

10. For a genre perspective on the accessibility relations between actual world and textual actual world of fiction, see Ryan 1991, Chapter 2.

readers who questioned the facts reported in the travel books, or claimed that these writers' fictions set in Africa were thinly disguised character assassinations (and, in this way, disguised forms of nonfiction). For instance, the setting and some of the characters and events in Simenon's novel *Le Coup de lune* (1933) were in some readers' minds so close to the reality in Libreville, in Gabon, that this resemblance led to a court case against the writer in 1934.[11] The author's lawyer, Maurice Garçon, successfully pleaded that the novelist had the right to draw from reality, and Simenon was acquitted. Likewise, Esme Barton's response to Evelyn Waugh's African novel *Black Mischief* (1932) has become well known. As Waugh sat in an Addis Ababa nightclub in 1935, Esme concluded their discussion by hurling champagne in his face (see Stannard 1986, 406). This was her protest against Waugh's satirical representation in that novel of Sir Samson Courteney, the head of the British Legation in Addis Ababa, a character modelled after Esme's father Sir Sidney Barton. Sir Samson Courteney's daughter, moreover, was portrayed as the naive and promiscuous Prudence Courteney. Graham Greene's travel book *Journey Without Maps*, in turn, was withdrawn from bookstores at the end of 1937 on account of a libel case brought against the writer for his depiction of certain people in Freetown, Sierra Leone.[12] The cause of the case is less significant than the principle it illustrates, namely that truthfulness in relation to actual places and people is usually expected of travel writing. Greene described in his travelogue a drunken party in Freetown, where he called one of the participants by the name of Pa Oakley, without apparently knowing that a certain Dr. P. D. Oakley was a real person, and was in fact head of the Sierra Leone Medical Service!

Such cases can be used to illustrate the importance of generic expectations and reaffirm a text's generic boundaries. The alleged breaches against the veracity of the travelogue, and the hidden insults in the fictions, were intimately tied to generic expectations: a travelogue needs to appear trustworthy, specifically in the sense of being true to the writer's experience in some actual place of travel, whereas a novelist has the freedom to manipulate real events, places, and people. By the latter I mean, more precisely, that a novel does not need to refer to reality, or if it does, it need not be accurate. Fiction may certainly have two intended audiences at the same time, for instance one audience reading the novel as fiction without any interest in relating the fiction to some actual historical reality or people, and another audience reading

---

11. Enraged by what they thought was their portrayal in the novel, a group of French woodcutters in Libreville paid the travel fare for a hotelkeeper's wife, who felt insulted by what she thought was her caricature in the novel, so that she could sue Simenon for libel in Paris.

12. As a result, the travel book remained out of print for almost a decade.

it as a satire that comments on real events, as an inside joke or a well-crafted insult aimed at real people. The potential for close ties with reality is there in Waugh's and Simenon's novels especially, and in particular for some of those novels' contemporary audiences, but this does not seriously undermine these novels' overall generic classification. With regard to the nonfiction travel narratives and journals that are investigated here, it is likely that, at the time of their publication, these works appealed specially to those readers who wished to learn more about the authors, aside from their better-known role as fiction writers. Loti and Gide also consciously used their journals and diaries to create a public image of themselves. This is an issue of the author's performance and book marketing, however, not just of generic classification. Conrad's brief African travel notes are an exception in this respect in that they were not meant to be published. As such, they did not have any intended audience except, perhaps, the writer himself.

Yet, while the distinction between fiction and nonfiction travel writing usually depends both on semantic and pragmatic criteria, and sometimes can be decided on pragmatic criteria alone, there are also certain textual and linguistic markers that may cue the reader to interpret a given text as fiction rather than as nonfiction. These textual features, such as the use of thought report (the narrator's representation of a character's thoughts) or free indirect discourse, where a character's utterances or thoughts are presented within a narrator's discourse, are never by themselves decisive in determining the text's classification, but they can function as important markers, or to borrow Dorrit Cohn's term, "signposts" of fictionality. Similarly, the "split" voice in many modern novels, where we can make a clear distinction between a fictional narrator-character and the real author, does not usually apply to nonfictional narratives.[13] While in fiction the narrative voice and the narrative world are mutually constitutive, meaning that they create each other as they refer to each other (see Cohn 1999, 13), the reader's inferences with regard to the "voice" and authorship of nonfiction travel writing are characteristically conditioned by the expectation of referentiality, that is, they are licensed by the assumption that the author bears truthful witness to the real world. The referential principle generally holds even if the writer-traveller's main objective is to create the impression of an interesting travelling persona, or to instill

---

13. Philippe Lejeune defines the autobiographical pact as the identity between the author, the narrator and the main character (1996, 15, 27–29). This influential definition is obviously not only a matter of detecting the right textual features (for instance, a fictional narrator or the lack thereof), but may be seen as a consequence of the pragmatic distinction between fiction and nonfiction (for instance, contextual information concerning a factual narrative tells us that the author and the narrator are the same person).

wonder in his tale, rather than to be accurate. With third-person travel literature, the default assumption is similar: the writer reports, in his own name, someone else's actual experience as truthfully as possible.

For Dorrit Cohn, the signposts of fiction include three basic criteria:

1. An adherence to a bi-level story/discourse model that assumes emancipation from the enforcement of a referential data base;
2. The representation of inner lives: that is, the employment of narrative situations that open to inside views of the characters' minds, the here and now of their lives; and the mind-reading experience, in which fiction can make the reader share in a character's experience of time; and
3. An articulation of narrative voices that can be detached from their authorial origin (1999, viii, 110–31).

The first criterion, the distinction between the order of the events and the order of their presentation (or story vs. discourse), can be highly relevant in various nonfiction genres such as historiography and, as we will see, in travel writing. Nonfiction travel writing can employ any or all of the conventions of dramatic structure that manipulate this relation, including the dramatic and narrative importance of beginnings (see also Chapter 1), rising and falling action, acceleration, deceleration and ellipsis, climax and dénouement; travel books can create effects of suspense and surprise, or start in the middle, the beginning or the end of the action. Moreover, the fact that much travel literature is written after the actual journey is also often reflected by the travel writer openly acknowledging the difference between the time of the travel experience and the time of the writing (as in Elias Canetti's carefully crafted *The Voices of Marrakesh*, published over a decade after the author's visit in Morocco). Cohn accepts that the bi-level story/discourse model may be relevant in historiography (1999, 112), and specifies that the crucial distinction in this regard is that one has to postulate another level of narrative analysis for nonfictional narratives: the referential level.[14] The third signpost (the "disjunctive theory") requires the reader to perform a contextualizing evaluation of the text in regard to the responsibility of the narrative voice: to evaluate, in other words, what the narrating voice is responsible for and whether, in case of so-called covert narrators, there is any narrative voice to be

---

14. Cohn is basically only interested in narratological indices of fiction. However, she does take paratextual indices into consideration in regard to Hildesheimer's fictional biography *Marbot* (1999, 92–95) and she evokes the question of (non)referentiality throughout *Distinction of Fiction*. See also Mikkonen 2006.

detected.¹⁵ Besides the three signposts listed, Cohn also refers to the principle of nonreferentiality. This is the idea, already mentioned above, that fiction itself creates the world to which it refers by actually referring to it, that is, fiction crafts a self-enclosed universe ruled by formal patterns. For Cohn, a fictional text is essentially a *literary nonreferential narrative:* it can refer to the real world but need not do so; the referentiality of fiction does not have to be accurate or exclusive (1999, 15). The signposts, therefore, are not sufficient in themselves to determine the classification of any text as fiction or nonfiction. The communally affirmed principles of referentiality and verifiability help one to decide what features of the text do or do not have a referent in the actual world, or whether one is to concentrate on them and why.

Two further clarifications in regard to the instability of any textual "indices" or signposts of fiction are necessary here. First, none of these indices are exclusive in the sense that nonfiction could not borrow and appropriate them. Cohn also admits that all the narrative features listed above can be imitated and used by various kinds of nonfiction texts—such simulation just requires more from the viewer for successful classification. As I will argue throughout this study, the mind-reading experience is crucial in much modern travel writing: its main benefit can be to make the reader share in the writer's experience of a foreign place and people. The question of split-narrative voice is another case in point. The concept of a travelling persona has been used to refer to the cases in travel writing where there is a clear difference between the travelling "I" of the travelogue and the author in real life (see Lidström 2005, 151). The difference between these two identities is not just based on the fact that travelogues differ from traditional autobiographies—for instance, in that they do not usually try to present the writer's personality comprehensively—but because the modern travelogue is also often similar to modern autobiographies that reinvent the author as a certain kind of persona. In travel writing, the writer can present himself or herself in a certain role, that is, as a certain kind of traveller or a travelling persona.¹⁶ This distinction between a travelling persona and the author in real life becomes increasingly evident in travel writing of the early twentieth century, when authors travelled in order to write about the experience, and will be a relevant question with regard to Graham Greene's and Evelyn Waugh's African travelogues in particular.¹⁷

---

15. See Ryan 2002, 362–64.

16. I borrow the concept of "travelling persona" from Carina Lidström, who has used it in her study of Swedish travel writing 1667–1879 (2003, 233–34; 2005, 151–52). Lidström's main types of travel persona include the adventurer, the scientific traveller, and the aesthete.

17. Blanton goes so far as to call the self-conscious mediating consciousness that monitors the journey, a "narrator" (2002, 4). While I agree that the impression of a mediating conscious-

Second, the function of such markers of fiction is profoundly conditioned by the readers' expectation and understanding of a text's genre: what may count as a signpost of fiction in one case may not apply in another case. For instance, the presentation of verbatim speech, shifts between external observation and an individual's inner reflection, or the author's (or the narrator's) interruptions between narrative levels, which are common in modern novels, may also be used in modern travel writing.

The Traveller's Mediating Mind

Much research agrees that in travel writing, characteristically, the journey events are monitored and organized by the traveller's mediating consciousness, even when the travel account is written in the third person. The traversed spaces are unified in the traveller's experience, impressions, and recounting, which is punctuated by episodes, names of places, and local descriptions. Modern travel writing typically involves, also when we are dealing with examples of pure description, the portrayal of human consciousness engaged in goal-oriented activity.[18] This may also explain why vicarious experience, understood both in the sense of learning about a foreign place through someone else's travel experience and learning about someone's experience in that place, is such a crucial feature of this genre. The fact that travel writing may encourage further travel, or discourage people from travelling, is another proof of the close association between travel writing and travel experience. The ability to convey a sense of "what it's like" or, more precisely, "what it's like to be somewhere else," is also comparable, in general terms, to the experience of reading fiction, that is, the way in which the writer and the reader imagine fictional experiences, lives, and worlds and, furthermore, may be able to imaginatively transport themselves into a fictional world. As has often been argued, one of the main features and attractions of reading fiction is to imagine what it is like to be someone else, that is, to think and feel like someone else, and to experience another world, place, and time through the imagination.[19]

---

ness is central in much modern travel writing, I refrain from using Blanton's concept so as to avoid a direct association with fiction at this level.

18. Recent approaches to the cognitive and experiential features of fiction have also shown how the understanding of fictional narratives is tied to the projection of a world. For Marie-Laure Ryan, fictional narrative is an imaginative "recentring" in another possible world (2001, 103–5). In this regard, travel narratives are prototypical cases of all narratives.

19. See, for instance, Cohn's theory of thought representation in fiction in *Transparent Minds* (1978), Ryan's theory of the reader's "recentring" into a fictional world (1991, 21–23),

The traveller's consciousness is central to the genre of travel writing and, unless we are talking about simple travel guides that compete with their stacks of information, the genre prefers, particularly when we come to the early twentieth century, a focalized perspective that reflects on the here and now of the travel experience, seeking to dramatize a particular engagement between a self and the world. For Odile Gannier, the personality of the modern author-traveller is "present, and in control" (2001, 51). Jean-Xavier Ridon argues similarly that "it is through the filter of a subjective experience that all travel stories develop" (2002, 15). For Gerard Cogez, likewise, modern travel writing is characterized by the consciousness of being "the only person to have this particular point of view on the world, the only one being able to record with objectivity the intimate repercussions of one's contact with elsewhere and novelty" (2004, 152). Furthermore, the traveller, according to Louis Marin, unavoidably "anthropomorphizes the wanderings of the text," by traversing a geographic and textual network that is thus raised "from anonymity" (1984, 42–43).[20] In other words, the basis of a modern travel narrative is the reconfiguration of a sequence of places by the experiencing self and his or her consciousness. Travel journals and narratives project worlds in this way, in a tension between the immediacy of perception and meaningful consequence, each crafting a subjective universe according to which its propositions are read. The notion of *narrative* that I will employ throughout this study emphasizes the importance of the travel writer's or the narrator's experiential frame vis-à-vis the sequencing of events, times, or places (see also Chapter 3).

Much travel writing underscores the centrality of the writer-traveller's mind, by making explicit the interdependence between the description of the world and the traveller's necessarily subjective and limited perspective. Typically, the modern travel writer wishes to be both objective and authentic in his

---

Fludernik's notion of experientiality (1996, 12–13, 28–30, 48–50), and David Herman's application of the concept of *qualia*, by which the philosophers of mind refer to the sense of what it's like for someone or something to have a particular experience, in connection with the reading of narratives (Herman 2009, 143–52).

20. Many other similar statements could be listed here. For Germaine Brée, similarly, the protagonist of a travel narrative moves as a focal point for actions and ideas, thus realizing narrative of the episodes of journey as an index of his digression (1968, 89). Furthermore, Pasquali has made the important point that the personalized point of view of travel writing is dependent on a double determination between the perspectives of the travel process and the order of a finalized text (1994, 112). See also the way in which Fussell (1980, 203) and Thompson (2011, 14–15) differentiate between the proper modern "travel book," as a form of autobiographical narrative, and the guide book. However, Thompson asserts important reservations about Fussell's definition of the travel book as a "sub-species of memoir," especially with regard to texts published before 1800 (2011, 17–27). I would like to thank John Calton for his helpful comments in this section of the Introduction.

vision, somewhat like an ethnographer or a scientist who relies first and foremost on his direct observations, but he is also clearly, if not blatantly, personal in his observation, distinguished by his impressions, particular sensitivities, and the individuality of his perception. In the foreword to his travel book *First Russia, Then Tibet* (1933), entitled "The Traveller's Confession," Robert Byron gave voice to this paradox. He explains that "the traveller is a slave to his senses; his grasp of a fact can only be complete when reinforced by sensory evidence; he can know the world, in fact, only when he sees, hears, and smells it" (1933, iv). The emphasis on experience, evidence, and sensory perception, however, is not merely indicative of empiricist epistemological principles, even if it is clearly indebted to them. Byron's empiricism also validates a personal voice and experience that is relatively independent of the principles of referentiality and reliability in description. In travel, Byron (or his travelling persona) acquires wholesome knowledge of the world, as opposed to modern specialized disciplines of knowledge.[21] The knowledge that comes out of travelling necessitates, in addition, a distance from the kinds of travellers who are too close to a geographer's, ethnographer's, or zoologist's vision. In his best-known travel book *The Road to Oxiana* (1937) Byron distinguishes himself sharply and ironically from

> these modern travellers, these over-grown prefects and pseudo-scientific bores despatched by congregations of extinguished officials to see if sand-dunes sing and snow is cold. Unlimited money, every kind of official influence support them; they penetrate the furthest recesses of the globe; and beyond ascertaining that sand-dunes do sing and snow is cold, what do they observe to enlarge the human mind? Nothing. (2007, 239)

And unlike the explorer, with whom the modern traveller and travel writer may share the excitement of the unpredictable and the unknown, Byron does not seek to explain away the strangeness of the experience or the place, or marginalize the pleasures of travel.[22] At the same time, and characteristically of the modern travel writer, Byron likes to distinguish himself from the tourist, who represents the safety of pure cliché, or the mere recording of impressions. The three categories of the tourist, the traveller, and the explorer are, nevertheless, mutually dependent, as is revealed by the way in which Byron self-consciously defines himself in contrast to the other two. The attempt to

---

21. Moreover, Byron's emphasis on direct observation betrays a spiritual necessity to travel, the discovery, as he says, of "organic harmony between all matter and all activity" (1933, xiv) that broadens the mind.

22. See also Fussell 1980, 39; Healey 2003, 22–23.

distinguish oneself as a traveller, or as a unique type of tourist (even if this gesture entails a kind of contradiction in terms), is similar to some of my main examples of modern travel writers, such as Waugh, who self-consciously portrayed the available roles of travel in his travelogues.

The various conversations in direct discourse included in *The Road to Oxiana* reveal yet another kind of paradox in a way that a travel writer enunciates his situation. This is that the sense of immediacy and spontaneity that characterizes Byron's dialogues with locals and fellow travellers, such as the one below, not only borrows from the conventions of fiction and theater, but may also be a product of pure invention:

> But at one camp two men stopped us. "Where is your kibitka?" they asked.
> "My what?"
> "Your kibitka?"
> "I don't understand."
> With expressions of contempt and irritation, they pointed to their own felt-and-wattle huts: "Your kibitka—you must have a kibitka. Where is it?"
> "In Inglistan."
> "Where is that?"
> "In Hindostan."
> "Is that in Russia?"
> "Yes." (2007, 115)

Byron's travel companion Christopher Sykes has explained that all the supposedly non-English conversations recorded in *The Road to Oxiana* were in fact invented. This is because, as Sykes claims, Byron was a "very poor linguist."[23] Yet why is it we can still read Byron's travelogue as nonfiction and not be bothered about the veracity of the words, let alone their accuracy, or the reality of the scene? Is it that, even if the reader expects that travel writing is committed to the principles of truthfulness—at least in the sense of being true to one's own travel experience—and verifiable documentation, he or she may equally expect that this genre may easily suspend this commitment, at least as far as it does not go beyond certain bounds of possibility?

Our willingness to accept such inventions, but still hold onto the principle of veracity and the category of nonfiction, raises an important epistemological question that characterizes the modern travel genre and its enunciative situation in general: the difference between the order and time of the travel and the order and time of writing. On the one hand, the reader may take the

---

23. Cited by Fussell in his introduction to *The Road to Oxiana* (Byron 2007, 15).

author as a "witness" rather than as a writer whose writing transfers, with no loss of persuasive power, the force of experience, and the meanings related to the time and the place of travel. On the other hand, the reader must know that this is not quite possible since the act of travel writing comes after the experience, it is a representation that is mediated by the traveller's mind after the event. In other words, travel writing is able to manipulate the relation between two kinds of temporality and causality: on the one hand, the chain of causes and effects that can be assumed to count for the traveller's movements during the travel and, on the other hand, the sense of time and causal relations in the organisation of the text that motivate the writer to issue reports about some aspects of those movements, but not others. In fact, the distance between the time of the travel experience and that of writing, may in itself be of interest in reading travel literature. For instance, the reader may pretend to believe that the dialogues included in a travelogue took place as they are transcribed, or that they might have taken place, assuming thus that travel writing does not require perfect accuracy. It may be of interest to Byron's readers, furthermore, to appreciate the way in which the invented dialogues make this experience more vivid, humorous, and at the same time more literary. Finally, the expectation that travel writing focuses on the marvellous and the unfamiliar through the traveller's subjective mind, may invite the reader to relax the expectation of accuracy or at least make it somewhat difficult to estimate the accuracy of the description.

The Reorientation of Description

Another expectation that is traditionally associated with travel writing is the requirement of documentary description, at least since Sir Francis Bacon's advice for travellers, in an essay "Of Travel" (1615), to adapt his empiricist principles, that is, to make careful observations about the world in a travel diary. "Let diaries, therefore, be brought in use," he advised. From then on, "empirical" travelogues, with their emphasis on direct observation as the basis of knowledge, developed ways to attain descriptive specificity in details about places and people; and put forward a style of witnessing.[24] At the same time, the modern novel, in particular in some of its realist forms, closely followed

---

24. Accordingly, Jaś Elsner and Joan-Pau Rubiés have identified, in reference to Richard Burton's pilgrimage to Mecca in 1853, the traveller's "rhetorical claim of authority as a direct observer" as perhaps the "fundamental literary mechanism of legitimation in the genre of travel literature" (1999, 3). Batten (1978, 82–115) has a comprehensive discussion of the principles and aims of description in eighteenth-century English travel literature.

these developments. In effect, several of the presuppositions that Philippe Hamon detects in what he calls descriptive realism in the novel (1973, 422) are highly relevant in the tradition of travel writing, and conform with Francis Bacon's advice. For example, both travel writing and the traditional realist novel presuppose that the world is rich in forms and details and, consequently, is worth describing. It may be further expected that the traveller's description of the world, or the author's/narrator's portrayal of a fictional world, has a unique capacity to transmit information concerning this diversity. Evelyn Waugh claims in *Remote People,* in yet another formulation of this principle, that he is concerned in his book with firsthand impressions (2003, 320) and how, moreover, these impressions could challenge some commonly held misconceptions, for instance, concerning life in the English settlements in Kenya. The same expectation of detailed description based on firsthand impressions may also be one of the reasons why readers of travel literature are willing to "naturalize" inconsistencies and inaccuracies in travel writing, that is, to reconcile what appears to them to be inconsistencies in this genre and to continue to read the text as coherent and factual.[25] For instance, while we suppose that Robert Byron invented his dialogues or that Marco Polo and Sir John Mandeville often wrote from hearsay or imagination, we may still expect that their geographical descriptions, and in Byron's case the depiction of his personal experience of places and people, reveal the way the world was seen at the time of writing.

The emphasis on direct observation is also apparent in my corpus in that many of these travelogues and reportages were written by authors who were working as journalists and had a keen investment in maintaining their credibility. In the 1930s, Graham Greene, Evelyn Waugh, and Georges Simenon were employed by newspapers and weeklies to cover their travels in sub-Saharan colonial Africa. André Gide, likewise, published articles on the French Congo after his long journey there. The basic functions of description, as a means of identifying and pointing at something in the world, providing objective information—filtered through the traveller's experience and evaluating mind—and communicating sense data that is based on the observation of a given reality, were essential to this endeavor.[26] Voicing problems concerning the colonial government that were suppressed and obscured by the contemporary mainstream press, Gide's African travel journal, and the writer's campaign against the cruelty of French colonialism, had important political consequences. The first parts of *Travels in the Congo* were published in

---

25. For the concept of naturalization, see Culler 1975, 134–60.
26. The three functions of description are derived from Werner Wolf's definition of the basic functions of the cognitive frame of the descriptive (2007, 12, 16–17).

France in the journal *La Nouvelle Revue Française* in the winter of 1926 and 1927, and the travel journal appeared as a book in June 1927, supplemented in October by the article "La détresse de notre Afrique Equatoriale" (The distress of our Equatorial Africa) in *La Revue de Paris*. These publications sparked off intense controversy, which soon spread to other parts of Europe, about the exploitation of African labor in the colonies. *Travels in the Congo* also served as documentation in a session of the Chamber of Deputies of France concerning large rubber concessions in the West African colonies, resulting in November 1927 in a promise from the minister of colonies, Léon Perrier, that such concessions would no longer be renewed (O'Brian 1953, 322; Putnam 1990, 157–59).[27] Gide's travel journal became an unlikely bestseller and was also well known in the English-speaking world through Dorothy Bussy's translation in 1929.[28] All in all, many of these writer-travellers, such as Greene, Gide, Simenon, Albert Londres (in his *Terre d'ébène*, 1929), the Italian Curzio Malaparte, and Michel Leiris, who took part in an ethnographic expedition in the early 1930s, were driven by a genuine impulse to see parts of Africa for themselves in order to counter predominant notions of Africa and the official truth about colonial rule there.[29]

At the same time, many of these writers' travels were motivated by the desire to find new authentic material for fiction. For instance, Greene explains in the introduction to his West African journals "Congo Journal" and "Convoy to West Africa" how his novels, such as those he set in West Africa, have always relied on notes as raw material for his novels: "for I have very little visual imagination and only a short memory" (1968, 7–8).

---

27. The main target of Gide's criticism was the so-called Large Concessions regime according to which part of French Equatorial Africa was conceded to a French company that promised to take charge of investments in the area and, in return, could freely exploit its people and natural resources. After the journey, Gide wrote a report to the minister of the colonies (July 1926), a number of letters to various colonial administrators and editors, and met with the Minister of Colonies, Léon Perrier. Gide also produced a documentary film with Allégret, *Voyage au Congo*, which was released in the summer of 1927. Complimentary copies of *Le retour du Tchad* were sent out to politicians in May 1928 to influence the debate about the problems in the French colonies. See also Durosay 1993.

28. The book's popularity is reflected, for instance, in Greene's and Waugh's references to it in their African travelogues and diaries from the 1930s. Waugh mentions that a copy of *Voyage au Congo* was lent to him at the end of November 1930 while he was in Aden (Waugh 1976, 340–41), but does not discuss the contents of the travelogue.

29. It has also been debated whether Greene's journey was in fact organized by the British Anti-Slavery Society in cooperation with the Foreign Office. In March 1935, after his return to England from Sierra Leone and Liberia, Greene addressed the annual general meeting of the Anti-Slavery and Aborigines' Protection Society about his travel. The society was concerned at this time about the situation at the rubber plantations in Liberia. See Butcher 2010b.

Travel notes and observations also inform, as we will see throughout this study, Loti's, Simenon's, Waugh's, Gide's, Conrad's, and Céline's fictions about Africa. In their divided interest of finding authentic material for both travel writing and fiction these writers had an earlier model in Henry M. Stanley who, after the success of his travel account *How I Found Livingstone in Central Africa* (1872) wrote the much less successful novel *My Kalulu, Prince, King, and Slave. A Story of Central Africa* (1873). It is not clear whether Stanley already had the idea of a fictional story during his journey, but in the Preface to the novel he underscored the close relation between the novel and the travel experience. While admitting that he had woven fiction with fact for the amusement of his readers—Stanley addressed the novel to adolescent male audience—he emphasized that the story was based on the knowledge he had acquired during his journey in search of Livingstone: "much of the book contains facts which I have witnessed myself, or which have come to my knowledge" (1890, vii). Furthermore, Stanley was careful to note that the fictional elements in his novel fell within the sphere of the possible (as opposed to the improbable).

Nevertheless, the expectation of the observer's authority as a witness, and the authenticity of his or her account, involves a major paradox that characterizes much modern travel writing: the assumption that one can arrive at a fresh and objective version of reality—in the sense of an accurate description of some part of our world that, in principle, could be revisited—by way of the subjective experience. It is probably because of the very emphasis on subjective experience of an existing reality of a place, whether related in first-person or third-person narration, that travel writing has traditionally been accused of lies. As an old English proverb has it: "Old men and far travellers may lie by authority."[30] The traveller's limitations in observation, the fallibility of his memory, false expectations, misunderstandings, deliberate fabrications and omissions have been the target of parodies at least since *Gulliver's Travels*, perhaps the best-known satire on travel stories which lack credibility and probability. Greene, Leiris, and Gide, among many other writers of this era, made an attempt to turn the paradox of objective subjectivity into a point of interest in their travelogues, and their occasional discomfort with the conventions of description also points to the same paradox.

With regard to travel writers in the early twentieth century, the requirement of careful observation and description often translates as the expectation of the traveller's receptivity and keen attention to diversity in the world and, moreover, an ability to convey a sense of this sensitivity and attentiveness

---

30. See John Ray's *Collection of English Proverbs*, 1st ed., 1670.

to their readers. At the same time, description becomes a crucial problem in modern travel writing where the traveller's way of travelling, even style, is foregrounded. The gap between writing (as representation of the world) and the inexhaustible reality under observation, is regularly acknowledged in this context, specifically with regard to the task of description. The French thinker of the exotic and the diverse, Victor Segalen, for example, noted in his posthumously published travel book *Équipée* (1929) that in description, which he defined as "the traveller's principal argument," the rhythm of the vision is often "in advance stereotyped in the phrases and cut up by indentations" (1983, 103).[31] The problem of description for Segalen, but also for many other French writers including Leiris and Claude Lévi-Strauss,[32] involves the intimate, but often ambiguous bond between the means of writing, imagination, and the presumed veracity of the traveller's experience of reality. The dilemma is similar to some of the key problems confronted in the emerging field of ethnography at the time: how does the ethnographic text constitute the world and not just describe it? Can the writing rediscover the specificity, the heterogeneity and the spontaneity of experience? Can the distant or the foreign culture be rendered in familiar terms without at the same time contributing to its loss?

Among the strongest denunciations of description in modern European travel writing, we can quote several daily notes from Leiris's travel diary *L'Afrique fantôme* that he kept during the Dakar-Djibouti ethnographic mission. In the entry for March 18, 1932, Leiris raised the question of description by referring to Gide's *Voyage au Congo*, a travel book that Leiris appreciated for its criticism of the atrocities in colonized Africa, whilst at the same time denigrating descriptions of landscape:

> Mais toutes les descriptions, si brèves soient-elles, sont décidément bien vaines—on ne peut retracer un paysage, mais tout au plus le *recréer*; à condition, alors, de n'essayer aucunement de décrire. (1981, 248)

---

31. The lead-in in *Équipée* is emblematic of the paradoxical situation of enunciation. At the end of this passage, Segalen writes that he has always believed the genre of travel and adventure story to be suspicious but that, nevertheless, *Équipée* belongs to this genre ("C'est pourtant un récit de ce genre, récit de voyage et d'aventures, que ce livre propose dans ses pages mesurées, mises bout à bout comme des étapes"; 1983, 11). In *Équipée*, Segalen dramatizes the collision between two fundamental tendencies of its poetry: the contact with the physical world on a sensory level and the poetic creation of a world through the imagination.

32. The anthropologist Claude Lévi-Strauss regarded his voyages as a confrontation with the heterogeneity of reality, and, consequently, with the limits of description. "Why," asks Lévi-Strauss in the opening chapter to his *Tristes Tropiques* (1955), where he claims to hate travel writing, "should I give a detailed account of so many trivial circumstances and insignificant happenings?" (1973, 17).

But all descriptions, no matter how short, are definitely quite useless—one cannot recall a landscape, but at most *recreate* it; provided, then, that one does not try at all to describe it. (my translation)

It is paradoxical that the assertion of the vanity of description does not prevent Leiris from engaging in relatively conventional descriptions of sub-Saharan landscape and Africans elsewhere in his travel journal. However, the problem that Leiris raises here is common to many modern travel writers and does not just point to the problematic notion of transparency in description, but rather opens the question of the very motivation of description. This questioning involves, furthermore, the importance that Leiris gives to the notion of the particular, the concrete, and the confrontation with the unknown in one's self:

Je décris peu. Je note des détails qu'il est loisible à chacun de déclarer déplacés ou futiles. J'en néglige d'autres, qu'on peut juger plus importants. Je n'ai pour ainsi dire rien fait, après coup, pour corriger ce qu'il y a là de trop individuel. Mais ce, afin de parvenir au *maximum de vérité*. Car rien n'est vrai que le concret. C'est en poussant à l'extrême le particulier que, bien souvent, on touche au général; en exhibant le coefficient personnel au grand jour qu'on permet le calcul de l'erreur; en portant la subjectivité à son comble qu'on atteint l'objectivité (1981, 264).

I describe little. I note down details that one could easily judge inappropriate or trivial. I neglect others that are perhaps more important. I have thus done nothing, in afterthought, to correct what is too individual. But this is in order to arrive at the maximum amount of truth. Because nothing is true other than the concrete. It is by taking the individual to the extreme that, very often, one arrives at the general; by exposing the personal coefficient to daylight one is able to calculate the error; by pushing subjectivity to its limit, one attains objectivity. (my translation)

Leiris finds that while Gide's travel journal tries its best to convey a sense of reality in the Congo, at the same time the description represses the reality that it wishes to reveal. Contrary to this, Leiris proposes the principle of careful notation of his own internal mental processes that would render visible the most personal, intense, and precise experience of the everyday instead of the exotic object of description that must always remain distant to the observer. The demand for description, thus, is not abandoned but the attention is reoriented toward the traveller's inner realm of experience.

The Africanist Field of Knowledge

A central feature of travel literature is that it inspires further travel, suggesting reasons why the reader might want to revisit the places depicted. This is reflected in the fact that travel books and guides are frequently the traveller's favorite companions en route. The close connection between travel writing and the reasons for travel, and the act of travelling, is also observable in the writer's need to reconcile his or her experiences with the authority of earlier accounts of the same places and routes. At the same time, the existing travel descriptions in the "library" of available references may constitute an obstacle to be overcome by the subsequent travelogue.[33] Obviously also, by offering the reader a form of vicarious experience, travel writing may obviate the reader's need to travel. Be that as it may, travel writing, and reading travel writing, are closely associated with actual travel—and if not with actual travel, then with potential travel. Much of the comical predicament in Evelyn Waugh's interwar travel books, for instance, is built on the insight that in order to be able to tell about foreign places one has to pass through many interpretive filters, including earlier travel literature or fictions about the same places.

As we shall see, the circulation of cultural givens concerning sub-Saharan people and spaces is one of the major thematic areas of interpenetration across the fiction/nonfiction divide in this body of work. The study of Orientalist discourse that Edward Said developed is helpful in this respect in showing how the Orient has been "Orientalised" in various Western representations, in learned studies of Islamic culture and languages, travel writing, literature, and other texts, in ways that can be attributed to a closed system of knowledge (1978, 65–70). What is especially worth considering here is what Said has called *strategic location* and *strategic formation*, involving a given author's relationship to the cultural material that he writes about, and the referential power of the textual field of knowledge to which his work contributes (1978, 20). More precisely, strategic location means that anyone "who writes about the Orient must locate himself vis-à-vis the Orient, translated into his

---

33. In her *Le voyage, le monde et la bibliothèque* (1997), Christine Montalbetti has described the aporias of referentiality that are characteristic of travel writing, including those of description. These include the disparities between the means of writing and the (visual) structures of the world to be described; between language and the object of description (the inadequacy of the lexicon in regard to the foreign, the exotic, the other); and between the order of the text and the disorder of the world (the necessary order of a written composition versus the lack of configuration in the world). Still another question of referentiality that emerges in my examples, but one that is not posed by Montalbetti, is the problem of narrativisation, that is, how to give narrative form to the travel experience.

text" (1978, 20). This may involve the type of narrative voice that the writer adopts, and the kinds of images, themes, and motifs that circulate in his text. Strategic formation, in contrast, points to an intertextual formation and concerns the way in which groups and types of texts, and textual genres "acquire mass, density, and referential power among themselves and thereafter in the culture at large" (1978, 20).[34]

The concept of "Africanism," meaning something that is represented as characteristically African, but that may also refer to implicit, underlying assumptions about Africa, has been applied in postcolonial studies as a sort of modification of Said's "Orientalism" to analyse the way in which certain images, themes, and motifs of Africa are employed within a discursive formation, as in European literary modernism. Christopher L. Miller has, for instance, claimed that Africanist texts have had a tendency toward polarized evaluations where "Africa" typically bears a double burden, that of representing "monstrousness *and* nobility, all imposed by a deeper condition of difference and instability (Pliny's 'newness')" (1985, 5).

However, the Orientalist or Africanist approach does not readily lend itself to a literary analysis, which prefers to focus on genre-specific questions, pertaining for instance to claims for referentiality and probability, or intergeneric relations and distinctions. As many critics have pointed out, Said's notion of the discursive construction of Orientalism is inflexible with regard to the individual features of texts and their genres on the one hand, and Western culture and its imperial ideology on the other. Said makes little substantive distinction between literary and nonliterary genres,[35] or between fiction and nonfiction, and hardly pays any attention to the differences in the Western writers' identity and agency in regard to their gender, language, religion, and other variables of cultural or social background.[36] For this reason, the investigation of Africanism in European literature, ethnology, and anthro-

---

34. Said explains these two concepts, the "principal methodological devices for studying authority," in the introduction to his *Orientalism*. See Said 1978, 19–21.

35. These are oft-noted problems in Said's theory of Orientalism. See, for instance, MacKenzie 1995, xi–xvii, 8–25; Porter 1994; Clifford 1988, 255–76; and Prendergast 2000, 83–100.

36. For Said, the Western writer, artist, and scholar has always been a more or less conscious proponent of his Orientalism. In postcolonial studies since the 1990s, in contrast, it has become increasingly acknowledged that the history of colonialism has an essentially contentious and instable nature. Ian Baucom has argued, for instance, in reference to the fact that much of the history of England has happened in the vast overseas Empire that is now lost, that "we should read imperialism not simply as the history of England's expansion and contraction but as the history of a cultivated confusion" (1999, 3–5). Behdad (1994, 11–15) serves as an example of a postcolonial study of European travel writing where the emphasis lies on Orientalism's discursive heterogeneity and ideological uncertainty.

pology has often resulted in monolithic images of the Western mind or short listings of negative stereotyping in different discourses of knowledge.[37]

As the question of genre and generic relations is of crucial importance to this study, our concern with "Africanism" must have a somewhat different emphasis from Said's Orientalism. Specifically with regard to the modern novel, it makes sense to ask more precise questions about narrative authority in terms of literary genre and convention, for instance whether the writer's strategic location is dependent on the kind of narrative voice that is adopted in a text.[38] In my corpus, a narrative voice may refer to a strategic location that is different from the actual writer's strategic location; it may also be at variance with the real author's opinions. Polyphonic narration, such as narratorial irony with regard to the main characters in Waugh's, Céline's, and Simenon's fiction that is set in Africa, typically, puts forward contradictory intentions of narrative authority for the reader's evaluation, thus illustrating multiple potential strategic locations in relation to the kinds of images and themes that are associated with Africa, the Africans and the colonials. Therefore, the question of hypothetical audience, that is, the kind of audience for whom the author wrote the text, becomes relevant. Both fiction and nonfiction narratives imply a reader, who shares some basic knowledge and values with the author, even if he or she does not have to, or may not be able to agree with these expressions of knowledge and value (i.e., the reader participates in the authorial audience). In fiction, however, the ideal reader of narrative audience may be asked to pretend that the fictional world, and the various voices of that world, constitute a possible world in which he or she can participate by way of imagination (while knowing it to be a fiction).[39] In nonfiction travel

---

37. Perhaps the main problem with the notion of Orientalist discourse is that it appears as a kind of total intercultural translation that has no particular reference, even if it presumes to know its reference best—for, as Robert Young has pointed out, there is no object to which it corresponds. Neither is there any inner conflict in this totality, as Young also argues, but Orientalism is defined as a simple will to dominate, the only possible conflicts arising from the intervention of some outsider critic, a kind of romantic alienated being (Young 1990, 135).

38. Christopher Prendergast, specifically, has posed the question of literary genre in representing realities in other cultures:

> To speak of empire in literary texts is not necessarily the same as speaking of empire as constructed *by* literary texts; the latter would require an analysis of the textuality of the text, its modes of functioning. This we are rarely given in either *Orientalism* or *Culture and Imperialism*. There is, for example, the important issue of literary genre, initially the category of genre itself. Said never discusses it. The manner in which the formal reality of a genre seeks to grasp and represent another culture demands a reflection on the constitution, and thus the constitutive power, of the genre in question. (Prendergast 2000, 95)

39. "Authorial audience" is Peter J. Rabinowitz's notion of the hypothetical audience (or a reader role) in which actual readers may participate so as to understand the text as much as

writing, a double hypothetical audience is also possible, but it takes different forms. For instance, when a travelogue creates a sense of the writer's travelling persona, this technique may require that the reader knows the persona to be different from the writer's actual self in some way or another. This, again, suggests a double consciousness for reading the text, that is, the reader knows that the narrative is meant to be read as nonfiction but, at the same time, is aware that accuracy in the description of the travel destination may not be as important as creating a credible subjective truth about a place or an interesting travelling persona who filters the experience. Furthermore, instead of being invited to participate in a fictional world by way of imagination, the ideal reader of travel literature is asked to imagine some experience in and of the actual world as a possible one.

Moreover, in these travel books and reportages, the redefinition of the meaning of "Europe" or Western culture is an inseparable element of the various images and conceptions of the African. The encounter with African spaces and cultures suggested for many of these writers a means by which to investigate the limits of Western literature, identity, and ethnonational boundaries, including the criteria that maintained these boundaries. The dilemma that most of these writer-travellers faced was what they saw as the disconcerting modernity and mass culture of their home country. The interest in so-called primitivism or primitive mentality that many of them (but not all) share, where the idea of cultural and creative origin is found in the margins of civilization, or in the depths of one's mind as reflecting this supposedly different kind of mentality, becomes understandable in this context, as a rejection of modern civilization.

As has often been argued, the various modernist primitivisms maintained the traditional opposition between the civilized and the primitive—based on late nineteenth-century evolutionist ideas of the progress of human societies from the primitive to the modern—while at the same time various early twentieth-century avant-garde movements aimed to disempower and redesign these categories. In this reevaluation, both the primitive and Europe (or the "West") were subjected to sweeping generalizations. This meant, typically, and as happens in many of my examples, that African cultures and artifacts functioned as a convenient mirror for Europe and, thus, European society often emerged as a kind of false stereotype of the primitive. Therefore, by taking into consideration the Occidentalism of the European writers—the

---

possible in the sense that the author wished. As members of the authorial audience, readers share the same knowledge, beliefs, and expectations with the intended readers, and if an intelligent reading of the text so requires, distance themselves from their own immediate needs and interests (1987, 21–25). The narrative audience, in turn, is the "imaginary audience for which the narrator is writing" (Rabinowitz 1977, 127).

way Europe or the West was perceived against the African exotic primitive (or other representatives of Africa)—as a necessary counterpart of its many Africanisms, and the modernist critique of modern civilization, we may be better placed to shed light on the complex dialectic through which European literature and travel writing has continuously constituted itself in opposition to the larger world.[40] Most writers who are included in this study resort to the opposition between the primitive and the civilized in one way or another, even if their differences in the definition and evaluation of this dichotomy are also notable and worthy of our attention.

Even if in the late nineteenth and early twentieth century Africa was no longer a terra incognita, the knowledge concerning its cultures, especially sub-Saharan and inland cultures, was blurred and fragmentary. We may presume that it was partly for this reason that Black Africa remained an intense locus of conflicting meanings, exhibiting alterity in European early twentieth-century travel writing and fiction. And this sense of alterity is, further, accentuated in my corpus in the often contradictory and uneasy confrontation with one's self-image—with the "internalised exotic" or the "primitive" self—that these works portray in the course of travel. Similarly, the notion of a different kind of psychology, a *mentalité primitive*, is prominent across interwar travel writing in sub-Saharan Africa. It is important to note, however, that this interest is not necessarily a result of actual readings of Lucien Lévy-Bruhl's 1922 influential book of the same name (*La mentalité primitive*), or the French anthropologist's other theories, but can often be perceived as a kind of common "knowledge" concerning primitive man, prototypically the black African. Some versions of this notion were conceptually related but not directly indebted to any pseudo-anthropological theories. For instance, Karen Blixen's memoir *Out of Africa* creates a personal myth of African lifestyle (and perhaps something we could also refer to as a cognitive style), with her emphasis on the Africans' innate freedom, nobility, and heroism. As one of the best-known accounts of colonial life in sub-Saharan Africa in the early twentieth century, *Out of Africa* has also contributed to much more recent stereotypes and cultural givens about the Noble Savage.

In many of these texts, however, and in fictions that take on the same themes, the sense of exotic authenticity that is situated in, or projected onto,

---

40. See Clifford (1988, 259, 272) for a similar emphasis; and Perloff (1995) who tackles the problem of Occidentalism in certain "postmodernist" critiques of Orientalism and primitivism. The specifically futurist forms of primitivism are treated expertly in White (1990, 288–358). Several recent studies on the complex status of "the primitive" within surrealism and futurism are also insightful and helpful in this regard. See especially Blachère (1996), Tythacott (2003), Sabot (2003), and Mikkonen (2009b).

Africa emerges as incompatible with modern historical consciousness and the colonial situation. Consequently, primitivism, or exoticism, is exposed as a myth. What results, then, from this loss of the great opposition, for instance in Greene's and Leiris's travelogues, is ambivalence between the search for an authentic experience, and disillusionment (or *Weltschmerz*). As to these writers' more or less outspoken stances concerning colonialism, they also represent a variety of positions. Waugh rejected exoticism as a myth, but he was also a staunch supporter of imperialism and colonialist rule, particularly in *Waugh in Abyssinia*, while others, most notably Gide and Leiris, but also Blixen and Simenon in their different ways, became outspoken critics of colonialism, later supporting the anticolonialist movement.

Imaginary Projections of the African Zone

To generalize, the case studies that form the basis of this study suggest that there are three basic types of cultural givens or assumptions concerning sub-Saharan Africa in this body of work. These categories include, first, the notion of Africa as a place of wonder and renewed perception; second, the discourses of exhaustion and excess, which I have grouped together under the term hermeneutic pessimism; and, third, the imperial concept of Black Africa as a place without history. All three categories appear in various combinations and with different emphases in the individual works.

First of all, one common feature in my corpus is the notion of "Black Africa" as a kind of theatrical stage of wonderful projections. In its most extreme forms, this fantastic space of Africa has no real object to which it could correspond; little or no accuracy is, therefore, required. One prototype of such imaginary space is the lost but rediscovered civilized world, as in H. Rider Haggard's *King Solomon's Mines* (1885) and *She* (1887) to which, for instance, Graham Greene refers in his African travelogue.[41] Another model would be Pierre Loti's semi-autobiographical novels set in various localities outside Europe, as in Polynesia, Turkey, Japan, and Senegal. In these novels, Loti used his travel journal as a catalyst and a kind of laboratory, thus exemplifying what Tzvetan Todorov has called the egocentric voyage, where the

---

41. Edward Said's observation that the Orient may function as an enclosed "stage" in the discipline of Orientalism is relevant here: "the Orient is the stage on which the whole East is confined. On this stage will appear figures whose role it is to represent the larger whole from which they emanate. The Orient then seems to be, not an unlimited extension beyond the familiar European world, but rather a closed field, a theatrical stage affixed to Europe" (Said 1978, 63).

foreign framework allows the traveller, as well as the novelist, to rediscover his taste for life (1993, 345).[42] Loti's work is seminal for the later French exoticist tradition, including writers like Gide, Céline, Leiris, and Simenon, not only as their predecessor in suggesting models for a literary description of a non-European milieu, but also as an outdated form of picturesque exoticism. A yet more radical version of imaginary Africa was perceived by Raymond Roussel, who depicted Black Africa, in *Impressions d'Afrique* (1910) and *Nouvelles Impressions d'Afrique* (1932), as a fictive pseudo-referent and a kind of immense museum of visual effects and fantastic machinery. Such a fantastic Africa, to which for instance Michel Leiris refers in his travel journal, does not have actual, psychosocial geography, but necessarily only exists *for* Europe and the Europeans, who appreciate the freedom of imagination to reinvent "Africa" as a man-made entity.

While the notion that Black Africa is a place of fantastic projections is not fully endorsed in my examples except, perhaps, for Loti and Céline, it still remains a powerful image in most of them. In her study *The Modernist Traveler* (2003), Kimberley Healey has underlined the potential in the French word *zone* to describe the heterogeneous and fluctuating nature of the spaces found in early twentieth-century travel writing, including for instance Henri Michaux's works. Healey writes that the conception of space as a zone transforms geography into a "liminal, latent, and often an imaginary rather than real demarcated space" (2003, 2). Similarly, we can find many instances in early twentieth-century writers' travelogues where the question of the African simulacrum becomes highly relevant, or where the traveller's own phantasms and preconceived notions become the focus of the text, as for instance is the case with Leiris's notion of the *phantomesque* Africa.

Louis-Ferdinand Céline's novels, which draw widely on the writer's personal experience, often seem to suggest that the real world is not just comparable to a fictional world, or vice versa, but that each may be assimilated into the other. The West Africa that Céline depicts in his writings regularly poses the question of the status of referential discourse by multiplying the worlds of reference—be they realistic, fantastic, picaresque, or pseudo-autobiographical worlds—and allowing them to constantly interpenetrate each another. Sometimes Céline also deliberately uses images of Africa to dramatize uncertainty about the degree of realism and reliability in his narration. However, the fantastic elements in Céline's colonial West Africa have not prevented many authors of nonfiction from using Céline's portrayal of Africa as a guarantor

---

42. For Todorov, "Loti's books are not deceptive, for they do not claim to be telling the truth about the country in question; all they propose to do is describe with sincerity the *effect* produced by the country on the narrator's soul" (1993, 310).

of reality in their travel books. For instance, in the "Finale" to his travelogue *Africa Dances: A Book about West African Negroes* (1935), the British anthropologist Geoffrey Gorer notes that "Dr 'L-F. Céline' has so well described the atmosphere of a colonial boat in his *Voyage au Bout de la Nuit* (1932) that it would be useless to improve on him, and otiose to repeat him" (2003, 282). The fantasy of fiction thus authenticates travel facts. In his African travelogue, Graham Greene similarly refers to Céline's descriptions.

In Céline's whole work, from the early play *L'Église* through *Journey to the End of the Night*, his anti-Semitic pamphlets and to his last pseudo-autobiographical novels, such as *Féerie pour une autre fois* (1952, *Fable for Another Time*), where there is also a short passage relating to nightlife in a Cameroonian forest, the West African "realities" and memories often reveal a probability which operates inside a larger artifice: an Africa that is at the same time real and imaginary, and an Africa that epitomizes the almost anarchist forces of nature. Even in Céline's letters from Cameroon in 1916–17, the trope of Black Africa is associated with the power to conjure up exciting scenes, and the ability to fuse material reality closely with the metaphorical or possible world, and unreliable narration. Some of Céline's first experiments in fiction, such as a story called "Des vagues," which is loosely based on the events on the steamer that took him back to Europe, are also included in these letters.

Hermeneutic Pessimism, or the Discourses of Exhaustion and "Fractal Travel"

The image of sub-Saharan Africa in my corpus is often characterized by a sense of hermeneutic pessimism, resulting from an awareness of the semiotic uncertainties of description, that is, a recognition of the gap between representation and the objects to be represented. The basic forms of such discrepancy between the signs and the world are the discourse of exhaustion and excess, both involving an elusive object of description, that is, an African reality which is just too rich, heterogeneous, strange, and detailed or disturbingly monotonous. Both the discourse of exhaustion and excess suggest that the ways in which the world can be classified and described is potentially endless and, consequently, description will always remain wanting in details and to some extent arbitrary.

This discourse of exhaustion often coincides with the sense of belatedness: there are no illusions left of the exotic outside of Western civilization.[43] Paul

---

43. Ali Behdad argues that mid- and late nineteenth-century writer-travellers in the Orient were characterized by their sense of belatedness, since the "European colonial power structure

Fussell has articulated the discourse of exhaustion in the context of interwar travel writing in relation to the growing tourist industry and the resulting opposition between a traveller, a tourist, and an anti-tourist. A traveller, at this time, was someone who conceived travel to be like study or scientific research, whereas a tourist did not presume to know anything of the places he visits. An anti-tourist,[44] in turn, was motivated by his class-conscious self-protection and vanity to think that he is like a traveller (even if he was much closer to a tourist) (Fussell 1980, 43–45). Accordingly, many twentieth-century travel writers, such as Robert Byron, defined "authentic" and individual forms of travel in contrast to mass tourism and its commercially determined circuits of travel.[45]

Sometimes an inseparable counterpart of the discourse of exhaustion in these works is the description of the African experience in terms of excess, haunted by a proliferation of signs, images, and potential meanings that are more or less uncontrollable. Such an effect may result, for instance, from the sense of overwhelming richness in reality or, equally, from the estranging monotony and irregular structures of reality that highlight the difficulty in making sense of the experience. What Michael Cronin has called the fractal dimension of travel is insightful in this respect (2000, 17). The "fractal" vision in travel involves a heightened awareness of and sensitivity to the details and particulars of the places of travel, such as the complexity and history of cultures, the language of description and, potentially, the complexities in the traveller's own identity that are revealed to him or her during the journey (2000, 18–19). The traveller's experience of movement may, further, heighten such fractal visions of complex structures. My case studies will show how the open-endedness of travel, and misadventure, function as a means by which the writer-traveller can undermine habitual patterns of thought and behaviour.

---

and the rise of tourism had transformed the exotic referent into the familiar sign of Western hegemony" (1994, 13).

44. James Buzard has claimed that "anti-tourism" has been an element of modern tourism from the start, and that it has "offered an important, even exemplary way of regarding one's own cultural experiences as authentic and unique, setting them against a backdrop of always assumed tourist vulgarity, repetition, and ignorance" (1993, 5).

45. Helen Carr has pointed out, in reference to Hilaire Belloc's *The Path to Rome* (1902), the modern traveller's desire not just to "put a distance between himself as traveller and the burgeoning droves of tourists," but the need to describe the byway, not the famous sights (2002, 79). Evelyn Waugh blames Belloc's travelogue for inventing a new kind of traveller, a type of antimodern pilgrim or a travel snob, who walks long distances in "shabby clothes," avoiding trains and hotels and, furthermore, manages not only "to get paid to write travel books" but find "peculiar relish in discomfort" (2003, 37).

Postimperial Melancholy and Africa That Has No History

A disturbing aspect in some of these travelogues and fictions is the sometimes close relationship between the search for an authentic, mythological Africa and the imperialist concept that Africa has no history. The view that Africa is a "land of childhood" that is outside or beyond any proper history was first articulated by G. W. F. Hegel in his *Lectures on the Philosophy of History* (1837) and established as knowledge during the era of colonialist expansion in Africa (from around the 1884–1885 Berlin Conference to the decolonization of Africa after the Second World War). The notion held that Africans were incapable of creating their own cultures, living in a nearly pure state of nature, and for this reason they could not have their own histories. The claim was further justified by presumed differences in race and mentality and, as in Hegel's lectures, in reference to Africa's supposed geographical isolation from the rest of the world—exempting Egypt and the Mediterranean coastline, a zone that Hegel called "European Africa"—and the lack of cross-cultural contacts.[46] Hegel saw the supposed geographical and cultural isolation of sub-Saharan Africa reflected also in the Africans' "primitive" religious practices and political systems.

In the light of this imperialist concept, the lack of reference to any explicit geographical and historical location in Joseph Conrad's novella *Heart of Darkness* (first published in serial form in 1899), a text which is evoked throughout my corpus, is profoundly ambivalent. Christopher L. Miller has pointed out how Conrad's suppression of historical places in the novella, where "every detail points to Africa but 'Africa' alone is missing," creates the ambiguous effect where the phrase "heart of darkness" can "never be wholly identified as either a repressed, encoded real referent or a fictive pseudo-referent, independent of the real world. *Heart of Darkness* is in fact deeply engaged in both projects at once" (1985, 175).[47] With regard to most writers who are included

---

46. Hegel writes in *The Philosophy of History* that

> At this point we leave Africa, not to mention it again. For it is no historical part of the World; it has no movement or development to exhibit. Historical movements in it—that is in its northern part—belong to the Asiatic or European World. Carthage displayed there an important transitory phase of civilization; but, as a Phoenician colony, it belongs to Asia. Egypt will be considered in reference to the passage of the human mind from its Eastern to its Western phase, but it does not belong to the African Spirit. What we properly understand by Africa, is the Unhistorical, Undeveloped Spirit, still involved in the conditions of mere nature, and which had to be presented here only as on the threshold of the World's History. (1956, 99)

47. However, *Heart of Darkness* also demystifies the great exotic other, Marlow's boyhood fantasy of Africa as "the biggest, the most blank" space on the world map. Conrad's novella

in this study, Conrad's novella functions as a central reference and textual authority, whose impact cuts across languages, literatures, and the divide between fiction and nonfiction. André Gide, who also translated Conrad, read *Heart of Darkness* for the fourth time during his West African journey in 1925 and 1926. Greene and Leiris quote Conrad in their travelogues. In Simenon's novel *45° à l'ombre*, the protagonist Donadieu concentrates on some unnamed Conrad novel, where the events take place on a cargo ship, while travelling back to Europe from Africa on an ocean liner, and so on.[48]

In this corpus, the ideal of (lost) exotic authenticity and nostalgia for absolute alterity sometimes belies the colonialist notion that Africa has no history of its own. Likewise, it is commonplace that some aspect of the Africans' life or their environment, be it real or imaginary, comes to epitomize them as a whole. This may become obvious, for instance, in what Arjun Appadurai has referred to as the "metonymic freezing" of the locals as "natives" (1988, 36–37). This occurs in some passages in Gide's African travel journal for instance, where the Africans in certain villages of the Congo are characterized by their supposed lack of individuality, distinction, and property. The same notion of non-distinction may be implied in descriptions of colonial imitation, as in Waugh's ridicule of the Africans' imitation of Western customs and dress in Addis Ababa, thus presupposing that the Ethiopians are unable to understand such customs and traditions. Equally, but with a very different emphasis, the same notion may be present in Blixen's admiration for the Africans' resistance to appropriation and forced imitation of Western civilisation, customs, and dress, thus presupposing that African nobility is beyond *our* (limited) notions of tradition and history. Still another strategy in description that relies on a similar preconceived notion is the emptying of African forest of everything human, as we will later see in relation to Conrad's, Greene's, and Céline's descriptions of the African forest.

Outline of This Book

Part I, "'Narrating and Describing West Africa," opens with two chapters that investigate the way in which certain descriptive passages in travel writing and in fiction foreground the writer's mental processes and trigger, further-

---

made it possible, as Miller further argues, to transform perception of African spaces and people, perhaps for the first time, so that it was "not so much the African object as the Africanist subject—the explorer, the writer—who was called into question" (1985, 170–71).

48. There is no evidence, however, of Evelyn Waugh having read *Heart of Darkness* (see Stannard 1986, 267).

more, the problem of the language of description. Chapter 1, "The Enchanted Arrival: Passage into West Africa in the Travel Writings of Blaise Cendrars, André Gide, and Graham Greene," analyzes three scenes of arrival in sub-Saharan West Africa where the travel writer (Cendrars, Gide, and Greene) perceives the passage into Black Africa as a relocation to another world. Typically, the scene of arrival dramatizes the traveller's cross-cultural encounters with local people or his or her experience of radical contingency. In terms of narrative organization, the arrival scenes function as another beginning in the story beyond the traveller's initial departure from home, and a set of instabilities that call for narrative explanation. Chapter 2, "The Rhetoric of the Mad African Forest in Joseph Conrad, Louis-Ferdinand Céline, and Graham Greene," investigates the description of African forests, which is a central shared topos across the fiction/nonfiction divide, focusing on Conrad's African notebooks and fictions, Céline's novel *Journey to the End of the Night*, and Greene's travelogue *Journey Without Maps*. The comparison between these works will show how the discourses of excess and exhaustion, that is, that the African reality is too overwhelming for representation, may be intertwined within one description. Chapter 3, "Travel Narrative between Spatial Sequence and Open Consequence in Graham Greene's *Journey Without Maps*" returns to Greene's African travelogue, and his novels set in Africa, but from a different angle that those in Chapters 1 and 2, developing the idea of narrativisation and narrative consequence that will be important throughout this study. The question of narrativisation will emerge especially in relation to the ways in which Greene manipulates the relationship between sequence and consequence, or between the spatio-temporal order of the journey and the personal experience of travel in his travelogue.

Part II, "Travel Writing and the Novel," consists of sustained close readings of travel writing and novels in three authors' works. These readings will amplify the theoretical basis of the research and illustrate some of the main research findings. The analyses include André Gide's travel journals *Voyage au Congo* and *Le retour du Tchad* (combined in the translation *Travels in the Congo*) and the novel *Les Faux-Monnayeurs* (*The Counterfeiters*); Evelyn Waugh's travel books *Remote People* and *Waugh in Abyssinia* and his novels *Black Mischief* and *Scoop*; and, finally, Georges Simenon's African reportages, along with his *Le Coup de lune* (*Tropic Moon*), *45° à l'ombre* (*Aboard the Aquitaine*), and *Le Blanc à lunettes* (*Talatala*), three novels set in Africa. Chapter 4, "The Immediacy of Reading: André Gide's Travel Fact and Travel Fictions," analyses, on the one hand, the features in Gide's major novel, *The Counterfeiters*, that evoke the themes of Africa and travel, including the Conradian trope of madness-inducing immersion in the "heart of darkness," and the metaphor of "writing as a journey." On the other hand, this chapter investigates the way in which Gide's travel journal *Travels in the Congo* evokes the question of fiction-writing and the reading of fiction. Chapter 5, "The Incongruous Worlds of Evelyn Waugh's Ethiopia," discusses the interplay between Waugh's travel writing and fiction especially in terms of the way in which fiction was a source of information, and even a kind of conceptual model for his East African travel books and reportages. It should be emphasized, however, that the objective of this investigation is not source-hunting in the authors' nonfiction travel writing but the two-way *interaction* between the genres. Waugh's writings about real and imaginary East African spaces reveal a symptomatic image of East Africa, common to all of his writings across the fiction/nonfiction divide, as a unique space of possible worlds and a source of endless comic or absurd juxtapositions of cultural incongruity. Chapter 6, "A Critique of the African Picturesque in Georges Simenon's Travel Reportages and Novels," discusses the ways in which Simenon's novels probe the relation between real circumstances and misconceived notions of Africa, particularly with regard to the notion of picturesque exotic, and do it similarly to or differently from his travel articles and essays. The comparison between Simenon's fiction and nonfiction requires that we carefully consider the narrative situation and voice in these novels, particularly pertaining to the changing distance between the narrator and the characters.

Part III, "Inventions of Life Narrative," opens with a critical investigation of generic potentiality in narrative texts, based on some passages in Pierre Loti's and Joseph Conrad's African fictions that refer to travel writing. Chapter 7, "Virtual Genres in Pierre Loti's and Joseph Conrad's African Travel Diaries and Fiction," expands the narratological notions of the disnarrated and narratorial counterfactual to encompass those generic frames that are evoked in these texts and that could have been adopted to depict the events, but that nevertheless remain unrealised projections. The two subsequent chapters in this section focus on the distinction between fiction and nonfiction in the context of autobiographical writing. Chapter 8, "Out of Europe: The African Palimpsest in Michel Leiris's *L'Afrique fantôme*" demonstrates how Leiris's travel journal anticipates his later experiments with autobiography and life writing. By listing his favorite literary (and other) images of Africa in his travel journal, Leiris dramatizes a loss of command of the exotic discourse and narrative authority, thus pointing to the cure of his exotic illusions, which the writer later associated with European egocentrism vis-à-vis other cultures. Chapter 9, "Africanist Paradoxes of Storytelling in Karen Blixen's *Out of Africa*," discusses the interrelation between Blixen's notions of Africa, Africans and storytelling in *Out of Africa*. Despite the fact that *Out of Africa* is a memoir and not a travel book, its inclusion in this study is justified in that Blixen explicitly takes issue with the fiction/nonfiction divide, and redefines the art of storytelling through her African experience in a way that is related to my other main examples.[49] Blixen's memoir, furthermore, raises the question of narrativisation and asks how fiction can contribute to autobiographical writing.

The Choice of Examples

It must be emphasized that the writers who are included in this study do not constitute a homogeneous group and that putting their works together in this way needs to be justified. The most important reasons for choosing these particular European writers are that they wrote both fiction and nonfiction (travel books or memoirs) that are set in sub-Saharan Africa and that their works have a number of themes, patterns, and techniques in common. Moreover, most of these works share the same Conradian intertext and many of these writers also refer to each other's works (Greene employs Céline's imagery; Leiris and Waugh refer to Gide's travelogue; Gide translated Conrad and read Simenon's African novels, and so on).

Despite these striking similarities, however, the differences are also significant. Karen Blixen was a settler in Kenya; she did not publish travel writing. Michel Leiris, by contrast, who belongs to the same generation as Simenon, Waugh, and Greene, is a case apart in the sense that he hardly published any fiction in his career after a short surrealist period in the 1920s. Pierre Loti and Georges Simenon, in turn, may be identified as writers of popular fiction. André Gide, by contrast, clearly belongs to the high modernist generation, and his *The Counterfeiters* can be counted among the most important early twentieth-century experiments with the novel form. Louis-Ferdinand Céline is, without question, distinct from the other authors in that he did not write any actual travelogue, reportage, or memoir from Africa. His letters from Cameroon in 1916–17 do not allow us to make extended comparisons

---

49. Blixen made four long trips back to Denmark during the years when she lived at her farm in Kenya, but does not describe the travelling as part of the African experience in her memoir, except for the story "Fellow-Travellers." Blixen travelled or stayed temporarily in Denmark, between April 1915 and November 1916; August 1919 and November 1920; March 1925 and February 1926; and May and December 1929. The distinction between travel and emigrant/immigrant writing is further complicated by the fact that not all travel books focus on the act of travelling but on a period spent in a foreign place. Thompson (2011, 18) makes the simple but helpful observation that the journey can be given a very different degree of prominence in narratives that count as travel writing.

with the writer's fiction either, even if they seek to undermine the fiction/nonfiction divide due to their invented and fictional elements. Céline's post–World War II works, in particular, would pose an interesting challenge to any simple distinction between fiction and autobiography, but since these works include only a few short passages about his life in Africa they are not included here. The trajectory of Céline's literary career is obviously also marked by the anti-Semitic pamphlets that he wrote in the late 1930s. In Waugh's travel writings, colonialism is much less problematic for the author than in the other examples.

Nevertheless, reading fiction and nonfiction side by side in these authors' works allows us to make relevant comparisons that suggest meaningful conclusions about the interplay and cross-fertilization between the respective genres. Blixen's description of scenes of storytelling indicates that, at some more profound level of a person's life story, the distinction between fictional and nonfictional sources of narrative loses its usefulness. Leiris's African travelogue pursues the issue of fictionality, and the relation between memory and the reality of a place, in a way that directly relates to the other writers included here. The reading of Simenon's travel writing together with his less known "exotic novels" or "romans du monde," which are set in the places of his travel, makes apparent some of the subtle strategies by which this writer constructed his realist fiction. Gide's African travelogue, in turn, marks a critical moment in the writer's career that is perhaps not given the attention that it deserves. The description of acts of reading in *Travels in the Congo*, for instance, suggests a sense of continuity with many questions that Gide, or his mouthpieces in *The Counterfeiters*, had raised about the novel genre prior to the journey. Moreover, his African travelogue opened up a new phase in his career in terms of politically engaged writing. Céline's novel *Journey to the End of the Night*, finally, since it exaggerates and thus undermines some common stereotypes of Black Africa, but also because his description of African colonial life acquired a certain authority in this time (similar to even if less influential than *Heart of Darkness*), allows us to investigate the distinction between factuality and fictionality that is at the core of this study.

PART I
Narrating and Describing West Africa

The Enchanted Arrival
Passage into West Africa in the Travel Writings of Blaise Cendrars, André Gide, and Graham Greene

A FAVORITE CONVENTION in travel writing is the portrayal of the traveller's arrival in a foreign country or culture. The first impressions and contacts at the border, the train station, the harbor or the airport are a stock item of modern travel literature. Typically, the scenes of arrival dramatize the traveller's cross-cultural encounters with local people or his or her experience of radical contingency. In terms of narrative organization, the arrival scene can function as another beginning in the story beyond the traveller's initial departure from home. The experience of arrival may also, as we will later see, require the traveller to reflect on his presuppositions concerning the place where he has travelled and make apparent the way in which he or she conceptualizes the meaning of his travel.

As a potential new beginning in a travel narrative, the arrival relates to what James Phelan has defined as a "launch" in his four-part conception of narrative beginnings in fiction. Different from exposition, and the rhetorical transactions of "initiation" or "entrance" that take place between the implied author, the narrator, and the reader, Phelan defines "launch" as "the first set of global instabilities or tensions in the narrative"—the launch thus makes the boundary between the narrative's beginning and the middle (2009, 197–98).[1]

---

1. Initiation refers to the initial rhetorical transactions—such as "rules of notice" (Peter J. Rabinowitz) concerning what counts as important in a given narrative—between the implied author and the narrator, on the one hand, and the flesh-and-blood reader and the hypotheti-

Conventionally, the arrival in the destination is a turning point in the nonfiction travel narrative and inaugurates an uncertainty—what will happen here? what will happen next? what is it going to be like?—or may suggest a preliminary conclusion to an uncertainty relating to the traveller's potentially conflicting expectations of "what it's like?" that he or she has developed prior to the arrival. In other words, the arrival scenes in travel writing typically serve the function of a "launch," establishing a new direction for the travel and the narrative, and marking the real beginning of the voyage.

In what follows, I will investigate three scenes of arrival in sub-Saharan West Africa in travel writing where the travel writer perceives the entryway as the real beginning of the voyage and, at the same time, more or less metaphorically, as a relocation in another world. The examples include Blaise Cendrars's collection of travel poems entitled *Feuilles de route* (1924–28), André Gide's travel journals *Voyage au Congo* (1927) and *Le retour du Tchad* (1928) (translated into English as *Travels in the Congo*), and Graham Greene's travelogue *Journey Without Maps* (1936). All three travel accounts describe the writer-traveller's arrival in West African port towns by boat—and all of them feature an arrival in Dakar, Senegal—suggesting a set of narrative and cognitive tensions that call for resolution. What interests me especially in their scenes of arrival are the ways in which they foreground the writer's mental processes and, simultaneously, evoke dense meanings of Africa as a "world" that makes a perfect contrast to the traveller's point of departure in Europe. My inquiry focuses on the way in which the travel writer portrays the space of arrival, and the people who are involved in that scene, thus creating a kind of symbolism of that space that helps to identify the real beginning of the voyage.[2] These scenes trigger, furthermore, the question of the language and means of description, pointing to the traveller's necessity to transform geography, space, and the experience of encounter into a description and the temporal structure of narrative. The African world into which these travellers enter requires, for instance, the writer to change the temporal frame of reference in which his or her earlier observations were made and recorded. The use of poetic language is another means by which the writers frame the tensions and instabilities of the arrival scene, and the expectations that are built around it, suggesting that poetic description may better describe the power and complexity of the experience than everyday language.

---

cal audience roles on the other (Phelan 2009, 198). Phelan defines "entrance" as "the flesh-and-blood reader's multi-leveled movement from outside the text to a specific location in the authorial audience" at the end of the launch—"authorial audience" meaning the hypothetical, ideal audience for whom the author constructs the text (Phelan 2009, 198).

2. See Requemora (2002) who has undertaken a similar investigation with regard to the representation of space in French seventeenth-century maritime travel literature.

Cendrars's Ideal Black Culture

On his first voyage to Brazil in 1924, Blaise Cendrars (1887–1961) had the chance to visit Dakar, where his ocean liner *Le Formose* made a short stopover on its way to Sao Paolo, Brazil. The port call took place on January 26, about two weeks after Cendrars had left Le Havre, and it remained the writer's only visit to Africa in his lifetime. Cendrars describes the visit in a series of entries in the first part of his lyrical travel book, *Feuilles de route*. These texts include a short account of the entry into the port of the town ("Dakar"), where Cendrars relates the sight of a red seawall, blue sky, and a dazzling white beach upon arrival; a poem about visiting the island of Gorée and its House of Slaves near the main port of Dakar ("Gorée"); an entry about listening to a French passenger's anecdote concerning the making of artificial eggs while he was waiting to disembark ("Œufs artificiels"); and a series of three poems about things that he saw in the town. The longest poem in this series is called "The Mumus" ("Les boubous"), which focuses on the dress and elegance of Senegalese women.

In Cendrars's career, *Feuilles de route* represents an important stage in his gradual move away from formally experimental writing and avant-garde aesthetics, such as his early *Prose du Transsibérien*, towards storytelling and prose genres, resulting in the publication of the biographical novel and international bestseller *L'Or* (*Sutter's Gold*) in 1925, and another novel, *Moravagine*, in the following year. Cendrars started writing *Sutter's Gold* on his return to Europe.[3] This shift in the author's career is reflected in a number of poems included in *Feuilles de route*, and also in the entries about the scene of arrival in Dakar. For instance, Cendrars's discomfort with the notion of poetry, including not just traditional definitions of poetry but also avant-garde aesthetics, is clearly reflected in his ironic take on Apollinaire's first visual poem, "Lettre-Océan," just prior to the arrival in Dakar. In Apollinaire's famous telegraphic message, which was addressed to his brother travelling in Mexico, Apollinaire used diverse typographies and explored the visual contours of the page by placing words in a series of concentric circles radiating outward from

---

3. The classification of the texts in this collection as poems is not altogether clear even though they are included in Cendrars's complete poems (*Poésies complètes*). The title of the book refers to a road map (*feuille de route*) in the sense of a military term for directions (marching orders) and Cendrars defines the entries as "ocean letters." Cendrars's lyrical travel entries, even though they have the appearance of separate, individually entitled poems, are hardly poetic in the sense that they contain very little metaphoric language and their style is prosaic, often elliptical, and summarizing. For instance, Cendrars systematically describes the contents of his baggage, records impressions of things that he has seen, and collects short anecdotes of encounters *en route*.

a circular centre.⁴ In contrast, Cendrars's poem "Lettre-Océan" is a practical telegram message cut up into short lines and written in prose style:

> La lettre-océan n'est pas un nouveau genre poétique / C'est un message pratique à tarif régressif et bien meilleur / marché qu'un radio (2001, 204)

> The ocean letter is not a new poetic genre / It's a practical message with a descending rate and a lot cheaper than a / radiogram / (1992, 150)

Cendrars explains that with his ocean letters his intention was not to write poetry. In contrast, an ocean letter forges a close relationship with the travel experience and the real world. The rejection of poetry for the sake of poetic experience somehow translates as being more real and instantaneous:

> La lettre-océan n'a pas été inventée pour faire de la / poésie / Mais quand on voyage quand on commerce quand on est / à bord quand on envoie des lettres-océan / On fait de la poésie. (2001, 204)

> The ocean letter was not invented for writing poetry / But when you travel when you do business when you're on board when / you send ocean letters / It's poetry. (1992, 150)

In lieu of attempting a literary invention, an ocean letter is a testimonial to the openness of the travel experience, which Cendrars sees in its own right as a poetic activity, free from all established forms and genres of literature.

The result was a hybrid genre of lyrical travel writing. In his poems (or ocean letters) about the arrival in Dakar, Cendrars reiterates the desire for open spaces and immediate experience that characterizes an ocean letter. What is apparent in the expression "Negro village" that Cendrars uses in "The Mumus" and in another of the Dakar poems, "Les charognards," is that it emphasizes the non-European nature of the world being described. In "The Mumus," Cendrars glorifies the African women he saw and met during the stopover, claiming that they are beyond any point of comparison with women in other continents, and especially in Europe:

> Aucune femme au monde ne possède cette distinction cette noblesse
>   cette démarche cette allure ce port cette élégance cette nonchalance

---

4. When the poem was first published in the journal *Les Soirées de Paris* in 1914, it almost had the status of a manifesto due to its radical visual style and collage technique.

ce raffinement cette propreté cette hygiène cette santé cet optimisme
cette inconscience cette jeunesse ce goût (2001, 207)

No other women in the world possess that distinctiveness that nobility
 that bearing that demeanor that carriage that elegance that
 nonchalance that refinement that neatness that hygiene that health
 that optimism that obliviousness that youthfulness that taste (1992, 152)

The writer then introduces a parade of non-African women who have nothing of the nobility, elegance and optimism that he had seen in Dakar, from the aristocratic English women of Hyde Park mornings and Spanish women on a Sunday evening walk to the most Parisian of the Parisian women. Cendrars celebrates the Senegalese women's tufts of hair, shiny braids, head ornaments, embroidery, rings, bracelets, tattoos, makeup, painted heels, *boubou* dresses of different length, belts and charms, heavenly turbans, and impeccable teeth. Re-evoking in this description the idealized black body of *l'art nègre*, Cendrars further compares the shine of these women's teeth and their gait to the fine movements of a luxury boat. For Cendrars, the most impressive aspects of these women are the subtle proportions of their bodies and the self-conscious nonchalance of their walk. Curiously, while Cendrars rejects the comparison to any other women who had left an impression on him during his travels, he evokes an analogy with an inanimate object. The comparison with a moving vehicle, a luxury boat, adds to the superiority of the Senegalese women given the writer's emphasis on his journey out of Europe as a means towards renewed perception, bodily transformation, and fulfilment.

The black body and African dress thus function as important metaphors for the promises of the journey ahead. The portrait presents to us a corporeal image of plenitude, abundance, confidence, optimism, and perfect movement that connote the sense of harmony with one's body and the surroundings. Furthermore, the Senegalese women's self-confidence and what seems to Cendrars as their perfect assimilation to their environment anticipate the characteristics that he was later to associate with the "Utopialand" of Brazil on his many travels to South America.

"The Mumus" is simultaneously a continuation and extension of the writer's earlier "poèmes nègres," with some important alterations in emphasis. If we look backward in his career, Cendrars's description of the African woman's body and dress in Dakar resonates with the mythical vision of the first black human being, the founder of civilization whom Cendrars had conceived of in the production of the "Swedish" ballet *La Création du monde* (1923) and earlier "poèmes nègres." As to their exotic primitivism, Cendrars's first "poèmes nègres," "Continent noir" et "Les grands fétiches," which were written around 1916 (and published in 1922), were not remarkably different from other avant-garde texts of the same period that were engaged with so-called primitive material, including for instance Dadaist "negro" songs and poems that used quasi-African names and sounds to underscore the interruptive and "instinctual" force of the expression. In "The Great Fetishes," Cendrars describes a series of African fetishes, meaning the statuettes and masks that he had seen in a museum catalogue, probably in the British Museum, including a male figure who "tears his belly / And worships his risen member" (1992, 96) ("déchire son ventre / Et adore son membre dressé"; 2001, 141) and a statuette of a female African that he "likes the best" and that has a "mouth shaped like a funnel" and a "gaze shining like a bugle" (1992, 98) ("une bouche en entonnoir" [. . .] "et le regard astiqué comme un cuivre"; 2001, 143). Similarly to "The Mumus," the speaker in the poem finds inspiration in direct observation of black bodies that are compared to inanimate objects (funnel, bugle).

The fashion of *l'art nègre* in early twentieth-century Europe, to which Cendrars contributed with his avant-garde poems and productions, adored African statues and black jazz dancers. The same fascinated perception frames Cendrars's experience of arrival in Africa but, at the same time, "The Mumus" and the other poems about Dakar in *Feuilles de route* reflect a fundamental contradiction within Cendrars's fascination, and often also identification, with black cultures. On the one hand, the African model, from the tradition of folktales that he researched to the image of the perfectly shaped and functioning black body, indicated for Cendrars the possibility to freely invent and mythologize his self, thus suggesting a form of escape not only from modernity and the avant-garde circles of Paris but the limitations of his own self and body. On the other hand, Black people and their cultures represented for Cendrars a common ground for all humanity that was lost and should be rediscovered.

Cendrars's identification with Black people, as also Judith Trachsel has pointed out, concerned both the identification with the people themselves and all objects that their cultures have produced (1992, 54). The desire for identification runs through his work and profoundly informs Cendrars's thinking about the origin of language and literature (1992, 55). However, by around the beginning of the 1920s it had become clear to Cendrars that the notion of so-called Negro poetry was no longer a means of revolt as it still was, for instance, for the Dadaists, but instead offered an important means by which to contest and broaden the Western concept of literature from within. Cendrars distanced himself from the exoticizing perspective of *l'art nègre* and the avant-garde "Negro poems" particularly in his reinterpretation of the

African art of storytelling in the last years of the 1910s and the early 1920s. To the extent that Cendrars underscored, in collecting and interpreting African folktales, spirituality and literature as an ideal and a model for the future, and not only as a civilization that was comparable to ours, he also questioned the ethnocentric gaze on *l'art nègre* that saw so-called primitive art as an incarnation of the original simplicity of expression or of pure instincts.[5]

The composition of l'*Anthologie nègre* (1921) and two other complementary volumes featuring traditional African stories, published later as *Petits contes nègres pour les enfants des blancs* (1928) and *Comment les blancs sont d'anciens noirs* (1930), reflect the same contradiction between the necessity to construct a vision of an original and mythopoetic Africa, as a part of the poet's personal mythology and process of self-fashioning, and the writer's careful attention to "black" literary tradition in its own right. By publishing these anthologies Cendrars promoted the idea of a mythological Africa, an Africa manifesting ancient ways of life, thought, and literature, and the plenitude of language (*plénitude du langage*) that he writes about in his notice to *Anthologie nègre*. At the same time, these anthologies elevate the African art of storytelling to the level of literature, thus allowing the Francophone Occident to read, perhaps for the first time, African stories as literature and not simply as ethnographic documents. Despite the writer's thematic organization and other manipulation of these materials that were originally collected by missionaries and colonisers, the anthologies pointed out to the readers the inherent value in the African tradition of storytelling, thus suggesting the possibility of transforming European literature from within, not only by appropriating the other but by giving them a voice, albeit a filtered and indirect one.

Cendrars's Broken Body Image

In the three poems that describe Cendrars's visit to Dakar, and in some earlier entries in *Feuilles de route* where he anticipates the arrival, the writer's antimodern, even Europhobic impulses become quite explicit. In "Bijou-Concert," Cendrars represents the European colonials of Dakar as hopelessly corrupt, as "filthy cows" (*sales vaches*) who are wasting their lives away from home, and explains, in a kind of wishful identification, how he wants to be the poor

---

5. Moreover, Cendrars's conception of "Negro" or black culture is not reducible to the academic notion of the prelogical primitive mentality, based on Lucien Lévy-Bruhl's pseudo-ethnographic theories. For Cendrars, the Africans were, above all, storytellers and in this role they also necessarily possessed a good sense of causal relations, as was required in storytelling.

African he sees in the street—"I want to be this poor black man I want to be this poor black who stands / in the doorway" (1992, 154) ("je voudrais être ce pauvre nègre je voudrais être ce pauvre nègre qui reste à la porte"; 2001, 208)— and states that he will never set his feet in these "colonial dives" ("beuglant colonial") again. This was to be so, since Cendrars never returned to Africa. In "En route pour Dakar," Cendrars writes twice his farewell to Europe, explaining the need to forget Europe and, further, to sleep with and merge with the rest of the world, including its animals and plants:

Adieu Europe que je quitte pour la première fois depuis 1914
Rien ne m'intéresse plus à ton bord plus que les émigrants de l'entrepont
    juifs russes basques espagnols portugais et saltimbanques allemands
    qui regrettent Paris
Je veux tout oublier ne plus parler tes langues et coucher avec des nègres
    et des négresses des indiens et des indiennes des animaux des plantes
Et prendre un bain et vivre dans l'eau
Et prendre un bain et vivre dans le soleil en compagnie d'un gros bananier
Et aimer le gros bourgeon de cette plante (2001, 200)

Goodbye Europe which I leave for the first time since 1914
I am no longer interested in you not even the emigrants in steerage the
    Jews Russians Basques
Spaniards Portuguese and German saltimbanques who miss Paris
I want to forget everything no longer speak your languages and sleep
    alongside black men and women and Indian men and women
    animals and plants
And take a bath and live in the water
And take a bath and live in the sun with a big banana tree
And love the big buds of that plant (1992, 147)

The non-European space, of which the town of Dakar is Cendrars's first actual point of reference in this journey, promises to the writer a multiform life in the water and the sun, in love with the bud of a banana tree, to the point of "segmenting my own self" or becoming a stone so as to freely fall from the heights. The image of bodily division and transformation included in this fantasy—"To segment my own self / And become hard as a rock" ("Me segmenter moi-même / Et devenir dur comme un caillou")—is particularly evocative when we consider the fact that Cendrars had lost one of his arms due to a war injury. Cendrars was seriously wounded in the line of fire in Champagne in September 1915 and his right arm was amputated a few months later (in

February 1916). The description of the fullness and optimism of the black body, and the desire to identify with the Africans—a desire that characterizes both the early "Negro poems" and the Dakar poems—may become more understandable in this context, the traveller still suffering from his lost arm and broken body image: "My body is steel" ("mon corps est d'acier").

Throughout the journey, Cendrars evokes the metaphor of the fragmented body in relation to the myth of Orion, the great blind hunter, who has the ability to heal the body with the help of cosmic forces. According to the myth, Orion was healed from blindness by the rising sun. In an entry entitled "Nuits étoilées," where Cendrars describes his observations of the sky at night time from the deck of *Le Formose,* he claims that Orion is his constellation ("sa constellation"; 2001, 211). The same stress on the cure offered by the stars and the sun also explains Cendrars's admiration for the dawn, of which he writes in the preceding entry ("Couchers de soleil")—an admiration he thinks is uncommon among travellers in comparison with the love of the tropical sunset. Throughout his journey, and especially on the way from Dakar to Brazil, Cendrars associates the sun, the stars, and the southern hemisphere, with the power of reinvigoration.

Shortly after the entries about the southern sky, Cendrars confirms the importance of the metaphoric blend between a hand and the constellation of Orion in the image of the one-handed Orion: "It's my star / It's in the form of a hand / It's my hand gone up into the sky" (1992, 159) ("C'est mon étoile / Elle a la forme d'une main / C'est ma main montée au ciel") and further,

> Aujourd'hui je l'ai [Orion] au-dessus de ma tête
> Le grand mât perce la paume de cette main qui doit souffrir
> Comme ma main coupée me fait souffrir percée qu'elle est par un dard continuel (2001, 214)

> I have it [Orion] above my head today
> The main mast pierces the palm of that hand which must hurt
> As my amputated hand hurts me pierced as it is by a continual stabbing pain (1992, 159)

Just like Orion who, after his death is transformed into a constellation, the lost but still painfully felt hand mutates in Cendrars's poems into a cosmic image.[6]

---

6. The poem "Orion" is not the first time that Cendrars evokes the same metaphor, however. He makes use of the Orion myth, for instance, in the unfinished poem "Au cœur du monde," the first fragment of which was published in 1919, though Cendrars had worked on it earlier in 1917: "Ma main coupée brille au ciel dans la constellation d'Orion" (2001, 303) ("My cut

The metaphor of the astral hand, which would remain a constant theme in Cendrars's oeuvre, thus contributes to the author's reinterpretation of his life as a myth (or the mythologization of his life narrative).

Therefore, upon his arrival in Dakar Cendrars contrasts his fragmented body with the idealized body of Black people. At the same time, it is important to note the affinity between the image of the body of plenitude and the experience of open vast spaces, and the power of the southern sun, in sea voyages. The non-European spaces in Cendrars's travelogue, from Dakar to Rio de Janeiro and Sao Paolo, from the vast ocean to the southern skies, are open spaces where liberty of thought and imagination, and bodily freedom, are constantly affirmed. The sky and ocean of the Great South, like the elegance and perfection that Cendrars finds in Senegalese women, occur as a response to the writer's almost obsessive need for exotic experiences that might heal his body. After Dakar, Cendrars perceives in "White Suit" ("Complet blanc"), pacing around the deck in the white suit that he had bought in Dakar, how he felt like a king, rich as a billionaire, and free as a man ("Heureux comme un roi / Riche comme un milliardaire / Libre comme un homme"; 2001, 212). At least some of Cendrars's expectations about the voyage seem to have been met at this point in the journey.

The sense of displacement in travel as a value in itself emerges in the entries immediately following Dakar, suggesting for Cendrars ever-new images and mythical analogies, and freedom of thought. He writes in "Cabin No.6": "Because tons of things go through my head but don't get out into the / cabin / I'm living in a breeze the porthole wide open and the fan whirring / Not reading" (1992, 157) ("Car des tas de choses me passent par la tête mais n'entrent pas / dans ma cabine / Je vis dans un courant d'air le hublot grand ouvert et le ventilateur / ronflant / Je ne lis rien"; 2001, 213). Reading and staying inside his cabin are here contrasted with the open spaces of the ocean. In further entries on the way to Brazil, Cendrars suggests that European civilization has lost its contact with myth and nature, as well as with optimism, burdened as it is with the past.

The stopover in Dakar marked for Cendrars the first major creative rupture from what he had started increasingly to see as the stagnation of European civilization. By contrast, the black women in Senegal imply to him the continuity of an ancient mythopoeic civilization, the "heart of the world," at once representative of the mythological past and the optimistic future. Furthermore, far removed from the concerns of the aesthetes and the avant-

---

off hand shines in the sky in the constellation of Orion"). For a more comprehensive analysis of bodily metaphors in *Feuilles de route* see Leroy, 1996, 155–66, and Mikkonen 2009a.

gardes of Paris, the non-European spaces and people, from Dakar on, stand in Cendrars's travelogue for the life-affirming forces of the art of storytelling: the ability of the storyteller to focus on what is important in his life, such as the contingency, immediacy, and dynamism of the experience, or the relationship with the forces of nature, and to transmit tested and mythical knowledge about ways of living from generation to generation. The invention of a new genre of travel writing, the nonpoetic poetry of the ocean letters, reflects the writer's high expectations of rupture with the past.

Gide's Lyricism

In *Travels in the Congo* Gide portrays his journey in West Africa with Marc Allégret, which started on the steamship *Asie* from Bordeaux in July 1925, as a gradual penetration into the continent, comprising a series of scenes of arrival that took him and his companion ever deeper into the interior of the continent. The arrival in coastal Africa, however, in the "French town" of Dakar on the July 26, 1925, was a clear disappointment to Gide. The "dreary," night-time town, with its narrow and deserted streets, was far detached from his expectations of the exotic ("rien de moins exotique, de plus laid"; 2002, 15; "Impossible to imagine anything less exotic or more ugly"; 1957, 5) even if he enjoyed, as he writes, being among the Negroes. In Dakar, Gide went to a small open-air cinema, and attempted to visit a native village outside the town. However, a lagoon that they could not get around prevented Gide from reaching the village. Here we could speak of a deferred "launch": the arrival in the destination does not establish a new direction for the journey, at least not immediately, and leaves the traveller in a state of anticipation for the real beginning of the voyage. In contrast, the subsequent stopovers in Conakry, Grand-Bassam, and Libreville along the coast were more promising. This is well reflected in Gide's descriptions of local people and nature. For instance, during the port call in Conakry on the July 29, Gide portrays the young black youth who was his rickshaw puller with a citation from Baudelaire's poem "Parfum exotique," calling him vigorous and slender ("mince et vigoureux"). A few days later in Libreville Gide draws from Baudelaire's poetic imagery about the happy shores of an "indolent isle" and a distant harbor where sweet, exotic indolence reigns to illustrate the atmosphere of that city. Here are the last five lines of the poem that Gide recalls upon his arrival in West Africa:

> Je vois un port rempli de voiles et de mâts
> Encor tout fatigués par la vague marine,

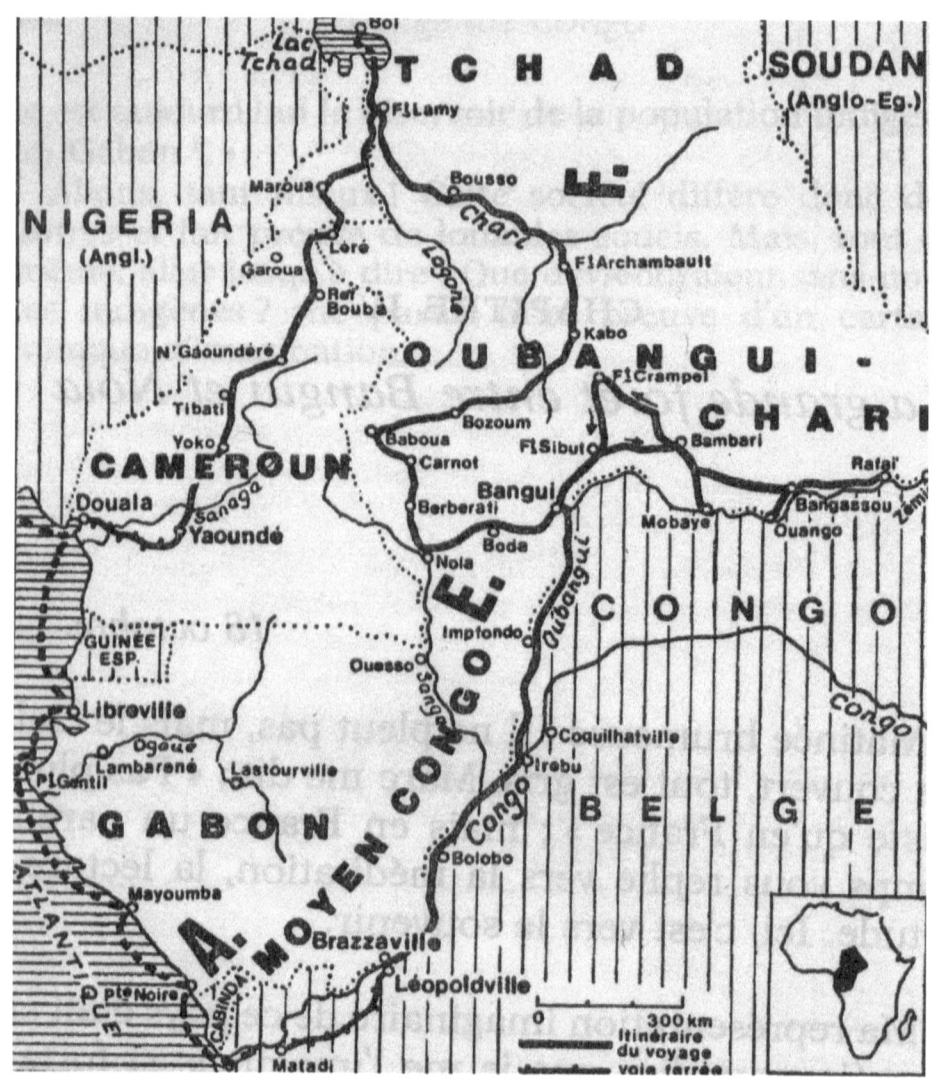

Figure 1. Map of Ubangi-Shari and Chad, showing André Gide's route between August 1925 and May 1926 (André Gide. *Voyage au Congo suivi de Le retour du Tchad. Carnets de route.* © Éditions Gallimard).

Pendant que le parfum des verts tamariniers,
Qui circule dans l'air et m'enfle la narine,
Se mêle dans mon âme au chant des mariniers. (Baudelaire 1991, 75)

I see a port filled with sails and rigging
Still utterly wearied by the waves of the sea,
While the perfume of the green tamarinds,
That permeates the air, and elates my nostrils,
Is mingled in my soul with the sailors' chanteys.[7]

Baudelaire's poem frames the early stages of the journey. Marvelling at the extraordinary silence and sweetness of the air in Conakry, Gide concludes the entry by noting how everything in this town and in its surroundings promised happiness, sensual pleasure and oblivion ("Tout ici semble promettre le Bonheur, la volupté, l'oubli"; 2002, 17). Grand-Bassam, then, confirms for Gide the sense of the exotic, with the sights of laughing and arguing, naked Negros and their "cannibal teeth" ("les nègres nus crient, rient et se querellent en montrant des dents des cannibales"; 2002, 18–19), the strange big trees that astonish the travellers, and the abundant vegetation. All this further suggests to Gide the exciting closeness of the real virgin forest ("l'immense forêt vierge, la vraie"; 2002, 18) that held the full exotic promise of the journey for him. In Libreville, Gide returns to "Parfum exotique," quoting the lines about the singular trees and the savory fruits ("où la nature donne / Des arbres singuliers et des fruits savoureux"; Gide 2002b, 18), inspired by what he calls the enchanting land. The lyricism that Gide associates with Libreville is marked with a difference however. While emphasizing the exoticism of the experience, Gide simultaneously underscores the famine in the city, thus juxtaposing harsh reality with his expectations of the exotic. He mentions, further, that the food shortage was supposed to be even greater in the interior of the country.

While moving down the African coast, anticipating the real beginning of the voyage, Gide continues to make use of Baudelairean imagery. In Mayumba, in Gabon, during one of the last stopovers before the *Asie* entered the Congo River, Gide writes about the lyricism of the black rowers of his canoe, focusing on the rhythm of the black men's singing and the movement of their bodies:

Lyrisme des pagayeurs, au dangereux franchissement de la barre. Les couplets et les refrains de leur chant rythmé se chevauchent. À chaque

---

7. Trans. William Aggeler (Baudelaire 1954).

> enfoncement dans le flot, la tige de la pagaie prend appui sur la cuisse nue. Beauté sauvage de ce chant semi-triste; allégresse musculaire; enthousiasme farouche. (2002, 21–22)

> The dangerous crossing of the bar was made to the accompaniment of the boatmen's lyrical chanting. The song and the refrain overlap each other. Every time the boat dips, the boatman uses his bare thigh as leverage for the pole of his paddle. There was a wild beauty in this half-plaintive chant; a joyous play of the muscles; a farouche enthusiasm. (1957, 10)

During the stopover in Mayumba Gide took a walk in the woods, noting the strangeness of the sights and the excitement of not having experienced such a vivid joy in twenty years. In these passages, Gide resorts to his old formula of sensualizing Africa, as manifested for instance in *Paludes* (1895), *Les nourritures terrestres* (1897) and *L'Immoraliste* (1902), in which he projects North Africa as a kind of refuge from the West where he could explore sexual freedoms unburdened by moral and family constraints. In *Paludes,* for instance, the narrator plans to fight the boredom of Paris by leaving for Biskra, Algeria, where Gide and the painter Paul-Albert Laurens had stayed during their nine-month journey in North Africa and Italy in the winter of 1893–94. It was during this journey that Gide had his first homosexual experiences with young Arab men in Sousse, Tunisia.

Many of the experiences after Dakar had a strong rejuvenating effect on the traveller. A desire to see what is not usually seen, and to step off the trodden path, so as to penetrate profoundly into the country, conditions the beginning of his journey:

> Ce que nous voulons, c'est précisément quitter les routes usuelles; c'est voir ce que l'on ne voit pas d'ordinaire, c'est pénétrer profondément, intimement, dans le pays. (2002, 97)

> What we want is precisely to leave the beaten track, to see what one does not see ordinarily, to enter profoundly, intimately, into the heart of the country. (1957, 61)

Beyond Dakar, entering the more distant towns, the river, and finally the jungle, the journey seemed to revive for Gide forgotten joys and pleasures. In entering the rivers of the Congo, again inspired by Baudelaire (and this time also Conrad), Gide remarks that

La joie est peut-être aussi vive; mais elle entre en moi moins avant; elle éveille un écho moins retentissant dans mon cœur. Ah! pouvoir ignorer que la vie rétrécit devant moi sa promesse . . . Mon cœur ne bat pas moins fort qu'à vingt ans. (2002, 23)

My joy is perhaps as keen; but it penetrates less deeply; it re-echoes in my heart less soundingly. Oh, if only I could forget that life's promises are closing in before me! . . . My heart beats as if I were twenty. (1957, 11)

Entering the Congo River held much promise for the traveller. For instance, Gide explains that he rediscovered the joys of a child and a young man in Brazzaville a few days later when he chased unknown insects and caught fine specimens of tailed butterflies by the river. By the Congo River, Gide portrays in his entries the invigorating effects of mere movement (or "lyrisme ambulatoire"; 2002, 186), exquisite bathing, the magnificent trees and forests, the chasing of insects and the observation of butterflies, the vigorous bodies of the Africans, the air, the forces of light and the sun. He also writes about the pleasures of reading and the reading lessons with Adoum, who is one of the carrier boys of his team. We will return to the importance of reading in Gide's travel in Part 2.

Nevertheless, the writer's disabilities never cease to haunt him. The sensation of numbness (*engourdissement*) that Gide had described on several occasions in his *Journal* prior to the journey becomes associated in the travel journal with the negative forces of apathy, feebleness, and aging. In Cuverville at the end of May 1925 Gide deplored in his *Journal,* for which *Travels in the Congo* is a direct continuation, his apathy, lack of concentration, and poor sight. For some of these problems, the journey suggested a possible remedy:

Je ne compte plus que sur le Congo pour m'en sortir. La préparation de ce voyage et l'attente des pays nouveaux a désenchanté le présent; j'éprouve combien il était vrai de dire que le bonheur habite l'instant. Rien ne me paraît plus que provisoire. (1951, 806)

I have given up counting on anything but the Congo to get me out of it [my apathy]. Preparations for this trip and the expectation of new landscapes have disenchanted the present. I am experiencing how true it was to say that happiness lies in the moment. Nothing seems to me anything but provisional now. (1967, 390)

And Gide writes further that

> Ma vue a beaucoup faibli ces derniers temps. Les lunettes subviennent à cette insuffisance. Que le cerveau ne peut-il également en porter! Difficulté qu'a mon esprit de « mettre au point » l'idée qu'il examine; analogue à celle de mon œil, aujourd'hui. Les contours restent flous. (1951, 806)

> My sight has weakened considerably of late. Spectacles relieve this deficiency. Would that the brain could wear them too! Difficulty my mind has in "focusing" on the idea it is examining; analogous to my eye's difficulty today. The outlines remain fuzzy. (1967, 390)

However, in the beginning of Gide's travel journal several different versions of numbness emerge: one that is clearly negative and a continuation of the kind of apathy that Gide lamented in his *Journal*—the "torpor" of his aging body (he was 56), weak sight and apathy of mind—and another that appears to be a specifically African in nature.

In the first occurrence of the term *engourdissement* in the travel journal, in an entry for August 30, 1925 in Brazzaville, the sensation of numbness equals a profound apathy and a sense of physical decline:

> Engourdissement, peut-être diminution. La vue baisse; l'oreille durcit, aussi bien portent-elles moins loin des désirs sans doute plus faibles. L'important, c'est que cette équation se maintienne entre l'impulsion de l'âme et l'obéissance du corps. Puissé-je, même alors et vieillissant, maintenir en moi l'harmonie. Je n'aime pas l'orgueilleux raidissement du stoïque; mais l'horreur de la mort, de la vieillesse et de tout ce qui ne se peut éviter, me semble impie. Je voudrais rendre à Dieu quoi qu'il m'advienne, une âme reconnaissante et ravie. (2002, 32)

> I recognize a numbness—perhaps a diminution. Eyes are less keen; ears duller; and they carry less far desires that are no doubt weaker. The important thing is that this equation between the urging of the soul and the obedience of the body should be maintained. Even when growing old, may I preserve within myself an undiminished harmony! I do not like the Stoic's proud stiffening of the lip; but the horror of death, of old age, of all that cannot be avoided, strikes me as impious. Whatever may be my fate, I should wish to return to God a grateful and enraptured soul. (1957, 17)

For Gide, this numbness threatened to destroy all sense of harmony between body and mind. During the journey, Gide keeps evoking the contradiction between an old body, which suffers from the decline of its physical forces, and the joys of a child. At one point in Bangui, Gide portrays this contrast as an interior battle between his reason and intuition: "my reason sometimes tells me that I am perhaps rather too old to plunge into the bush and into a life of adventure—but I do not believe my reason" (1957, 61) ("ma raison me dit parfois que je suis peut-être un peu vieux pour me lancer dans la brousse et dans l'aventure; mais je ne le crois pas"; 2002, 97). At the same time, we must note how Gide's inner battle against numbness and apathy is reflected in some of his observations about Africans. Contrary to the ideal harmony of body and mind that Gide sought in his travel, the African jungle and the African crowds in forest villages, the two often being interwoven in the description, become marked, as the journey advances, by the writer's profound uncertainty about whether the battle against apathy and age is really possible.

Beyond the ports of West Africa, and the Congo River, entering the great forests of the interior constitutes the most powerful and final scene of arrival in Gide's travel journal, marking the frontier between the beginning and the middle of the travel narrative. The African jungle, and some of the African crowds, are for Gide, in his sensualizing and exoticizing vision, Janus-faced, characteristically multiple and mobile.[8] The immense forest and the Africans in forest villages alternatively suggest to the traveller the possibility of invigoration and further numbness. As we can see in his travelogue, the space of "the great virgin forest—the real forest" attracted Gide profoundly and promised to him the escape he so desperately longed for. After Dakar, Gide occasionally gets carried away by a lyricism of the exotic, inspired by Baudelaire. The final threshold of this exoticism was the vast jungles of Africa, and after that there is much less poetry in Gide's journal. Gide portrays the entrance in the forest as a transforming experience, as in Conrad's *Heart of Darkness*, that might allow the traveller to forget all sense of time and place, even himself. Gide's desire to forge an immediate relation with the jungle is also reflected in his attempts to get rid of the carriers who, nevertheless, made possible his journey through the Congo and Chad in the first place:

Ici la forêt vous enveloppe et se fait plus charmante encore [. . .] J'avance dans un état de ravissement et d'exaltation indicibles (sans me douter hélas! que nous ne reverrions rien d'aussi beau). Ah! pouvoir s'arrêter ici,

---

8. See also Scott (2004, 163) on Gide's means of description of the African jungle.

pouvoir y revenir sans cette escorte de porteurs qui fait s'enfuir au loin tout le gibier . . . Parfois cette constante compagnie m'importune, m'excède. Désireux de goûter ma solitude et l'enveloppement étroit de la forêt, je presse le pas, m'échappe en courant, tâchant de distancer les porteurs. Mais aussitôt ils partent tous au petit trot pour me rejoindre (2002, 107)

The forest closes in here and becomes still more enchanting . . . . I cannot describe my rapture and excitement as I walked on (not suspecting, alas, that we should never see anything so beautiful again). Oh! If one could only have stopped! If one could only come back without an escort of porters, who put every wild creature to flight! At times this constant company irks me, exasperates me. Wanting to get a taste of solitude and feel more intimately the closeness of the forest, I quickened my step and began to run, in an attempt to escape, to out-distance the porters. In vain! They all immediately started off at a trot to catch me. (1957, 68–69)

The disturbing presence of the carriers evidently prevents Gide, or so he believed, from enjoying the full excitement of the immense jungle. In this quotation, in the parentheses, Gide also reveals in hindsight that the journey became a disappointment after the arrival in the forest. From this point on, getting closer to the middle of his journey, Gide had to give up the notion of an exotic world—perhaps a product of what Gide calls his lively, imaginary, and ultimately false, idea of the country in the first place—and the sense of numbness takes over. From then on, Gide also turns his attention to the colonial situation. This shift in perspective, marking the end of the new beginnings, turns the travel journal into a testimony of the problems of colonial rule.

Inside the tropical forest the exoticism of the experience soon wore out and Gide started to notice all-too-familiar aspects in his surroundings. Gide points out, for instance, that the forest reminded him of Italy:

Forêt des plus monotones, et très peu exotique d'aspect. Elle ressemblerait à telle forêt italienne, celle d'Albano par exemple, ou de Némi, n'était parfois quelque arbre gigantesque, deux fois plus haut qu'aucun de nos arbres d'Europe. (2002, 114)

The forest is extremely monotonous and hardly at all exotic-looking. It would be like an Italian forest—the one at Albano or the one at Nemi—except that there sometimes appears a gigantic tree (twice as tall as any of our European trees). (1957, 73–74)

As Gide penetrated deeper into the jungle the monotony of the experience became a predominant sensation. He remarks on the "perfect monotony" and the interminable quality of the jungle. He associates the forest with a disagreeable nightmare (2002, 147), shapelessness ("l'informe") (2002, 184), and "the savage, the embryonic, and the non-existent" (2002, 192) that he desired to leave behind as soon as possible, and uses mythical connotations of an infernal itinerary, comparing the forest to hell or being buried in limbo (2002, 220). The terrifying forest, finally, evokes for Gide the oppressive state of being enveloped, of suffocation, or even, to use Gide's vocabulary, a form of cannibalism, the fear of being eaten alive.

As to the Africans in the forest villages in these descriptions, Gide often writes about them as members of a large group with an essentially monotonous outlook. The village crowds and the endless jungle are both marked by the absence of individual characteristics. After four months of travel, in December 1925, Gide explains that the "absence of individuality" in the Africans had become equated in his mind with the uniformity of the landscape, "The absence of individuality, of individualization—the impossibility of differentiating" (1957, 137) ("L'absence d'individualité, d'individualisation, l'impossibilité d'arriver à une différenciation"; 2002, 195). Further, he made observations on "the population of children all alike, all equally agreeable, etc." (1957, 137) ("le peuple d'enfants tous pareils, indifféremment agréables, etc."; 195), and the "droves of human cattle with the same looks, tastes, customs, possibilities, etc." (1957, 137) ("bétail humain uniforme d'aspect, de goûts, de mœurs, de possibilités"; 2002, 195). At this point in his journey the fear of being suffocated by the crowds, and of cannibalism becomes frequent. For instance, on the way to Bosoum, upon arriving in the village of Pakori, Gide writes that "the whole population crowds round one, pressing eagerly up to have the joy of shaking the hand one holds out—all shouting and laughing in a kind of lyrical demonstration of affection—almost cannibalism!" (1957, 99) ("tout ce peuple vous enveloppe, s'empresse pour la joie de serrer la main qu'on leur tend [. . .] C'est presque du cannibalisme"; 2002, 148). Soon after, Gide writes that the residents of another village hurried up to welcome them after nightfall, "crowding round us with cannibal-like expressions of joy, and so close as almost to suffocate us" (1957, 130) ("avec des manifestations de cannibales, si serrés contre nous qu'on suffoquait"; 2002, 186).

However, in close proximity with his reports about suffocation and monotony, Gide refers to a different kind of numbness, a delicious sensation that is again reminiscent of the atmosphere in Baudelaire's "Parfum exotique" and the earlier scenes of arrival. Notably, soon after the passage where Gide describes the most profound apathy of the small villages that seemed to lack all individuality, he entered another native village that appeared to him to be completely different. Here, as Gide reports, he saw many details that pleased him, such as a group of small hanging granaries, which made these minute settlements look to him like "a Lilliputian village, built on piles" (1957, 158) ("l'aspect d'un village de Lilliput, sur pilotis"; 2002, 221). The atmosphere of this village enhanced for him the

> sentiment d'étalement des heures, de lenteur, de paresse et d'engourdissement voluptueux. Une indéfinissable atmosphère de paix, d'oubli, de bonheur. Ces gens sont tous souriants; oui, même les infirmes, les malades. (2002, 221)

> sensation of long-drawn-out hours, of slowness, of idleness, of sinking into a delicious dream. The atmosphere is one of peace, forgetfulness, happiness; the people here are all smiling; yes, even the suffering, even the sick. (1957, 158)

The delicious and voluptuous numbness that characterizes Gide's arrival in this village, and the sense of agreeable laziness and oblivion, thus affirms the exotic quality of Africa that Gide still continued to seek despite the "terrible entanglement of colonial problems" (2002, 30, 112) that he started noticing in Libreville and Brazzaville. This is yet another glimpse of the healthy and robust physicality that Gide associated with "the heart of Africa," and the young male Africans in particular, and that suggested to him at once spiritual and physical reinvigoration.

Finally, we have to account for the "demonic" motivation of travel that Gide evokes in the beginning of his travel journal and that frames his description of the series of scenes of arrival from Dakar to the jungle. In the first entry in his travel journal, Gide likens the departure for Africa to throwing himself into an abyss without full consciousness or self-control:

> Je me suis précipité dans ce voyage comme Curtius dans le gouffre. Il ne me semble déjà plus que précisément je l'aie voulu (encore que depuis des mois ma volonté se soit tendue vers lui); mais plutôt qu'il s'est imposé à moi par une sorte de fatalité inéluctable—comme tous les événements importants de ma vie. Et j'en viens à presque oublier que ce n'est là qu'un « projet de jeunesse réalisé dans l'âge mur » ce voyage au Congo, je n'avais pas vingt ans que déjà je me promettais de le faire; il y a trente-six ans de cela. (2002, 14)

> I have plunged into this journey like Curtius into the gulf. I feel already as if I had not so much willed it (though for many months past I have been stringing my will up to it) as had it imposed upon me by a sort of ineluctable fatality—like all the important events of my life. And I come near forgetting that it is nothing but a project made in youth and realized in maturity; I was barely twenty when I first made up my mind to make this journey to the Congo—thirty-six years ago. (1957, 4)

Gide thus claims that the journey was imposed on him as some nearly mythical fatality, just as the legendary Roman hero Marcus Curtius had to sacrifice himself for his people by leaping on horseback into a deep chasm that had opened up in the Roman Forum. It is noteworthy that Gide uses similar images of "le gouffre," the abyss, to describe the mysterious appeal of Africa, both in the travel journal and his novel *The Counterfeiters*. Africa has a demonic force that fatally pulls Gide's characters Vincent, Lilian, and Alexandre away from the "closed" European spaces, as if through magic, or indeed because of some demonic impulse, which may also enable the traveller to realize his fantasies. A few months into the journey, Gide asks himself about the nature of the forces that pushed him to Africa in the first place: "What demon drove me to Africa? What did I come out to find in this country? I was at peace. I know now. I must speak" (Gide 1957, 72) ("Quel démon m'a poussé en Afrique? Qu'allais-je donc chercher dans ce pays? J'étais tranquille. À présent je sais; je dois parler"; 2002, 113). Later the passage into the abyss of the great jungle becomes the ultimate and decisive response to the mysterious appeal of Africa.

Much later, in his memoir *Ainsi soit-il ou les jeux sont faits* (1952), Gide returned to the expectations that he had had at the time, explaining that his arrival in Black Africa with his companion and male friend Marc Allégret in 1925, and the commencement of their trek on a narrow path into the "mysterious forest," was one of the moments of his life that he would most like to be able to relive, despite the disillusionment that then followed (1952, 136–37). Reminiscing about the memorable entrance into the "virgin" forest, Gide writes how he and Allégret naively thought that the strangeness and the charm of the experience would only increase as they penetrated deeper into the forest. Little did they know how wrong they were. The continuation of Gide's journey after the entry in the forest is marked, in the retrospective mode of the time of writing, by disillusionment and regret. The post-Dakar scenes of arrival were to remain, in many ways, the high point of his travel experience.

Greene's Reminder of Darkness

Graham Greene (1904–1991) travelled on a cargo ship from Liverpool to Freetown, Sierra Leone, by way of Madeira and Tenerife, in January 1935, accompanied by his cousin Barbara Greene. The steamship SS *David Livingstone* of the Elder Dempster line made its first African stopover in Dakar. Greene describes the arrival in the port and his impressions of the town in a fragment (or subchapter) entitled "Dakar" included in the chapter "The Cargo Ship" in *Journey Without Maps*.

At first, when Greene's ship had just arrived in the port, he had the impression that the world was "already over-familiar" (2002, 32). The reason for the impression was that the other passengers on board had constantly been talking about *the* Coast, by which they meant West African coast towns such as Dakar. Upon disembarking, however, Greene was struck by something unexpected: the sight of African men, and especially the behavior of two men, who seemed to spend the whole day by the quay and the ships, without doing "a stroke of work" (2002, 33). These men, as Greene reports, strolled up and down the quay hand-in-hand, sometimes putting arms around each other's necks, and "laughing sleepily together under the blinding vertical glare" (2002, 33). Greene notes twice in this passage how the men's behavior was not anything "we" could understand, it was not love for instance. The pronoun "we" refers to the few European passengers on their cargo ship, such as himself and his cousin, but likely also to his expected Western readers. The men's behavior suggested to Greene a deeper insight into Africa and the Africans: "They gave to the blinding day, to the first sight of Africa, a sense of warm and sleepy beauty, of enjoyment divorced from activity and the weariness of willing" (2002, 33). Greene, then, associates this image with a citation from Baudelaire's poem "L'invitation au voyage"—the refrain "There all is order and beauty, / Luxury, peace, and pleasure"[9] ("Là, tout n'est qu'ordre et beauté, / Luxe, calme et volupté"). Greene further points out that he found it hard to believe that Baudelaire had never been to Africa and did not know Dakar but just Jeanne Duval (his lover), the "mulatto tart from *Le Théâtre du Panthéon*" (2002, 33). Evidently, Greene was not aware that Charles Baudelaire made a trip to Mauritius and back around the coast of Africa, including a port call in Cape Town, when the poet was only twenty years old (1841–1842).

Greene's arrival in Dakar triggers in the author's mind a series of textual sources in a kind of kaleidoscopic reflection. The references complement each other by way of contrast. Besides Baudelaire's poem about the mys-

---

9. Trans. William Aggeler (Baudelaire 1954).

terious charms and sensuous pleasures of distant places, the arrival brings to Greene's mind René Clair's 1931 classic comedy film *Le Million*, with "its happy lyrical absurdity" (2002, 33). Greene writes that Dakar "was the Baudelaire of *L'Invitation au Voyage*, when it was not the René Clair of *Le Million*" (2002, 33). Moreover, Greene evokes in this passage anthropologist Geoffrey Gorer's travel book *Africa Dances*, and cites from the beginning of Cecil Day-Lewis's poem "Do not expect again a phoenix hour," which ends with the line "Sudden the rain of gold and heart's first ease . . ." (2002, 34). Greene contrasts Gorer's realistic description of the town with Baudelaire on the one hand and Clair's film on the other. Both Baudelaire's poem and Clair's film relate to the "sharp differentiated pictorial quality" (2002, 33–34) of Greene's impressions in Dakar, and the women in the market in particular. Gorer's arrival in, and notes on, Dakar, or what Greene calls the inanition and hopelessness of life in the town—"He stayed too long," writes Greene, "and saw too much" (2002, 34)—are far-removed from the light atmosphere of Clair's comedy where a young Parisian artist, heavily in debt, wins a lottery only to lose his ticket. Day-Lewis's poem, in turn, seems to complement Greene's impression of the idle men's happiness and lightheartedness. Furthermore, the poem illustrates the idea of wish fulfilment similarly to Baudelaire and René Clair.

In this sequence of references Greene thus plays different contrasting and complementary textual sources against each other to illustrate the complexity of his experience and the movements of his mind upon arrival. Clair's *Le Million* and the poems, moreover, point out to Greene that something important was "momentarily shining through" or "breaking through" the predominantly poor, harsh, and even depressing West African reality. In other words, this is some more authentic form of life than "as one had been made to live it" (2002, 34). As the *SS David Livingstone* moved ahead and Greene found more evidence of the poverty of the Coast, and continued to discover signs of yellow fever and hopelessness among the people, he realized that his first impression "was not the Coast" (2002, 34). By contrast, he accepted that the first impression was just an impression, and the happiness in the image was related to his limited experience as a traveller, as someone who was merely passing through. Greene ends the scene of his arrival with a grim image, relating how the Captain of his ship shot a hawk that was sitting in the rigging. The dusty body of the bird fell on the deck, "like a reminder of darkness" (2002, 35).

The same words, "reminder of darkness," that end the arrival scene of the Dakar section start the subsequent fragment entitled "The Shape of Africa," where Greene parades a series of memories of "darkness" from England and Europe. Greene thus ties the scene of the arrival, and the notion of African darkness, with a series of memories concerning the ambivalent experience of the "pleasure of cruelty," which means for him the simultaneous sensation of happiness and pain. In the beginning of this fragment, in a kind of frame story, Greene relates a memory of a weeping girl whom he had observed near Leicester Square in a bar called the Queen's bar. Greene points out that the girl's tears indicated to him something enviable, that is, the experience of lost love and happiness that was unfamiliar to him at that time. In the frame narrative Greene then embeds other memories from his childhood, and some more recent experiences, including the happiness of a quick impression when his airplane landed safely at night in dark Berlin, while on the ground in the city, "among the swastikas, one saw pain at every yard" (2002, 36). Furthermore, Greene recalls the memory of seeing from a hotel window in Paris in 1924 a man and a woman copulating in the street, "like two people who are supporting and comforting each other in the pain of some sickness" (2002, 36). He also mentions the first thing that he remembered at all. This involved a dead dog that his nurse had placed at the bottom of his pram and that he had perceived with the "admirable objectivity" of a child. Greene also relates how when he was fourteen he realized the pleasure of cruelty and pain. This was because of a girl in his neighborhood to whom he "wanted to do things" (2002, 37). He loitered outside the girl's door but could not do anything else, or did not know what to do since he was not old enough, but at the same time felt deeply happy about the experience.

The frame narrative of "The Shape of Africa" that embeds these associations, involving various instances of symbolic darkness, explains the title and elaborates the thematic structure of the fragment. The key moment in the memory of the weeping girl in the Queen's bar for Greene was another association: a subtle relationship that his mind forged between the girl and the idea of Africa that dawned on him at that moment. The weeping and drinking girl whom he was watching from the other end of the bar, and around whom a space of empty chairs had been cleared, had made Greene think "for some reason" about Africa as a kind of shape:

> not a particular place, but a shape, a strangeness, a wanting to know. The unconscious mind is often sentimental; I have written 'a shape,' and the shape, of course, is roughly that of the human heart. (2002, 37)

The Africa of the memory, thus, illustrates both a raw emotional state and the workings of the writer's mind through association. Africa stands, on the one hand, for raw sentimentality that is oblivious to one's surroundings and any sense of embarrassment and shame. The girl, overwhelmed by her emotions, represented to Greene a form of Africa as such an emotional state.

The empty space around the girl further emphasized the raw and unrefined quality of her emotion. On the other hand, the memory displays for Greene an associative and perhaps unconscious logic that builds on connections and similarities between seemingly distinct mental imagery. In other words, the girl's emotional state triggered in Greene's mind an associative process that is further reflected in the structure of the fragment, meaning the logic of a loosely connected series of memories that reveal a deep stratum of experience, relating to powerful feelings of mixed happiness and pain (or "darkness") in the writer's life.

Dakar and Freetown, however, which inspire these reflections and memories, did not fully evoke for Greene the true, seedy, and unconscious side of Africa that he was looking for. This was due to the dominant European quality of these towns (as we saw above, a similar lack of "authenticity" bothered Gide). Greene soon found the excitements in Freetown to be very English, and those of Dakar very French. Freetown, especially, was for Greene a European town and, as he writes, "everything ugly" in Freetown, such as the stores, the churches, the government offices, and the two hotels, was European (2002, 38). The following train trip through Sierra Leone to the town of Pendembu, in contrast, restored the sense of strangeness, and of Greene's "wanting to know." This was partly due to the extreme slowness of the train as it climbed up-country but also to the great heat and dampness that Greene had never experienced before, and the sight of naked women at the stations. Furthermore, the arrival in the village of Kailahun, situated on the borders of both French Guinea and Liberia, where Greene was forced to delay his departure, allowed him to evaluate the presence of Western civilization—it was worth very little in his mind, except being a smokescreen for the exploitation of the African people. Greene also points out at this point in the travelogue that the "noble savage" no longer existed, and perhaps had never existed (2002, 61), even if he was able to detect in some of the young people in Kailahun "something lovely, happy and unenslaved" that was perhaps related to it (2002, 61). At Kailahun, and upon entering the Republic of Liberia, as Greene was able to judge in retrospect, his journey was transformed because he had to change his relation to time and maps. This meant, as Greene writes, that in the interior he had to realize how "there was no such thing as time; the best watches couldn't stand the climate" (2002, 65). Instead, Greene learns to let himself "drift with Africa" (2002, 66).

Greene enjoyed the first trek into the Liberian forests before growing tired of the monotony of the landscape. The difference between Gide's and Greene's experiences of the monotony of the West African forest, however, is that Greene continued to see his journey in terms of a kind of self-analysis that enabled him to study the inner contradictions of his mind, whereas Gide transformed his travel journal, started as a realization of a childhood dream and a youthful fantasy of sexual and physical fulfillment, into a critical commentary on colonialism. Greene writes that

> The method of psychoanalysis is to bring the patient back to the idea which he is repressing: a long journey backwards without maps, catching a clue here and a clue there, as I caught the names of the villages from this man and that, until one has to face the general idea, the pain or the memory. (2002, 97)

In this way, the sense of travel by drifting from one village to the next reiterates the unconscious logic of association and emotional complexity that Greene closely associated with his arrival in Dakar. The method of his journey thus echoes the form of self-analysis that is based on the free associations of one's mind.

Conclusion

When these three writers draw attention to the language of their description in the scenes of arrival, for instance by poetic imagery of the exotic (Gide, Greene), or the primitive mentality of *l'art nègre* (Cendrars), and by resorting to other literary sources, films, and personal memories, they highlight the traveller's desire to mentally relocate himself in a different world. The focus on the style, form, and genre of the writing in these passages further points to the traveller's necessity to reevaluate his language of description and, subsequently, to reflect critically on his everyday understanding of time, space or what is real and possible. In other words, the arrival in sub-Saharan Africa and the real beginning of the voyage (or the expectation of it) is dramatized in these works as an entrance into another world that requires the traveller to adopt a different mindset. To a significant degree, the three writers evoke similar imagery in reference to their arrivals in West African coastal towns: the mystery and the luxury of the seemingly idle lifestyle, the promise of heightened and unusual sensual pleasures, the bodily splendor and lyricism, and complex entanglements of pain and pleasure. However, not all Gide's and Greene's expectations are met upon the arrival. The contradiction between the expectation of a real beginning of the adventure and the actual experience calls for resolution in the narrative that unfolds. Later, in Gide's and Greene's travel books, the lyricism of the exotic becomes entangled with the striking contradictions that the writers found between colonialism and the supposedly authentic forms of living.

In all of these examples, the scenes of arrival portray the traveller's heightened sensitivity to both his surroundings and the processes of his mind as well as raise new expectations and inaugurate new uncertainties. This heightened state of mind, furthermore, suggests a close connection between the traveller's inner and outer world. The sense of wonder or disappointment that the travellers associate with their experiences of arrival thus functions as a narrative means by which the text gives the reader access to the African "world" that is experientially, symbolically, logically, and perhaps even ontologically, different from Europe. Moreover, by accentuating the exotic difference of Africa, the scenes of arrival attempt to induce a sense of wonder in the reader, manipulating thus the distinction between actual and fantastic (or ideal) reality, between truthfulness—the travel writer's role as a witness of a geographical place—and the subjective meanings of the experience of arrival.

David Scott's formulation, in his *Semiologies of Travel* (2004), about the paradoxical relation in travel writing between a rite of passage to the real (the link with reality) and the ideal, meaning the need to liberate the writer's and the reader's imagination, illustrates well the contradiction between referentiality (or accuracy) and the ideal reality that is foregrounded in these examples of arrival:

> Travel writing is a paradox in that it is a rite of passage both to the *real*—that is, to an epistemic system different from that of the writer and which thus provokes a profound re-assessment of experience and values—and to the *ideal*—that is, to a world of renewed and heightened meaning. (2004, 5–6)

Traditionally, travel writing proposes a textual model that is both linked to the real and yet, as Scott writes, one that tries to liberate the imagination "through a complex layering of signs" (2004, 5). In my analysis of Cendrars's, Gide's, and Greene's travel writing I have not applied a semiotic theoretical frame but, nevertheless, the analysis points to similar results. The paradox that my examples present is the contrast between the desire to reveal reality as it is and the desire to heighten the sense of reality and, subsequently, find means for describing the experience of such heightened reality. These scenes of arrival function as key moments in the travel narrative, marking the passage between the narrative's beginning and its middle, and bring the traveller's mental processes, deeper sense of identity, and the language of description fully to the fore.

Beyond suggesting a change of perspective and indicating the end of the narrative's beginning, the scene of arrival is also a risky moment in the journey since it opens up new alternatives and uncertainties, introducing the traveller to the unknown of a new beginning. In these examples, the arrival scenes also suggest a new challenge to the writer's expectations. As these scenes reveal, the experience of arrival may lead to the traveller's evaluation of the motivation and the consequences of his decision to embark on a journey in the first place. In this sense, fulfilling multiple functions at once, the scenes of arrival act as nodal points in the narrative of the journey, both closing out uncertainties and introducing many new ones, pointing to that which lies ahead.

2

The Rhetoric of the Mad African Forest in Joseph Conrad, Louis-Ferdinand Céline, and Graham Greene

IN CERTAIN privileged moments of description in Greene's travelogue *Journey Without Maps* and Louis-Ferdinand Céline's novel *Journey to the End of the Night* the language of description ceases to represent thought as the sane contemplation of an object and instead invents ways to imitate the irrational mental processes of dreams, hallucination, or madness. These privileged instances of cultivated confusion draw especially on the effects of stupefying detail—or its opposite, the stupefying lack of detail—in their language and logic of description. Such scenes suggest an analogy between the landscape of the forest and the landscape of the mind; the descriptions of the landscape are continually bearing the signs of the traveller's disintegrating mind, so that they also become vehicles for its representation. What further contributes to the rhetoric of madness in these descriptions is the conflation of the space of the forest with the portrayals of Africans, colonials, and fellow travellers. As Shoshana Felman argues, the rhetoric of madness involves the thematization of a certain discourse about madness in literature, which, "mobilizing all the linguistic resonances of eloquence, asserts madness as the meaning, the *statement* of the text" (1985, 251). In the light of this, I intend to examine the way the description of African forests identifies certain "mad" properties of the place as well as of the persons within that space and, subsequently, dramatizes the relationship between reason and unreason and between the object and the means of description.

My choice of texts is motivated not only by their common themes and similarities in description but by their mutual debt to Joseph Conrad's portrayal of the African landscape. Céline's novel develops the many-layered symbolic meanings of Conrad's "darkness" and sense of immensity in the West African forest, and can be seen as another variation on the motif of losing one's sense of the (European, rational) self in Africa. Greene's travelogue explicitly evokes a connected group of texts on Africa that includes Conrad's *Congo Diary* (1890) and *Heart of Darkness* (1902) as well as Céline's description of the African landscape in *Voyage*.

Conrad's Madness-Inducing Jungle

Many colonial novels from the era of high imperialism—from Joseph Conrad to Rudyard Kipling, from Pierre Loti to André Gide and Georges Simenon—were preoccupied with the white man's degeneration and miscegenation in the colonies.[1] Popular fiction of the late nineteenth and early twentieth centuries, for which Patrick Brantlinger has coined the phrase "imperial Gothic," centred on the three principal themes of the individual regression or going native, the invasion of civilization by the forces of barbarism and demonism, and the diminution of opportunities for adventure and heroism in the modern world. This fiction thus conveyed the widespread anxieties of the time about the declining British Empire, for instance by cultivating a sense of confusion between the civilized (or rational) mindset and the primitive (or the occult).[2]

At one extreme in these stories of colonial regression or anxiety is the portrayal of a mental disintegration that threatens the colonial adventurer with madness. In Joseph Conrad's *Heart of Darkness*, the question of mental disequilibrium is first evoked in relation to Marlow's motivation for travelling to Africa. During a physical examination before the journey begins, the colonial company doctor asks whether there was any madness in Marlow's family. Irritated by the question, Marlow retorts, "Is that question in the interest of science, too?" (1994, 17). The doctor explains that he has a "little theory" about the mental changes from which individuals suffer in the African colonies. What this colonial madness might involve, however, is left unexplained.

---

1. See, for instance, Kipling's stories "Beyond the Pale" (1888), "The Phantom Rickshaw" (1888), "The Mark of the Beast" (1891), and the novel *The Light that Failed* (1890); Pierre Loti's *Le Roman d'un spahi*; André Gide's *L'immoraliste* (1902); and Claude Farrère's *Les civilisés* (1905).

2. See Brantlinger 1988, 227–30. The novels of H. Rider Haggard are a case in point.

Earlier, anticipating the theme of the menacing irrationality of the African forest, Marlow had explained his desire to travel to Africa in terms of an irrational fascination with blank spaces on the map, while topographical details had already "charmed" him as a boy, like the big river on the map that resembled a snake uncoiled: "And as I looked at the map of it in a shop-window, it fascinated me as a snake would a bird—a silly little bird" (1994, 17).

Later in the novel, the question of madness becomes part of an interpretive framework, both for the African experience and for Kurtz's mental state. Upon Marlow's arrival in Africa, the question reemerges when he sees a French man-of-war anchored off the coast blazing away at some unseen enemy on land. The event, Marlow explains, scared away his false sense of belonging in the world of straightforward facts, introducing instead "a touch of insanity" to his adventure. As for Kurtz, whom he is searching, Marlow refers to his soul as "mad" instead of acknowledging his intelligence: "being alone in the wilderness, it had looked within itself, and, by heavens! I tell you, it had gone mad" (1994, 95).

Specifically, what interests me here is the association made in Marlow's narrative between a growing sense of madness and the forest wilderness as he moves up the great African river in search of an explanation for Kurtz's behavior. By this I mean especially the split quality of the description: on the one hand, it represents *thought* engaged in the contemplation of an object; on the other hand, the observing mind projects imaginary and madness-inducing qualities onto the immense forest. In this forest the earth, as Marlow paradoxically sees it, appears unearthly. The paradox of this description is at once exterior and interior to the observing mind:

> Going up that river was like travelling back to the earliest beginnings of the world, when vegetation rioted on the earth and the big trees were kings. An empty stream, a great silence, an impenetrable forest. The air was warm, thick, heavy, sluggish. There was no joy in the brilliance of sunshine. (Conrad 1994, 48)

The forest has a face and a gaze, sometimes a masked face, "with a vengeful aspect" (Conrad 1994, 49), which can never be fully looked back upon. The reality of such looking back has a deeply disorienting, numbing effect that is able to hold the observer captive.

The African landscape in *Heart of Darkness*, as Graham Huggan has suggested, highlights a tension between the indigenous and the cultural landscape and thus symbolizes a rupture in the balance between man and his environment (1989, 22). Marlow travels back in time into the realm of vegetation to be overwhelmed by the force of nature that makes his steamboat—the symbol of the conquest of nature—look like "a sluggish beetle crawling on the floor of a lofty portico" (Conrad 1994, 50). In thus projecting a mind onto the forest and the forest back onto the mind, Marlow also reveals the observer's unfathomability to himself. The observer-narrator succumbs to the view widely held in the early twentieth century that the so-called primitive mentality lives somehow within the modern mind. What also contributes to the personification of the forest is the conflation of the description with the Africans who "were not inhuman." "Well, you know," Marlow explains, "that was the worst of it—this suspicion of their not being inhuman" (Conrad 1994, 51). The thrill that Marlow finds in the Africans' "wild and passionate uproar" and in the "ugliness" of their behavior suggests to him the idea, at once monstrous and liberating, of a mind capable of anything, containing both the past and the future (Conrad 1994, 52). The anthropomorphized but still strangely inhuman forest and its all-too-human inhabitants threaten the modern mind with disintegration but at the same time suggest a maddening escape from the bounds of rational thought.

Céline's Railway Forest Station

The Bambola-Bragamance section of Louis-Ferdinand Céline's *Voyage au bout de la nuit* builds on a tension between the imaginary and the real geographical space of Africa and exaggerates this tension to the point of obliteration. The protagonist of the novel, Ferdinand Bardamu, rejects what he calls the "poésie des Tropiques," yet his descriptions of African landscapes affirm this same poetry of the impenetrable jungle. One key moment of the novel's ambiguous exoticism is the depiction of the African twilight as a tragic spectacle:

> Les crépuscules dans cet enfer africain se révélaient fameux. On n'y coupait pas. Tragiques chaque fois comme d'énormes assassinats du soleil. Un immense chiqué. Seulement c'était beaucoup d'admiration pour un seul homme. Le ciel pendant une heure paradait tout giclé d'un bout à l'autre d'écarlate en délire, et puis le vert éclatait au milieu des arbres et montait du sol en traînées tremblantes jusqu'aux premières étoiles. Après ça le gris reprenait tout l'horizon et puis le rouge encore, mais alors fatigué le rouge et pas pour longtemps. Ça se terminait ainsi. Toutes les couleurs retombaient en lambeaux, avachies sur la forêt comme des oripeaux après la centième. Chaque jour sur les six heures exactement que ça se passait.

Et la nuit avec tous ses monstres entrait alors dans la danse parmi ses mille et mille bruits de gueules de crapauds.

La forêt n'attend que leur signal pour se mettre à trembler, siffler, mugir de toutes ses profondeurs. Une énorme gare amoureuse et sans lumière. Pleine à craquer. Des arbres entiers bouffis de gueuletons vivants, d'érections mutilées, d'horreur. (Céline 1961, 168)

The sunsets in that African hell proved to be fabulous. They never missed. As tragic every time as a monumental murder of the sun! [An immense bluff.] But the marvel was too great for one man alone. For a whole hour the sun paraded in great delirious spurts of scarlet from end to end; after that the green of the trees exploded and rose up in quivering trails to meet the first stars. Then the whole horizon turned grey again and the red, but this time a tired red that didn't last too long. That was the end. All the colors fell back down on the forest in tatters, like streamers after the hundredth performance. It happened every day at exactly six o'clock.

Then the night set in with all its monsters and its thousands and thousands of croaking toads.

The forest is only waiting for their signal to start trembling, hissing, and roaring from its depths. An enormous, love-maddened, unlighted railway station, full to bursting. Whole trees bristling with living noise-makers, mutilated erections, horror. (Céline 1983, 144–45)[3]

The horror and mutilation, the fusion of the organic (forest) with the mechanical (train station), the color transformations from scarlet to grey and to green and to "tired" red followed by absolute darkness are central elements of the description. The quality of darkness designates both an outside reality and the observer's mental landscape, similar to Marlow's description of the forest in *Heart of Darkness*. Furthermore, the Darkness that extinguishes all colors relates metaphorically to other forms of mutilation, madness, and death that are everywhere present in Céline's colonial Africa.

There are three madness-inducing forces in Bardamu's description of the forest twilight that I specifically wish to discuss here. These include the madness of stupefying detail, the sense of the mechanical within the organic, and the sense of madness caused by the disorientation in travel. First of all, as in Conrad, there is a sense of anonymous threat in the landscape, something more than can be appropriated, and something that is all-too-much,

---

3. The reference to simulation or bluff (*chiqué*) is lost in the English translation and I have added it here in brackets.

that evokes a spectacle of monstrous decay, mutilation, and death. Africa is more detailed, more vibrant, more colorful, more everything. Moreover, and again as in Conrad, the forest is impassable, just as the traveller's mind can be unfathomable. As Bardamu explains, this forest could only be penetrated by a river or—as by a rat—through some tunnel. What is quite different from the millions of massive trees in Conrad, and from Pierre Loti's romantic melancholy, however, is that here the multitude of forest trees is eroticized as one enormous living organism ("Une énorme gare amoureuse") and, further, that this eroticization is closely tied to the horror of castration and death ("d'érections mutilées").[4] Indeed, the eroticization of African nature and space is a recurrent trope in Céline's writings. In a postcard from Cameroon to Simone Saintu signed June 1916, Céline refers to the African towns as the anti-chambers of hell—"nauseatingly unhealthy, black-hot, humid" ("nauséabond malsain. chaud noir, humide"). A few days later in another letter to the same friend, however, the writer is eager to talk about "negro life" ("vivre à la nègre") as a form of perfect liberty ("la grande, totale, absolue liberté") with obvious erotic connotations (Céline 1978, 38, 43). In one of his later novels, *Féerie pour une autre fois* (1952), the narrator refers to the Cameroonian night forests as "ces orchestrations de forêts! . . . de nuit, hein! . . . de nuit! . . . faut entendre les égorgements des énormes amours animales!" ("these orchestrations of the forests! of the night! Yes, the night! Listen to the cut throat great animal passions") and "le choeur des gourmets de la nuit qu'était couvert encore lui-même par la bacchanale animale, éventreries, égorgeries, amoureries de vingt-cinq Zoos!" ("and the chorus of the nighttime gourmets that in turn was surpassed by the sounds of the animal bacchanal, the disemboweling, the throat cuttings and the lovemaking of twenty-five zoos!") (Céline 1952, 183, 185). A similarly "lascivious" African atmosphere is recalled in a ballet script included in Céline's most notorious pamphlet, *Bagatelles pour un massacre* (1937).

However, Bardamu ties sexual relations constantly with disease and transgression, and at times also with the European officials' lust for power. The eroticism of the colonial Africa, thus, instead of being associated with the bodies of African women, or virile black men—homosexuality, however, is sometimes implied—corresponds to the environment, "decadent" nature, and sexual diseases. Peter Dunwoodie is right in claiming that the images of black women in Céline's novel have never the sensuality, the beauty, the grace, or the sense of Orientalist seduction that they have in Pierre Loti's

---

4. See Dunwoodie (1993, 148) on Céline's pastiche of Loti in the African section of the novel.

fiction and journals (Dunwoodie 1993, 145). But it would be an exaggeration to claim that Céline's novel does not follow the theme of a libidinous white man. Libidinal constraints, and the eroticizing of the other's body, structures Bardamu's African journey precisely because the narrator continuously rejects the pattern of an erotic conquest. The rejection of the black woman's body dramatizes and internalizes the contradictions of colonial desire. Furthermore, the overt eroticism of African societies is already present in the names Céline invents for his African places. The name of Bardamu's destination Bambola-Fort Gono, more precisely the city of "Fort Gono" in the colony of "Bambola-Bragamance," fuses the connotations of a wild party and a sexually transmitted disease. "Bambola" evokes the name "la bamboula", a party in military slang, or an African dance to the beat of a drum, while "Gono" points to "le gonocoque," a special microbe of the venereal disease gonorrhea. Bragamance, in turn, refers to "braguette," the trouser's fly, "San Tapeta" implies a "tapette" (French slang for a homosexual) and the boat "Infanta Combitta" includes another slang word "bite" (penis).

Throughout Bardamu's African experience in *Voyage au bout de la nuit* the forces of heat, light, rain, and fever contribute to the obliteration of limits between things, a dissolving objecthood accompanied by a sense of a disintegrating self. For Bardamu, it is difficult to see things in the tropics fully and accurately.

> Il est difficile de regarder en conscience les gens et les choses des Tropiques à cause des couleurs qui en émanent. Elles sont en ébullition les couleurs et les choses. Une petite boîte de sardines ouverte en plein midi sur la chaussée projette tant de reflets divers qu'elle prend pour les yeux l'importance d'un accident. Faut faire attention. Il n'y a pas là-bas que les hommes d'hystériques, les choses aussi s'y mettent. La vie ne devient guère tolérable qu'à la tombée de la nuit, mais encore l'obscurité est-elle accaparée presque immédiatement par les moustiques en essaims. (Céline 1961, 126)

> It is hard to get a faithful look at people and things in the tropics because of the colors that emanate from them. In the tropics colors and things are in a turmoil. To the eye, a small sardine can lying upon the road at midday can take on the dimensions of an accident. You've got to watch out. It's not just the people who are hysterical down there, objects are the same way. Life only becomes tolerable at nightfall, but then almost immediately the darkness is taken over by swarms of mosquitoes. (Céline 1983, 108)

This is the most explicit statement in the whole of *Voyage,* regarding the difficulty of talking about the mad object of description.[5] Life is teeming with stupefying colors, things, and their transformations; a box of sardines may project so many reflections that it may be likened to a traffic accident, a case of hysteria, the chaos of war, or an attack of mosquitoes.

In the African chapters of *Voyage au bout de la nuit* perception is always framed by the haunting prospect of delirium and hermeneutic pessimism. In *Heart of Darkness,* Marlow's perception of his surroundings is often difficult, especially when he confronts the gaze of the forest, and sometimes his vision seems wilfully obscured, as for instance when he describes the primeval forest in the moonlight:

> The high stillness of primeval forest was before my eyes; there were shiny patches on the black creek. The moon had spread over everything a thin layer of silver—over the rank grass, over the mud, upon the wall of matted vegetation standing higher that the wall of a temple, over the great river I would see through a sombre gap glittering, glittering, as it flowed broadly by without a murmur. (Conrad 1994, 38)

But the metamorphosis of natural objects is never experienced as fully or pessimistically in Conrad as it is in Céline. The sentence rhythm of Céline's semi-autobiographical narrator is also characteristically close to (stylized) oral delivery. The personal style and voice of his narration thus reflects the speaker's mental and emotional state much more explicitly than in Conrad. Towards the end of the African episode in *Voyage,* we hear Bardamu's refusal to appreciate the happy immanence of substance:

> À moi donc seul le paysage! J'aurais désormais tout le temps d'y revenir, songeais-je, à la surface, à la profondeur de cette immensité de feuillages, de cet océan de rouge, de marbré jaune, de salaisons flamboyantes magnifiques sans doute pour ceux qui aiment la nature. Je ne l'aimais décidément pas. La poésie des Tropiques me dégoûtait. Mon regard, ma pensée sur ces ensembles me revenaient comme du thon. On aura beau dire, ça sera

---

5. Dunwoodie (1983, 90–91) has investigated the ways in which Céline plays with the impossibilities of the referent in his novels. Dunwoodie argues that the marvelous in Céline, combining farce and grotesque and often interrupted by the protagonist's satirical comments, begs not so much the credibility as, rather, the reader's understanding of how the marvelous element has a cathartic, distancing function in relation to the satirical and violent content of the narrative.

toujours un pays pour les moustiques et les panthères. Chacun sa place. (Céline 1961, 171)

So the whole landscape was mine! I'd have all the time I needed, I thought, to study the surface and the depths of this leafy immensity, this ocean of red, of mottled yellow, of flamboyant hams and head cheeses, magnificent no doubt for people who love nature. I definitely didn't. The poetry of the tropics turned my stomach. The thought of all those vistas repeated on me like tuna fish. Say what you like, it will never be anything but a country of mosquitoes and panthers. And not for me. (Céline 1983, 147)

Bardamu's disgust and flattening of his feelings towards the immanence of Africa show us a traveller who is not simply admitting the impossibility of incorporating all of the visual details and information that offer themselves to him, a sign of anxious rejection when facing too much detail; there is, rather, a delirious debunking of any possible way of speaking about or experiencing the tropical object of description.

Moreover, the forest in Bardamu's description is not so much anthropomorphized *à la* Conrad as it is associated with the mechanical. The visual details and the sounds of a forest, teeming with hissing and roaring life, are superimposed on the urban space of a love-maddened railway station, a machine-like monster that follows a strict schedule punctuated by signals that propel action. The fusion between the mechanical and the organic further plays out fractally within Bardamu's perception. By this I mean that Bardamu is *inclined* to perceive structures within structures in the object of observation. The African object of description is hysterical, in constant turmoil, but so is the mind of the observer, the often irritated and disgusted narrator ("In the tropics colors and things are in a turmoil"; "It's not just the people who are hysterical down there, objects are the same way"). In his perception, different experiential domains, such as the streets and railway stations of a modern city, the twilight spectacle over the wild forest, the state of being madly in love, are posited within each other's conceptual fields so that they may produce infinite reflections of each other's forms.

Finally, while Céline presents an erotically-charged dream of fever and madness in his African forest, *Journey to the End of the Night* as a whole is also a dramatization, through a modern rendition of the episodic picaresque form, of the *madness of travel*, or dromomania. The African episode in *Voyage* is framed by the structuring device of the journey and is itself structured as a journey with an itinerary of three destinations (Fort Gono, Topo, Bikimimbo) and a shorter stop in the middle at San Tapeta. All these trips are framed by the voyages to and from Africa on the *Amiral Bragueton* and the galley boat *Infanta Combitta*. For Bardamu, furthermore, travel to Africa functions indirectly as a means to move somewhere else, namely North America. Bardamu's constant passing through places is akin to the transient pathological case of the fugue or *dromomanie* as Ian Hacking defines this condition in his *Mad Travellers* (1998, 8, 84). Mad travellers like Bardamu travel obsessively and uncontrollably, in states of obscured consciousness, not always knowing who they are or why and where they have travelled. In Céline's picaresque account, travel gives delirious forms to colonial imagery, in the process transmuting the modernist poetics of perception, of epiphany, and the possibility of discovering an individual myth that is associated with such perception. This mutation may also lead to the total obliteration of limits between things, a dissolution of objecthood accompanied by pangs of anxiety:

> On avait à peine le temps de les voir disparaître, les hommes, les jours et les choses dans cette verdure, ce climat, la chaleur et les moustiques. Tout y passait, c'était dégoûtant, par bouts, par phrases, par membres, par regrets, par globules, ils se perdaient au soleil, fondaient dans le torrent de la lumière et des couleurs, et le goût et le temps avec, tout y passait. Il n'y avait que de l'angoisse étincelante dans l'air. (Céline 1961, 147)

> Men, days, things—they passed before you knew it in this hotbed of vegetation, heat, humidity, and mosquitoes. Everything passed, disgustingly, in little pieces, in phrases, particles of flesh and bone, in regrets and corpuscles; demolished by the sun, they melted away in a torrent of light and colors, and taste and time went with them, everything went. Nothing remained but shimmering dread. (Céline 1983, 126)

The modernist moment of sudden revelation, and of the derangement of the senses, is a by-product of the transformations of Bardamu's perception in travel and deliberate exile. The perceiving self, having trouble distinguishing between things, is itself in the process of disintegrating. At the end of his African visit, Bardamu, an early twentieth-century colonial having come to the continent on a boat full of drunkards, is transformed into an eighteenth-century galley slave without any individual agency. Feverish and unconscious, he has to leave Africa for other mad destinations in America.

Similarly, in Céline's personal letters from Cameroon between 1916 and 1917, when he worked as a plantation manager for the *Société forestière Sangha Oubangui* in Bikomimbo, the monstrosity of Africa is aligned with a sense of multiplicity in its forms of life, an intensity of material. In these letters, furthermore, Céline constantly fuses the material with the metaphorical. Especially in his letters to his friend Simone Saintu, he invents imaginary people whom he supposedly has met, such as Père de Lestrée and Père Delestré (whose names are homonyms). He also imagines a rendezvous with the Austrian emperor F. J. d'Habsbourg and says, falsely, that he is not married—"je ne suis pas (marié) et me marierai jamais, surtout en Afrique" (1978, 73) ("I am not married and will never get married, especially not in Africa")—even though he had married discreetly in England six months prior to the voyage. Céline's first known experiments in poetry and fiction-writing are also included in the letters. These include two Orientalist poems, "Gnomographie" and "Le grand chêne" that are accompanied with illustrations, and the short story "Des vagues" that takes place in a smoking room on board the moving passenger ship, *Tarconia*, resembling closely *R. M. S. Tarquah*, on which Céline returned from Africa to Europe by way of Liverpool in May 1917.

Greene's Dead and Empty Forest

From the outset of his travelogue *Journey Without Maps*, Graham Greene makes explicit that he is preoccupied with African landscape as the landscape of his mind. This travel narrative is as much an investigation of the writer's psyche and his dreams as it is the report of a real travel experience in geographical space. Discussing the motive for his travel, Greene suggests that it "is not the fully conscious mind which chooses West Africa in preference to Switzerland" (2002, 20). By this he means that there is a certain Africa that represents more to him than he can put into words. This Africa is not the well-known British colonies of South Africa, Rhodesia, or Kenya, but the less known West Africa that Greene associates with a certain darkness, a kind of mental image built on Marlow's idea that Africa had ceased to represent "a blank space of delightful mystery" and instead had become "a place of darkness" (Conrad, *Heart*, 12). This Africa, as much imaginary as it is real, retains the quality of the inexplicable, of an unexplained brutality as portrayed in Conrad's *Congo Diary*, or the kind of despair one may find in Céline's *Journey to the End of the Night*, two of the texts quoted by Greene. Other fictions that encapsulate the essence of Africa for Greene in *Journey Without Maps* include H. Rider Haggard's and Kurt Heuser's novels, and *Heart of Darkness*—all novels that describe the European travellers' quest in the unexplored interior of Africa. Greene explains in the beginning of the travelogue that there are a thousand names for what he was searching:

King Solomon's Mines, the "heart of darkness" if one is romantically inclined, or more simply, as Herr Heuser puts it in his African novel, *The Inner Journey*, one's place in time, based on a knowledge not only of one's present but of the past from which one has emerged. (2002, 19–20)

In Heuser's novel *The Journey Inward* (*Die Reise ins Innere*, 1931), the young hero, Jeronimo, who is disappointed in love and fascinated by the "true native" of Africa, flees from the civilized West to a colony in Portuguese East Africa. In Africa, he is given the job of mapping the unknown interior where he finally disappears. H. Rider Haggard's *King Solomon's Mines* (1885), in turn, was Greene's favorite novel when he was ten years old and a book that, as he explains in the essay, "The Lost Childhood," influenced his future to the extent that the "the odd African fixation," meaning a fascination with regions of the imagination and of uncertainty, always remained with him (1969, 15–16).

As to Conrad, his "Congo Diary" and *Heart of Darkness* had a lasting effect on Greene's mind and, as Greene also feared, on his literary style. Greene voices such concerns in his "Congo Journal" where he notes that he was once again reading Conrad, the novels *Youth* and *The Heart of Darkness*, in the Congo in February 1959. Greene claims that he had abandoned Conrad "about 1932 because his influence on me was too great and too disastrous" (1968, 42). In the Congo in 1959, however, he hoped that he had lived long enough to be safe from this "corruption." Later in the same entry of February 13, 1959, Greene writes more poignantly that

> Conrad's *Heart of Darkness* still a fine story, but its faults show now. The language too inflated for the situation. Kurtz never comes really alive. It is as if Conrad had taken an episode in his own life and tried to lend it, for the sake of "literature," a greater significance than it will hold. And how often he compares something concrete to something abstract. Is this a trick that I have caught? (1968, 44)

Greene makes at least three complaints here: the supposedly inflated language in *Heart of Darkness*, the projection of actual experience onto a fictional character so as to be able to sublimate one's life, and the abstraction of the concrete. Greene is again anxious over Conrad's influence, struggling with similar "faults" himself as he was trying to give shape to his new novel that was set in West Africa, *A Burnt-Out Case* (1960). At the same time, he defends his own notion of novelistic realism and matter-of-factness against what he sees as Conrad's abstractions.

As Greene explains in *Journey Without Maps*, the Africa that he had in mind before embarking on his first voyage to Freetown was a powerful mental image capable of evoking immediate associations in which a "crowd of words and images, witches and death, unhappiness and the Gare St Lazare, the huge smoky viaduct over a Paris slum, crowd together and block the way to full consciousness" (2002, 20). We may note that Greene here employs an association between urban and forest space similar to Céline's, but his forest has no erotic force. The forest is suspected of harboring evil forces and unhappiness, of inscrutable intentions as in Conrad, but it is also a place where one can sleep and have vivid dreams of some distant and lost past.[6] For both Conrad's Marlow and for Greene, the empty, silent, and impenetrable forest is intimately associated with the idea of travelling back to the earliest beginnings of the world. Yet, while Conrad and Céline locate a certain destructive and self-destructive force in their African forests, for Greene the monotonous environment involves no apparent danger in the form of an exterior force beyond malaria, dysentery, other diseases, or rebellious carriers. In contrast to Céline, Greene's black Africa functions as a projection screen for self-exploration, "not a particular place, but a shape, a strangeness, a wanting to know," and this non-place, further, has a shape of "roughly that of the human heart" (2002, 37).[7] His fictional characters, such as Querry in *A Burnt-Out Case,* may desire to lose themselves for ever in Africa, but such a desire does not come from the environment (even if it may be amplified by the African setting). In Greene's variation on the motif of the African forest, furthermore, the threat implied by the landscape is intimately associated with the traveller's own uncertain state of mind and spiritual search. Greene redefines Conrad's symbolic heart of darkness as a human heart, encapsulating the despair and the evil of human experience, with help from Bardamu's vision of the shapeless, animated machine monster, at once horrifying and fascinating. In Greene's other major novel set in Africa, *Heart of the Matter* (1948), Major Henry Scobie explains that what he loved about living in his African colony was that there human nature had no time to disguise itself but was exposed in its most basic forms, including cruelty and meanness.

---

6. Greene quotes Conrad's description of an "empty stream, a great silence, an impenetrable forest" also in his "Congo Diary" when he was in Yonda in the Congo (Greene 1968, 18).

7. Compare with the beginning of *Heart of Darkness,* where Marlow relates that the farthest point of his navigation in the heart of Africa, and meeting with Kurtz, "seemed somehow to throw a kind of light on everything about me—and into my thoughts" (Conrad 1994, 11). Greene repeats the idea of Africa having the shape of a human heart at the end of his "Convoy to West Africa" (1941) in reference to the sweet hot smell from the land near Freetown: "It will always be to me the smell of Africa, and Africa will always be the Africa of the Victorian atlas, the blank unexplored continent the shape of the human heart" (1968, 106).

Greene's exotic, antimodern self-exploration retains much of the customary meanings of the civilized and the primitive. Sub-Saharan Africa represents to him the raw, primitive experiences of terror and pleasure, of seediness and humanity in its untamed childhood. Yet, what interests me especially here is the moment of disillusionment in the middle of the travelogue: the experience of a Liberian forest that does not at all correspond to the traveller's expectations. It is at this particular moment, in a passage entitled "The Dead Forest," that Greene realizes he is no longer able to find himself anew, to reinvent himself beyond the limits of civilization. Instead, he becomes painfully aware of the disjointed nature of the experience, the impossibility of integrating it to give it a coherent meaning: Greene finds no interesting, dangerous life in the Liberian forest—in fact, he finds no life at all: "The word 'forest' to me had always conveyed a sense of wildness and beauty, of an active natural force, but this forest was simply a green wilderness, and not even so very green" (2002, 156). The reason for this numbing experience is in many ways the opposite of Marlow's need to repress the dangerous "face" of the forest and to cut himself off from the threatening shores that swarm with life. Because of the "quality of deadness" (2002, 157), the landscape cannot be aestheticized: what Greene calls his aesthetic eye ceases to respond to the world around him. There is nothing in Greene's field of vision to give a particular order to his description, no interesting detail or panoramic view to concentrate on: "there was no view, no change of scene, nothing to distract the eyes, and even if there had been, we couldn't have enjoyed the sight, for the eyes had to be kept on the ground all the way, to avoid the roots and boulders" (2002, 156).

What emerges in the narrative then is the traveller's failed excursion into his personal reference library, one that includes Conrad, Céline, A. E. Housman, Wordsworth, and other English nature poets. Greene appeals first to a series of writers, starting with Céline, who, in their descriptions of Africa, have "complained" about the noise and savagery of the jungle. He cites from *Journey to the End of the Night* the passage discussed earlier about the association between the forest and a railway station, and laments, "How we would have welcomed the moans and whistles of that station" (2002, 157).[8]

It may be symptomatic of a certain arrogance in Greene's viewpoint that he finds the West African forest to be without any signs of life, reminding

---

8. In the beginning of his travelogue, Greene also quotes from Céline's novel: "Hidden away in all this flowering forest of twisted vegetation, a few decimated tribes of natives squatted among fleas and flies, crushed by taboos and eating nothing all the time but rotten tapioca." Images and observations like these, Greene explains, "seem like the images in a dream to stand for something of importance to myself" (2002, 21).

us of the kind of colonial rhetoric that wishes to discover empty spaces to be conquered (or rather in this case "empty" spaces to be appropriated as metaphors for a mental state). Greene for example also refers to "the shell of a house on a bankrupt housing estate" that had remained uninhabited (2002, 157). It is only in Greene's imagination, however, that the emptiness of the forest has a highly negative quality, signifying a total lack of human presence and a threat to his project of self-discovery. In a short story, "A Chance for Mr Lever" (1936) that Greene partly based on his travel experience in Liberia, a description of a Liberian forest mirrors closely that in *Journey Without Maps*:

> Forest conveys a sense of wildness and beauty, of an active natural force, but this Liberian forest was simply a dull green wilderness. You passed, on the path a foot or so wide, through an endless back garden of tangled weeds, it didn't seem to be growing round you, so much as dying. There was no life at all, except for a few large birds whose wings creaked overhead through the invisible sky like an unoiled door. There was no view, no way out for the eyes, no change of scene. It wasn't the heat that tired so much as the boredom; you had to think of things to think about. (1947, 117)

At the end of the story, the narrator further underscores that in the "drab empty forest" through which the protagonist Mr. Lever was moving, infected by dysentery, it was "impossible to believe in any spiritual life, in anything outside the nature dying round you, the shrivelling of the weeds" (1947, 124). In *A Burnt-Out Case,* the African forest is described in similar terms of emptiness and lifelessness through the protagonist Querry's perspective:

> There was little in the forest to appeal to the romantic. It was completely empty. It had never been humanized, like the woods of Europe, with witches and charcoal-burners and cottages of marzipan; no one had ever walked under these trees lamenting lost love, nor had anyone listened to the silence and communed like a lake-poet with his heart. For there was no silence; if a man here wished to be heard at night he had to raise his voice to counter the continuous chatter of the insects as in some monstrous factory where thousands of sewing-machines were being driven against time by myriads of needy seamstresses. Only for an hour or so, in the midday heat, silence fell, the siesta of the insect. (Greene 1975, 54)[9]

---

9. Greene also explains in a letter to Docteur Michel Lechat, which is included in the beginning of *A Burnt-Out Case,* that the Congo of this novel is a "region of the mind" that cannot be found in any maps (1975, 5).

While Greene's description of the empty African forest, in fiction and nonfiction alike, plays upon the common metaphor of colonial Africa being the "white man's grave," it also dramatizes the traveller's own misplaced intentions. The empty, anti-poetic forest reveals a kind of mad logic of travel where the "heart of darkness" or the "end of the night" that the traveller is seeking always lies somewhere else. After citing Céline in *Journey Without Maps*, Greene quotes a poem from A. E. Housman's *Last Poems*. Its first line, "Tell me not here, it needs not saying, / What tune the enchantress plays" (Housman 1922, 75–76), Greene explains, had a curious fascination for him during the weeks of his travel. In the dead forest, however, even this last resort ceased to carry any meaning: "It was impossible here to think of Nature in such terms of enchantment and nostalgia; it would have been like cherishing a dead weed in a pot, a sign of mental derangement" (2002, 158). Greene's description of an African forest thus implies the dangers in the rhetoric of madness, the madness of habit in clinging to misleading literary allusions.

We must also note that Greene's image of the dead, inhuman forest is based on tropical imagery, drawn from the same sources, including Conrad and Céline, which Greene now interprets as inadequate. For Marlow, there is no joy in the West African sunshine. His forest, after all, has the impenetrable quality of stillness that "was the stillness of an implacable force brooding over an inscrutable intention" (Conrad 1994, 48), even able to make the traveller doubt his memory of himself. Céline, in turn, develops a sense of the difficulty of distinguishing between dead matter and living organisms. In Housman's poem, the idea of possessing the "pillared forest" during an autumn walk is, likewise, the melancholic traveller's illusion. In fact, the last stanza of the poem, not included in Greene's quotation, speaks of "inhuman" nature perfectly indifferent to the characteristics of any individuals who may pass through it, and also indifferent to any claims of ownership:

> For nature, heartless, witless nature,
> Will neither care nor know
> What stranger's feet may find the meadow
> And trespass there and go,
> Nor ask amid the dews of morning
> If they are mine or no. (Housman 1922, 25–30)

If misguided trust in literary description appears to Greene to be a sign of mental derangement, then his own revision of forest imagery reveals the rhetoric of intertextual "madness." After all, Greene resorts to his favorite references even when he rejects their value.

Conclusion

Colonial discourse analysis and critical histories of ethnology and anthropology have recently shown us how the black African, especially in the era of high imperialism in the late nineteenth and early twentieth centuries, has been used to represent a primitive mentality ruled by belief in magic, by intuition and habit, or by "mindless" sensuality. Similarly, in colonial literature, the African space has symbolized the primitive state of historical development that has served as a privileged site for the disintegration of the European mind. Christopher L. Miller, for instance, has argued that in what he calls Africanist discourse there is always a European subject who represents *thought*, the sane contemplation of an object recognized as the other, as opposed to *hallucination*, the illusory identification with the non-self (1985, 64).[10] As for Conrad, Céline, and Greene, the madness of their descriptions of the African forest subverts the presumed distinction between the primitive and the civilized mind. These descriptions thus portray a space that reveals its capacity to collect and exhibit otherness, including the traveller's unfathomability to himself. The forest experiences of Marlow, Bardamu, and Graham Greene also illustrate modern exoticism to the extent that for all of them, the African forest represents a sense of refuge from overbearing modernity and rationality that denies the possibility of self-realization. Even when such escape is revealed to be illusory, as happens especially in Céline's demystification of colonial adventure, the wild African forest reveals a perception-shattering and madness-inducing force. Paradoxically, African space is used to construct a historical image of the formlessness of modern experience and to evoke dream-sensations that can never be fully described, since they are too evasive, too powerful, as we see in Marlow's struggle with the possibility of conveying a sense of lived life or dream content through narration: "no relation of a dream can convey the dream-sensation, that commingling of absurdity, surprise, and bewilderment in a tremor of struggling revolt, that notion of being captured by the incredible which is of the very essence of dreams" (Conrad 1994, 39).

What is perhaps most characteristic of these descriptions, in terms of the way they portray an observing consciousness and not just an object of observation, is that they build on the sense of discrepancy between the means of description and what is seen. Marlow's forest, like Bardamu's and Greene's, is a metaphor for the traveller's mind: not manageable, not possible to domesticate. The rhetoric of madness in *Heart of Darkness* culminates in Marlow's

---

10. See also Loomba 1998, 136–39.

idea of the madness of the soul as opposed to the madness of intelligence, and overlaps with other questions about a modern mind whose faculties are subject to change. Insofar as civilization may be identified with the mastery of nature, including the mastery of the human body, the wild forest questions the distinction between the civilized mindset, on the one hand, and the primitive (or tyrannical), on the other. In Céline's novel, the monstrosity of Africa is less aligned with its nobility and dream-like qualities than with the sense of the mechanical within the organic, an intensity of material and colors that thematizes the question of the limits of perception. No longer nostalgic for the exotic enterprise, Bardamu, in his compulsive travel and aimless wandering, suggests a madness of perception and travel, driven by impulses that one does not understand, or has ceased to want to understand.

Journey Without Maps, by contrast, is an exploration through travel of the lost primitive within oneself, in associative style. In Greene's imagination, Africa stands for violence, and a sense of concrete, palpable evil within oneself that contributed to his conversion to Catholicism. In his later fictional renditions of West Africa, the novels *The Heart of the Matter* and *A Burnt-Out Case,* by projecting such moral questions and notions of the beginnings of human life on the African landscape, Greene portrays the tragic ends of two Western male protagonists, the colonialist major Scobie and the architect Querry. Scobie and Querry face difficult moral dilemmas concerning personal responsibility, involving adultery in both novels, suicide in *The Heart of the Matter,* and apathy and indifference in *A Burnt-Out Case.* The burnt-out Querry's travel into the interior of the Congo follows closely in the footsteps of Marlow and Bardamu and Greene's own experience of the dead forest and the later journey in the Congo in 1959. As do his literary predecessors, Querry enters the mythical "heart" or "centre" of Africa—Greene uses both expressions consciously in reference to Conrad and other narratives about journeys into the interior of Africa—on a small passenger boat. But unlike Marlow and Bardamu, he seeks an empty place where nothing can remind him of the past and of being alive, which in his case means especially the lost capacity to love and suffer. Later, when he is settled at a Congolese leper village, Querry is portrayed in the press, much to his disliking, as a Kurtz-like mysterious figure, surrounded by faithful natives. He is then shot to death for adultery that he, for the first time in his life, had not committed.

Journey Without Maps does not involve similar scenes of self-destruction. Yet the description of the inhuman, empty forest suggests a momentary, disturbing rupture in the traveller's projections of the lost primitive onto the African forest space. At the end of the passage set in the forest Greene resolves the dilemma caused by his expectations by referring to the boredom that a child may experience when he or she feels apart from everyone. Greene likens the experience to a child's sense of boredom:

> that agonizing boredom of 'apartness' which came before one had learnt the fatal trick of transferring emotion, to flash back enchantingly all day long one's image, a period when other people were as distinct from oneself as this Liberian forest. (2002, 158)[11]

Travel writing thus has to come to terms with the boring and the monotonous that the rational traveller cannot blot out of his mind. Querry's isolation in *A Burnt-Out Case* is another description of and response to the same dilemma. This time only the burnt-out mind has lost its capacity to transfer emotion and to be enchantingly captured by its own image.

---

11. In the travel book *The Lawless Roads* (1939), Greene re-evokes the "appalling" experience of Nature, meaning a kind of nature that is "unemployed or unemployable," such "as the beauty of the African bush or the Cornish coast" (Greene 2002b, 62).

3

Travel Narrative between Spatial Sequence and Open Consequence in Graham Greene's *Journey Without Maps*

IN THE FORMALIST VEIN of narrative theory, where much of the effort has been to think the minimum story, the travel concept has tended to function as a model for the organization of a narrative, for the ordering of narrated events. The Russian formalist conception of the genre of travel writing, and the journey plot in the structuralist theory of plot functions, point out the importance of both temporal and causal dimensions in narrative. At the same time, they reveal that the constitutive forces of cause and effect are often difficult to separate. These two overlap easily, not least because the reader is inclined to experience causality in a temporal order.[1] Boris Tomashevsky, for instance, argued that all narratives require causality in their organization, in addition to temporal sequencing, and justified the claim with reference to travel accounts: "If the account is only about the sights and not about the personal adventures of the travellers, we have exposition without story. The weaker the causal connection, the stronger the purely chronological connection" (1965, 66). Without causal connection, therefore, there is no story but a

---

1. Todorov, for instance, sees that temporal order and causality are closely linked and easily confused and further that "the logical series is in the reader's eyes a much stronger relation than the temporal series; if the two go together, he sees only the first" (1981, 42). For Rimmon-Kenan, by contrast, temporal succession is a sufficient condition for a narrative since "causality can often (always?) be projected onto temporality" (1983, 18).

mere exposition, a list, or a chronicle.² Ultimately, these investigations into travel writing and the journey plot also reveal that the causal organization of the elements of a narrative cannot be separated from the mediating perspective of the traveller's personal experience, whether in the form of a narrator or character, through which the sequence of the events is seen.

In this theoretical tradition, travel writing plays out the rival conceptions of temporal succession and causal connection and has helped to establish the approximate point of demarcation between the narrative and the non-narrative. Travel writing occupies both the role of the episodic tale that fails to possess a sense of causality—because it portrays a mere sequence of places or events (the raw material of a story)—and so lacks narrativity, and also occupies the role of the simple narrative proper, a prototype of storytelling. This ambivalent positioning between narratives proper and their outside, the "not yet" narrative or the non-narrative, is related to two basic assumptions concerning the travel genre. On the one hand, a travel story is believed to possess clear temporal and spatial order: the traveller's itinerary and his or her physical journey through some space structures the experience of time, be it the first-person narrative of an eccentric journey around one's room (Xavier de Maistre's *Voyage autour de ma chambre*, 1795) or a third-person narrative on a trans-Antarctic expedition (Alfred Lansing's *Endurance: Shackleton's Incredible Voyage*, 1959). In travel writing, time can be, as it were, compressed into space. On the other hand, the causal connection between places, events, and their meanings in travel, that is, the translation of space into the time of writing and some particular narrative order, is a crucial feature of the genre. The characteristic causal connection, however, may remain profoundly open in terms of its form and pattern.

Hence, one reason why the travel story, or travel writing in general, so easily lends itself to be considered both a borderline and nascent case of narratives is that it foregrounds a tension between consecutiveness and consequence. For instance, the order of telling in a travelogue may be quite different from the order of the travel events. "Anachronies," by which Gérard Genette refers especially to forms of anticipation (prolepsis) and flashback (analepsis),³ and the effects of duration, speed and frequency, which result from alterations in the narrative order of events, can be found in literary fiction and travel narratives alike. The chronological presentation of the events of travel can be seen as the predominant form and expectation of the genre of travel writing but, at the same time, it can be powerful to temporarily let go of this expecta-

---

2. See Mikkonen 2007a.
3. See Genette 1972, 80; Genette 1980, 35–36, 40.

tion, for instance, by interrupting the narrative of the places and events with recollections, anecdotes, and anticipations.[4] Similarly, discrepancies between the time of the experience and the time of the writing can become as palpable and important in travel narratives as in some forms of autobiography or first-person fiction. The travel writers manipulate the relation between the order of events and the order of telling also in quite conventional narrative accounts of journeys such as Lansing's *Endurance,* which starts in the middle of the Antarctic expedition as Sir Ernest Shackleton's men are leaving their boat.

The history of the genre of travel writing, and the theoretical findings of the Russian formalists, suggest strongly that in order for a travel account to become a narrative in the proper sense, and not remain a mere chronicle of a journey, it needs to create a sufficient causal connection between the events or the places that it depicts. The travel writer's, the narrator's, or the character's experiential frame, meaning his or her personalizing point of view, is a central means for establishing such causal links between events. In a travel journal, perhaps the genre's most prototypical form, the speaker is expected to be constrained at some level by the immediate environment and the objects available there for description. At the same time, the mental processing of a world is also a means of engrossing the reader in the world of the story. As with Graham Greene's *Journey Without Maps,* a literary version of a journey that is based on a travel diary, the reader is witness to the mental process by which the writer forms the representation of a world (a place, a destination, a home). The traveller's movement and mental processing, therefore, realize the potential of the given space for experience.

The cultivated tension or "confusion" between sequence and consequence, further, is an indication of narrativity and often features in travel writing. This dynamic may be illustrated through the question of turning points in the narrative. Roland Barthes observed in his essay "Introduction to the Structural Analysis of Narratives" that

> Everything suggests, indeed, that the mainspring of narrative is precisely the confusion of consecution and consequence, what comes *after* being read in narrative as what is *caused by;* in which case narrative would be a systematic application of the logical fallacy denounced by Scholasticism in the formula *post hoc, ergo propter hoc*—a good motto for Destiny. (Barthes 1977, 94)

---

4. See Korte 2008, 33–35, for a helpful application of Genettean temporal structures in travel narratives; and Cohn 1999, 117, on similarity between fictional and nonfictional narratives in this respect. Korte also argues, rightly I think, that as far as the order of the events is concerned, "travelogues tend strongly towards chronological narration" (2008, 33).

Barthes's scheme of narrative units, which we can see as an attempt to come to terms with the logical fallacy of "after this, therefore because of this" that he sees as characteristic of all narratives, is based on the sharp distinction between the purely chronological functionality of *catalyzers* on the one hand and the *cardinal functions* (or *nuclei*) on the other hand. The cardinal functions, the turning points of the narrative, are both consecutive and consequential functions that can be recognized as such when the action to which they refer "open (or continue, or close) an alternative that is of direct consequence for the subsequent development of the story" (Barthes 1977, 94). The opening and closing of alternatives in the journey, given specific form as the crossroads and the directions that are available in the physical itinerary of the journey, are a key feature in the genre of travel literature, and especially so when the travel account takes a narrative form. Within the conventions of this genre there are various potential, often foregrounded conceptual matches for the cardinal narrative units: the "launch" of the real beginning of the voyage (after the departure from home); the "telescoping" of logic and temporality in travel experience through the traveller's moving perspective and points of attention, emphasizing the importance of a certain moment or experience in travel; the direction of movement and the choices at the crossroads open up alternatives and close them; the idea and experience of "turning back" (towards home or the place where the journey began); a sudden reversal of circumstances (*peripeteia*); chance encounters involve risks that both move the narrative forward and structure it; the landmarks and the description of places can be used to gauge progress in movement but also the unfolding of the travel narrative; and the return. Beyond this scheme, another obvious means through which travel writing builds on the relationship between consecutiveness and consequence are maps and itineraries. The maps, with their itineraries, show the physical route of the journey and the sequence of places, while the accompanying text describes the travel experience and gives it a causal form. All these conventions can increase narrativity in the story, combine consecution with consequence, quite possibly confusing them, and thus are potential nuclei of travel narratives.

By the same token, while the path schema provides the travel writing with a basic narrative structure, or a conceptual frame of a narrative,[5] travel writing is also typically marked by a sense of profound openness as to the causal mechanisms that motivate a travelling character or narrator to issue reports about the aspects of his or her movement through space. This means that

---

5. On the conceptual metaphors of LIFE IS A JOURNEY, CHOICES IN LIFE ARE CROSSROADS (or DECISIONS ARE JUNCTIONS IN THE ROAD) see Lakoff and Turner 1989, 3–4, and for applications of these metaphors see Mikkonen 2007a and Dannenberg 2008.

what comes after in the temporally ordered events in travel is not necessarily triggered by what went before. In other words, not just the sequencing of the travel events but also the traveller's experience of an event or a place, the meaning given to that event or place in relation to what has happened before, an impression or feeling of the time that has passed (see Korte 2008, 26), as well as the anticipation of what may happen next, are all essential features in travel *narratives*. To further illustrate these arguments about narrative organization, I now return to discuss Greene's *Journey Without Maps* and consider the question of the relation between narrative consecutiveness and consequence in this travelogue and, furthermore, how this question involves the distinction between travel writing and fictional narratives. I will develop the ideas of consecutiveness and consequence around two specific generic features and expectations of travel narratives. On the one hand, travel experience and travel writing presuppose the sense of a consecution of places, and events happening in particular places. The travel concept, and especially the journey plot pattern, manifests a specific model of temporality and causality—travel entails the arrangement of points of actuality in temporal order. On the other hand, the notion of travel is prone to confer identity and narrativity to a series of events since it "humanizes" the experience of time and space.[6] A travel story is dependent on the projection and experience of a world from a particular perspective, person, or group of people moving through space in a given time, thus enabling the treatment of space as a stage for possible narrative action. Narrative progress, therefore, is intimately related to, even if it does not always equal, the representation of the traveller's experience of space and time.

Greene's travel narrative is particularly pertinent to the questions raised here since it foregrounds the relationship between consecutiveness and consequence by questioning the meaning of maps and itineraries, and by projecting, as I aim to show briefly, a narrative voice concerned with the issue of how to narrativize the flow of travel experience in the first place. By "consequence" I mean more precisely the sense of logical relation that the writer-traveller constructs between the places and events of travel, intimately related to the traveller's personal experience of space and time. The notion of "experientality," which comes from Monika Fludernik, is helpful in this regard. Narrative experientiality means that narratives project on someone's state of mind, that is, they are based on the reporting, evaluation, and interpretation of someone's experience of an event, such as what is surprising, exciting, or terrible

---

6. In the sense that Frank Kermode (*The Sense of an Ending*, 1967) and Paul Ricoeur (*Time and Narrative*, 1983–85) discuss the function of emplotment.

in some event, filtered through consciousness (Fludernik 1996, 48–50; 2009, 59, 109).⁷

Open-Ended Travel

Journey Without Maps chronicles Greene's travel to West Africa, from January to April 1935. The itinerary of Greene's and his cousin Barbara Greene's 350-mile, four-week trek from Sierra Leone through Liberia, accompanied by a party of native guides and carriers, serves as a basis for the book's division into three parts and subchapters. The first section of the travelogue describes the journey from England to Freetown, the capital of Sierra Leone, and the train ride to the Liberian border; the second part tells about events on the trek from the border to the Liberian village of Ganta, including a passage in French Guinea; and the last part relates the trip from Ganta to Grand Bassa on the coast and the return boat to Monrovia, including a short note on the journey back from Freetown to Dover, England. The text, however, constantly diverges from the given chronological order of travel. The travel events, episodes, and impressions are punctuated by descriptions of people and acts of reading; the text includes anticipatory passages, memories and reflections on people and matters at home. Greene explained later, in his autobiography *Ways of Escape* (1980), how he had conceived the form for the book to be neither a political essay like Gide's *Voyage au Congo* nor an adventure story like Peter Fleming's travelogues. Furthermore, he wanted to avoid narrative structure in the sense of simple chronology or a sequence of places and travel events:

> The idea of A to Z has always scared me, like the thought in childhood of the long summer term, and I have always broken the continuity of a story with the memories of my chief character, just as I was now to break the continuity of the journey with the memories of 'I.' (1980, 48)

The "I" is in quotation marks, since this "I" indicates the writer's self-consciously abstracted persona, a second reflective self. At the same time, Greene excluded any mention of his cousin during the journey, for the sake of the

---

7. In Greene's fiction, there also emerges a Catholic sense of consequence that I do not discuss here, meaning the consequences from one's actions and sins. The notion is explored for instance in *The Heart of Matter*, where the protagonist Scobie (or perhaps the narrator in free indirect discourse) uses the expression of being "condemned to consequences" (1965, 154).

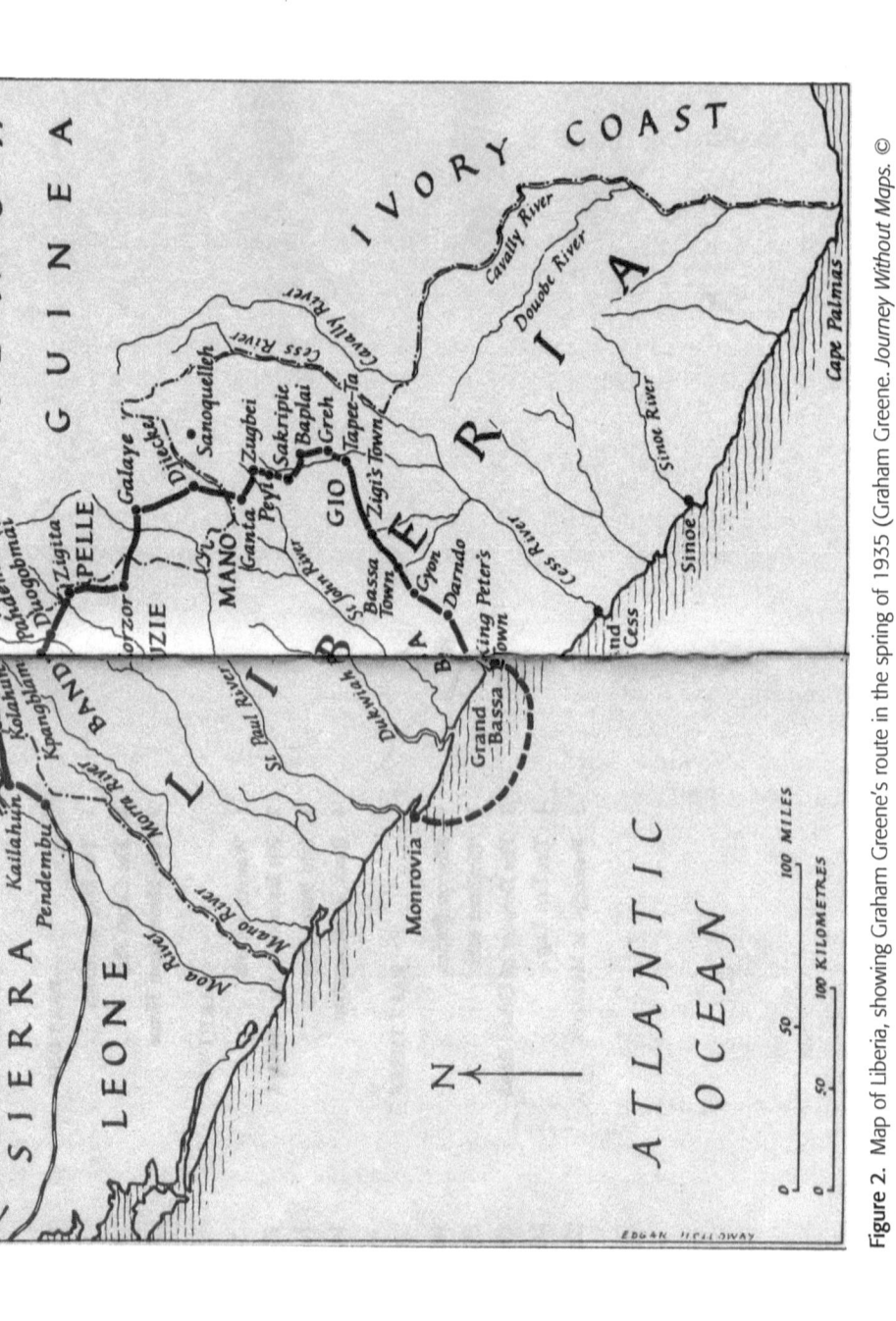

Figure 2. Map of Liberia, showing Graham Greene's route in the spring of 1935 (Graham Greene. *Journey Without Maps*. © Graham Greene).

abstracted perspective.[8] He thought that the outer journey into the unknown interior of West Africa needed to be intertwined with an inner dimension of personal experience, a journey into his mind, for the travel book to have any real meaning and interest:

> The account of a journey—a slow footsore journey into an interior literally unknown—was only of interest if it paralleled another journey. It would lose the triviality of a personal travel diary only if it became more completely personal. It is a disadvantage to have an 'I' who is not a fictional figure, and the only way to deal with 'I' was to make him an abstraction. (1980, 48)

The narrative of *Journey Without Maps* thus alternates systematically with memories and reflections of the writer's personal life, supporting, as Greene says, "the uneventful record with memories, dreams, word-associations" (1980, 48). As the quotation also shows, Greene's choice of narrative voice and perspective was made self-consciously in relation to kinds of choices that were available to him in writing fiction. The exclusion of his cousin from the narrative enabled Greene to focus on his own mind instead of dialogue and interaction with a companion. The choice is made for literary purposes and analogous to choosing between different direct or indirect modes of presenting consciousness, speech, and perception in fiction.

The title of Greene's travel book is not literally true, at least not as far as Greene's actual journey through Liberia is concerned. The travelogue also includes a small, sketchy map of Sierra Leone and Liberia.[9] In fact, the title serves as a guide for numerous possible interpretations and calls for the reader's response in terms of the relation between travel and narrative, potentially also drawing attention to the illusory transparency of maps, their illusion of referentiality. One of its meanings is almost true: in 1935 Greene and his cousin entered a relatively unmapped area of Liberia. The maps the Greenes were able

---

8. Greene mentions Barbara a few times in the book, however, and thanks her for accompanying him (2002, 21). In *Ways of Escape*, Greene explains further that "only in one thing did she [Barbara] disappoint me—she wrote a book. However, her generosity was apparent even there, for she waited several years, until my own book had appeared" (1980, 47). Barbara Greene's travel book from the same journey, *Too Late to Turn Back: Barbara and Graham Greene in Liberia*, was published in 1938 (originally it was entitled *Land Benighted*). In *Ways of Escape*, Greene compares the notes in his diary, Barbara's account in *Land Benighted*, and the description in *Journey Without Maps*, in what comes to the turning point of his sickness during the trek (1980, 49–54).

9. See Thacker for an analysis on the symbolic differences in the maps of the various editions of the book (the editions of 1936, 1953, and 1978) (2002, 13–16).

to find for Sierra Leone and Liberia showed whole areas left blank; they were inaccurate, useless, and imaginary (see Greene 2002a, 45–46; Sherry 1989, 512, 528–29). For example, an American military map of the area included empty spaces with remarks of the whereabouts of "cannibals." Another aspect of the travel experience suggested by the title indicates is practical knowledge about the travel conditions. During his journey in Sierra Leone and Liberia Greene realized that travel which followed a timetable was impossible and that the only way to plan the journey was "to know the next town or village ahead and repeat it as you go" (2002a, 47). Therefore, instead of using maps and itineraries, he gradually became used to "drifting with Africa" (2002a, 66).

Andrew Thacker has pointed out that the title of Greene's travelogue draws attention, on the one hand, to the ambiguous status of pictorial maps in travel writing as illustrations of a written text, posing as seemingly supplementary textual features while, on the other hand, suggesting how maps also act as a kind of guide to the journey, thus altering the way we travel and read works of travel writing (2002, 11). Thacker, moreover, interprets Greene's emphasis on travelling without maps as a metaphor for "a covert exploration of unknown territory" (2002, 17), meaning both the archaic cartographic status of Liberia and the unknown, archaic qualities of the writer's mind. Some features in the maps included in the earlier editions of the book, particularly the 1936 and 1953 editions, such as absent names or decorative African patterns, further emphasize Greene's self-identification as an explorer rather than a traveller or a tourist (Thacker 2002, 13–17). To some extent we may also speak of Greene's desire to identify himself with earlier famous British explorers in the region, such as Mungo Park, Mary Kingsley, or Sir Alfred Sharpe. The first half of Greene's route followed roughly Sir Alfred Sharpe's 1919 journey from Freetown through the roadless hinterland of Liberia (Greene 2002a, 109, 118, 164). Greene's predecessors obviously had even less cartographical support.

The practical meanings of poorly-mapped forest areas are inseparable from various metaphorical and ideological connotations in a mapless West Africa. The latter include, for instance, a writer's search for new, unexpected material; a means of self-analysis; and the colonial notion of African space as void of history and culture. Thacker argues convincingly that Greene's anti-cartographic discourse is deeply embedded in a spatial history of Africa that has been constructed by "European imperialist views of the continent's seeming achronicity" (2002, 19)[10] Here, however, I will concentrate on another

---

10. By "self-analysis" I mean that West Africa serves Greene in *Journey Without Maps* as scenery for posing moral questions about oneself and one's culture. Further, the lack of maps is a religious-philosophical allegory—involving the intention to know "one's place in time"

specific meaning of Greene's cultivated resistance to maps and itinerary that bears significance in terms of the problem of narrative consecutiveness/consequence. Greene's growing determination to drift on unmapped paths reveals an excitement not only in unstructured adventure and open-ended travel but also in travel writing that does not respect the structure given by maps and itineraries. This drifting involves, further, a hesitation to use the conventional "life is a journey" and "life is a narrative" metaphors of an autobiography, at least in the sense that there could be a neat analogy between the experience of life, the order of travel, and the order of narratives. In this respect the book's second epigraph, by the American physician and poet Oliver Wendell Holmes, becomes important. In the passage that Greene cites, Holmes claims that

> The life of an individual is in many respects like a child's dissected map. If I could live a hundred years, keeping my intelligence to the last, I feel as if I could put the pieces together until they made a properly connected whole. As it is, I, like all others, find a certain number of connected fragments, and a large number of disjointed pieces, which I might in time place in their natural connection. Many of these pieces seem fragmentary, but would in time show themselves as essential parts of the whole. What strikes me very forcibly is the arbitrary and as it were accidental way in which the lines of junction appear to run irregularly among the fragments. With every decade I find some new pieces coming into place. Blanks which have been left in former years find their complement among the undistributed fragments. If I could look back on the whole, as we look at the child's map when it is put together, I feel that I should have my whole life intelligently laid out before me. (Greene 2002a, 7; Holmes 1896, 28–29)

The central metaphors of this passage, the problem of the "dissected map," the "fragmentary pieces" of life and the arbitrary "lines of junction," link Greene's travel narrative to the metaphorical notion of "life is a journey" in the form of a question: in what sense, if at all, can life (and travel as a microcosm of life)

(2002, 19)—for searching what has been lost in European culture (sense of seediness, brutality, childhood, primitive virtue). Among the cultural and ideological "maps" evoked by Greene's commentary in the book is the lop-sided information about West Africa by British newspapers and Government sources. In the same category we can count Greene's own Africanism, meaning the frequent superimposition of notions of childhood and primitive virtue on African spaces—"a quality of darkness is needed, of the inexplicable" (2002, 20)—that recalls colonialist notions of Africa as void of history and any advanced human culture. For more on Greene's "anti-cartographic discourse" and its relationship with imperialist views of Africa's achronicity, see Thacker 2002, 19–20.

be experienced as a connected whole like a narrative? Or can one, so to say, live out narratives?[11] The metaphor of a child's dissected map in the Holmes epigraph evokes the dilemma that characterizes Greene's travel book and the meaning of travel as "drifting": the contradiction between the promise of understanding one's life as a connected whole—life has not only a spatialized temporal order like a map and an itinerary, but it is also causally organized like a narrative—and the distrust of that very same possibility (since life is an ongoing process without clear beginning or end). Two further dimensions of this piecing together, and ones that Greene occasionally evokes in the travelogue, are psychoanalysis—the method of bringing the patient back to the repressed idea, "the pain or the memory" (2002a, 96–97)—and fiction, the possibility in fiction to give life a narrative form.

Greene's idea of a travelling that is not fully conscious—"it is not the fully conscious mind which chooses West Africa in preference to Switzerland" (2002a, 20)—since it is repressed in the traveller's mind, draws on psychoanalysis and the idea of a specifically African "unconsciousness." At the same time, this idea reflects the ambiguous dynamic of plotting between a grasp of the connected whole and a sense of an open-ended process. *Journey Without Maps* suggests that there is always potential ambiguity in the status of the itinerary just as there is in the concept of the *fabula* (i.e. the set of narrated situations and events in their chronological order, see Prince 2003, 29). Itinerary is, on the one hand, the map that the traveller follows (temporal and spatial order), but, on the other hand, it is also a history of travels—the map as narrative (combining temporal and causal orders in the told story). In the same way the narrative sequence of the story may be thought to exist both before and after the discourse (in the sense of the order of presentation, as distinct from *fabula*). The notion of journeying as drifting celebrates the open-ended and not fully conscious possibilities of both travel and narrative but also draws attention to the topos, since rivers and droves are obvious conduits in difficult, roadless terrain.

The Itinerary and the Map

An important feature of graphic maps in classical travel narratives is that they concreticize the *fabula* of a travel story; or at least the fabula can be conceived

---

11. This is, of course, a much debated question in interdisciplinary narrative studies and narrative theory. See Alasdair MacIntyre (1984, 212) for the famous claim that we live out stories before they are told, "except in the case of fiction," and Jerome Bruner for a similar claim that "in the end, we *become* the autobiographical narratives by which we tell about our lives" (1987, 15). For an antithesis to this Narrativist thesis of identity, see Strawson (2012).

of, with the help of the map, in terms of actual space, of geography. In the event that the map is missing, travel stories often prompt their readers to provide a map: in various editions or on the internet one can, for instance, find a large amount of competing maps of Odysseus's travels. The number of people who are driven to draw maps of Odysseus's itinerary is indicative of the seemingly inherent potential of travel narrative, be it fiction or nonfiction, to be thought of as a substantial spatial configuration.[12] The great variety of these maps points to the relative openness in the fabula, at least in the sense that Odysseus's route can be conceived in different ways within certain basic parameters (major events and locations) while it is also evidence of divergence in reader response.

In their function as a graphic interpretation of the sequence of places and events, and as potential narrative programs, the map and the itinerary suggest further affinities between travel and narrative. In this analogy, the map indicates both the route followed and the trace that is interpreted as a story. Often the map, in its graphic form, also suggests possibilities of choice, possible lines of travel that are not chosen. The map, therefore, is not only a model of a referential world, affirming the referentiality of travel writing, but may presuppose a narrative. The itinerary, the succession of traversed spaces in the map, is already a part of the transformation of travel into narrative. The map indicates the literal space of places and events but it is also realized and practiced by the traveller.[13] The itinerary, whether in graphic form on the map, a written list of places and times, or implied in the reported events, mediates between the possibilities of the space of the map and the transformation of the experience of space in writing. The itinerary traces the order and the direction of travel, its sequence.

However, if the itinerary in travel writing may function as an index of narrative structure, there remains the difficult question of the relation of the itinerary to the process and experience of travel. This difficulty is due to the fact that the order in a journey is often only created in the very act of travelling itself (in its open-ended temporal process) or can be known only after the journey (as a retrospective outcome of the experience). For more the-

---

12. Gibson's insights that the various spaces in *The Odyssey* are rigorously separated but "cannot be reduced to any homogeneous or global whole," or that "the mythical adventure of Odysseus is nothing more or less than the connecting up of these incommensurable spaces," are in line with the idea of the incomparable maps (1996, 17). On the complexities involved in charting a map of a fictional world, see Ryan 2003.

13. There are, naturally, great differences between maps in regards to the way a map can be incorporated in the verbal narrative, how text and image interact within the map, or how visible the map's enunciation as narrative discourse may be. Such differences are discussed, for instance, by Jacob 1992, 247–51.

oretical insight into the relation of the map and the itinerary to temporal and causal narrative structure, we can turn to Louis Marin's study of utopian spaces and signifying practices, *Utopiques. Jeux d'espaces* (1973), and Michel de Certeau's *L'invention du quotidien* (1980), a theory of everyday practices. Both Marin and de Certeau develop an analogy between the map-itinerary opposition, on the one hand, and the Russian formalist (and later narratological) distinction between fabula and *syuzhet,* or story and discourse, on the other. Moreover, their theories involve an interactional model of the relation between the map and the itinerary, a sense of a meaning-making process between the two. Marin argues, for instance, that the itinerary of travel narrative also "constitutes the map, which is, as representation, the product of the narrative" (1984, 44). For de Certeau, similarly, the spatial reference of the map implies the structure of the narrative by pointing to the transformation of geographic inscription into discourse, space into time.[14] In de Certeau's model, the narrative nature of walking in a city can thus be distinguished as an interaction between "place" (*lieu*) and "space" (*espace*). Place, for de Certeau, is "the order (of whatever kind) in accord with which elements are distributed in relationships of coexistence," while space is composed of intersections of mobile elements: space "occurs as the effect produced by the operations that orient it" (1984, 117). A sense of space, in other words, is a practiced place.[15]

The title and the second epigraph of Greene's travel book rely on the analogy between travel and narrative, but also on the dilemma between a conception of travel as a meaningful, connected whole of events, in the form of a pre-understanding or retrospective knowledge, and the uncontrollable process of the disjointed experiences travelling often includes. The emphasis on the importance of going astray and drifting in a mapless territory, excitement of travelling to "unmapped" Africa, instead of colonial British Africa, involves an interruption in the relation de Certeau describes as obtaining between place and space. The excitement of travel and unknown territory is,

---

14. Franco Moretti is also principally in line with this argument as he suggests that the literary map enjoys a position between the pattern of experience, or chronotope, which is described in the story and that may also structure the story, and narrative discourse (or "narrative flow" as he calls it). Moretti argues, more precisely, that even if the literary map may not be an explanation itself of the spatial and temporal pattern of the story, it is a specific form of knowledge that shows to the reader "that there is something that needs to be explained" (2004, 84). For a more extended application of de Certeau's concepts to Greene's book, see Thacker 2002, 21–25.

15. The idea equals Mieke Bal's distinction between "frame-space" and "thematized space," the first meaning the place of action and the latter meaning "acting place" or space transformed into a story (1997, 136).

furthermore, implied in the travelogue's first epigraph, the second stanza from W. H. Auden's "O Where Are You Going?," and the beginning of the narrative.[16] In Auden's poem, which is structured around a dialogue between a passive and an active person, the active agent, who is called a "rider," "fearer," and "hearer," boldly moves onwards, regardless of the passive speaker's threats and warnings about the dangers and uncertainties of travel. The first subchapter of *Journey Without Maps*, entitled "Harvest Festival," revolves around an experience of losing the sense of fixed points of direction. The book starts with Greene entering, by accident, the harvest festival preparations in the vestry of St. Dunstan's Church while trying to find the Liberian consulate.

As the title, the epigraphs, and the narrative's beginning suggest, travel is always to some extent multidirectional and even threatens to be nonnarrative because too much can be recounted, even the boring and the uninteresting, or simply because a chronological account of the journey from A to Z would be too tedious, too uninteresting. Traditionally, travel narrative is organized by the cumulative, observational enterprise of documenting geography, landscape, flora, fauna, people, and customs in the chronological order of the journey. We can easily recall the ocular obsessions of sightseeing guidebooks. An important single event in this respect, building on but also questioning this convention, is Greene's description of the Liberian forest as lacking any interesting detail, and the accompanying confusion of the sense of time discussed in the previous chapter.

However, the passage that Greene quotes from Oliver Wendell Holmes also strongly implies that one may discover an important meaning in pieces

---

16. W. H. Auden: "O Where Are You Going?"

"O where are you going?" said reader to rider,
"That valley is fatal where furnaces burn,
Yonder's the midden whose odours will madden,
That gap is the grave where the tall return."

"O do you imagine," said fearer to farer,
"That dusk will delay on your path to the pass,
Your diligent looking discover the lacking,
Your footsteps feel from granite to grass?"

"O what was that bird," said horror to hearer,
"Did you see that shape in the twisted trees?
Behind you swiftly the figure comes softly,
The spot on your skin is a shocking disease."

"Out of this house," said rider to reader,
"Yours never will," said farer to fearer
"They're looking for you," said hearer to horror,
As he left them there, as he left them there. (Auden 1991 [1931], 59–69)

of a dissected map in retrospect, upon discovering a hidden structure of the whole or new pieces that may join and complement the fragment. The fact that the itinerary can usually only be known after the end of travel exemplifies not only the backward logic of causal relation—the possibility of looking back on the whole experience—but also points to the importance of the crucial experiences of unresolved direction, unrealized possibilities, and shattered expectations during travel. Digression and chronological deviation, typical of odyssey and nomadism, increase the sense of narrativity by upsetting expectations about the agents' goal. Most classical, episodic travel stories, from Homer to Joyce, capitalize on detouring, and explore the experience of dislocation. They occlude causal relations, present examples of the discontinuous, the amorphous, and the surprising; in the case of *Journey Without Maps*, the path of travel, while structuring the time and space of narrative, suggests contingency, chance meetings, and ever-new associations. An open-ended journey, such as drifting in a mapless territory with no sense of time, is at one end of the spectrum of travel experiences. Another ultimate metaphor for digressive narration is the experience of being stuck in a labyrinth or a maze, a sense of journey in which all possible itineraries are predetermined. A labyrinth has only a single path but it is maximally circuitous. A maze is emblematic of narrative mechanisms that threaten reversible sequence with irreversible consequence and a closed-up space. In a maze, every turn in direction is fatal not only since all sequences have different consequences but since all points in space are part of a closure and confusingly similar.

In *Journey Without Maps*, the sense of (nearly) directionless drifting, as well as the experience of acute boredom in the middle of the great monotonous forest, are framed by the time of writing, the retrospective frame of the narration that connects the various events together. The moment of writing, as distinct from the time of travelling, provides the text with connections based on circularity between departure and return. Retrospective knowledge of the final shape of the itinerary is clearly there right from the book's opening lines: "later sitting before a hut in French Guinea, where I never meant to find myself, I remembered this first going astray, the buses passing at the corner and the pale autumn sun" (2002a, 15). Different moments and memories of travel overlap, and the time of writing, including the creation of stylized memories and literary portraits, constantly interrupts the time of travel. At the same time, a sense of consequence between places and events becomes apparent, entirely distinct from the temporal order of movement through space.

The complex relation between sequence and consequence in Greene's travelogue suggests that the circular hermeneutics between departure and return can be thought of as a retrospective memorial reconstruction of a series of events and experiences. However, the relation between the travel experience and the travel narrative is also a theme in *Journey Without Maps* that invites questions about their order and causal connection. Jean-Didier Urbain has argued, with regard to travel writing in general, that the relationship between travel and story (*récit*) can also be circular in the sense that the story is a structure within or simultaneous to the travel experience, and not merely an a posteriori frame of travel, a literary translation of the experience. It is therefore also possible to write about travel first and experience it later, or to experience travel while writing about it, thus making the real journey a citation of the preceding narrative ("la citation jouée d'un récit antérieur"; 1998, 370). In Greene's travelogue, the time of the writing and the time of the travel experience are generally clearly distinguishable, but at the same time, the narrated moments of travel, the author's memories and associations, and the perspective of the time of writing inform one another reciprocally.

Over the course of the narrative, *Journey Without Maps*, wanderings without maps gradually make more room for contingency, chance encounter, and the risks of travel. The traveller begins to repeat the sense of the present (he could only know the name of the next village). At the same time, however, the hermeneutics of departure and return is always re-affirmed by the writer's retrospective point of view, where the goal of remembrance is to integrate events into a well-crafted narrative. Greene's travel book makes manifest to us the complexities and the rich possibilities in the relationship between narrative and travel, or narrative sequence and consequence by evoking (but also questioning) travel metaphors like "life is a journey" and "narrative is travel" (or "travel is narrative"), and by questioning the bias towards chronological organization in travel writing.

Potential Characters

Greene's constant and skillful manipulation of the relation between the order of the events and the order of their presentation in his travelogue makes manifest that nonfiction travel narrative and fiction can be indistinguishable in terms of the complexity of their temporal organization. The fact that *Journey Without Maps* is finely segmented into three parts, twelve chapters, and over sixty subchapters also facilitates constant transitions in perspective, time, and place, between the more descriptive observations of places and events en route and Greene's personal memories, associations, and storytelling. The structure is clearly indebted to the form of a modern novel.

In some cases, chapter divisions reflect transitions not only of perspective, narrative mode, time, and topic, but create juxtapositions of time and place that may remind one of the functions of segmentation and chapter divisions in fiction. Perhaps the most interesting case in this respect is the subchapter "The Way Back," which ends the first part of the book, and which consists of a series of short literary portraits and caricatures of people at home in England whom Greene remembers during the journey. The subchapter has an important structural function in the travelogue and, moreover, frames these portraits in relation to fiction-writing, as potential material for the creation of literary characters. Thus another area of interplay between travel writing and fiction opens up.

"The Way Back" subchapter is placed in between two passages that describe Greene's arrival at the Liberian border and his encounter with the customs officers. The interruption of the journey creates a juxtaposition of place and time that is only partially explained by the transitions into and out of the subchapter. At the end of the previous passage, entitled "To the Frontier," Greene had related his amazement at seeing twenty-five carriers obeying his orders, and the "odd feeling of pleasure" and "an absurd sense of pride" that had resulted from it (2002a, 68). Upon arriving at the border, Greene then explains that

> One couldn't help having, however unjustifiably, a sense of the dramatic; the way forward through the clearing was as broad as the primrose way, as open as a trap; the way back was narrow, hidden, difficult, to the English scene. (2002a, 68)

The transition points to the fact that the narration, and the direction of Greene's thoughts, shifts backwards at this point, back to the "English scene" and memories of the people he had met or heard about. The character portraits that then follow include Major Grant who frequents brothels; Miss Kilvane who is a follower of the religious prophetess, Joanna Southcott; a runaway gypsy boy called Buckland, who pretends to know how to milk a cow so as to be employed; and Mr. Charles Seitz, the mystery of whose madness and death by freezing had attracted many rival stories. At the very end of the subchapter, Greene then hints at the reason why his journey was interrupted:

> We turned away from Major Grant and Miss Kilvane, from the peace under the down and the flat off the Strand, from the holy and the depraved individualists to the old, the unfamiliar, the communal life beyond the clearing. (2002a, 74)

It now becomes evident that the portraits highlight Greene's impression of the differences between English individualism and the West African communal lifestyle, while they also dramatize the contrast between the harsh winter in London and the heat of the African noon sun. The notion of West African communal lifestyle is reflected, for instance, in Greene's description, just prior to the subchapter, of the twenty-five carriers who act as a group and are set in motion "like a long mechanical toy" (2002a, 68). At the same time, Greene associates his reminiscing with a movement in space, as moving on a path that may narrow or broaden at will. After the "The Way Back" subchapter begins Part Two of the book, where the narrative returns to the present moment of the journey, Greene's arrival at the Liberian border.

Major Grant and Miss Kilvane represent to Greene the kinds of people who are of high interest to the novelist from a creative point of view. Greene collects such stories, as for instance is evident in his "Congo Diary" that is included in *In Search of a Character*, as rough material to be used, transformed and sometimes caricatured in his fiction. At a later point in *Journey Without Maps*, at the very end of the second part of the book, the author returns to Grant and Kilvane as potential literary characters. They are reintroduced by way of an encounter with an interesting Liberian called Wordsworth:

> Already he [Wordsworth] was intent on joining that odd assortment of "characters" (the Grants and the Kilvanes) one collects through life, vivid grotesques, people so simple that they always have the same side turned to one, damned by their unself-consciousness to be material for the novelist, to supply the minor characters, to be endlessly caricatured, to make in their multiplicity one's world. (2002a, 165)

The mention of the Grants and the Kilvanes points back to the division into Books One and Two, but also marks the transition between Books Two and Three. Later in Book Three, Greene gives a description of meeting with Mr. Wordsworth, junior, whose father was the District Commissioner and "like a stern and sadistic papa in a Victorian children's story" (2002a, 299). For the third and last time Major Grant and Miss Kilvane are brought up at the end of the travel book, where Greene reveals that they and others like them, people of the mythical Coast, represent to him a Western version of "central darkness," that is, the sense of being close to an ancestral, communal life "with its terror and its gentleness" (2002a, 249). For that reason, these people make good characters. Here, Greene associates the mental image of "Miss Kilvane listening to the ghost of Joanna" with a circle of black Africans in Tailahun listening to the enigmatic speech of Landow, a leader of a local religious movement. All the book's three major segments, through their closure, are thus tied to the question of characterization and the process of fiction writing. In this way, the travel, and the travel book, anticipates the novel, illustrating how interesting and credible characters may be found and constructed.

Greene made the analogy between travel, and in particular travel into an unknown territory, and the invention of fictional characters explicit in his 1952 essay "The Explorers." Here he asks: "Is it that the explorer has the same creative sickness as the writer or the artist and that to fill in the map, as to fill in the character or features of a human being, requires the urge to surrender and self-destruction?" (Greene 1969, 318). Greene's question actually involves two different comparisons between travel and literary narrative: to create a fictional entity, such as a literary character, is like exploring an unknown territory and, subsequently, both the travel exploration and the creation of characters may necessitate that the agent, the traveller or the writer, to some extent effaces himself in the process. In Greene's "Congo Journal" (1959), the analogue between exploring a territory and creating new characters is further enhanced by the idea of mysterious African space. During his 1959 trip to the Congo as he was working on his next African novel (*A Burnt-Out Case*), Greene wrote about the demands of creating characters based on his travel and the atmosphere of (Conradian) West African mystique. In planning the narrative perspective for his next novel, Greene insisted that the story should not be told through the main character's eyes and, moreover, that the author "should not penetrate into the thoughts of any character—which must be indicated only in action and dialogue. This makes for the mood of mystery which I wish to catch" (1968, 20). In his earlier novels, Greene had made ample use of free indirect discourse, but in *A Burnt-Out Case* the device is rarely used.[17] Only on a few occasions does the narrator's report of a character's thoughts and emotions include words, phrases, or questions that might come from the character. Direct presentation of his thoughts, except for the frequent dialogue scenes, is similarly exceptional and brief. In the first chapter of this novel in particular Greene carries out his principle of mysterious indirection effectively by giving the reader very limited access to the protagonist's mind. The only exception is the initial and intriguing quotation, a parody of Descartes, from the character's diary: "I feel discomfort, therefore I am alive" (Greene 1975, 9). The protagonist's identity, who is not yet called Querry but some anonymous "passenger" moving deeper into Africa on the Congo River, and the reason for what he has written, remain open and mysterious.

---

17. See also Bergonzi 2006, 153.

Only gradually will the reader learn that this sense of secrecy and anonymity, and a rejection of a life that feels like a story, is something that Querry seeks by travelling to the Congo in the first place.

The Writing Process

Many of Graham Greene's travels involve a multiphase and multilayered process of writing, and a two-way movement between nonfiction and fiction, similarly to the texts written by Evelyn Waugh, Georges Simenon, and André Gide that we will discuss in the next sections of this study. On his travels Greene usually kept a diary. He wrote two important travel books, *Journey Without Maps* and *The Lawless Roads* (1939) (also published as *Another Mexico*), which were to some extent based on the travel diary. This also becomes evident in Greene's references to and quotations from his Diary in *Journey Without Maps* (see Greene 2002a, 128, 214). Furthermore, the travel diaries and the travel books are continuous with the writer's fictions set up in the same locations. Greene's journey through Liberia in 1935 produced a short story, "A Chance for Mr Lever" (*London Mercury*, January 1936) that was later included in *Nineteen Stories* (1947). The story mirrors closely the writer's experience, for instance in relation to the notion of travel in Liberia without maps, or the protagonist Mr. Lever's difficult confrontation with the carriers who want a raise in their pay. *Lawless Roads*, describing Greene's five-week trip in Mexico, when he was investigating the effects of the government's campaign of forced anti-Catholic secularization, and the novel *The Power and the Glory* (1940), share the same Mexican background and describe some shared events. In *The Heart of the Matter*, in turn, the exact West African location of the events remains anonymous, but is generally held to be Sierra Leone, where Greene was stationed as an intelligence officer in 1942–43. Some details from Greene's earlier journey in Liberia are also reused in this novel.[18] Greene's travel to the Belgian Congo in 1959 had the purpose of gathering material for *A Burnt-Out Case*. *In Search of a Character* (1961) includes the diary of that same journey ("Congo Journal"), and an earlier short diary, "Convoy to West Africa," consisting of diary entries made in December 1941 and the first days of 1942, when Greene travelled from Liverpool to Free-

---

18. We find, for instance, a place called "France" in *The Heart of the Matter* (1965, 105), while in *Journey Without Maps* the colony of French Guinea is known as "France" among the natives of the Liberian Republic (2002, 145). However, Greene's stay in Lagos and Freetown during the war was different from most of his other travels in that he could not keep a diary for security reasons.

town. The story of *The Comedians* (1966) draws on Greene's travel to Haiti, and so on.

The relation between Greene's travels and fictions was often seen to be so close that the writer thought it was important to list, in the beginning of his autobiography *Ways of Escape* (1980), those of his travels, such as his reportages on the Mau Mau rebellion in Kenya in the 1950s, which had not produced any novels or stories. Here he claimed that he was not purposely looking to find material during his travels, but that the material just came his way: "More rarely than might be supposed the places I visited proved sources for my novels. I wasn't seeking sources, I stumbled on them" (1980, 9).[19] Be that as it may, Greene's travel diaries also confirm the close relation between his travels and fiction.

Conclusion

A travel narrative such as Greene's *Journey Without Maps* provides us with a model for negotiating the relationship between the process of experience and narrative order, the difference between the shape of experience and the shape of narrative. What adds to this capacity is that to write about travel usually means to reenact earlier journeys and to succumb to pre-existing literary models. Greene, for instance, uses preexisting texts—mainly canonical works of fiction and poetry—as an intertextual filter to mediate the gap between the "open" order of the travelling experience and the order of writing. Quotations from books and descriptions of reading experiences punctuate the travel throughout *Journey Without Maps* and, as in the disturbing case of going through a dull, dead forest, the writer is engaged in reevaluating earlier readings in regard to the travel experience.

The experience of distance and the foreignness of the described world also increase narrativity in Greene's travelogue. The "exhausted discourse" of certain modern travel writing, even if it challenges the possibility of evoking an authentic foreign world, is based on the premise of constructing a world through negation (as a reaction against the others' experience of the exotic, the strange and the marvelous). Greene's "mapless" Africa is, at least partly, a personal and imaginary construct rather than a strictly real, geographic space. The literary references, the interspersed memories, and the juxtaposition of the time of travel and the time of writing help to impose a spatial-temporal

---

19. Greene also claims in the introduction to his "Congo Diary" that "I have very little visual imagination and only a short memory" (1968, 8).

method on the static, map-like structuring of space. Writing thus resists the notion of space as a static entity.

To summarize, Greene's *Journey Without Maps* helps to raise the question of the process-versus-product aspect of narrative in a palpable way: how to represent freedom and contingency within a structure? Travel writing shows explicitly how causality and chronology, narrative consequence and temporal sequence can fuse. But typically travel stories tend to break this conjunction, at least provisionally, during the course of the narrative. As regards the increase of narrativity, the very suggestion of travel produces narrative, or increases narrativity, since the idea of travel personalizes the experience of time and space through the subjective perspective of movement and of perceiving a world. Greene's African travel narrative explores the ways in which time can be personalized as a narrative and how the traveller's viewpoint introduces a sense of consequence to the sequence of places and events.

PART II
Travel Writing and the Novel

The Immediacy of Reading
André Gide's Travel Fact and Travel Fictions

ANDRÉ GIDE'S (1869–1951) travel journal from colonial West and Central Africa, *Travels in the Congo,* was a continuation of the writer's intimate *Journal,* which he interrupted during the journey between July 1925 and June 1926. Gide had conceived of the African journey as a kind of turning point in his life, not just as another journey. Before his departure from Bordeaux with Marc Allégret on July 14, 1925, Gide had sold his villa in Auteuil and part of his library. He had also finished a major novel, *Les Faux-Monnayeurs* (*The Counterfeiters,* 1925). An entry on November 1, 1924 in *Journal des Faux-Monnayeurs,* which is Gide's journal dedicated to the process of writing *The Counterfeiters,*[1] reveals that the writer had postponed his departure for Africa until the following June in the hope that he could finish the novel before then (2008, 90).[2] In an entry from his *Journal* at the end of May 1925, when Gide notes that he had finished typing the final version of five chapters from the

---

1. Gide kept this journal throughout the writing process, from the summer of 1919 until May 1925. Gide's *Journal 1889–1939,* which was published in 1939 in the Bibliothèque de la Pléiade collection, was the first in the series of published journals that the author edited from his complete journal. The latter came out in the same collection in 1996–97.

2. Gide refers here to some other important reason for postponing the journey, but does not give any details. The reason was probably his lover Marc Allégret's examinations in the fall of 1924, which are mentioned in an entry in Gide's *Journal* on October 26 of that year (see also O'Brien 1953, 264–65). Justin O'Brien has translated the notebook about the writing of *The Counterfeiters* as *Logbook of The Coiners* (1952).

novel, he refers to his high expectations of the Congo, distressed as he was by the apathy he felt:

> Je ne compte plus que sur le Congo pour m'en sortir. La préparation de ce voyage et l'attente des pays nouveaux a désenchanté le présent; j'éprouve combien il était vrai de dire que le bonheur habite l'instant. Rien ne me paraît plus que provisoire. (Gide 1951a, 805–6)

> I have given up counting on anything but the Congo to get me out of it [my apathy]. Preparations for this trip and the expectation of new landscapes have disenchanted the present. I am experiencing how true it was to say that happiness lies in the moment. Nothing seems to me anything but provisional now. (Gide 1967, 390)

Furthermore, two brief subsequent entries from the summer of 1925 suggest that the finishing of the novel and the journey were directly connected: "8 June: Finished *Les Faux-Monnayeurs*; 14 July: Departure for the Congo" (Gide 1967, 390) ("8 juin: Achevé *les Faux-Monnayeurs*; 14 juillet: Départ pour le Congo"; Gide 1948, 806).

Inspired by the biographical relation between the novel and Gide's departure for Africa, as well as the writer's *Journal* entries from the summer of 1925, Gérard Cogez has argued that Gide's travel was motivated by a desire to distance himself from the limitations of the novel genre: "How could one not see that this was for the writer an escape from the novelistic trap, and one which enabled him to take a helpful and, perhaps, definitive critical distance from the genre?" (2004, 215).[3] The journey would thus have been for Gide a means of turning away from the novel genre with which he had recently, and amply, expressed his dissatisfaction, especially in *Le Journal des Faux-Monnayeurs*, where Gide, for instance, explains how, in writing *The Counterfeiters*, he sought to reinvent the novel form. Gide, as he explains in his journal about writing the novel, was particularly concerned about the construction of fictional characters and sought to find powerful verbal expressions, tones of voice and nuanced gestures that would reveal the characters' minds, instead of using the novelistic convention of narrative access to the characters' thoughts and emotions (Gide 2008, 82–85). The journal of writer-character Edouard, of which fragments are included in *The Counterfeiters*, voices similar concerns about novelistic pretensions of verisimilitude, based

---

3. My translation of "Comment n'entendrait-on pas qu'il s'agit bien pour l'écrivain de se sortir du piège romanesque, de prendre avec le genre une salutaire, et peut-être définitive, distance critique?"

on descriptive realism, and about traditional means for portraying the characters' dialogue, action, and states of mind.

However, the assumption that Gide travelled "away from" the novel or that he did so "in hatred of the novel" (Cogez 2004, 212) is not easily reconciled with the fact that the writer had in his luggage several novels and that during the journey he commented on his novel-reading with much pleasure. Furthermore, Gide not only writes in his travel journal about the immersive qualities of fiction, but also structures much of his experience in Africa with the help of fiction, especially in reference to Joseph Conrad's *Heart of Darkness*. In addition, there are some striking thematic affinities between *The Counterfeiters* and the travel journal that suggest a sense of continuity in the writer's thinking about the novel genre at this time. Gide, for instance, continues in his travel journal to inquire into the relation between mediated reality and the facts of reality, or between the power of imagination and the resistance of facts—questions that are extensively developed in *The Counterfeiters*. In Gide's career after the journey, there is also no definitive break in writing longer prose fiction—*L'Ecole des femmes* and *Robert* came out in 1929—even if, admittedly, he was no longer interested in questioning the conventions of the genre through ambitious experiments such as *The Counterfeiters*. The fact that *The Counterfeiters* was the only book that Gide called a novel among his works, classifying his earlier undertakings in prose fiction as satires (*soties*) or stories (*récits*), underscores the author's attempt to rethink the novel genre at this time. However, as to the misgivings about novel-writing that Gide voices in *Le Journal des Faux-Monnayeurs*, or through his mouthpieces in *The Counterfeiters*, these involve mainly his critique of traditional novelistic conventions in characterization and description. All in all, it seems more justified to claim that Gide sought to write a novel that would present its characters and their minds differently from his earlier works (with a sense of outer flatness, for instance),[4] and, at the same time, reject traditional forms of realism that he disliked, rather than to reject the novel genre as a whole.

Below, I will explore the relationship between Gide's major novel and his African travel journal in more detail, with specific attention given to the question of the possibilities and limitations of the novel as a genre. Such an inquiry involves, on the one hand, an analysis of the features in *The Counterfeiters* that evoke the themes of Africa and travel and, on the other hand, how

---

4. The "flatness" of the characters refers here to Gide's intention to respect the mystery of his characters' intimate lives, including, for instance, the principle that the novelist should not penetrate into the character's intimate thoughts by reporting them with the help of introductory phrases such as "He thought that . . ." (see also Gide 1952, 65).

Travels in the Congo reflects on the question of fiction-writing and the reading of fiction.[5] First, I will discuss three interrelated elements in *The Counterfeiters:* the Conradian trope of madness-inducing immersion in the "heart of darkness," the question of belief in magic, and the metaphor of "writing as a journey." All of these elements point to the necessity for some of the characters to leave Europe and move to Black Africa. As to *Travels in the Congo*, I will then develop a detailed analysis of the functions of reading in Gide's travel, in particular with regard to the author's systematic exploitation of fictions as a structuring device for his travel experience. My ultimate aim in this investigation is to illuminate the effects of the complex game of generic mirroring, borrowing, and transformation between Gide's travel writing (or journal-keeping in a broader sense) and his fiction.

Aspects of Africa in *The Counterfeiters*

The Counterfeiters, which, in a dedication to fellow writer Roger Martin du Gard, Gide called his first novel, describes colonial adventure in Africa through the destinies of Alexandre Vedel, a tradesman in the French West African colonies, and two lovers, Vincent Molinier and Lady Lilian Griffith, who leave France for the same Casamance region of Senegal where Vedel had made a living. We are told that Alexandre "ran away to Africa" where he found some success after a rough start, making his living in rubber and the ivory trade. Vincent, a young physician interested in sea life and botany, and his lover Lilian, an American, disappear from the European scene around the middle of the novel. Later we hear about their fate indirectly in two letters that some other characters read and discuss. In the first instance, the novel's main writer-character, Edouard, reads part of Lilian's letter from Dakar, sent to her friend Comte de Passavant. In her letter, Lilian describes the boredom and desperation during the couple's voyage to Senegal. She also depicts the tightening "clutches of the demon of adventure" and the growing hatred that the lovers now feel for each other:

> Oui, mon cher, l'amour nous paraissant trop fade, nous avons pris le parti de nous haïr. A vrai dire, ça a commencé bien avant; oui, dès notre embarquement; d'abord, ce n'était que de l'irritation, une sourde animosité qui

---

5. Gide first published his travel journal in these two volumes, but in subsequent editions they have been usually united. *Le retour du Tchad* starts where *Voyage au Congo* ends, on February 20, 1926 in Fort-Lamy in Chad. This was the midpoint in Gide's journey after which his team returned to the Cameroonian coast, first on the Logone River.

n'empêchait pas le corps à corps. Ah! je sais à présent ce que c'est que d'éprouver de la passion pour quelqu'un . . . (Gide 2002a, 314)

Yes, my dear, love seemed too tasteless, so we have gone in for hating each other. In reality it began long before; really, as soon as we got on board; at first it was only irritation, a smouldering animosity, which didn't prevent closer encounters. With the fine weather, it became ferocious. Oh! I know now what it is to feel passion for someone . . . (Gide 1966, 287)

In the second instance, Olivier Molinier reads part of Alexandre's letter from Senegal destined for Alexandre's brother Armand. In his letter, Alexandre mentions an unnamed "singular" companion (Vincent), who thinks he is the devil and has spells of madness and whom Alexandre suspects of having drowned the woman (Lilian) who accompanied him.

Both letters from Senegal convey images of a mythical Africa of violence, madness, and possession fantasies, but also of freedom from conventional morality. In his letter, Alexandre explains that he wants "less and less" to go back to civilization, likening it to a starched collar and a straitjacket.[6] Alexandre's letter does not reveal the names of the couple, but the narrator establishes the connection with Vincent and Lilian. The madman's obsession with cut hands also clearly recalls Lilian's earlier story about the shipwreck of *The Bourgogne* in the first part of the novel. In this story two sailors in a lifeboat, one of them a black man, hacked off peoples' fingers and hands to prevent them from getting into the boat and overloading it. Lilian's interest in this story had revealed to her listeners an inclination to see life in terms of a constant struggle to survive. In the letter, when the same image of severed hands comes up, the hands stand metonymically for Lilian's drowning and possible murder.[7]

The uncontrollable "demonic" forces that mark Vincent and Lilian's journey to the Casamance are closely related to the questions of magic and possession that emerge elsewhere in *The Counterfeiters*. While it is not possible to delve here into the complex theme of the devil, which informs various aspects of Gide's novel, we must note how the demonic features are

---

6. Alexandre's ironic reference to the "badge of civilization" re-evokes the critique of the writer-character Edouard, laid out elsewhere in the novel, of rules and conventions that atrophy human potential. Edouard observes in his journal: "I lean with a fearful attraction over the depths of each creature's possibilities and weep for all that lies atrophied under the heavy lid of custom and morality" (Gide 1966, 105).

7. The violent vision may further remind of the imperial practices in King Leopold's Congo, where the failure to meet rubber collection quotas was sometimes punished by having one's hands cut off.

frequently associated both with Africa and with the impulse to travel. It is significant, first of all, how the metaphor of the demon is intimately associated with the most significant departures in the novel, as a metaphor for the impulse to seek independence, adventure, and sexual gratification.[8] In the beginning of *The Counterfeiters* the narrator explains that some "demonic" force pushes Bernard Profitendieu to leave his home and renounce his foster father. The discovery of letters from his mother's lover and, later, the reading of Edouard's journal, open for Bernard an adventure into a world of surprising unknowns. Similarly, a "demon" supposedly hints to Vincent that he needs to go gambling, and, as the narrator reveals, the "devil" watches over him in amusement as he goes back to Lilian instead of to Laura, who is pregnant with his child.

Secondly, the demonic forces in *The Counterfeiters* are also associated with a childlike belief in magic. The question of magic surfaces specifically in relation to two schoolboys, Boris and his friend Baptistin Kraft, who share a "primitive" belief in talismans and magic spells. The boys' notion of magic is based on some vague ideas of something they had read, concerning the idea of an unlimited power that "enables one in some mysterious way to gain possession of what one wishes for" (Gide 1966, 184). Magic thinking in this sense holds the supernatural to be present in all reality. Boris's nurse, Mme Sophroniska, explains the boys' magic practice as a failed effort to cope with "nervous illness" and as a form of mental laziness. Edouard, however, objects strongly to Mme Sophroniska's rationalism: "Sophroniska takes to bits the innermost wheels of his mental organism and spreads them out in the broad daylight, like a watchmaker cleaning the works of a clock" (Gide 1966, 183). Edouard clearly distances himself from Mme Sophroniska at this point in the novel, interested as he is in investigating the relationship between magic practices and literary imagination, even if he does not seem to believe in magic in the same sense as Boris and Baptistin. The controversy between Edouard and Mme Sophroniska is noteworthy in that Edouard often voices the author's views.

In this regard, it is significant how Edouard suggests that he himself might follow a kind of belief in magic. Having just explained that the rivalry between

---

8. The novel ends with Edouard's notes about La Pérouse's agonizing discourse over what he sees as the similarity between God and the devil, and the cruelty of God in sacrificing his son (here, Christ also symbolizes La Pérouse's grandson Boris who has committed suicide). The various meanings of the demon metaphor in *The Counterfeiters* have been well demonstrated in Gide scholarship, for instance, in relation to Gide's personal theology, the theme of sexual desire, and the significance that the writer gives to chance and circumstance in artistic creativity. See, for instance, Brosman 1986. Gide makes the association between sexuality and the demon explicit in his published *Journal* (1951, 540–41).

the real world and the representation is the deep-lying subject of his novel yet to be written (Gide 1966, 183), Edouard admits that his constant talk of an unfinished novel may appear as a kind of mysticism to people around him. The problem that Edouard thus seems to be posing is whether novel-writing in his case—since he does not adhere to a realism that pretends to start with pure facts—constitutes a kind of magical belief system in its own right, perhaps no better or no worse than the use of a talisman and a belief in the power of incantation. In Edouard's "magic" practice, the writer tries to impose his interpretation on the outside world, even when he knows that the "resistance of facts" is likely to invite him to imagine ideal constructions of reality.

The question of realism and magic is yet another instance in the novel where Gide's personal concerns seem to be voiced through Edouard. In his *Travels in the Congo* Gide makes explicit the relation between primitive mentality and Africa and displays a similar ambivalence towards mysticism, or belief in magic, as does Edouard in the novel. In the course of the journey, however, the nature of the demonic force that pulls Gide forward seems to change, at least with regard to what he reveals to his readers. Instead of the demonic forces within his mind, or the intense sensual and sexual pleasures that Gide associates with this continent (since the early 1890s), the demonic is gradually associated with the horrors of the colonial situation behind the façade of the French colonial government.

In *The Counterfeiters,* Edouard's idea of poetic existence is based on the premise that constant change is a prerequisite for an intensive life, while this idea also suggests that imagination and reality are always intertwined. In a conversation with Bernard, Edouard explains to his companion's deaf ears that he has often thought

> qu'en art, et en littérature en particulier, ceux-là seuls comptent qui se lancent vers l'inconnu. On ne découvre pas de terre nouvelle sans consentir à perdre de vue, d'abord et longtemps, tout rivage. Mais nos écrivains craignent le large; ce ne sont que des côtoyeurs. (Gide 2002a, 338)

> that in art, and particularly in literature, the only people who count are those who launch out on to unknown seas, one doesn't discover new lands without consenting to lose sight of the shore for a very long time. But our writers are afraid of the open; they are mere coasters. (Gide 1966, 309)

The metaphorical journey and the actual journey are thus closely associated in Edouard's thinking, similar to certain passages in Gide's travel journal. It is telling that Edouard's curiosity about a boy called Georges Molinier, whom he discovers stealing a book from a secondhand bookshop, increases as he realizes that the book in question is a guide book of Algeria, revealing the boy's possible propensity for vagabondage. In *Journal des Faux-Monnayeurs* (2008, 39–42), in an entry on May 3, 1921, Gide writes about a similar incidence on meeting a teenager from the Lycée Henri-IV. As a crucial context for understanding the meaning of this encounter for Gide, and the excitement that he associates with vagabondage in Algeria, we need to recall Gide's literary autobiography *Si le grain ne meurt* (*If It Die: An Autobiography*), which was published in commercial form in 1924, where Gide described his discovery of homosexuality in Algeria in the early 1890s.[9]

From these references to Africa and travel in *The Counterfeiters*, there emerges an image of Africa that has a mythical, even immoral quality as a den of iniquity, a place of regression, perhaps self-destruction, and madness, and a state of determined exile. Yet the inevitable mystery and force of Africa also invites further travel and adventure and suggests the discovery of new pleasures without the moral and family issues of home. To describe the boredom of a sea passage in her letter from Africa, Lilian quotes Baudelaire's lines "... grand miroir / De mon désespoir," thus superimposing the landscape of travel on the landscape of the mind. Baudelaire's poem "La Musique" is one of the poet's many descriptions of what he called the abyss:

> Je sens vibrer en moi toutes les passions
>   D'un vaisseau qui souffre;
>   Le bon vent, la tempête et ses convulsions
>
>   Sur l'immense gouffre
> Me bercent. D'autre fois, calme plat, grand miroir
>   De mon désespoir!
>   (Baudelaire 1991)

> I feel vibrating within me all the passions
>   Of ships in distress;
>   The good wind and the tempest with its convulsions

---

9. See also Aldrich (2003, 331–44), who discusses Gide's romantic attachments to "the irresistible youths of the classical Mediterranean or exotic North Africa." However, Aldrich points out that in his African travel journal, Gide, while occasionally commenting on the attractive physical attributes of blacks, only rarely describes his erotic feelings or the cultural empathy that were "constants of his contacts with North Africa" (2003, 343). For the ways in which Gide's sexuality is affected by his African travels, see also Michaud 1961 and Chadourne 1968.

Over the vast gulf
Cradle me. At other times, dead calm, great mirror
Of my despair!
(Baudelaire 1954)

Lilian's and Vincent's voyage to Senegal is characterized by inevitability: her drowning in the abyss of Africa, both in the metaphorical and the literal sense, is already predicted in the story of the shipwreck of *The Bourgogne* earlier in the novel. Furthermore, Vincent's fate conforms to the narrator's definition of exoticism, which the narrator gives in a detailed description of Vincent:

> On appelle « exotisme », je crois, tout repli diapré de la Maya, devant quoi notre âme se sent étrangère; qui la prive de points d'appui. Parfois telle vertu résisterait, que le diable avant d'attaquer, dépayse. (Gide 2002a, 143)

> The name "*exoticism*" is, I believe, given to those of Maia's iridescent folds which make the soul feel itself a stranger, which deprive it of points of contact. There are some whose virtue would resist, but that the devil, before attacking it, transplants them. (Gide 1966, 130)

Vincent easily feels that he is in a foreign land, even at home, suffering from a sense of estrangement that culminates with his arrival in Senegal.

Finally, to account fully for the African presence in Gide's major novel, we have to consider the author's (or the author figure's) metaphor of writing as a form of travel, which surfaces explicitly in the last chapter of the second part of the novel, entitled "The Author Reviews His Characters," where the author speaks in his own name. This is a turning point in the novel in many ways, since Gide not only adds another narrative level to his text, but also evaluates the main personalities in his novel and reflects on the direction of his tale. The author begins this midpoint evaluation with the travel metaphor:

> Le voyageur, parvenu au haut de la colline, s'assied et regarde avant de reprendre sa marche, à présent déclinante: il cherche à distinguer où le conduit enfin ce chemin sinueux qu'il a pris, qui lui semble se perdre dans l'ombre et, car le soir tombe, dans la nuit. Ainsi l'auteur imprévoyant s'arrête un instant, reprend souffle, et se demande avec inquiétude où va le mener son récit. (Gide 2002a, 215)

> The traveller, having reached the top of the hill, sits down and looks about him before continuing his journey, which henceforward lies all downhill.

He seeks to distinguish in the darkness—for night is falling—where the winding path he has chosen is leading him. So the undiscerning author stops awhile to regain his breath, and wonders with some anxiety where his tale will take him. (Gide 1966, 195)

The perspective from above enables the author, and possibly also the reader, to see the story as a whole at this point in the narrative: to examine the ramifications of the story and to develop ideas about the main characters' possible future itineraries. At the same time, the metaphor of narrative as travel suggests the idea that the story may not be wholly within the writer's control, but that the events confronted in the course of writing, as in travel, might freely impose themselves on the writing mind. While the author thus makes himself much more visible than in his earlier short interventions, he also pretends to distance himself from his work as if his writing was something happening by itself, by surprise or the like fate, which dictates itself to him, or like some open-ended journey on which he has embarked. Novel-writing, thus, is like a journey, and we are advised to think the same about novel-reading as well.

Novel-Reading in Fiction and the Travel Journal

Reading is a central activity in *The Counterfeiters*, in which almost everyone is an avid reader, if not also a writer. Reading literature, letters, and journals determines much of the characters' experience and punctuates the whole narrative of the novel. Reactions to books, journals, and letters and shared readings have an important function in characterization, as they reveal the character's inner thoughts, emotions, and interests, and create relations and contrasts between different personalities. Reading can also play a significant role in terms of perspectival change. Reading someone else's journal or letter without permission, or by accident, which happens quite often in this novel, always reflects both the reader's and the writer's state of mind, their motivation to read, and the nature of their emotional involvement with each other and with what they read. Such changes in perspective further mirror the novel's larger structure in which excerpts from the writer-character Edouard's journal are continuously interspersed in the narration, thus imposing on the text a structure of crisscross reading between the predominant third-person narration and a first-person journal.

The various moments of reading described in *The Counterfeiters*, from the readings of letters, journals, and talismans to Edouard rereading his journal notes, facilitate the shifts between third-person narration and first-person writing. Scenes of reading, for instance, allow for the narrator-author to intervene ironically in the characters' situations, as happens in the passages about the reading of the two letters from Senegal. The readers of these letters, Edouard and Olivier, are surprisingly uninterested in what they read, much less interested than the letters' recipients (Passavant and Armand), nor do they understand the text's full implications. Edouard explains that he does not want to bother his head with Lady Lilian's "outrageous feelings," as he calls them, and thus does not really pay attention to what he reads. The nonchalant reaction mortifies Passavant, who considers Edouard's lack of curiosity about his friends' destiny a personal affront. The narrator then explains, in indirect discourse, Passavant's complex feelings about the letter, feelings that motivated him to show it to Edouard in the first place: Passavant's original delight in receiving the letter, the memory of his affection for Lilian and Vincent, the self-satisfaction at being able to be kind to them, then the malicious pleasure in hearing about their failed attempt to find "perfect bliss" in Africa. The scene thus emphasizes the distance between the two writer-characters, Edouard and Passavant, as Passavant fails to have the desired effect on his competitor.

Olivier, in turn, who reads a passage from Vincent's letter to Armand Vedel, does not have anything to say about the letter. He does not even understand that the mad murderer mentioned in the text might be his brother Vincent. The narrator's intervention, which ends the scene and the chapter in question, further emphasizes Olivier's indifference towards his brother: "To tell the truth, Olivier did not trouble much about him" (Gide 1966, 330). This is important information about Olivier, but even more is said about Armand, who controls Olivier's reading by pointing out that only one sheet of the long letter contains interesting information. The exotic passage about a mad white man, a hideous negro, a murder by the river, and a flourishing ivory business accentuates Armand's own wish to follow Alexandre to Africa, a plan that he might realize were he not already expected to do military service. Another important aspect of the description of this scene is Armand's notion of his brother's self-confident character, calling him "a kind of donkey, something in my style" (Gide 1966, 329). These qualities Armand seems to detect in his brother's writing as well.

Furthermore, besides serving important functions in constructing and presenting the characters' minds, or indicating changes in focus and narrative level, the consequences of these reading scenes are part and parcel of the novel's evolving plot, in which reading incites various departures and motivates key choices. Gerald Prince has in fact argued, in view of the impressive number of readers and scenes of reading in this novel, that reading provides the novelist a way to control and measure narrative voices and to set in motion the story's evolution, adding to the complexity of narration in indirect exposition (Prince 1973, 20). Prince argues further that *The Counterfeiters* is structured around a series of readings: the evolution of the story and its resolution are in some sense direct consequences of reading and the read (1973, 20). The tragic quality in some of these reading scenes further adds to their importance as structuring devices in the novel. *The Counterfeiters* starts with Bernard finding and reading letters from his mother's lover. The discovery that his biological father is someone other than the man he has known as his father spurs Bernard to leave home; reading also inspires him to become Edouard's secretary; a letter makes Olivier feel closer to Comte de Passavant; and the reading of the five mysterious words of a talisman provokes the death of young Boris (or this at least is what some of the boys believe). The importance of reading is also highlighted in that the characters who spend the most time with literature, especially Edouard and Bernard, seem to be the least likely to fall victims to the evil present everywhere in their world—even if in some ways Edouard, being possessed by his novel-writing project, is driven by "demonic" forces. As Prince further perceives, the characters who read the least, or the ones who never read, like Lady Griffith or Vincent, are most likely to become victims of forces that they cannot control (see Prince 1973, 22). Perhaps if Lady Griffith and Vincent had been readers, they could have avoided their tragic fate.

But what do we find if we turn our focus from *The Counterfeiters* to *Travels in the Congo* and consider the many scenes of reading embedded in the travel journal? First of all, it is important to note that in his travel journal Gide never comments on his writing or on the act of keeping the journal. The reader is not invited, as happens in *The Counterfeiters,* to assist in the different phases and hazards of writing or to scrutinize the construction of the text or indeed of a fictional world, from a series of different perspectives, voices, and narrative levels. Second, the travel journal highlights the act of reading as immersion, accentuated by the movement and disorientation in travel and the changing scenery. The various pleasures and displeasures of travel are framed, complemented, and to some extent controlled by the pleasures of reading, as the traveller constantly dives into the classics of Western literature, and novels in particular, during the journey. Gide's motivation for the travel, as he describes in his first notes in the travelogue, was precisely "voyager pour le plaisir" (2002b, 13), and the sense of pleasure is constantly associated not just with the environment, but also with the experience of reading during the course of the journey.

Reading accompanies Gide's penetration into the "heart" of Africa as a joyful state of being embedded in a book.[10] Commentary on readings in *Travels in the Congo* is at least as frequent as in Gide's *Journal*, inviting the reader to share the intimate effects and pleasures of books. Gide discusses his readings so frequently in the travel journal that this made Michel Leiris feel the need to reproach him for it. However, as Leiris advanced further in his own African trek, he explains that he came to understand perfectly why Gide wrote about reading so much, having had similar discussions about literature and aesthetics with his travel companions.[11] Gide's reading and immersion in the books enhances, for instance, the experience of entering another world, but it has a number of other important functions as well. Gide usually reads before and after each leg of his journey, in the morning and the evening, during the breaks. The books that he had with him filled many boxes, including classics of French and English literature, such as the fables of La Fontaine, Milton's epic poem *Paradise Lost* and his tragedy *Samson Agonistes*, Shakespeare's *Romeo and Juliet*, plays by Molière (*Le Misanthrope*), Corneille (*Cinna, Horace*), and Racine (*Iphigénie*), poems by Robert Browning, and Chekhov's travel story "The Steppe." Among the longer fictions were, most notably, Conrad's *Heart of Darkness*, Goethe's *Elective Affinities* and *Faust*, the latter two included in a leather-bound Goethe collection in the original German, and Robert Louis Stevenson's *The Master of Ballantrae*. Gide also had with him a number of nonfiction and philosophical texts, for instance, some of Jacques-Bénigne Bossuet's writings (*Traité de la concupiscence; Discours sur la vie cachée en Dieu*), Cuthbert Christy's travel book *Big Game and Pigmies* (1924), André Cresson's *Position actuelle des problèmes philosophiques* (1924), autobiographical fiction (*The Autobiography of Mark Rutherford*), some liter-

---

10. Gide uses the metaphor of the heart (*cœur*) of Africa at the end of September 1925 in a way that reveals the intimate tie between this metaphor and the expectation of the exotic. Entering an unnamed village in the forest, he writes that "a village so strange and so beautiful that we felt we had found in it the very reason of our journey and its very core" (1957, 42) ("village si beau, si étrange qu'il nous semblait trouver ici la raison de notre voyage, entrer au cœur de son sujet"; Gide 2002, 65); again the next day, feeling somewhat disappointed about the exotic, he writes: "The shrubs and plants are not, it must be admitted, the least exotic in appearance, and if it were not for a strange little island of pandanus with its aerial roots, nothing would remind one that this is almost the heart of Africa" (Gide 1957, 43) ("arbustes et plantes d'aspect, à vrai dire, fort peu exotique et, sans un étrange îlot de pandanus aux racines aériennes, un peu en amont de la chute, rien ne rappellerait ici qu'on est presque au cœur de l'Afrique"; Gide 2002, 66).

11. "Autrefois je reprochais à Gide de parler fréquemment, dans le récit de son voyage en Afrique, de ses lectures, par exemple Milton ou Bossuet. Je m'aperçois maintenant que c'est très naturel. Le voyage nous change que par moments. La plupart du temps vous restez tristement pareil à ce que vous aviez toujours été. Je me rends compte en constatant que très souvent Schaeffner et moi avons des conversations sur des sujets littéraires ou esthétiques" (1981, 225).

ary periodicals and Parisian journals, and a *Concise Oxford Dictionary*. Gide also cites Baudelaire and Flaubert, but this he probably does by heart; he does not mention having the actual books with him.

Commentary on literature also marks the beginning of the travel journal, where Gide praises La Fontaine, calling his fables a miracle of culture, and wonders if they are indeed the best literature ever written. La Fontaine's stories demonstrate for Gide, as he explains in the first entry in his travel journal, a model of sensitivity in observation and reading. Furthermore, the ease and delicacy of La Fontaine's expression guarantee for Gide a richness of ideas and density of observation: "There is nothing one cannot find in him, provided one knows how to look; but the eye that looks must be a skilful one, his touch is often so light and so delicate. He is a miracle of culture—Montaigne's wisdom; Mozart's sensibility" (Gide 1957, 4) ("Celui qui sait bien voir peut y trouver trace de tout; mais il faut un oeil averti, tant la touché, souvent, est légère. C'est un miracle de culture. Sage comme Montaigne; sensible comme Mozart"; Gide 2002b, 14). These remarks establish the expectation of a world that is rich in details and suggest a kind of sensitivity that the writer-traveller attempts to emulate in his observations.[12]

To understand better the many meanings of Gide's readings during his journey, we can turn to David Scott, who has cogently identified the basic functions of these readings in organizing Gide's travel experience and in what Gide chose to report of this experience. Scott sees that Gide's travel journal is profoundly marked by a "search for *découpages* that will cut the amorphous mass of jungle experience into comprehensible units" (Scott 2004, 164). The various reading scenes respond to this search as types of framing devices that help the writer come to terms with the foreign and sometimes frustrating reality around him. This framing and cutting-out process, Scott argues, involves both the level of the sign, such as "clichés, *instantanés* and other images," and the "interpretant," meaning the mental process of interpreting the signs of African reality. The latter include "mental images, memories, associated ideas, taxonomies, whether personal, scientific or cultural," together with other materials derived from the readings (Scott 2004, 164). Literature thus served Gide both as an underlying explanatory frame of experience, as a structuring device that helped him to sharpen a given image or experience vis-à-vis the context, as an interlude between scene changes, and, as Scott puts it, as "a curtain to blot out the unfathomable monotony or impenetrability of the jungle scene" (Scott 2004, 168).

---

12. See also Warehime 1995, 459–60, who points out that La Fontaine is "the most obvious 'internal' model" for Gide as observer.

Gide immerses himself in the fictional world of *The Master of Ballantrae* when he cannot do anything else, for instance, when he is forced to stay put due to the brutally hot afternoon temperatures, or because his leg is aching too much to move. The author explains that he reads Stevenson with much pleasure ("avec délices") to round off a perfect day. Citations from this or other novels can sum up for the traveller his complex feelings of hope, regret, and courage or mark the episodes of the journey. Having reached the turning point of his travels somewhere in Chad, and realizing that he has already turned back towards home, Gide quotes the character Hoffnung in Goethe's *Faust*: "Sicherlich, es muss das Beste Irgendwo zu finden sein" (Gide 2002b, 264) ("It is certain that the best is somewhere to be found"). Feeling more courageous than ever, Gide explains, he thus lets his reading mark the return from his journey and lead the way towards future discoveries.

In addition to the general functions of reading as a semiotic framework for experience or as a kind of cognitive blackout, as defined by Scott, we may be able to tease out more precise functions of fiction- and novel-reading in Gide's travel journal. In relying on narrative fiction as a major point of reference, especially with regard to *Heart of Darkness*, but also to some extent in relation to Goethe's *Die Wahlverwandtschaften* (*Elective Affinities*, 1809) and Stevenson's adventure novel, Gide not only organizes the travel experience, but also poses the question of the reality of fiction, prompting us to ask what constitutes and produces the pleasure in reading fiction during travel. We can phrase this latent question as a problem of immediacy, which is familiar to us from *The Counterfeiters:* How can fiction achieve immediacy, realism, and accuracy and do so perhaps better than a nonfiction description of the world in a journal? Or how can the sense of immediacy in journal form contribute to and contrast with third-person perspectives? Gide's reading and interpretation of Conrad's and Goethe's fiction during his travel suggests some answers to these questions.

On Conrad

In his travel journal, which is dedicated to the memory of Joseph Conrad,[13] Gide uses Conrad's fiction not only as a major point of reference to frame and explain his perceptions during the travel, but also to affirm the reality and truth-value of Conrad's novella with regard to the circumstances of his travel

---

13. Gide had also contributed an account of his friendship with the writer, who had died in 1924, to a special issue of *La Nouvelle Revue Française* (December 1924) entitled "Hommage à Conrad."

and the African ways of life that he witnesses. More than any other work, *Heart of Darkness* provides Gide with a kind of global frame of reference that extends from the journal's beginning to its end.

Gide makes the first reference to Conrad in a long footnote, appended to one of the first entries in the travel journal. The comment stands out from the other references as a significant metacommentary on the reality of Conrad's fiction, explaining the need to cite from *Heart of Darkness* and to resort to this novella as an authority on the Congo. In this note Gide first explains that the town of Pointe-Noire was the starting point for the Brazzaville-Océan railroad. This leads him to mention Conrad's travels in the same region ten years prior to the construction of the railroad and to underscore the importance of Conrad's "admirable" book that remains still

> profondément vrai, j'ai pu m'en convaincre, et que j'aurai souvent à citer. Aucune outrance dans ses peintures: elles sont cruellement exactes; mais ce qui les désassombrit, c'est la réussite de ce projet qui, dans son livre, paraît si vain. (Gide 2002b, 23n2)

> profoundly true and I shall often have occasion to quote it. There is no exaggeration in his picture; it is cruelly exact; but what lightens its gloom is the success of the project which in his pages appears so vain. (Gide 1957, 11n2)

The statement suggests not only that *Heart of Darkness* is "profoundly real," but that the novella acts as a kind of guarantee for the reality of the travel experience, just as the travel experience affirms the reality of the novella (even if, in Gide's opinion, the railroad project turned out to be more successful than Conrad might have expected). This tendency to read Conrad's novella as fact, or at least as nonfiction, is evident again in an entry for March 25, 1926, when Gide, after reading Conrad's novella for the fourth time, realizes that it is only after having seen the country about which Conrad writes that he is able to understand the excellence of the description (Gide 2002b, 399).

What is consistent in the references to Conrad's fiction, mainly *Heart of Darkness* and, to a lesser degree, *Typhoon*, which Gide himself had translated into French, is Gide's persistent view of these novels as accurate representations of reality and, perhaps even more, as more accurate descriptions of reality than the best nonfiction. In addition to the instances that I have already mentioned, Gide praises the description of a storm in *Typhoon*, which he thinks gives the reader free rein to imagine the real horror of the event. Gide also explains a mistake in the French translation of *Heart of Darkness* (*Au coeur des ténèbres*) in which the measure of half a kilo (*livre*) in a carrier's luggage is confused with a kilo (he points out in a footnote that the load should weigh thirty rather than fifteen kilos). Furthermore, the function of *Heart of Darkness* as an authority against which observations of the Congo can be tested and corrected, and the realities checked, becomes evident when Gide refers to Conrad's "admirable" way of talking about the "extraordinary efforts of imagination" that have been required of Europeans wanting to see black Africans as their enemies (2002b, 245n1). In this footnote, Gide undermines this hostile perception, drawing from Conrad's disclosure of such contradictions in his critique of colonialist rhetoric by means of fiction.

The passage from *Heart of Darkness* that Gide quotes at this point in the travel journal may, however, be much more radical in its implications than Gide is ready to admit. The passage includes Marlow's description of six chained black men who walk in file, passing him within a mere six inches: "but these men could by no stretch of imagination be called enemies. They were called criminals, and the outraged law, like the bursting shells, had come to them, an insoluble mystery from the sea" (Conrad 1994, 22). What follows, then, is Marlow's depiction of the reaction of a "reclaimed" black man, who accompanies these prisoners and hoists his weapon to his shoulder whenever he sees a white European. From the gesture Marlow infers that "this was simple prudence, white men being so much alike at a distance that he could not tell who I might be" (Conrad 1994, 23). Marlow's observation indicates a complex understanding of the racial situation in which the African, not only wrongly perceived as an enemy, may also see white men as a group without clear differentiation between individuals, just as the colonials, and indeed Marlow and Gide himself, may have seen the Africans as one mass of people. This is diametrically opposed to Gide's lament about the terrible "non-différenciation" of the Africans, meaning his impression of the lack of individuality among the Africans, to which I will return later, and which Gide made about a month before the above citation.[14] Gide, while he undermines one preconceived notion of the Africans, thus affirms another.

In these references to Conrad's fiction, real geography confirms the referentiality of fictional literature and literary value (or vice versa). In one of the most comprehensive discussions of the relation between Conrad's fiction and Gide's travel journal, Russell West offers an insightful, but somewhat one-sided interpretation of Gide's use of *Heart of Darkness* in his travel journal. West shows how *Heart of Darkness* fundamentally structures the travel journal and that, as we have already seen, Gide seems to read the novel to a large

---

14. See Gide 2002, 195, 220, and developed in 220n1.

extent as a documentary (1996, 149). What is problematic in West's argument, however, is that he assumes that Gide gives the novella a secondary status as nonfiction. In other words, it is not clear why Gide's emphasis on Conrad's novella as a true description, and a form of (potential) nonfiction, would be a sign of the book's secondary role, particularly if *Heart of Darkness* so thoroughly informs the travel journal's structure. Gide's emphasis on the reality and actuality of Conrad's fiction may in fact speak to the contrary.

More precisely, West claims that Gide *reduces* the status of *Heart of Darkness* to that of a documentary, thus relegating the novel "to a secondary position, subordinated to the relentlessly 'realist' nature of Gide's travel document" (West 1996, 142). The argument might be supported, for instance, by a psychologizing "anxiety of influence" thesis, claiming that perhaps Gide constantly reevoked Conrad's novella so that he could better negate its influence (similar to what takes place in Graham Greene's *In Search of a Character*, where Greene laments Conrad's influence on his novels). In giving Conrad such an authoritative position, Gide may have wished to show that he could outdo Conrad on his own territory. Or we might want to suggest, as West does, that Gide remained oblivious to the way in which *Heart of Darkness* informed his vision of Africa, and that Conrad's powerful presence in the travel journal was somehow a blind spot to the writer. While such speculation is interesting, it seems more likely, keeping in mind that the travel journal is dedicated to Conrad's memory, that the references to the novella are not unmindful or that they are simple corroborations of Gide's firsthand observations based on Conrad's fiction, as West would have it. We may, moreover, ask whether the idea of the novella's (nearly) documentary status was really a negative evaluation for Gide during this time when he wished to report honestly on colonial Africa's realities, or whether the reality that Gide discovered in the novella was another argument in favour of Conrad's writing (as fiction that surpasses its limits as fiction and by so doing rivals the truth-value of documentary nonfiction).

Be that as it may, Gide's reliance on Conrad as an authority on the Congo relocates *Heart of Darkness* closer to the domain of travel writing. Gide reassesses the value of Conrad's novella in his travel journal, that is, he turns it into a kind of documentary, while his own travel writing testifies to the novella's ability to create an accurate image of reality. The status that Gide gives to the novella suggests that fiction has the capacity to capture a sense and experience of reality in the full sense of the term, not just create a reality of its own. Simultaneously, travel writing is relocated closer to the domain of fiction. Reading Gide's African travelogue together with *The Counterfeiters*, we may see how the travel journal takes on various Conradian themes and imagery prevalent in the novel. *Travels in the Congo* starts where *The Counterfeiters* closes, that is, with Vincent's letter from Africa, the contents of which West appropriately calls a "treasure-trove of Conradian tropes" (1996, 136). The beginning of the travel journal evokes the same madness-inducing forces of Africa, the metaphor of the demon that pulls Gide towards the scorching sun, the immense forest, or the abyss, thus illustrating the traveller's wish to escape from civilization and Western rationalism, renew his perceptions, and perhaps discover unforeseen pleasures.

Gide's description of the immersive and mimetic qualities of fiction in his travel journal creates an interesting contrast with the author's poetics of the so-called pure novel, which he develops in his journals and in the fragments of Edouard's journal that are incorporated in the novel.[15] In *The Counterfeiters*, Edouard even provocatively states that if journals of the composition of *Sentimental Education* or *The Brothers Karamazov* existed, they would be much more exciting and interesting than the novels themselves (2002a, 186).[16] As I mentioned above, Edouard is often a mouthpiece for the writer, and the character's theory of fiction and his uncertainties about his novel-writing project may reflect Gide's difficulties in composing the kind of novel that Gide had in mind. The close relationship between author and character is also confirmed by the fact that Edouard is engaged in writing a novel that has the same title as the novel in which he is a character, and he keeps a journal that, as Gide himself claims, emulates what Gide's *Journal des Faux-Monnayeurs* had become (see Gide 2008, 36–37). Yet, at the same time, Edouard's poetics of the pure novel cannot be wholly equated with Gide's stance on this question. Gide explains in *Journal des Faux-Monnayeurs* that he had given much of himself to the character, while also wanting to portray Edouard as an amateur writer. Gide also saw that Edouard, partly owing to his "judicious" views, fails to write the ideal, "pure" novel that Edouard has in mind (Gide 2008, 61, 67). For these reasons, as there is a sliding scale from consonance to dissonance between author (and narrator) and character, we cannot make an easy distinction between their views on the novel genre. Further, this enables us to speculate that Edouard's take on the issue is both more judicious and more extreme than that of his creator.

---

15. See, for instance, Gide 2008, 64–65.

16. On Gide's adherence to Oscar Wilde's paradoxical principle that nature should imitate art, see Gide 2008, 33.

On Goethe

In late November and early December 1925 in the course of his journey Gide rereads Goethe's *Elective Affinities*. He starts reading the novel one night after having finished Stevenson's *The Master of Ballantrae*, sitting by a small table outdoors, surrounded by the sounds of drumming and dancing from a nearby village. The insufficient light of his lantern accentuates the sense of the immensity of the night: "I feel surrounded on all sides by the strange immensity of the night" (Gide 1957, 111) ("Je sens m'environner de toutes parts l'étrange immensité de la nuit"; Gide 2002b, 163). Once again, the text that he is reading appears to envelop the environment, while the environment frames the reading, and thus the experience of reading is metaphorically associated with the qualities of the surrounding landscape and life.

Elective Affinities is one of the books about which Gide writes most enthusiastically in his travel journal, and one that he also frequently uses to emphasize or, alternatively, to blot out certain travel experiences (such as numbness, monotony, and exhaustion). In later references to Goethe's novel, Gide mentions that he had finished his day by "diving" and "diving again" into the novel, sometimes reading it in "rapture" (*ravissement*). These evening readings were regularly followed by a bath or accompanied by reading lessons that Gide gave to an Arab boy called Adoum, one of his and Marc Allégret's assistants. Gide also associates the joyful reading of this novel with the purity and gentleness of the air, and explains how the reading of Goethe's novel helps him to forget the monotony of the road after completing the day's journey. Gide quotes from this novel too, using a famous proverb by the character Ottilie: "Durch nichts bezeichnen die Menschen mehr ihren Charakter als durch das, was sie lächerlich finden" (Nothing so characterizes a man as what he finds ridiculous[17])—to comment ironically on a recent article by a critic who had called Gide's fiction "abstruse" (*abscons*) (Gide 2002b, 200). Gide congratulates himself that he is able to read the novel easily in the original German, without the help of a dictionary.

There are some important structural similarities between Goethe's and Gide's novels, including the important role given to scenes of reading. On more than one occasion Goethe's *Elective Affinities* focuses on the act of reading, and such scenes serve characterization and plot development in important ways. Reading in *Elective Affinities*, as in *The Counterfeiters*, is always significant in terms of understanding the characters' minds, revealing the nature of their thoughts and their underlying emotional relations and atti-

---

17. Goethe 1994, 140.

tudes, such as distance from or closeness to each other. Acts of reading also move the story forward. To mention only two such instances, Baron Eduard's lack of "affinity" with his wife Charlotte is revealed through an act of reading early in the novel. Here the narrator explains that Eduard cannot stand it if someone even looks at the book he is reading.[18] And when Charlotte indeed looks at his book, Eduard feels as if he were torn apart. Eduard's anger, we are told, is due to his emotional attachment to reading as a form of thinking: for him, reading the written text equals thinking and mental privacy. Thus, for Eduard, to interrupt the act of reading by looking at his book from behind his back is not different from trying to intrude upon his privacy violently. Similarly, Ottilie's love for Eduard, and the deep emotional closeness between these two characters, becomes manifest during another reading scene when, upon reading a text that Ottilie has copied for him, Eduard realizes that she has imitated his handwriting. For Eduard, and for the reader, the imitation implies emotional involvement or "affinity," to use Goethe's pseudoscientific concept, suggesting that Ottilie is able not only to understand Eduard's thoughts, but also to share them at some deeper level.

Elective Affinities is mostly narrated in external perspective with frequent narratorial reports about the thoughts and feelings of Eduard and his wife, but it also includes other modes of narration, in particular, shifts from third- to first-person narration, which are relevant here. Such changes occur mainly through quoted letters and journals. Various letters are interspersed with the narration; they include those from Eduard to his wife and to Ottilie, and from Ottilie to her friends. The excerpts from Ottilie's journal in the second part of the novel create a further contrast to the predominant third-person narration. These entries, however, are atypical journal notes in that they reveal relatively little of the journal-keeper's thoughts and feelings. The excerpts are only loosely related to the novel's events and consist mostly of philosophical generalizations or commonplaces, save perhaps the question of life without love, which has a direct personal meaning for their writer. Some of these entries comprise aphorisms about the nature of art or human nature, including meditations on the development of natural science, moral questions, or the passing of time. As the novel gives no account of Ottilie's unspoken thoughts in third-person narration, either through the use of free indirect discourse or by other means, Ottilie's mind seems to shun penetration, remaining a kind of mystery even when the reader seems to have access to her at the moment of writing.[19]

---

18. "Eine seiner besonderen Eigenheiten, die er jedoch vielleicht mit mehreren Menschen teilt, war die, daß es ihm unerträglich fiel, wenn jemand ihm beim Lesen in das Buch sah" (Goethe 1965, 36–37).

19. See also Leacock 2002.

What is important in Goethe's novel with regard to our question of the fiction/nonfiction divide is that *Elective Affinities* is one of the first modern novels systematically to cite passages from an intimate fictional journal. The shifts of perspective in the second part of *Elective Affinities* between third-person narration, with an omniscient narrator, and the first-person voice of the journal writer create the effect of juxtaposed points of view and suggest a prototype of a kind of fictional blend of genres that Gide later employs and expands in *The Counterfeiters*.

To read *The Counterfeiters* in an intelligent way, it is essential to follow similar changes in the point of view as in *Elective Affinities*, involving shifts between the narrator's third-person and first-person narration (Edouard's journal), as well as the author's direct interventions, and between the reality of the fictional world and what the novelist pretends to make of that reality, integrating information from the different sources.[20] The narrator's relentlessly changing distance from the world of his characters—between the "objective" third-person narration and direct intervention, including occasional "subjective" evaluation of his characters or expressions of uncertainty about their thoughts and motives[21]—is a seminal element of Gide's novel. However, at the same time, the reader never has much direct access to the characters' minds. While the narrator's report on the characters' thoughts are frequent in this novel, free indirect discourse, in which the narrator can appropriate parts of a character's speech or thoughts, remains fairly rare. In the chapters in third-person narration, and often also in the excerpts from Edouard's journal, dialogue and thought reports dominate, thus leaving the boundaries between who speaks (or thinks) and who narrates relatively intact. The characters' thoughts and their whole intimate world remain in some sense a mystery, unless some bits and pieces are revealed in letters or, in Edouard's case, in his journal. The reading scenes make an exception in this respect, as they allow the narrator to report more closely on the characters' minds.[22]

---

20. Another structural resemblance between Gide's and Goethe's novels is the double "elective affinity" between a married couple, Eduard (or Edward in the English translation) and Charlotte, and their two good friends, the Captain and Ottilie, in Goethe's novel, and the intricate relations between the two boys, Bernard and Olivier, and the two writer figures, Edouard and Robert de Passavant.

21. Henri Godard has pointed out how Gide multiplies his "confessions" of uncertainty in his interpretation of the characters during the novel and thus pretends to place the novel-writer on the same level as the actual readers. The frequent use of the first-person plural pronoun may also associate the narrator with the reader (Godard 2006, 109–10).

22. With regard to his use of dialogue, Gide often deletes the reporting verb of "saying" and conjunction. This gives the appearance of the immediacy of the event, but also prompts

By contrast, in the travel journal, there is hardly any verbatim speech, with the exception of some short direct citations. For the most part, the perspective remains internal and fixed; even the subtle shifts between the more objective and the more subjective descriptions, between the descriptions of the outside world and the descriptions of the traveller's experience and state of mind follow the conventions of travel writing.[23] Yet the method of multiplied and contrasted viewpoints is relevant with regard to the way in which Gide writes about his reading experiences and the effects of reading during the journey. Consider an example from Gide's entry on March 9, 1926 in Logone-Gana, where he moves from describing the rediscovery of a dead body in the river to his reading of Browning and Milton during the same day:

> Je n'aurai pas dressé le bilan exact de ce jour si j'omets Browning et Milton. Relu avec ravissement, transport, quelques sonnets, le début de *Samson* et de longs passages du *Paradise lost*; avec moins d'enthousiasme *In a Balcony* de Browning, qui m'avait laissé meilleur souvenir. Il y a souvent avantage à ne point parfaitement comprendre. Mon imagination prêtait au mirage et diaprait généreusement mes incertitudes. À présent que j'y vois plus net, je suis un peu déçu.
>
> Étendu sous ma moustiquaire, j'ai lu avec une sorte de frénésie (qui a fini par me donner un fort mal de tête). Je ne me souviens pas avoir jamais porté sur un texte un regard plus perspicace, plus avide et plus frémissant, ni chargé de plus d'appétit. (Gide 2002b, 348)

> I shall not have drawn up an accurate balance of the day's proceedings if I omit Browning and Milton. I re-read with delight, with rapture, some of the sonnets, the opening of *Samson*, and long passages of *Paradise Lost*, with less enthusiasm Browning's *In a Balcony*, of which I had kept a better recollection. It is often an advantage not to understand too perfectly. My imagination readily succumbed to mirage in those days and generously invested my uncertainties with the colours of enchantment. Now that I see more clearly, I am a little disappointed.
>
> I lay down under my mosquito-net with a kind of frenzy (which ended by giving me a bad headache). I cannot remember having ever brought to

---

the reader to pay careful attention to who is speaking and to be conscious of the changing perspectives.

23. Even if there are more descriptive or "objective" passages in *Travels in the Congo*, these do not suggest a third-person perspective.

bear on any text a keener, a more sensitive, a more perspicacious—or a hungrier—attention. (Gide 1957, 253)

On the one hand, the description of the reading experience allows Gide to blot out the disturbing and frustrating elements of the day's journey. Earlier in the same journal entry, Gide had described the nauseating smell of the place where he had slept, the monotony of the country he had seen, and an encounter with the swollen corpse of a drowned man. On the other hand, the description of the reading experience allows Gide to reflect on his state of mind, noting how his evaluation of Browning had changed, how his imagination is able to compensate for his misunderstandings, and how attentive and sensitive his mind becomes during reading. We must also note the strong physical sensations that accompany Gide's sense of heightened attention and visual perception in this passage: the frenzy of reading, the subsequent headache, and the great hunger that he has for the books. The passage is followed by a quotation from Milton's *Samson,* where Samson laments that the sense of sight is not distributed across the whole surface of the body like the sense of touch ("Why was the sight to such a tender ball as th'eye confin'd?"), and by Gide's remarks pertaining to his great desire to take a walk after the passage on a whaleboat. Thus, the description of the reading and the Milton citation illustrate the power of fiction to imagine alternative models of bodily configuration and sensual experience. Further, by multiplying perspectives the description of the reading experience enables Gide to move from the outside world to his inner experience. In other words, by allowing him to present different states of his mind, the subtle changes in his mind, and different sensations, the reading experience deepens the subjectivity of the description.

The importance that Gide gives to La Fontaine, Milton, Conrad, and Goethe suggests the potential of fiction to create a sense of a mind and an illusion of reality that captures the traveller, but that may also help the traveller to understand himself. We may perhaps think of the relation between *The Counterfeiters* and Gide's journal about writing this novel in the same way, as a ceaseless dynamic between reality and fiction in which the two opposites constantly inform each other. In his journal about novel-writing, Gide wanted to show how his novel both borrowed from and transformed actual reality. Furthermore, he made explicit the interdependence between his novel and journal-keeping by publishing the *Journal des Faux-Monnayeurs* almost simultaneously with *The Counterfeiters*. The interdependence between the two books, and their respective genres, is also mirrored in the structure of *The Counterfeiters,* where journal- and novel-writing alternate constantly.

Poetics of the Novel

What, then, is the significance of the dynamic between third- and first-person narration, which characterizes Goethe's and Gide's novels, for the travel journal, in which the writer-traveller remains the sole observing consciousness and voice of the text? The argument that I will develop at the end of this chapter is that Gide's poetics of the novel, especially his interest in the multiplicity of individual perspectives and voices, profoundly informs his reading experience during the journey and that this is exemplified, among other ways, in how he writes en route about novels, Conrad's novella, and other literature, such as Milton and La Fontaine.

As I have shown above, Gide not only underscores the immersive qualities of fiction in his travel journal, but also structures much of his travel experience with the help of literature. Furthermore, in his travelogue, Gide continues to inquire into the relation between mediated reality and the facts of reality, or between imagination and the resistance of facts—themes that are central to *The Counterfeiters*—even if he never poses questions about travel writing or journal-keeping as a genre. In his commentary on the literature that he reads, however, Gide postulates two versions of immediacy: the immediacy of travel and that of reading, which may shed some light on the way he conceived the purpose of his travel journal. On the one hand, in the entries in his travel journal Gide focuses on the immediacy of the travel experience, by which I mean the immediacy of life as the simultaneous flux of things and events. Such immediacy has the potential to rejuvenate the traveller, even renew him physically, putting an end to apathy, as happens, for instance, when Gide feels the joy of a child chasing some unknown insects in Brazzaville at the beginning of the journey (Gide 2002b, 25). Insofar as the travel experience is not only told, but is also an intimately felt experience of reality, and one that cannot be wholly captured in any narrative or description, Gide thus conceives travel and travel writing as a way to register the action that is "close" to reality, the experience that imposes itself on the observer. Such a perspective is evident in the writer's desire to penetrate profoundly into Africa—"to enter profoundly, intimately, into the heart of the country" (1957, 61) ("pénétrer profondément, intimement, dans le pays"; Gide 2002b, 97)[24]—and in the many

---

24. The full passage reads: "What we want is precisely to leave the beaten track, to see what one does not see ordinarily, to enter profoundly, intimately, into the heart of the country" (Gide 1957, 61) ("Ce que nous voulons, c'est précisément quitter les routes usuelles; c'est voir ce que l'on ne voit pas d'ordinaire, c'est pénétrer profondément, intimement, dans le pays"; Gide 2002, 97).

references to the screens of civilization that tend to blur his vision. Gide is eager, for instance, to leave behind the "French" Dakar, and the film that civilization interposes ("écran de la civilization") in Brazzaville, as well as his boat, since the boat makes the landscape seem like décor and hardly real (2002b, 35). At times, as we saw earlier, Gide is also irritated at the porters who deny him, by their mere presence, direct contact with the nature of Africa.

We come across the same hope of discovering some nonmediated reality in pure expression in *The Counterfeiters*, especially in Edouard's poetics of the novel and his contradictory wish to let the reality dictate the novel to him instead of having to plan its composition (Gide 2002a, 185; Gide 1966, 169). The question of mimesis—the outspoken subject of Edouard's novel—essentially involves the relation between the reality as it appears to the writer and the reality that is translated as literature, or as Edouard himself puts it, "the struggle between the facts presented by reality and the ideal reality" ("la lutte entre les faits proposés par la réalité, et la réalité idéale"; Gide 2002a, 185). The novel's author-narrator refers to these ideas as the incompatible requirements in Edouard's thinking. The author's own metaphor of novel-writing as a form of open-ended travel reiterates the view.

The embedding of Edouard's poetics of the "pure novel" in the excerpts of his journal in *The Counterfeiters* is paradoxical in the sense that this theory evokes competing notions of what is possible to achieve in novels. In principle, Edouard, echoing Gide in his *Journal des Faux-Monnayeurs* (entry for November 1, 1922), argues for the possibility of a pure novel. By the "pure novel" Edouard and Gide mean that the novel should cast aside all elements that do not specifically belong to it, such as "outward events, accidents, traumatisms" that can more accurately be shown in the cinema, or realistic dialogue that the phonograph may record more faithfully. Furthermore, Edouard argues in *The Counterfeiters* that "even the description of the characters does not seem to me the business of the *pure* novel (and in art, as in everything else, purity is the only thing I care about)" (Gide 1966, 71). Later on, Edouard points out that the novel is perhaps the most lawless of literary genres (Gide 1966, 182–83). The statement may discount the possibility of any poetics of the novel, while it is again part of a general critique of the predominant forms of realism that, for Edouard and Gide alike, cheaply give up the genre's freedom for outdated forms of verisimilitude.[25]

---

25. However, what Edouard sees as being most specific to the novel, beyond the narration of action, description, and dialogue, is left frustratingly open. It is nearly impossible to draw out any coherent poetics of the novel from the fragments of Edouard's journal, other than perhaps by way of negation. Edouard is also intentionally inconsistent. Whenever he is asked about his plan for the novel, he talks about it in a new light. The inconsistency was Gide's way of pointing out that Edouard was bluffing and afraid that he would never finish the

Edouard's and Gide's debate about the pure novel can be rephrased as a problem of immediacy. In *The Counterfeiters*, the strategy of superposition between third-person omniscient and first-person narration, framed as a juxtaposition between (fictional) reality and the nonfiction journal, reflects this problem: it invites the reader to imagine that the two modes of narration—the novel and the journal, or Edouard's fictional journal and the author's actual journals—complement each other while also trying to improve upon each other. Thus juxtaposed, the third-person novel and the first-person journal illuminate each other's specific limitations and potential for creating an illusion of immediacy.

At the end of his travel journal, Gide returns to the question of pure genres, having just read in recent French journals and periodicals some unnamed contributions to the ongoing debate about "Poésie pure" (Gide 2002b, 494–495). Despite the fact that Gide thinks it is "extraordinary and somewhat vain," the debate about pure poetry spurs the writer to defend the purity of literary genres against their "confusion." Poetry, as Gide sees it, should focus on what is specific to it, conveying meaning, but in an "essentially untranslatable" form, by way of its sonorous and rhythmic nature, and not succumb to calls to be like music or painting. "Symphonic poems," writes Gide, make him run away from concerts. The same journal entry ends with a reference to *The Counterfeiters*, which is the only mention of the novel in the travel journal and, for this reason, important. The novel is thus indirectly associated with the question of specific genres.[26] At the very end of this reference, Gide mentions some unfavorable reviews ("quelques éreintements") of his novel, which he has seen in the same magazines and laconically points out that this must mean that *The Counterfeiters* has come out (the novel was published in book form in February 1926 when Gide was still in Africa).[27] Thus,

---

novel (see Gide 2008, 61). Another difficulty in detecting any clear poetics of the "pure novel" in *The Counterfeiters* is that Gide ironically distances himself from his protagonist in both the novel and the accompanying journal—since, as Gide himself carefully points out (2008, 67), Edouard fails to write his "pure" novel. This failure may be Gide's as well, but then again, perhaps his notion of the pure novel was never to be taken too literally.

26. The problem of false or insincere representation surfaces in the travelogue in September 1925 when the writer articulates his reasons for not liking Molière's *Le Misanthrope* on the basis of true impression and genre-specificity. Gide argues that the problem in *Le Misanthrope* lies in the character Alceste, whose acts are too poorly justified, whose object of mockery is often unclear, and whose gestures he finds to be contrived and forced. In creating this character, Gide contends, Molière did not pay enough attention to the differences between the theater and the novel, that is, between what can be shown on stage and what needs to be told.

27. Five instalments of the novel had already been published in *La Nouvelle Revue Française* between March and August 1925. André Ruyters's translation of Conrad's *Heart of Darkness* was serialized in the same journal in December 1924 and January 1925. *Voyage au Congo* was

while the seeds of a journey to Africa may have already been planted in this novel, the travel journal in turn closes with the writer's muted reaction to the controversial reception of his novel.

The contradiction concerning true representation in Edouard's theory of the novel reflects similar concerns about verisimilitude voiced elsewhere in *The Counterfeiters* or in Gide's travel journal. For instance, the characters who leave European civilization behind, including Vincent, Lady Griffith, and Alexandre Vedel, seem to want to realize, even if it means self-destruction, the full potential of the principle of immediacy, that is, the immediacy of experience. Their desire to travel is intimately related to a desire to renew perception, to enhance sensual pleasure, or to experience another form of reality, and possibly to become wealthy. Likewise, Bernard's interest in Arthur Rimbaud as someone who presumably exits from literature via action is similarly motivated. In Gide's travel writing, in turn, it appears that the writer-traveller has momentarily resolved the problem of mimesis, since he projects an image of himself as someone who by nature is not a counterfeiter, a producer of *factice* (false, fake) as are the novelists in *The Counterfeiters,* but someone who is capable of immersing himself in the reality of the world around him. During the journey, Gide is able to see more clearly and accurately—despite the disappointments, exhaustion, and the harsh realities of colonial rule that gradually became more and more disturbing to him—since the reality under observation is inevitably close. The travel experience appears to be immediate and the world of travel something that is seen and felt, instead of told.

On the other hand, we are left with the paradox that so much of Gide's travel experience is mediated by literature and that at some level Gide is also aware that he has a more intense relation with the literature he reads than with anything else. The journey helps him to read more intensively, that is, to transport himself more completely into the world of fiction. However, Gide's (re)readings, and especially novel-reading, also suggest that the experience of travel lacks intensity in some important way and that perhaps journal-keeping is in need of another kind of immediacy, the immersion in the world of fiction, the world as a text. The readings thus not only blot out the monotony or the heterogeneity in his experience, heighten the joys of travel, or guide him in how to pay better attention to what he sees, but also affirm the reality around him, as an experience of reality that to a significant degree is indebted to imagination and his literary sensitivity. Gide's remarks on *Heart of Darkness,* Goethe's *Elective Affinities,* Milton, and others illustrate how effectively

---

first published in *La Nouvelle Revue Française* in a serial form from November 1926 to April 1927.

fiction may mediate the experience of reality, but also how his mind works through imagination, by generously investing his uncertainties "with the colours of enchantment."

A further complexity in this regard involves the thorny issue of first impressions. Gide displays sensitivity to nuances of reference, for example, one foggy morning in October of 1925, when he claims that bad weather in Africa turns the mind towards memories, whereas in France a grey sky would inspire the mind to read and meditate. However, the statement is clearly contradictory in that Gide is constantly inspired to read during the journey, regardless of the weather, and he hardly reflects on personal memories of any kind in his travel journal. In effect, the monotony of the forest or the bad weather enables Gide to read "in rapture" and appreciate certain texts, such as La Fontaine, Milton, or Conrad, differently and more fully than at home. Furthermore, what is important from our perspective is that some of Gide's entries suggest that his mind and imagination have the power to alter his observations of reality. For instance, Gide writes that his imagination of Africa had been so lively and powerful that he is no longer sure whether he remembers the town of Bangui as it really is or as he first imagined it (Gide 2002b, 95). Thus, his first impression had the capacity to alter profoundly the reality of perception, yet, at the same time, the freshness of this perception could never be maintained in a longer reflection:

> Tout l'effort de l'esprit ne parvient pas à créer cette émotion de la surprise qui ajoute au charme de l'objet une étrangeté ravissante. La beauté du monde extérieur reste la même, mais la virginité du regard s'est perdue. (Gide 2002b, 95)

> However much the mind tries, it cannot recapture that emotion of surprise which adds a strange enchantment to the object. The beauty of the exterior world remains the same, but the eye's virginity is lost. (Gide 1957, 60)

Gide's concern is that the immediacy of the first impression cannot be reclaimed. The same dilemma connects the otherwise different experiences of travel and reading fiction. Both travel and fiction have the capacity to make life seem new and unfamiliar, but both can also easily lose this power. The novels and other favorite readings, however, which can be read over and over again, seem to provide the traveller with a temporary antidote to losing the freshness of the first impression. What happens in the journal, in spite of the writer's outspoken claim here, is that the rereading of La Fontaine, Milton, Conrad, and Goethe revives for Gide at least the meaning and intensity of these books, if not also the experience of travel in new places, and thus prolongs the sense of the first impression.

Gide's difficulty with the presumed lack of individuality in landscape and people perhaps becomes more understandable in the same light, with regard to the author's stress on and search for renewed perception and sensitivity to nuances of reference. The assumed absence of the Africans' individualization, however, which Gide elaborates on in more detail after about three and a half months of travel, also runs contrary to his poetics of writing, and of the novel in particular, where he prioritizes the effect of multiplicity and counterpoint in specific, individual perspectives. Moreover, besides killing fresh perception, the experience of the Africans' nondifferentiation undermines the principle of sensitivity that Gide holds in high esteem, as exemplified in his discussion of the fables of La Fontaine. Furthermore, the remarks on African monotony and uniformity, which may equally concern the landscape and the people, are in stark contrast to the notion of poetical existence and the experience of travel that could allow the raw particulars of reality to impose itself freely on the traveller.

In Bosoum in December 1925 Gide writes that African children, especially in the first villages that he visited, looked the same and were indifferently likeable, that the village huts were all similar, and that the people in these villages seemed to him to be "droves of human cattle" ("un bétail humain"), all uniform in their looks, tastes, habits, and potential. Moreover, he explains that the landscape did not have a single feature that attracted his attention or made him feel as if he simply had to see it. Contrasted with Gide's earlier remarks on the fascinating qualities of the natural surroundings, such as the purity of the air, the beauty of the light, or the delightful warmth, the monotony that the traveller's frustrated gaze discovers in the people and the landscapes clarifies for him the value of differentiation:

> Cette notion de la différenciation, que j'acquiers ici, d'où dépend à la fois l'exquis et le rare, est si importante qu'elle me paraît le principal enseignement à remporter de ce pays. (Gide 2002b, 196)

> This notion of differentiation, which I have acquired here, and from which proceeds the sense both of the exquisite and of the rare, is so important that it seems to me the principal thing I shall bring away from this country. (Gide 1957, 137–38)

In this passage, Gide sees the black African as inseparable from his group, characterized by a certain primitive mentality that both attracts and terrifies him.[28] For instance, during a night spent in the village of Baboua, in November 1925, Gide depicts the village dance by way of its attractive "stupidity":

> On n'imagine rien de plus morne et de plus stupide que cette danse, d'un lyrisme que plus rien de spirituel ne soulève. . . . Telle est l'expression de leur ivresse, la manifestation de leur joie. Au clair de lune, cette obscure cérémonie semble la célébration d'on ne sait quel mystère infernal, que je contemple longuement, sur lequel je me penche comme sur un abîme, comme Antoine sur la bêtise du catoblépas: "Sa stupidité m'attire." (Gide 2002b, 176–77)

> It would be impossible to imagine anything more dismal and more stupid than this dance, unrelieved as it was by any breath of spirituality. . . . This is how they express their emotion—manifest their joy! By the light of the moon this obscure ceremony seemed the celebration of some infernal mystery; I stayed gazing at it for a long time, fascinated by it as by an abyss—like St. Anthony by the stupidity of the catoblepas: "Sa stupidité m'attire." (Gide 1957, 122–23)

The traveller is again on the verge of experiencing terror, facing the mystery and the mythical hell of Africa, similar to the moments when he had sensations of suffocating and even of being cannibalized (see Chapter 1).

When Gide was revising the travelogue and came upon his notes on the Africans' supposed lack of individuality, he could not help feeling that he had to explain himself. Perhaps also hearing the racist undertone in his remarks, Gide argues in a footnote, which he added to the manuscript, that the implications of the notes on non-differentiation of the individual and the herd ("tristes troupeaux humains") now appear to him certainly exaggerated. Trying to justify himself, furthermore, Gide explains that at the time he wrote these notes, his team had hardly emerged from the frustrating "limbo" of the forest into which they had plunged (Gide 2002b, 220n1).

Gide's description of the black Africans in these passages amounts to a trivialized version of Lucien Lévy-Bruhl's refuted ethnographic theory about prelogical primitive mentality. Soon after his return to France, Gide read Lévy-Bruhl's *La Mentalité Primitive* that he then cites, retrospectively, in several footnotes that he added to the travel journal. In the footnotes, Gide refers to the notion of a primitive mind, in contrast to the Western mind, and

---

28. See also Fraiture (2007, 228) who claims that in his attitude towards the Africans Gide oscillated between contempt and paternalistic kindness or admiration.

the idea of unity between the natural and the supernatural, to explain some of the observations that he had made during the journey. For instance, Gide justifies his observation that the relation of cause and effect seemed not to exist for the Africans with a reference to Lévy-Bruhl (Gide 1957, 241). Similarly, he explains in another footnote, where he cites at length Lévy-Bruhl's ideas on the indispensable role of magic in primitive mentality, how these ideas also explain the seeming lack of affection among a group of Arabs and black Africans who watched a man drown in a river almost before their eyes. Yet Lévy-Bruhl's theory also functions as a kind of correction to negative occidental stereotypes of the Africans, for instance, the Europeans' tendency to exaggerate "the lasciviousness and sexual precocity of the blacks, and the obscene signification of their dances" (Gide 1957, 138) ("la salacité et la précocité sexuelle des noirs et l'obscène signification de leurs danses"; Gide 2002b, 196), even if this does not prevent Gide from employing some of the same images elsewhere in his travelogue, such as in the description of the attractive stupidity, or the stupid lyricism, of a village dance. Gide further notes that he had made "the foolish mistake" of not reading Lévy-Bruhl before his return, since this would have spared him "numberless errors and shed light in many dark places" (1957, 241) ("Ils m'eussent épargné nombre de bévues, éclairé bien des ténèbres"; Gide 2002b, 335). The observation may not be so sincere, however, since prior to having actually read Lévy-Bruhl, Gide was already employing a similar, nontheoretical notion of primitive mentality to express his views of black Africans.[29] Lévy-Bruhl's theory is but another means by which the writer is able to give, retrospectively, a more authoritative formulation to his preconceived notions and observations. In this sense, there is also a clear difference in Gide's use of Lévy-Bruhl and Conrad as authorities on Black Africa in that he reread *Heart of Darkness* during the journey; the novella informs the very motivation for his travel from beginning to end and from the entries to the footnotes.

With the benefit of hindsight, we may, speculate upon whether the pleasures that Gide derives from evening readings, or from bath-taking, pure air,

---

29. Pierre Masson has pointed out, rightly I think, that Gide is never racist nor does he despise the indigenous Africans, but that the overt sensuality in his descriptions of Africa and the Africans recalls earlier forms of exoticism such as Loti's caricatures of Jean Peyral and his lover Fatou-gaye (1983, 20). Gide's preconceived notions of the black Africans' sensuality and their hyper-sensibility with regard to superstitious beliefs were also confirmed during his meetings in Bosoum with a colonial administrator, Yves Morel, whose remarks about the natives seemed to Gide "especially just, as they confirm the result of my own observations" (Gide 1957, 138).

warmth, and the elegance and attractiveness of certain Africans, are always sincere. The intensity of some of his descriptions about black African men in particular seems to point to homosexual experiences and desires that the writer could not express outright in the journal (despite being open about his sexual orientation in the second part of *If It Die* two years earlier). What we know, for instance, from Gide's later confessions in *So be it: or, The chips are down* (*Ainsi soit-il*, 1952), or from Marc Allégret's posthumously published travelogue, *Carnets du Congo: Voyage avec Gide* (1993), some of Gide's evening pleasures might indicate sexual encounters and the exploitation of young African men. In *So be it*, Gide is explicit, for instance, about nighttime encounters with a boy called Mala in the secrecy of the writer's mosquito net. Gide explains that his memories of the "most perfect" sensual pleasure, as in the memory of "sweet" Mala, who is mentioned only in passing in *Travels in the Congo*, as having a perfect figure, and being a *companion de luxe* (2002b, 444), are always accompanied by the sense of being surrounded by a landscape that absorbs him:

> C'est bien aussi pourquoi mes souvenirs de volupté les plus parfaits sont ceux qu'accompagne l'enveloppement d'un paysage qui l'absorbe et où je me paraisse me résorber. Dans celui que je viens d'évoquer de ces transes auprès de Mala, ce n'est pas seulement le beau corps pâmé de cet enfant que je revois, mais tout l'alentour mystérieux et formidable de la forêt équatoriale. (Gide 1952, 151)

> This is why my most perfect memories of sensual delight are those enveloped in a landscape which absorbs it and in which I seem to be swallowed up. In the one I have just evoked of those transports with Mala, it is not only the beautiful swooning body of the child I see again, but the whole mysterious and fearful surrounding of the equatorial forest. (Gide 1960, 126–27)

The passage about Mala in *So be it* gives a clear sexual meaning to Gide's depiction of the immensity of the forest and his need to feel enveloped in this immensity. Here the author, once again, resorts to his formula of sensualizing and eroticizing Africa through the young male body. The traveller's mind thus continues to be projected onto the environment, and the environment is projected into his mind, but the emphasis of this mutual implication is quite different from the original description in the travel journal.

Conclusion

Reading Gide's major novel *The Counterfeiters* side by side with his *Journal* and the two African travel books illustrates the effects of the game of generic mirroring, borrowing, and transformation between these works. *The Counterfeiters* stands out in Gide's oeuvre as a unique formal experimentation with the novel structure and character building. Partly due to the novel's elaborate narrative situation that combines alternating third- and first-person narration at different levels, *The Counterfeiters* appears to draw less from the author's life and autobiography than his other works of fiction. However, the many themes and references that the novel shares with the travel journal, including the question of "demonic" impulses and the metaphors of novel-writing and novel-reading as a journey, invite comparisons and suggest a sense of continuity across the fiction/nonfiction divide.

As I have discussed at length above, Gide structures much of his experience in Africa with the help of fiction and constant reading (both fiction and nonfiction). His readings and interpretation of Conrad's works upon the journey thus reveal how the travel experience can encourage a new (subjective) evaluation of the referential value of fiction. I will later return to the question of the reappraisal of a text's referentiality from the perspective of hypothetical genres and ask how the author's, the narrator's, or the character's evoking of possible or counterfactual genres, such as claims about fiction having specific potential as nonfiction, may function as an important dimension of cross-generic interplay.

5

The Incongruous Worlds of Evelyn Waugh's Ethiopia

EVELYN WAUGH'S (1903–1966) novels *Black Mischief* (1932) and *Scoop* (1938) are intimately related with the writer's travel books *Remote People* (1931) and *Waugh in Abyssinia* (1936) that draw from his experience as a correspondent in Ethiopia. *Remote People* includes a report of Emperor Haile Selassie's coronation in Addis Ababa in November 1930, commissioned by *The Times*, while *Waugh in Abyssinia* was the outcome of Waugh's work as a war correspondent for the *Daily Mail*, when he was covering the Italo-Ethiopian war from August to December 1935 and the Italian occupation of Addis Ababa in August 1936.[1] *Black Mischief*, written soon after Waugh's first visit to Ethiopia,[2] is set in an imaginary East African island state called Azania. The events of *Scoop*, in turn, take place in the fictional East African country of Ishmaelia, which is also embroiled in civil war.

The many correspondences between Waugh's African travel books and the novels have been thoroughly investigated in biographies and criticism

---

1. Twelve dispatches appeared in *The Times* between October 27 and November 13, 1930. Waugh also published three articles about his travel in *The Graphic*, and five dispatches appeared in the *Daily Express* between October 29 and November 6 (Gallagher 1983, 110). Sections of chapters from *Waugh in Abyssinia* were also published in the *English Review*.

2. In English-language historical contexts, and in Waugh's writings, Ethiopia was commonly called "Abyssinia" and its inhabitants "Abyssinians." This study uses the terms Ethiopia and Ethiopians except in quotations or summary where the use is Waugh's. The choice of the terms is similar, for instance, to Salwen's (2001b, 161).

that have shown how Waugh's fiction uses and transforms the facts of his travel experience (Salwen 2001a, 2001b; Stannard 1986, 301–4, 470–75). In what follows, I will pose the question of the relation between Waugh's travel writing and fiction from the opposite direction: in what sense was fiction also a source of information, and even a kind of conceptual model, for Waugh's travel books and reportages? How, further, are the novels and travel writing also significantly different from each other? Furthermore, I work from the assumption that Waugh's writings about real and imaginary East African spaces reveal a symptomatic image of Africa, common to all of his writings across the generic divide. By this I mean the projection of Ethiopia, and East Africa, as a unique space of potentiality and possible worlds, and a source of endless comic or absurd juxtapositions of cultural incongruity. Waugh refers to such juxtapositions in *Remote People*, for instance, as the "unique stage of the interpenetration" of Ethiopian and European cultures (2003, 212), and as a "system of life in a tangle of modernism and barbarity," consisting of a unique blend of European, American, and African cultural elements (2003, 220).

To answer these questions, and so as to make some progress toward a fuller characterization of the complex relation between travel writing and the novel in Waugh's work, I will read his African fiction and nonfiction side by side without privileging either side of the comparison. Before going any further, however, it must be noted that it is difficult and perhaps impossible to classify *Waugh in Abyssinia* within one nonfiction category. In *Waugh in Abyssinia*, unlike in *Remote People*, Waugh clearly attempted to influence public opinion, especially in the last two chapters, to become more favorable toward Italian intervention in Ethiopia. The first chapter of the book, moreover, focuses on the history of Ethiopia and colonialism in Africa without describing the author's travel. Given the political tendentiousness, and the relative distance of the perspective from the travel experience in the book's beginning and end, *Waugh in Abyssinia* is much less clearly a travel book than *Remote People*. Waugh's descriptions and observations are, furthermore, based on two separate visits to Ethiopia. This is reflected in the book's outline as well, chapters two to five describing the situation before and during the opening stages of the war in the fall of 1935, and chapters six and seven concentrating on the situation after the war in occupied Addis Ababa in August 1936. Yet, simultaneously, the main body of the book, from the second to the fifth chapter, is structured around the writer's travel experience in Addis Ababa and elsewhere in Ethiopia. This is similar to *Remote People* where the perspective consistently follows the traveller's movements and observations through Ethiopia, Aden, Zanzibar, Kenya, and the Congo. *Waugh in*

Abyssinia can thus be classified as a hybrid text between travel writing and a journalistic-political tract and, as such, it stands out among the other examples of travel writing included here.³

Motivation for Travel

In his travel books, Waugh often made it clear to the reader that his descriptions were not pure mimesis but shaped by his subjective vision and other travellers' descriptions. Typically, Waugh self-consciously stressed his lack of knowledge and innocence about the destination in the beginning of his travel account. In his first travelogue, *Labels: A Mediterranean Journal* (1930), the writer claims that "I did not really know where I was going, so, when anyone asked me, I said to Russia. Thus my trip started, like an autobiography, upon a rather nicely qualified basis of falsehood and self-glorification" (2003, 7). In *Remote People,* Waugh explains that six weeks prior to the journey he had barely heard of the name Ras Tafari (to be called Haile Selassie upon his ascension to the status of an emperor).

Escape and the thrill of estrangement were a strong, if not the main motivation for Waugh's travels. The writer explains in his article "Travel—and Escape from Your Friends" in the *Daily Mail* in January 1933 that

> I do not wish to pretend that we travellers are in a perpetual state of high courage, being ambushed by cannibals, pounced by lions, hissed at by snakes, but that as soon as one leaves the ordinary highways of civilization there is a certain agreeable sense of danger never very far away. (Gallagher 1983, 133)

In *Ninety-Two Days* (1934), where Waugh describes his travels in British Guiana and Brazil in 1932, he writes in the same spirit, emphasizing the vividness of the travel experience, which is also a source of inspiration for his writing:

---

3. Salwen (2001a) goes so far as to claim that it would be incorrect to describe *Waugh in Abyssinia* as a travel book, even if a segment of the book had been included in the first edited collection of his travel writings (*When the Going Was Good,* 1943). Salwen tries to justify the claim by stating that Waugh was not an "insouciant travel writer" when he wrote the book, but a war correspondent. I would hesitate to make such a strict distinction between the genres, however, and instead would characterize the book as a generic hybrid between travel writing and war journalism. *Waugh in Abyssinia* describes various episodes of actual travel and largely consists of material that was not published in newspapers. The book has also been included in a collection of Waugh's travel writing in Everyman's Library (2003).

> One does not travel, any more than one falls in love, to collect material. It is simply part of one's life. Some writers have a devotion for rural England; they settle in Sussex, identify themselves with the village, the farm, and the hedgerow and, inevitably, they write about it; others move into high society; for myself and many better than me, there is a fascination in distant and barbarous places, and particularly in the borderlands of conflicting cultures and states of development, where ideas, uprooted from their traditions, become oddly changed in their transplantation. It is there that I find the experiences vivid enough to demand translation into literary form. (2003, 379)

Likewise, the central characters in *Black Mischief* and *Scoop*, Basil Seal and John Courteney Boot, are motivated to travel to Azania and Ishmaelia, of which they hardly know anything, simply out of the promise of adventure in a distant location—a sense of adventure created by a similar expectation of oddly transformed ideas and experiences—and boredom with their everyday life in London. These travellers' self-conscious naiveté, just like Waugh's own cultivated and controlled desire for estrangement, is then contrasted over the course of their journey with the reputation of the place and the other travellers' hackneyed notions. As to the choice of the title *Labels*, Waugh explains that it also stems from the sense of the traveller's belatedness:

> I have called this book *Labels* for the reason that all the places I visited on this trip are already fully labelled. I was no adventurer of the sort who can write books with such names as *Off the Beaten Track in Surrey* or *Plunges into Unknown Herts*. I suppose there is no track quite so soundly beaten as the Mediterranean seaboard; no towns so constantly and completely overrun with tourists as those I intend to describe. (2003, 13)

What appears, thus, interesting to Waugh is the reputation of the famous destinations, in contrast with his own experiences, impressions, and interpretation that gradually disqualify this reputation. Waugh's tone is mockingly sensitive when he discusses in *Labels* the thick layer of descriptions that some places, like Paris, have attracted over time. He argues that the "overwhelming variety" of reputations, and fictions, has made the historical French city almost fade away:

> The fiction of Paris, conceived by Hollywood and the popular imagination, seems yearly to impose its identity more and more as the real city of Richelieu and Napoleon and Verlaine fades into the distance. This fictitious city expresses itself in dress parades, studios, and night clubs. (2003, 14)

Waugh makes a point, then, about having missed the authentic experience of Paris, and the difficulty of finding a topic "about which one can get down one's seventy thousand words without obvious plagiarism" (2003, 15). Yet, at the same time, his travel books convey the sense that, despite all disappointments, deception and false reputation, the challenge of finding a new ironic angle on travel experience and the famous places are worth the effort.

The self-consciousness in which Waugh implicates himself in his text is a central element in the early travel books. What was important for Waugh in travel writing at this time, as he makes clear in an approving reference to Gide's *Voyage au Congo* (Gallagher 1983, 129),[4] was the opportunity to present the writer's personality, not his material or the destination. Valentine Cunningham has made the important observation that Waugh's self-conscious, self-mirroring travel writings, including his text-side chats with the reader, blend "into those few moments in his fiction that are, formally speaking, more obviously serious disruptions of traditional narrative's claims on realism" (1989, 393). Such disruptions in his novels include, for instance, the narrator's reflections on the nature of Paul Pennyfeather's existence in Waugh's first novel *Decline and Fall* (1928). Further, in his early travel writing, Waugh does not look back in nostalgia, but may be even fascinated, in his self-ironic way, by the lack of authenticity, such as various aspects of modern "fictitious" Paris, involving the "inscrutable" world of fashion and women's clothing. In his last African travel book, *A Tourist in Africa* (1960), similarly, Waugh seems to enjoy the layered legends, and the false reputation, of certain African attractions, and the provocative clash between the ancient and the modern that these attractions evoke in his mind. While in Aden, he explains that

> Most of the passengers drove off to see the water-tanks ascribed to King Solomon. In a thousand years' time, will Central African guides show tourists the mighty ruins of the Kariba dam as one of the works of Solomon? I wish I could think so. (2003, 972)

Again, as so often in reading Waugh, the reader faces the difficulty of knowing the extent and the direction of the writer's irony. What if anything is Waugh mocking when he explains that he wishes to think that future guides will attribute the ruins of a modern dam to King Solomon? The irony is potentially directed toward the other passengers, but also the whole culture of tourism, our feeble sense of history and, further, the traveller himself, who is keenly "looking for remembered landmarks and finding none" (2003, 972).

---

4. Waugh made this point in a critique of Max Grühl's travel book *The Citadels of Ethiopia* (*Spectator*, April 9, 1932).

Waugh's dilemma as a travel writer consists, therefore, not so much in knowing whether the space in question blocks in advance interpretative passage due to the traveller's belatedness—since this blockage is taken as a given, and sometimes even an inspiration for his writing—but knowing what exactly the traveller makes of this blockage: how effectively, and by which means, the writer can manipulate the legends, stories, and reputations of places for his own purposes.

Paul Fussell has suggested that Waugh's dilemma in *Labels*, with regard to the Mediterranean locales that were already fully labelled, was the need to "disclose the odd in the familiar, that is, to spot anomalies" (1980, 178–79). In other words, the emphasis on the strange and the anomalous in much-travelled Mediterranean places functioned for Waugh as a means by which he could differentiate himself from previous travelling writers and their accounts. In Waugh's East African travel books, the traveller's sensitivity to the strange, the absurd and the incongruous around him is the writer's central focus. However, the strangeness that he associates with Ethiopia is quite different in quality from his strange experiences in the Mediterranean. This may in part be because the Ethiopian places and the people were not at all familiar to Waugh or his readers, but also because he kept on perceiving and finding unexpected blends of the familiar (European, English, colonial) and the unfamiliar (African, primitive, the archaic).

Fiction in Waugh's Travel Writing

With regard to *Remote People* and *Waugh in Abyssinia*, the question of the discrepancy between the object of description, the East African realities, and the traveller's expectations is perhaps even more significant than in *Labels*. Despite the writer's seeming seriousness in wanting to tell accurately about Haile Selassie's coronation or the East African political situation, Waugh's African travel books from the 1930s foreground the paradox of the subjective viewpoint, thus exploring the gap between expectations, reputation, and the reality of a foreign place. Waugh pays much attention in these books to the foreign, which appears to him strangely familiar, and to any odd blends of the ancient and the modern, the primitive and the civilized, splendor and banality. In *Remote People,* while visiting the British settlement in Kenya, for instance, he conveys the impression that the real Africa is somewhere else: "In Kenya it is easy to forget that one is in Africa; then one is reminded of it suddenly, and the awakening is agreeable" (2003, 332). The appeal of such moments for Waugh stems from a complex interplay between the familiar and the strange, involving the transplantation of the West in the African setting on the one hand, and the African interruptions in this transplanted Western presence on the other. At one point in Kenya, Waugh was sitting with a group of settlers on a terrace, drinking cocktails and listening to a gramophone—"all very much like the South of France" (2003, 332)—when suddenly a Kikuyu woman and her son "came lolloping over the lawn" asking for a pill for her son's pain. While this African "intrusion" has elements of the comical and stereotypical (the lolloping of the Kikuyu woman), Waugh's rendition of the event emphasized its absurdity and enabled the writer, once again, to make comparisons with England. Waugh concludes that the Kikuyu passion for pills is only equalled by similar passions in English Bohemia or the way Europeans might beg for sixpences. England remains always the touchstone in Waugh's impressions of strangely altered forms of life.

Waugh also sometimes highlights the gap between expectation and East African realities by a reference to fictional worlds and creates, thus, an effect of superimposed worlds of fact and fiction. Especially in the Ethiopian section of *Remote People,* the writer conjures up absurd juxtapositions that reveal a heterogeneous and nearly fantastic reality. In a central, opening description of the Emperor's coronation in Addis Ababa, Waugh resorts to fiction as the only possible means of access to the reality around him:

> In fact, it is to *Alice in Wonderland* that my thoughts recur in seeking some historical parallel for life in Addis Ababa. There are others: Israel in the time of Saul, the Scotland of Shakespeare's *Macbeth,* the Sublime Porte as one sees it revealed in the dispatches of the late eighteenth century, but it is in *Alice* only that one finds the peculiar flavour of galvanised and translated reality, where animals carry watches in their waistcoat pockets, royalty paces the croquet lawn beside the chief executioner, and litigation ends in a flutter of playing-cards. How to recapture, how retail, the crazy enchantment of these Ethiopian days? (2003, 200)

His observations prompt the writer to formulate a notion of a translated reality, where fact and fiction become ever more intertwined. Attempting to find historical parallels to the coronation ceremonies and the new town of Addis Ababa, where nothing "appears to be really finished" (2003, 200), Waugh's description thus turns to fiction as the most, and possibly only, accurate point of comparison, becoming itself hyperbolic by way of the imaginary, with the help of the fantastic. The difficulty in closing the gap between the demands of description and the world even leads Waugh to suggest a new definition for reality: reality as the translated reality of metamorphoses, mixed forms, and strange juxtapositions, or the galvanized reality, that is, a reality stimulated to action by administering a shock.

For Waugh, there is a specific kind of appeal in the *Alice*-like Addis Ababa with its systematic lack of regularity, punctuality, and logic: "In Addis Ababa everything was haphazard and incongruous; one learned always to expect the unusual and yet was always surprised" (2003, 228). The surprise effects in Waugh's East African reportages, and particularly the peculiar flavor of the "preposterous *Alice in Wonderland* fortnight" (2003, 199) during the Emperor's coronation, are to a large extent inspired by the charm and potentiality that he found in the strange blends between the ancient and the modern, the European and the African:

> After all, there really was something there to report that was quite new to the European public; a succession of events of startling spectacular character, and a system of life, in a tangle of modernism and barbarity, European, African, and American, of definite, individual character. (2003, 220)

At the end of the chapters that portray the Emperor's coronation in *Remote People*, as well as in one of his dispatches that appeared in *The Times* in December 1930, Waugh summarized what seemed to him the most typical characteristic of these ceremonies, that is, their "absurdity." Late one evening when he was returning to his hotel in Addis Ababa, he found that the insight of profound absurdity was affirmed as he noticed "on one side the primitive song of unfathomable antiquity; on the other, the preposterously dressed European, with a stockade between them" (Gallagher 1983, 118; see also Waugh 2003, 232). The European here was Waugh himself, dressed in evening clothes and white gloves and, what he calls the absurd white tie and tall hat of civilization. The "primitive," then, was the wakeful Ethiopian party in one of the "native huts" close to his hotel, and their monotonous music, drumming, and clapping. The modern and the primitive are thus, again, juxtaposed in Waugh's mind and a strange affinity is forged between the two. Waugh was, after all, returning from a party at one of the legations only to witness yet another party. At the same time, Waugh caricatures himself as an absurd figure in his own right, ridiculously removed from his proper context.

It is important to note, further, that the references to the French poet Arthur Rimbaud, made both in *Remote People* and in Waugh's *Diary* entries from the end of 1930, tie the fictional and the factual together. The story of the romantic figure of the gun-runner poet Arthur Rimbaud's life in Harar, in Ethiopia, structures Waugh's experience in this town around a wish to find new information on the poet. Yet, here again, the passage reveals a wide schism between the traveller's expectations and the reality of the travel experience, and one that Waugh does not fail to exploit. The description of his inquiries into Rimbaud while meeting with the famous Monsignor Jerome, the Bishop of Harar, is marked by self-irony. Hoping to find some new details on the poet's life—"perhaps even to encounter a half-caste son keeping a shop in some back street" (2003, 261)—Waugh insisted on posing questions to Monsignor Jerome who allegedly knew the poet. The irony is that in their interview in French, Monsignor Jerome confuses Waugh's "poète" for "prêtre" and maintains for a long time that no Father Rimbaud had ever ministered in Ethiopia. Later, the confusion is cleared up, but the information that Waugh received was a disappointment. Monsignor Jerome shared his memories of the poet's seriousness, sadness, and life with a woman from Tigre, but, as Waugh is keen to note, those memories were of no great significance ("It was rather a disappointing interview"; 2003, 261).[5]

The discrepancy between reputation and Waugh's experience of reality, and the blends between the primitive and the modern, on which he focused during his visits in Ethiopia, was in part dependent on two mediating sources of misinformation: Haile Selassie's propaganda efforts, specifically the Emperor's ongoing project to modernize the country, and the Western journalists and their practices, in particular their battle for scoops. On the one hand, as Waugh saw it, the Emperor had been at pains to impress foreign visitors as the natural ruler of a powerful, organized, modern state, and his own countrymen as an absolute monarch. Most of the modernizing project, however, was clearly unfinished and unconvincing. In reality, Addis Ababa was still, as Waugh reports, in a rudimentary stage of construction with half-finished buildings at every corner. On the other hand, the journalists who were covering the coronation, and later the Italo-Ethiopian war that Waugh covered as a war journalist, created a kind of parallel world of their own, a form of reality, or a blend of reality and invention, transformed into news.

A similar clash between the primitive and the modern is a central theme in *Black Mischief*. In this novel, the Azanian Emperor Amurath has just died and his grandson Seth, who has a bachelor's degree from Oxford, has returned from Europe to claim the small East African Empire. Seth, inspired by the technological progress and modern lifestyle of the West, but also by the socialism of the Soviet Union, is determined to fight what he sees as the barbarism of his country, be that the use of traditional languages or the lack of communal physical exercises. Seth's honorary title also dramatizes the para-

---

5. Rimbaud's legend is also a potential source of parody in Waugh's fiction. In *Scoop*, we learn that the writer John Courteney Boot began his career with a life of Rimbaud (2000a, 5).

doxical blend of savagery and modern society: "Emperor of Azania, Chief of Chiefs of Sakuyu, Lord of Wanda, and Tyrant of the Seas, Bachelor of the Arts of Oxford University" (Waugh 1960, 9).[6] Seth's efforts in modernization, including the military, school system, birth control, and many other institutions and areas of social life, are futile and unfortunate, however. What highlights the futility of Seth's idealistic projects further is that he suffers a nervous breakdown amidst the chaotic situation of misguided social reform and the ongoing civil war:

> The earnest and rather puzzled young man became suddenly capricious and volatile; ideas bubbled up within him, bearing to the surface a confused sediment of phrase and theory, scraps of learning half understood and fantastically translated. (Waugh 1960, 195)

Seth is clearly reminiscent of Waugh's caricature of Haile Selassie and his unstable empire in *Remote People* but, at the same time, just like all characters in this novel, he is a self-consciously made composite character. Seth is also a satirical caricature with little psychological depth.

Furthermore, as Waugh writes in *Remote People*, the international world of reporters and colonialists "jumbled together" in this "rich African setting" (2003, 228), contributed to the sense of ceaseless, and sometimes absurd, translations of meaning, reality, and truth. The journalists and photographers in Addis Ababa, as Waugh reports in *Waugh in Abyssinia*, "showed almost every diversity which the human species produces" (2003, 625). Both in *Remote People* and *Waugh in Abyssinia*, much of Waugh's attention is directed at the other Western travellers, officials, diplomats, settlers, and journalists and their views and fabrications. The driving question that Waugh repeats in the beginning of *Remote People* is "Why all the fuss?" pointing to his puzzlement over the justification for the sudden international press interest in Haile Selassie's coronation. In the rest of the travel account, unable to fully answer this question, Waugh describes the many fabrications of the Western press. The Associated Press, for instance, as Waugh claims, turned the Emperor's nighttime ride from his palace to the church, which in reality had a minimum of display, into a spectacular event at dawn, during which scores of natives were supposedly "trampled in the dust" (2003, 217). The reason for such inventions was, as Waugh argues, that the London newspapers, to win the battle for scoops, preferred any "incomplete, inaccurate, and insignificant report" of

---

6. Haile Selassie I, Emperor of Ethiopia, had the titles King of Kings, Lord of Lords, Conquering Lion of the Tribe of Judah, Elect of God, and Power of the Trinity.

an event, "provided that it came in time for an earlier edition than its rivals" (2003, 218).

In *Waugh in Abyssinia*, Waugh's criticism of journalism is even more biting, and he points out how the pressure to produce news from Ethiopia regularly forced writers to combine fantastic rumor and trivial gossip with "here and there embedded, a few facts of genuine personal observation" (2003, 631). Waugh gave much space both in *Waugh in Abyssinia* and *Scoop* to portray the manipulation of reality as news, not by discovering new realities but by inventing materials. Both the travel book and the novel point out how news may be made by carefully manipulating the frames of reference and reception, that is, by giving them credence as historical facts, regardless of their truth value. All statements of fact may thus imply a re-elaboration, as with the hermetic language of radiograms that was used by the journalists in Addis Ababa, and that creates its own model for a world of reference, as is made explicit in the many hilarious exchanges of telegrams in *Scoop*. Consequently, the empirical argument concerning that which has actually happened is exposed as inadequate, even as absurd, when the hunger for news scoops about the Italo-Ethiopian war overrides the principles of veracity and accuracy. Similar satire is found in Waugh's short story "Incident in Azania" (1932), where an anonymous "star journalist," who has the habit of writing his news stories in advance, based on what he expects to happen, gets involved in a rescue operation concerning a supposedly kidnapped young English woman. The journalist finds out that the "journey was in all respects totally unlike his narrative" (2000, 106).[7]

However, to focus on the illusions and fabrications of reality, or references to fictional worlds like *Alice in Wonderland*, does not necessarily "fictionalize" Waugh's travel writing, that is, make it any more fictional. The *Alice* reference functions, to a large extent, in the same way as the nonfiction that Waugh read or recalled in his mind while travelling. For instance, the travel literature with which Waugh was familiar served him as a point of comparison that justified to him or, perhaps more importantly, failed to justify to him the reputation of a place, and gave practical hints about when and where to travel, what to avoid, or how to focus one's attention. On various occasions during the journey, travel literature, legends, and fiction alike enabled the writer to position himself and his writing in relation to earlier interpretations. Potentially, the readings also suggested a way to close the gap between the expectations that he had before the journey, involving for instance ideas

---

7. See Salwen 2001a and 2001b for Waugh's journalism criticism, and the correspondences between *Scoop* and actual news coverage in Ethiopia during the Italo-Ethiopian war.

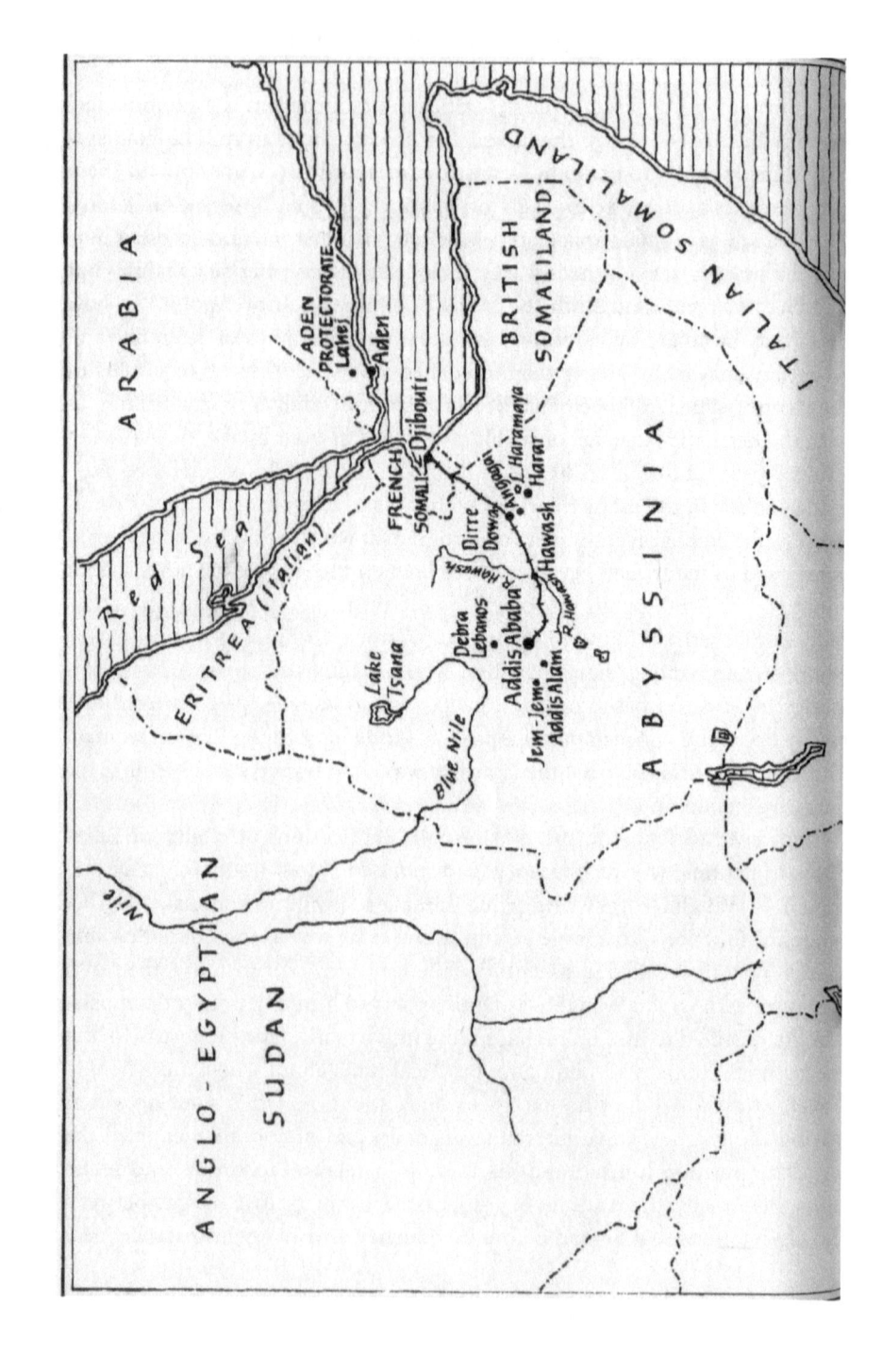

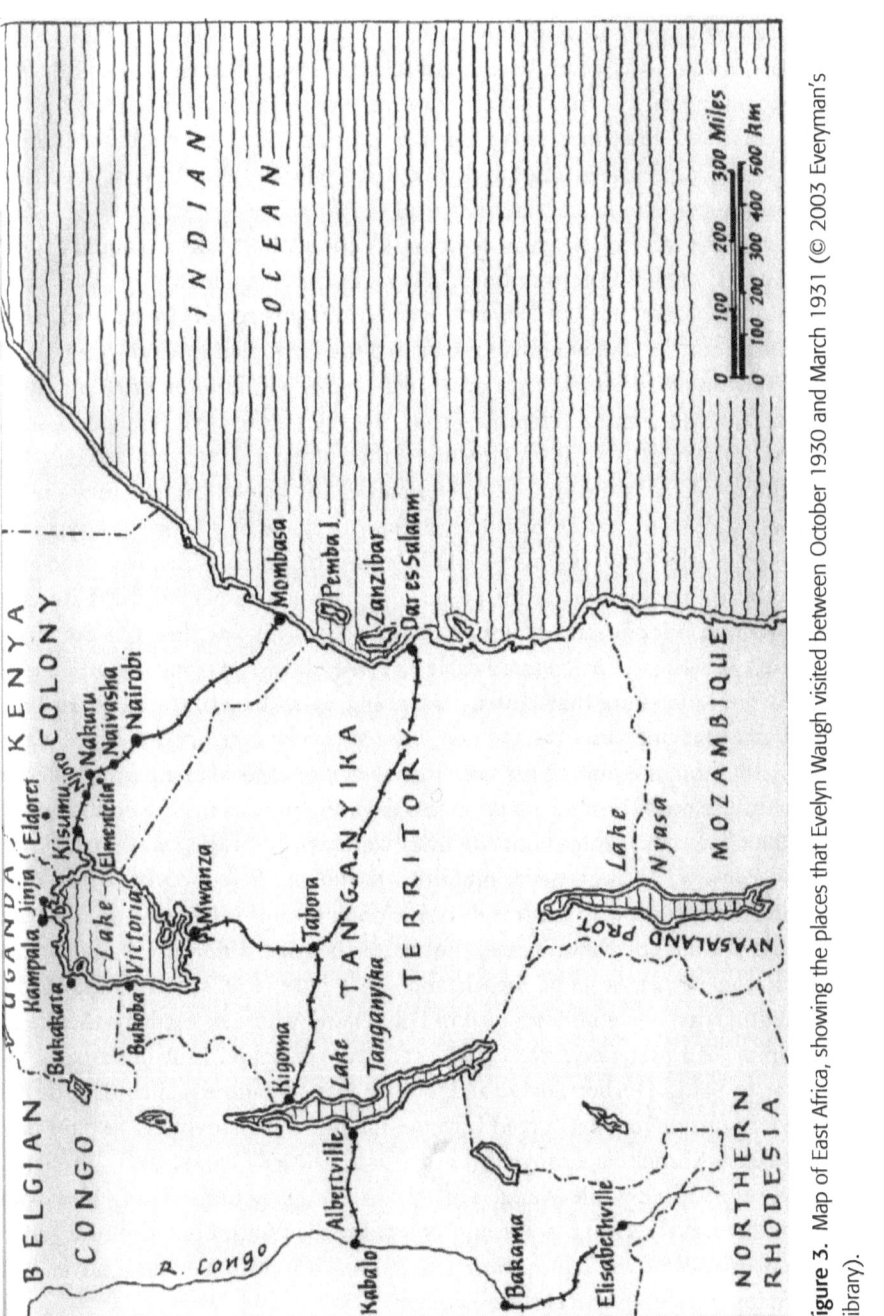

Figure 3. Map of East Africa, showing the places that Evelyn Waugh visited between October 1930 and March 1931 (© 2003 Everyman's Library).

of astonishing Ethiopian glamor (2003, 187), and the less glamorous reality. The many graphic descriptions of the train journey between Djibouti and Addis Ababa, with which Waugh familiarized himself on his way to Ethiopia, function literally in this way, giving him useful advice as to when to get on the train and what to expect from the journey. Waugh's own description of the same journey seems not to invalidate the earlier descriptions, the anonymous "many" books that he had read between West Meath and Marseille, but rather gives added value to remarks about the trains' frequent failures and parts of the line getting washed away, or the "primarily homicidal" interests of the Galla and the Danakil, who live in this region (2003, 194). Later, after the coronation, when Waugh visited the Ethiopian town of Harar, Richard Burton's *First Footsteps in East Africa or, An Exploration of Harar* (1856), stood out as his main reference (2003, 252, 257; 1976, 337). Burton's descriptions of the marketplace, and the beautiful women of Harar, and his drawings of the town from the side of the Somali coast, helped Waugh to frame his observations of what he calls the unique spectacle of a Moslem city also in *Waugh in Abyssinia*, but also to differentiate his impressions from the more glamorous associations of his predecessor. Waugh respected the distinction between nonfiction and fiction, for instance, in his few direct references to the act of writing. In *Remote People* and *Waugh in Abyssinia*, he emphasizes on a few occasions that he was travelling so as to write, that is, in order to write and publish a travel book. One such instance occurs when Waugh explains near the end of his travel in *Remote People* that to fight boredom aboard the boat *Prince Leopold* that was taking him from Kabalo to Bukama in the Congo, he ground out the first two chapters of the travel book (2003, 357). However, Waugh never mentions in *Remote People* or *Waugh in Abyssinia* that the events of his travels or his observations might end up in fiction. In his private correspondence, the matter is quite different. Waugh speaks of fiction-writing openly, for instance, in a letter to Catherine and Arthur Waugh, dated November 16, 1930 in Dire Dawa, where he explains that he has the plot "of a first-rate novel" (1980, 51). Five years later in Addis Ababa, in a letter to Laura Herbert, dated in October 1935, Waugh explains that, despite the circumstances that forced him to stay put in the town for several days, "all this will make a funny novel so it isn't wasted" (1980, 100). The letters thus suggest that while Waugh wished to keep his fiction-writing ideas away from his travel writing, and thus respect the distinction between the genres, the processes of writing in these two genres, a travelogue and a novel, were perhaps not so far apart as it may seem.

However, while the distinction between Waugh's African travel fact and fiction remains relatively intact, accuracy and adequacy in description is always at issue in Waugh's travel writing. The emphasis on the traveller's subjective experience is not only manifest in the importance that Waugh gives to his reactions to various layers of interpretation and reputation, including the fabrications of the Ethiopian government or Western reporters, but also in the undermining of other travel writing. These adjustments, including disappointments, surprises, and correctives, reenact the author's consciousness that is trying to capture some here and now of actual East African reality. For instance, in *Waugh in Abyssinia,* the example of Burton's *First Footsteps in East Africa* helped Waugh to position himself in relation to contemporary colonial politics in Ethiopia. Here Waugh explains that Burton's support for English interference in the region in the nineteenth century affected his description of the people of Harar to the extent that he tended to portray them as vicious and tyrannical. Waugh explains that Burton's description was "no doubt somewhat modified by his [Burton's] desire to make out a good case for interference" (2003, 607). Similarly, Waugh himself could not avoid being caught up in the politics of the 1930s Ethiopia and the question of Western intervention. While speaking for the Hararis, Waugh's criticism of the Ethiopian government, including its authoritarianism, propaganda, and military involvement in the town, is motivated by an attempt to justify the approaching Italian intervention.

The way in which the *Alice* reference differs, however, from the travelogues and legends that structure Waugh's travel writing, is the sense of extended possibility and the potentiality of a fictional world. This potential in fiction suggests a kind of model for the absurd juxtapositions and the metamorphosis of space and time that the writer was trying to capture.[8] What is also quite specific in the *Alice* reference is that it enables Waugh to rethink the category of reality in terms of the notion of a translated or galvanized reality, or of many intertwined realities reacting to each other.

The Superimposed Worlds in Fiction

The same idea of many superimposed worlds and their transformed realities emerges strongly in Waugh's African novels. Consider, for instance, how in *Black Mischief* Waugh appropriated the ancient name Azania that had been used in relation to various parts of sub-Saharan Africa since the Roman times, including for instance the East African coast in "The Periplus

---

8. A possible world, if we take this notion to mean constructs of the mind concerning possible worlds and the grounds of their possibility (Ryan 1991, 19), could be another way to describe this principle of potentiality.

of the Erythraean Sea" (A.D. 60). In Waugh's version, the name resonates with the sound elements of *Abyssinia* and *Zanzibar*, fusing these two together. Another explicit reference is to Cunard liners like Aurania, Albania, or Alaunia, and, closest of them all, Ascania. The allusion to Cunard ships surfaces in the novel when some anonymous Londoner who, having just heard the name, remarks "Azania? It sounds like a Cunarder to me" (1960, 86). The composite structure of Waugh's Azania includes, further, the enclosed world of Western colonials, diplomats, and adventurers, and the enlightened Emperor Seth's imitation of Western institutions—all of whom are somewhat detached from the realities of their actual (textual) world, as if they were travelling on a cruise ship or living out their own fantasies of possibility.[9]

Onto the Azanian geographical microcosm are also projected other isolated spaces and zones. The impression of many superimposed worlds emerges again in the novel's ending where Gilbert and Sullivan's popular comic opera *The Mikado* (1885) is heard played by a gramophone in the Portuguese Fort in the coastal town of Matodi. The fragments from the two songs "Three Little Maids From School Are We" and "Willow, tit-willow" (or "On a tree by a river") function here as a structuring device, providing the narrative with a sense of closure, while they also emphasize the hilarious absurdity of Seth's imperial commands, modernising mission, and planned economy. The songs ring clear, as the narrator explains, over the silent city, the harbor and the water that softly laps against the sea-wall of the port. The Azanian city is quiet since, according to new "modern" regulations, the stray dogs have been killed and all restaurants have to close before ten-thirty. The last song from *The Mikado* that is quoted, "Willow, tit-willow," is sung in the comic opera by a character called Ko-Ko,[10] who is the lord executioner of Titipu, to an elderly lady called Katisha:

> On a tree by a river a little tom-tit
> Sang "Willow, tit-willow, tit-willow!"
> And I said to him, "Dicky bird, why do you sit
> Singing Willow, tit-willow, tit-willow?"
> "Is it weakness of intellect, birdie?" I cried,

---

9. In Roman times, the name Azania referred to an area of the Southeast African coast south of the Horn of Africa. A later imaginary projection onto Azania is the interest of some leaders of the South African political organization Pan-African Congress (PAC) who, familiar with Waugh's novel, wanted to use "Azania" to rename South Africa in the 1960s.

10. Many of the names in the opera, for instance, such as Yum-Yum, Nanki-Poo, or Titipu are not Japanese at all but perfectly understandable as English "baby talk."

"Or a rather tough worm in your little inside?"
With a shake of his poor little head, he replied,
"Oh, willow, tit-willow, tit-willow!" (1960, 311)

At this point in the opera, Katisha has rebuffed Ko-Ko who begs her hand in marriage. Incorporated at the end of Waugh's novel, however, the reference to *The Mikado*, and the scene describing Katisha's initial indifference and Ko-Ko's desperate insistence to repeat the question, can be given different meanings. The song is a possible parable for the events in the novel in that it is perhaps similarly meaningless or even absurd, to ask why a bird would sit and sing, as it is to pretend to modernize a country like Azania. As unchangeable as Azania, the bird simply sings by pure instinct, because singing is in its nature. At the same time, however, this scene of Katisha's deception is a pivotal scene at the end of the opera. The speaking and feeling bird is Ko-Ko's desperate fabrication to save himself, by way of marriage to Katisha, from the execution that the Emperor has ordered. The bird's words and feelings are Ko-Ko's words and feelings, not because he is in love with Katisha, but to the extent that Ko-Ko is certain of his death if Katisha remains "callous and obdurate."

Through *The Mikado*, further, an imaginary Japan is superimposed on Azania. As Azania is loosely connected with Abyssinia and Zanzibar, the romance of *The Mikado*, set in Japan, does not try to be very authentic in its presentation of Japanese culture. It might have been of interest to Waugh that the imaginary Japan in *The Mikado*, which is ruled by strange laws and royal commands, allowed Gilbert to freely satirize English politics and institutions by disguising them as Japanese. The invention of Azania enabled Waugh, in turn, to poke fun at the colonial administration, the civilizing mission in Africa, and travelling snobs such as Basil Seal, who are on the lookout for an authentic adventure and primitive culture in the tropics.

The drawn map of the Azanian Empire included in the beginning of *Black Mischief*, mimicking the cartographic impulse of travel writing, where maps are placed in the beginning of the book, functions as another model of a porous reference world. Here, the map's simplicity may remind us of maps of utopian islands and fantastic worlds. The Azanian island that is shown in the map is relatively large in size in comparison to the Italian Somaliland that Azania faces across the Sakuyu channel—"Sakuyu" being a name for a local tribe (like Kikuyu) but also another possible reference to Japan. The empire includes only a few towns, most importantly the coastal town of Matodi and the new capital Dire Dawa, a monastery, one railway, a jungle called Wanda, some swampland, and hills. The name Debra-Dowa is obviously close to the

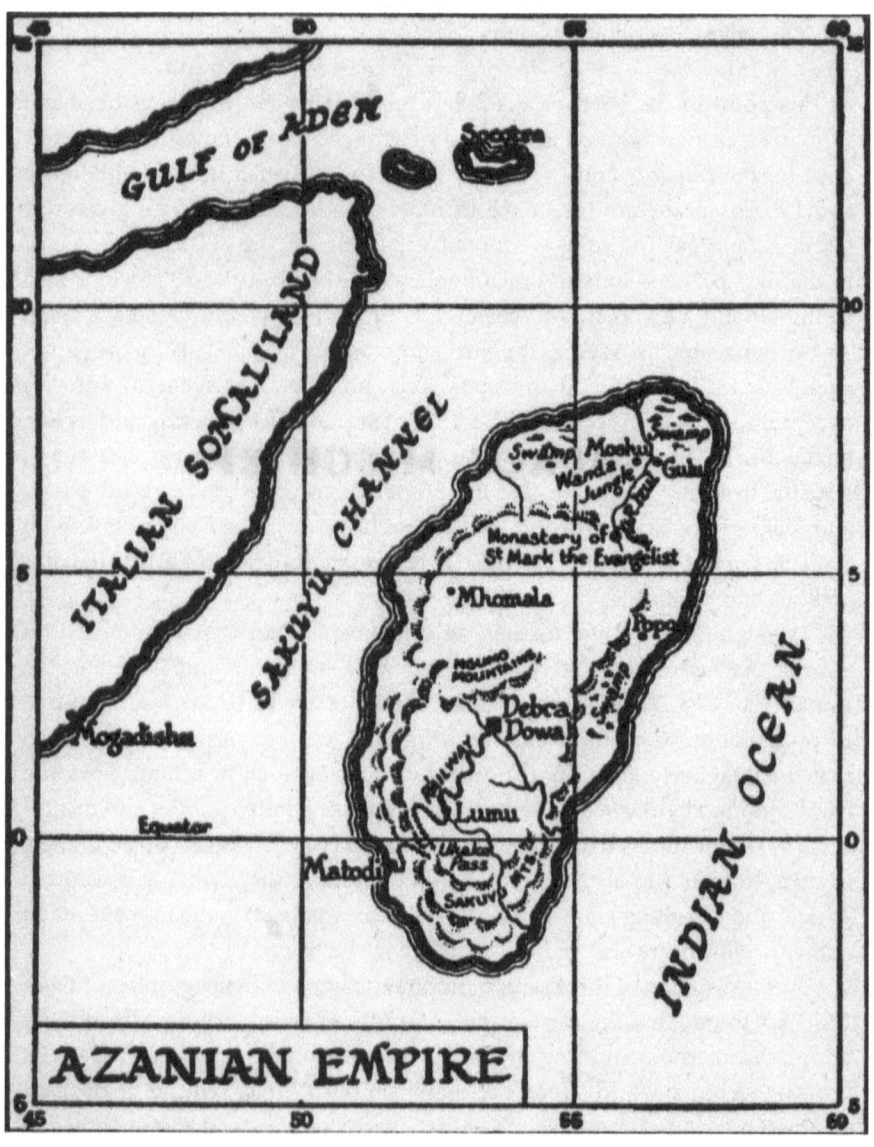

Figure 4. Fictional map from *Black Mischief* by Evelyn Waugh. (Copyright © 1932 by Evelyn Waugh. By permission of Little, Brown, and Company. All rights reserved.)

Ethiopian town of Dire Dawa (or "Dirre Dowa" in *Remote People*) that was part of Waugh's itinerary in 1930.

In *Scoop*, there is no graphic map of Ishmaelia, but the question over the "wildly deceptive map" of the country contributes, in a similar fashion, to the theme of a disorganized world of reference, suggesting a sense of profound deception in space and time. It is, for instance, told about the map of Ishmaelia that there is a place called Laku, which means "I don't know" in the local language (Waugh 2000a, 99). This town was born at the very moment when it was drawn on a map: once when a member of a boundary commission that was on its way to Sudan asked one of their boys for the name of a nearby hill, they received "Laku" as an answer. "Laku" was then copied onto the map and all subsequent maps from then on. Later, the Ishmaelite president Jackson had Laku marked large in the maps since he wanted the country to look important on atlases (2000a, 99). In the fictional world of *Scoop*, further, in another absurd superimposition of space, some features of the contemporary Spanish Civil War, as well as the history of Liberia, have been transported into the caricature of Ishmaelia. Instead of Italian fascist troops and Ethiopians, the warring parties in this novel are local fascists (the whites) and communists (the reds), resembling the opposed forces of the Spanish Civil War (1936–39), the Nationalists having close ideological ties with Nazi Germany while the Republicans were supported by the Soviet Union. At the same time, like the history of Liberia, the presidents and the ruling elite of the country have a past heritage as freed American slaves. The narrator tells us, for instance, that an African-American, or perhaps rather Americo-Ishmaelite, family, called Jackson, has been in power for so long that General Elections were called, according to the ruler's name, "Jackson Gnomas" whenever they were held (2000a, 75). Finally, we may consider the name Ishmaelia that, through its various possible connotations, including Islam, the Hebrew Bible and Melville, also contributes to the sense of multiple worlds.

Waugh's Model Traveller

The question of multiple intertwined worlds, and the effect of absurd spatial juxtapositions that characterize Waugh's novels, may enable us to read some aspects of the author's travel writing in a new light. By this I mean the question of potentiality and possible worlds that comes forth particularly in *Remote People*. In this respect it is relevant to refer to Waugh's interest in Count Hermann Keyserling's *The Travel Diary of a Philosopher* (*Das Reisetagebuch eines Philosophen*, 1919). Keyserling's notion of the "impulse" that drove him into the wide world was not curiosity for foreign places and cultures, but the desire for self-realization through controlled estrangement:

> I therefore begin my journey round the world. Europe has nothing more to give me. Its life is too familiar to force my being to new developments. Apart from this, it is too narrowly confined. The whole of Europe is essentially of one spirit. I wish to go to latitudes where my life must become quite different to make existence possible, where understanding necessitates a radical renewal of one's means of comprehension, latitudes where I will be forced to forget that which up to now I knew and was as much as possible. I want to let the climate of the tropics, the Indian mode of consciousness, the Chinese code of life and many other factors, which I cannot envisage in advance, work their spell upon me one after the other, and then watch what will become of me. (1925, 16)[11]

Keyserling's ideal travel journal was one that could be read like a novel. Keyserling explained that despite *The Travel Diary of a Philosopher* being inspired by the external stimulus of a journey round the world, and although the travelogue contains various more or less objective descriptions of places, the book represents, "nevertheless, an inwardly conceived and inwardly coherent work of fiction, and only those who regard it as such will understand its real meaning" (1925, 9).[12]

In *Labels*, Waugh self-consciously casts himself as a particular kind of traveller: a detached figure who, happily nonchalant about the routes and destination of journey, simply wants to keep on moving and forget his whereabouts, and to experience the potential in estrangement. Trying to avoid the pitfalls and expectations of typical tourists, he travels so as to write. Waugh thus positions himself in opposition to the tourist, especially when tourism means haste and compulsion, or the ridiculous "machinery of the uplift" (2003, 38), but also in opposition to the antimodern antitourist, meaning the travel snob

---

11. So trete ich den eine Weltreise an. Europa fördert mich nicht mehr. Zu vertraut ist mir schon diese Welt, um meine Seele zu neuen Gestaltungen zu zwingen. Und dann ist sie an sich auch zu beschränkt. Ganz Europa ist wesetlich eines Geistes. Ich will in Breiten hinaus, woselbst mein Leben ganz anders werden muβ, um zu bestehen, wo das Verständnis eine radikale Erneuerung der Begriffsmittel verlangt, wo ich möglichst viel von dem vergessen muβ, was ich ehedem wuβte und war. Ich will das Klima der Tropen, die indische Bewuβtseinslage, die chinesische Daseinsform und viele andere Momente, die ich gar nicht vorausberechnen kann, umschichtig auf mich einwirken lassen und zusehen, was aus mir wird (Keyserling 1920, 7).

12. See also Fussell (1980, 177) who has suggested that Waugh's wish in his travel writing to do justice to the potentialities of subjective meaning and experience, and the inwardly coherent work of fiction, rather than facts, is indebted to Keyserling's philosophy of travel.

or the pretentious pilgrim who, as Waugh explains in reference to Hilaire Belloc and his *The Path to Rome* (1902), believes the world to be his oyster and finds "peculiar relish in discomfort" (2003, 36–37). Waugh also focused, self-critically, on the potential of travel experience to change his state of mind when he had just left for Ethiopia in October 1930 and writes in his *Diary*, in relation to other passengers on the ship, that "I become slightly hypocritical as soon as I am away from my own background, adopting an unfamiliar manner of speech and code of judgments" (2003, 330). In *Remote People*, much more than in his *Diary*, Waugh makes observations of his changing state of mind during travel, almost as much as he is interested in the behavior and intentions of his fellow travellers. In contrast, he has little to say about the potentiality of actual foreign ways of life or, for instance, what it might feel like to be an Ethiopian. Self-realization and self-estrangement is also a central theme in *Scoop*, which is structured around a series of crisscrossing, mistaken identities and *quid pro quo*: the horticulture writer William Boot is taken for his distant cousin, the fashionable novelist John Courteney Boot, and sent to cover the civil war in Ishmaelia, while John Boot is thought to be William Boot. In the same novel, a character called "Mr Baldwin," who speaks many languages fluently, claims to be able to "dissemble one's nationality" whenever necessary (2000a 174). In another substitution of identity, "Mr Baldwin" takes William Boot's place and writes a news dispatch in Boot's name to satisfy, as he claims, the expectations of the editors at home.

Yet, Waugh also portrays himself as a kind of tourist with a difference. Pleasure cruising, for instance, suggests to him a new system of travel, wholly dedicated to comfort and pleasure, without the haste and other negative aspects of tourism (2003, 38). Waugh's position may be interpreted as an acceptance of what John Urry would call the posttourist version of the tourist gaze, by which he means a playful approval of inauthenticity, and the reproducibility of the travel experience. This involves a way of seeing that regards the institution of tourism as a kind of game with inauthenticity, or series of games that can be played for the sake of personal amusement (Urry 2002, 12).[13]

The provincial garden columnist William Boot in *Scoop*, who enters a "foreign and hostile world" whenever he has to leave his ancestral home (2000a 24), Boot Magna, and who has never been abroad before going to Ishmaelia, is the converse of all the hypocritical travellers, travel snobs and men of the world, whom Waugh portrays in his travel writing. In contrast, the

---

13. Waugh also describes his position vis-à-vis tourism in the article "The Tourist's Manual," published in *Vogue*, 1 July 1935 (included in Gallagher 1983, 170–76).

Armenian hotelkeeper in Harar called Bergebedgian, whom Waugh described fondly in *Remote People,* and his less likable and more egotistical double Mr. Krikor Youkoumian in *Black Mischief,* are men of the world that serve Waugh as another point of contrast in his self-portrait, or self-caricature as a traveller. For Waugh, Armenians like Bergebedgian are the only genuine men of the world, highly competent journeymen, who are tolerant, sociable, and have no scruples concerning race, creed, or morals (2003, 258). These enviable Armenians, as Waugh sees them, easily adjust to new situations and simply take advantage of them. Given his exceptional capability and energy to survive under any circumstances, this man of the world is perhaps comparable only to characters in fiction. Having described Bergebedgian at length, Waugh feels that

> However I deplore it, I shall never in actual fact become a "hardboiled man of the world" of the kind I read about in the novels I sometimes obtain at bookstalls for short railway journeys; that I shall always be ill at ease with nine out of every ten people I meet. (2003, 267)

In Waugh's pessimistic view, men like himself, even if they sometimes may wish to picture themselves as having some of the same qualities as Bergebedgian, or envy their friends' cosmopolitanism, hospitality, and adaptability to diverse company, cannot cut themselves off from the most conventional prejudices. Waugh makes a case in his travel writing about the persistence of his identity, such as his unwillingness to fully adapt to the foreign environment. It may be, in fact, that he finds some forms of colonial life to be quite comfortable, particularly in the isolated settler communities in Port Said, Aden, and British Kenya, since these settler communities showcase to him a way of life that is scarcely different from Britain.

It is debatable how sympathetic the narrator is toward the character Youkoumian in *Black Mischief.* Youkoumian, the Armenian jack-of-all-trades in Debra-Dowa and later Basil Seal's financial secretary, puts his wife's life at risk to make a profit and is indifferent to her suffering. Martin Stannard points out in his biography of Waugh that in the novel's manuscript Youkoumian appears for many pages under the name "Youkonmi" (1986, 302), implying thus "conning" and "con man." It is significant that, besides *Black Mischief,* the resourceful Mr. Youkoumian also emerges in "Incident in Azania," where his personality and qualities cast the members of the English community in an ironic light. At one point in the short story, the narrator explains that the Azanian English community accepted Mr. Youkoumian as "a foreigner who so completely fulfilled their ideal of all that a foreigner should be" (Waugh

2000b, 101). In this story, Mr. Youkoumian helps the heroine, Prunella Brooks, and her future husband, in a great swindle, involving a fake kidnapping by a local rogue. Much of the joke is on the Europeans and their prejudices concerning African native men. Prejudice, however, also seems inevitable; it may even be tied, as a specific condition, to the existence of a moral standpoint. In contrast to the prejudiced English in this story, who may still be honest, Youkoumian's loyalty and honesty never seem that certain. Particularly in *Black Mischief*, Youkoumian is caricatured as a man without moral values. His opportunism is contrasted with the stubborn persistence and prejudiced viewpoint of Western identity.

Narrative Techniques in Waugh's African Novels

While Waugh's fiction often complements the descriptions of East Africa in his travel writing, the historical and the autobiographical also penetrate into his novels. As was already mentioned, much of *Black Mischief* and *Scoop* is grounded in actual travel experience. These correspondences include many individuals and events, not just the pseudo-African setting and geography in the novels, thus creating an effect of continuity between fiction, travel writing, and travel experience. The descriptions of individuals such as Bergebedgian in *Remote People* and Youkoumian in *Black Mischief* and "Incident in Azania," appear to be complementary despite the slight differences in the focus of these characters' traits (Bergebedgian's ingenuity versus Youkoumian's opportunism and lack of morality).

However, what interests me specifically in Waugh's use of autobiographical material is that it not only allows us to make comparisons between fiction and travel writing (for instance, it permits us to check how facts are transformed in fiction) but that it may also prompt us to reflect on the generic divide between travel writing and fiction. More difficult considerations about the nature of the correspondences between these texts arise, for instance, when we compare the narrative mode of the novels and the travel-writer's narrative perspective. First of all, the observing point of view of an anonymous narrator in the novels, or what narratology would define as the heterodiegetic narrator, may recall Waugh's perspective as a travelling journalist, at least as far as the descriptive sections in his travel writing are concerned. Second, the descriptive passages in the novels, concerning especially the history of Azania and Ishmaelia, or the description of the present political situation in these imaginary countries, easily calls to mind Waugh's style in travel writing.

Third, the focalization of the novels through the antiheroic main characters Basil Seal and William Boot may also remind one of Waugh's self-caricature and the often embarrassing situations where the travelling writer found himself. Humphrey Carpenter has, in fact, argued that *Remote People* and *Black Mischief* are "evidently meant to be complementary, which is possibly why Waugh omits any sort of 'control' character from the novel, a Paul Pennyfeather or Adam Fenwick-Symes who can view the cavortings of its inmates without being entirely drawn into their lives" (1989, 238). Carpenter, thus, claims that Waugh is by implication present in his third novel as observer and critic, as he is explicitly present in *Remote People* (1989, 238). Carpenter does not specify what he means by a "control" character, but in *Black Mischief* it is at least true that the fictional world is relatively rarely focalized through Basil Seal, whom we may take as the novel's most central character. In fact, since there is no extended internal focalization of any character in the novel, no one can enjoy any extended privileged perspective over the events. I mean by internal focalization the presentation of the perceptual and conceptual position in the story mediated through a character's perspective (Prince 2003, 31–32). What further relativizes the importance of Basil Seal's viewpoint in the novel is that he is introduced relatively late in the text, and becomes a more constant focus of attention only in the second part of the novel, when he acts as the High Commissioner and Controller General of Emperor Seth's modernization project. Carpenter's argument about Basil Seal's potential role as one of the writer's self-portraits, or rather self-caricatures, can be further justified by calling to mind that after *Black Mischief*, Basil Seal becomes a recurrent figure in Waugh's works. He is featured as a central character in the novel *Put Out More Flags* (1942),[14] as a side character in the unfinished novel "Work Suspended" (1942), and the main character in Waugh's final fiction, "Basil Seal Rides Again" (1963).

The similarities in narrative and descriptive techniques across the genres seem to be more superficial than profound, however. Basil Seal's relative distance from the point of perception in the novel creates a stark contrast with the constant presence of the author's mediating consciousness in his travel books. What, furthermore, distinguishes Waugh's fiction from his nonfic-

---

14. Basil Seal's Azanian experience is mentioned in *Put Out More Flags* when his sister Barbara asks: "D'you remember how he took mother's emeralds, the time he went to Azania?" (Waugh 1961, 16), and again when the narrator explains that "from time to time he disappeared from the civilized area and returned with tales to which no one attached much credence—of having worked for the secret police in Bolivia and advised the Emperor of Azania on the modernization of his country" (Waugh 1961, 49). The intrafictional references in Waugh's novels, including recurring characters such as Basil Seal and Lady Metroland, further authenticate a sense of a sovereign fictional reference world.

tion in this respect are the dynamic means of focalization and the use of uninterrupted passages of dialogue that report speech verbatim. Throughout *Black Mischief,* for instance, the narrative follows, from a more or less equal distance, various characters and units of characters, including Basil Seal, the Armenian Krikor Youkoumian, Emperor Seth, General Connolly, who has defeated Prince Seyid's army, as well as the English diplomats at the British Legation (William Bland, Sir Samson Courteney, and Prudence Courteney). The focus falls consistently on these characters' actions and dialogue, and sometimes sense perceptions, rather than the contents or inner movements of their minds. In mediating the dialogue, further, the narrator typically shifts between various windows of focalization, following different characters from one chapter to another, often from one passage to another. If there is thought report, or free indirect discourse, it remains localized and brief. This limitation on direct access to the characters' minds, as well as scarce use of the narrator's direct discourse and description, is a common feature in much of Waugh's fiction (see Palmer 2004, 206). Frequently in *Black Mischief, Scoop,* and in many of Waugh's other novels, the characters' thoughts, feelings, and motivations are presented in and through what they say, in short narratorial descriptions of their manner of speaking and acting, and in their behavior and actions. Exceptions from this general rule often serve a comical purpose. The longest passages in first-person discourse in *Black Mischief,* for instance, involve entries from Dame Mildred Porch's travel diary in the sixth chapter. These citations highlight, also owing to their exceptional narrative mode, the comical aspect of Dame Mildred Porch's and her companion Sarah Tin's sufferings. The two women are leaders of an animal rights organization, the League of Dumb Chums, whose attempt to introduce the idea of compassion for animals is seriously misunderstood throughout their visit in Azania. Due to problems in translation, it is understood among the Azanians that the two women wish to educate Africans about modern methods of cruelty to animals.

We know from various extratextual sources, paratexts and the marketing of *Black Mischief* and *Scoop* that they are indeed meant to be read as novels, despite their thick layers of autobiographical materials and their perspectival techniques that may remind us of descriptive passages in travel writing. Their status as fiction, as novels, is further affirmed by a number of stylistic and narrative features that Waugh does not use in his travel books. The significance of the distinction between the impersonal narrator and the characters, which often allows the narrator an ironic distance towards the characters, clearly sets Waugh's novels apart from his nonfiction.[15] The role and func-

---

15. Waugh realized that he had taken his poetic license too much for granted, however.

tion of narratorial mediation, and the narrator's changing attitude towards the characters, is an essential part of the novels' meaning, unlike in travel writing. Moreover, much of *Black Mischief* and *Scoop* presents speech verbatim. This device plunges the text and the reader into the here and now of conversation, portraying the individuals who are engaged in conversation and action, in a manner that might pose problems of accuracy to much nonfiction.[16]

In Waugh's fiction and nonfiction alike, and as I have already shown, the recurring themes of spatial and temporal deception, or disorganized world of reference, further contribute to the problem of referentiality. Yet, in the two African novels, the question of spatial and temporal disorganization and deception is not only a thematic emphasis but characterizes the ambivalent ontological status of the fictional world and is, further, related to the formal experiments in the novels. Beyond the confusing maps of Azania and Ishmaelia, which multiply the worlds of reference, also the compositional device of literary montage contributes to a similar effect. For instance, in the beginning of the third chapter of *Black Mischief*, the cut up fragments of "direct" conversation by various Londoners, who are glancing through their evening papers in different places, and who are unimpressed by reports about the battle of Ukaka in Azania, create an illusion of various simultaneous spaces and situations. The juxtaposed fragments of conversations suggest a many-voiced, but unanimous world of discourse that exists somewhere at the back of the events described in the novel. There is no scenic description and most of the voices are not identifiable:

Namely, the satire of the European population and the Ethiopian regime in this novel, together with Waugh's known pro-Italian sentiments, had created a bad reputation for the writer in Addis Ababa by the time he returned there in 1935. Waugh writes in a letter, dated August 24, 1935 in Addis Ababa, to his future wife Laura Herbert that

> I am universally regarded as an Italian spy. In fact my name is mud all around—with the Legation because of a novel I wrote which they think was about them (it wasnt) [sic] with the Ethiopians because of the *Mail*'s policy, with the other journalists because I'm not really a journalist and it is black leg labour. (1980, 97)

16. The use of these narrative techniques and devices, however, should not to be thought of as determining the text's genre, but rather as cues for interpretation that are dependent on the overall interpretative frame of the text's genre. As Genette has suggested, the "indices" of fiction are not all narratological in nature, but also involve thematic and stylistic conventions, or generic markers such as the use of a certain kind of a beginning and end or a character's name. Perhaps the most stable indices, as Genette implies, are not textual in kind but paratextual, including for instance a book's generic indication (as a "novel," for instance), another writer's authorized preface, a dust jacket definition, a review, or the marketing style for the book (2004, 163–164). *Scoop* has the subtitle "A *Novel* about journalists" (my emphasis).

"It came in a cross-word quite lately. *Independent native principality.* You would have it was Turkey."

"Azania? It sounds like a Cunarder to me."
"But, my dear, surely you remember that *madly* attractive blackamoor at Balliol."

"Run up and see if you can find the atlas, deary. . . . Yes, where it always is, behind the stand in father's study."

"Things look quieter in East Africa. That Azanian business cleared up at last."

"Care to see the evening paper? There's nothing in it." (Waugh 1960, 86–87)

The two-page passage from which this quotation is taken is only one of the several instances of inventive use of dialogue in long uninterrupted passages in Waugh's novels, including the devices of stichomythia (dialogue in alternating lines), innuendo, incomplete sentences, ellipses (see Carens 1966, 5–6), and multiparty talk, in which the representation of the speech of a group foregrounds the sense of fragmentation and chaos (Thomas 2002; 2012, 85–86). Such techniques do not occur in any significant way in Waugh's travel writing, where the writer uses dialogue sparingly, if at all.

In a subchapter to the second book of *Scoop*, in turn, the shifts in perspective, or what I have also called windows of focalization, are given a spatial form as the narrator presents the residents of the Hotel Liberty in their respective rooms in the capital city of Jacksonburg in Ishmaelia. The passage is structured around an effect of simultaneity, a kind of montage of juxtaposed scenes, with different people in different spaces of the hotel, engaged in various activities separately from each other. The patroness of the hotel is reading the Bible and smoking her pipe in the lounge while a complacent British star correspondent is writing a book about English social life in his room, four furious Frenchman are composing a "memorandum of their wrongs" in another room, and in yet another room four European journalists are playing cards (2000a, 79–82). The literary montage suggests that there is an "uneventful" world of many simultaneous but separate realities and activities. In Waugh's travel writing such montages of juxtaposed scenes are not used, even if the relationship between the traveller's subjective perspective, and persona, and the experiences of others in the same spaces of travel is a central concern.

Generic Framing in the Novels

Certain passages in the two novels specifically draw attention to the divide between fiction and nonfiction. Let us focus, for instance, on the satire of Sir Samson Courteney, the Envoy Extraordinary in charge of the British legation in Debra-Dowa in *Black Mischief,* and thought to have been modelled after Sir Sydney Barton, who was the British Minister Extraordinary and Plenipotentiary in Addis Ababa before the Italian invasion. In the beginning of chapter seven, in a rare case of free indirect discourse in the novel, we can read Sir Samson Courteney's inner thoughts quoted in a few sentences. One morning, as it is told, when Sir Samson is in a "mood of high displeasure," having had to host too many visitors at his legation the previous night, we hear his thoughts in direct discourse: "Never known anything like it [. . .] These wretched people don't seem to realize that a legation is a place of business. How can I be expected to get through the day's work, with my whole house overrun with uninvited guests?" (1960, 261). The narrator then relates that

> First there had been the Bishop, who arrived during tea with two breathless curates and an absurd story about another revolution and shooting in the streets. Well, why not? You couldn't expect the calm of *Barchester Towers* in a place like Azania. Missionary work was known to involve some physical work. Nincompoops. (1960, 261)

The use of free indirect discourse—the citation of Sir Samson Courteney's words ("absurd," "Nincompoops") and question ("Well, why not?") inside the narrator's discourse—foregrounds the envoy's personality and way of thinking, revealing his self-importance. At the same time, the question over the fictional world of the novel is inherent in this passage by way of Sir Samson's reference to Anthony Trollope's *Barchester Towers* (1857). The mention of the calm of the world of *Barchester Towers* adds to the satire of the colonials and the diplomats, who have created a form of traditional British upper class life style in the colonies, gardening and tea parties, listening to gramophone records and playing bridge, bagatelle, and croquet. Sir Samson ridicules here one of his visitors, the Anglican Bishop Goodchild, for mixing African reality with the supposed calm of home, for trying to find the peacefulness of *Barchester Towers* in Azania. Yet, at the same time, Sir Samson himself is one of the narrator's targets of satire.

The Trollope reference opens up the question of correspondences between the two fictions of Azania and Barsetshire. Azania, just like Trollope's Barsetshire and the fictitious town of Barchester, is another version of a make-believe microcosm. However, Sir Samson's reference to the calm of *Barchester Towers* is somewhat misleading, considering that *Barchester Towers* is a novel about many intrigues, including a vicious battle for the position of Bishop of Barchester with the added issues of who should take over Hiram's Hospital and who will marry Eleanor Harding. Unless we limit ourselves to thinking that at the end of Trollope's novel life in the cathedral city of Barchester returns to its quiet ways, or that the fictional county of Barsetshire represents British "calm" in comparison to a (marginal) African country in a state of civil war, the peacefulness of *Barchester Towers* is a misguided notion. Much of the comic effect in *Black Mischief* is based on the stubborn refusal of the people at the British legation, as implied in Sir Samson's comments, to adapt to their surroundings. The satire of the British is contrasted and further amplified by the satire of the Azanian Emperor's refusal to accept reality, that is, his futile attempt at changing his surroundings according to misconceived ideals. Dame Mildred and Miss Tin's ludicrous campaign against the Azanians' cruelty to animals is similarly guided by ideals that are foreign and unreal to the local culture. The conservative British imaginary projections are no less comical and tragic than those of the ridiculed social reformers in the novel, but the author's sympathies may lie with the former. This becomes apparent, in particular, when we read Waugh's fiction and travel writing side by side.[17]

In addition to its ironic potential, the Trollope reference activates a kind of multireferential process of signification in the author's oeuvre. In his travel books, specifically in *Remote People,* Waugh uses "Barsetshire" as a metaphor for a certain national temperament of the white colonial settlers, a type of British mentality that persists in spite of time and, seemingly, change of place. When defending British imperialism in Kenya, Waugh points out the settlers' attempt "to re-create Barsetshire on the equator" that some might regard as Quixotic (2003, 324). These settlers have re-created, quite out of tune with their time and place, a comfortable version of traditional English lifestyle, squirearchy, and society in the African colony. Their only weakness may be a Quixotic temperament: to be foolishly impractical and old-fashioned, and to believe too much in the power of imaginary projection. They are not "pirates or landgrabbers" as their critics have claimed, but "perfectly normal, respectable Englishmen" (2003, 324). In Waugh's travel writing, therefore, the Barsetshire metaphor indicates a certain traditional mindset and colonial version of

---

17. See also Thomas who argues cogently, in her analysis of multiparty talk in *Black Mischief,* that "Waugh seems to delight in the dogged determination of the Legation members to pursue their own pleasures and in their total refusal to adapt to their surroundings" (2002, 668).

a mentality that projects traditional and in some ideal and fictional spaces in equatorial Africa and, in Waugh's opinion, succeeds in living out these projections. At the same time, this mentality is characterized by an ambiguous combination of fear of the primitive, or chaos, and anarchy (and sometimes delight in chaos), and a sense of superiority.

Later in *Remote People*, Waugh's Barsetshire metaphor reemerges as part of a discussion on racial fear. The travelling Northern races, Waugh believes, as they are unaccustomed to the reality of race antagonism, have an inborn fear of "domination or infection by a coloured race" (2003, 329). This fear, Waugh argues, is irrational, but also basically understandable given the multicultural complexities of East Africa. The issue of race becomes also evident when the writer once again refers to the specific temperament of the "equatorial Barsetshire" (2003, 330) and suggests, and not only jokingly, that "it is just worth considering the possibility that there may be something valuable behind the indefensible and inexplicable assumption of superiority by the Anglo-Saxon race" (2003, 330). As Waugh's biographer, Martin Stannard, has pointed out, there is little doubt that Waugh shared this assumption (1986, 263)

Still another way in which Waugh's two African novels draw attention to their genre and generic framing is the parody of journalistic practices. Just one of the many instances of such parody in *Scoop* is the moment near the end of the novel where the main character, the gardening columnist William Boot, returns home to Britain from Ishmaelia. While travelling through France in a train, Boot finds a copy of the *Beast*, the newspaper that had employed him in Ishmaelia, and, to his surprise, in this paper a framed notice on the front page promising an in-depth article by himself the next day. Boot has not heard about the arrangement. The story of the following day will be told, as the notice claims, in Boot's own personal way, revealing the "inner story" of the reporter's experience:

BOOT IS BACK
The man who made journalistic history, Boot of the *Beast*, will tomorrow tell in his own inimitable way the inner story of his meteoric leap to fame. How does it feel to tell the truth to two million registered readers? How does it feel to have risen in a single week to the highest pinnacle of fame? Boot will tell you. (Waugh 2000a, 185)

The article in question, which Boot also finds on his way through Dover, is authenticated with his photo and a facsimile of his signature. The text is written, as promised, in first-person discourse. Thus, in direct violation of the principles of journalism, the editors of his newspaper had invented a form of direct discourse and concealed it as authentic first-person (nonfiction) discourse. For the readers of this fictional world, in contrast, the story is true and genuine since it has been framed as such and they have no reason to believe that the frame is a fabrication. The ultimate fabrication, the invention of the author's inner self, stands as another proof for the story's veracity. What matters to the press, therefore, is to create an impression of the overall interpretative frame of the text's genre, its global nonfictional frame of enunciation—since readers are likely to appreciate and value the impression of accuracy in description and the witness perspective in itself—not the reliability of facts.

The "Boot is Back" incident dramatizes Waugh's criticism of journalistic practices in *Remote People* and *Waugh in Abyssinia*. In his travel writing, Waugh points out that the historical interest of news does not depend on the reality of the events, but on the framing of something, such as the coronation of an African emperor, *as* news and as historically important. Waugh points out in *Remote People* that events in newspapers "become amusing and thrilling just in so far as they are given credence as historical facts" and delight the readers with "unexpected byways of life" (2003, 219). If these events or byways of life, Waugh believes, were offered to the readers as fiction, they would become utterly insignificant and uninteresting (ibid.). Waugh thus stresses the importance of generic expectations: when something is presented and read as news it is given a value and credence as an interesting event at the same time. It is here that Waugh also makes one of his most direct statements about the distinction between fiction and nonfiction, or what he calls the "great gulf" between the novelist and the journalist:

> The value of a novel depends on the standards each book evolves for itself; incidents which have no value as news are given any degree of importance according to their place in the book's structure and their relation to other incidents in the composition, just as subdued colours attain great intensity in certain pictures. (2003, 219)

The value of the novel, as Waugh sees it, relies on the standards of composition that govern the whole narrative. In other words, the events of a novel have a compositional function as parts of a whole and, thus, reflect the way in which a fictional narrative—but possibly also other types of narratives in contrast to mere news items—is conventionally read, that is, as a meaningful composition. The stress is again on the overall structure and effect of the narrative, not its potential reference to actual reality.

Conclusion:
Imaginary Ethiopia and Imperialist Ideology

Reading Waugh's African fiction and travel writing side by side prompts questions about the differences, similarities, and possible continuity across the genres. Why, for instance, are certain real spaces in the author's travel writing characterized by fictional worlds and characters? How, further, does the postulation of referentiality work differently in travel writing and how does it affect the reading of a text? And in what sense may fictional worlds be a model for world construction in travel writing?

The similarities between Waugh's fiction and nonfiction include, as I have shown above, an ironic narrative voice, the pseudo-objective perspective of description, and the effect of multiple realities, that is, the effect of constructing possible worlds of different referential status superimposed on each other. With regard to Waugh's African travel books, especially *Remote People* stages an epistemological spectacle where the traveller, perhaps too constrained by rules of authentication, is at pains to understand the world around him. Much of the comic predicament in this travel book is built on the insight that in order to represent facts and historical events one has to pass through many interpretive filters, not only the traveller's personalized, and in many ways openly prejudiced viewpoint, but the social space of interpretation and representation on which the individual experience depends to a large extent.

Ethiopia, and to a lesser extent Zanzibar and Kenya, were for Waugh a composite reality, consisting of diverse elements, including various layers of fabrication. The unexpected and the surprising that attracted Waugh in Eastern Africa relates to the potentiality in certain fictional worlds and persisting fictions, like *Alice in Wonderland* or *Barchester Towers*, which have the capacity to provide the experience with ever new meanings. Due to its spectacular heterogeneity and fantastic features, "Abyssinia" is a festive body for Waugh, but the charm that it holds, as I have argued above, does not derive from any notion of the premodern, "primitive" or authentic exotic.[18]

The fictional worlds of Azania and Ishmaelia, by way of their various points of contact with other fictional spaces, but also with the real Ethiopia, create the effect of many superimposed worlds. This potentiality in fiction is reflected in the potentiality of the real world to create strange and incongruous cultural blends. We can thus perceive in Waugh's fictional depiction of East Africa a kind of heteronomy of imaginary relays, including also

---

18. However, Waugh's emphasis on the geographical plurality of location in his descriptions of Ethiopia, Azania, and Ishmaelia is intimately related to traditional European representations of Ethiopia, at least since medieval times (see Campbell 2009).

the stacking of cliché images, such as the dark humor stemming from cannibalism at the end of *Black Mischief* where Basil Seal unknowingly eats his sweetheart at a cannibal feast. In *Scoop,* similarly, the narrator exploits the stereotype of cannibalistic Africans when describing the history and political situation of Ishmaelia, as he explains that none of the first European visitors ever returned from this land:

> They were eaten, every one of them; some raw, others stewed and seasoned—according to local usage and the calendar (for the better sort of Ishmaelites have been Christians for many centuries and will not publicly eat human flesh, uncooked, in Lent, without special and costly dispensation from their bishop). (2000a, 74)

While the cliché image of African cannibals, and colonial Africa as the white man's grave, is exaggerated beyond any exotic appeal, and the joke is on the travel snob Basil Seal, who unknowingly becomes involved in eating human flesh, the cliché images are at the same time affirmed as part of this absurd world where Christianity does not necessarily exclude cannibalism.

In contrast to his ambivalent and later hostile attitude toward independent Ethiopia, Waugh's clearly positive experience in colonial Kenya, as outlined in the end of *Remote People,* is based on the writer's impression of the seemingly peaceful coexistence between the coloniser and the colonized, and the comfortable isolation of the former from the latter. More precisely, in the Kenyan section of the book, Waugh's sympathy is with the permanent European population in the area, not with the officials or commercial agents or the liberal "African Nationalists" who seek to defend the Africans' right to their land. What seems particularly appealing to Waugh in this colonial society, as in the society of pleasure cruisers (portrayed in *Labels*), the businessmen in Port Said in Egypt, or the English bachelor community of the Aden protectorate, is the persistence of their ways of life and English traditions, in comfortable isolation also from modern Europe. Members of these communities, moreover, lack any compulsion to understand authentic local experience—an attitude that for Waugh stands for a realistic worldview. Waugh's visit to the Kenyan colony offered him a true respite both from the modern world that he rejected and the confusion of Ethiopia.

Waugh's notion of the strange and incongruous in Ethiopia was far removed from any notion of the authentic exotic. This is in line with the anti-exotic emphasis in his worldview. Waugh had ridiculed the Westerners' search for the exotic other already in the Egyptian section of *Labels,* where he explained that he envied the agreeable life and good fellowship of the colonial businessmen and officials in Port Said, since there was "no nonsense of tropical romance; no indomitable jungle, no contact with raw nature, no malaria, delirium tremens, or 'mammy-palaver'; no one showed the smallest inclination to 'go native'" (2003, 64).

In *Waugh in Abyssinia*, Waugh continues the same mockery of the "extreme lovers of the picturesque" (2003, 573), who desired to find an unspoiled African Ethiopia. Just that this time it was charged with political and ideological meaning, Waugh siding strongly with Mussolini and the Italian intervention. He also ridiculed what he saw as sentimentalizing comparisons that were made by the "apologists" of Haile Selassie's regime between the Ethiopian monarchy and culture and some romanticized idea of medieval Europe (2003, 641–42). The same wish to downplay Ethiopian culture and history is prominent in Waugh's other pro-Italian writings at the time.[19] For instance, in an article entitled "We Can Applaud Italy" in the *Evening Standard* in February 1935, Waugh tried to question Haile Selassie's historical right to govern the country (portraying the Ethiopian Emperor as another coloniser with no particular rights to the country), emphasized the barbarism of his rule, and again mocked what he saw as the sentimentalist views held by the Emperor's supporters in Europe. The Ethiopian strangeness and the incongruity that Waugh construed and tried to capture more open-mindedly in *Remote People* had then become a negative value or another reason for a European intervention.

In *Waugh in Abyssinia*, Waugh emphasized less the sense of the absurd in Ethiopian society and culture and, instead, focused on the condescending idea of an empty culture that could, and should, be replaced by a new civilization.[20] Waugh saw that Ethiopian culture lacked any true content, "aesthetic stimu-

---

19. It is also worth remembering that the *Daily Mail* for which Waugh covered the Italian-Abyssinian war, was one of the few British newspapers that were sympathetic to the Fascist cause.

20. The difference concerning the importance of politics and ideology between the two travel books is of degree, not kind. At the end of *Remote People,* Waugh is unambiguous in his defence of British imperialism in Kenya against its detractors, as he claims,

> I am concerned in this book with first-hand impressions, and wish to avoid, as far as possible, raising issues which it is not in my scope to discuss at length, but personal experiences are dependent on general conditions and I cannot hope to make my emotions about Kenya intelligible unless I devote a few sentences to dissipating some of the humbug which has grown about it. (2003, 320)

Waugh critiques, for instance, Mr William Macgregor Ross's *Kenya from Within* which, he feels, inconsistently portrays settlers as "a gang of rapacious adventurers" (2003, 320). Waugh's belief in the benefits of colonialism is also reflected in the end of *Black Mischief* where, after the death of all Azanian competing emperors, the country is mandated by the League of Nations as a joint protectorate between England and France.

lus," or artistic significance, and that for this reason, it should be controlled by a more advanced, that is, Roman/Italian/Catholic nation.[21] Waugh also tried to justify his support for the Italian intervention by referring to what he saw as the stagnation of Addis Ababa and Ethiopia, that is, his impression of the lack of improvements between 1930 and 1935. The author claimed that the Ethiopians "had nothing to give their subject peoples, nothing to teach them" (2003, 569) and that "It was extraordinary to find a people with an ancient and continuous habit of life who had produced so little," and, further, that "They build nothing; they made no gardens; they could not dance" (2003, 593). The notion of an empty and historyless culture, in association with the writer's racist views of an "inferior race" (2003, 574), was yet another justification for the Italian intervention. Towards the end of *Waugh in Abyssinia*, Waugh, unabashedly, celebrates the Italian "expansion of a race," in contrast to English colonialism that he thinks favors the expansion of the ruling class and capitalism. He refers to the establishment "of new pastures and cities" in a barren land, comparable only to the history of American settlements (2003, 709–710), and glorifies the Italians' "inestimable gifts of fine workmanship and clear judgement" (2003, 712). Waugh's earlier observations of cultural incongruity and strange blends are thus associated with a lack of culture and history and given a much more disconcerting ideological meaning than before.

We can always decide to read Waugh's African fictions, and their satire that combines many different targets of ridicule, against the writer's outspoken imperialist ideology in his travel writing, especially in *Waugh in Abyssinia*. This kind of ideological self-transgression is still another way that travel fiction can inform travel fact. However, it is also quite plausible to read the other way around, so that the author's open imperialist ideology in his travel writing informs the interpretation of his African novels (if we are interested in determining, for instance, the most salient values and beliefs to which the novels and their author respond). In other words, Waugh's travel writing can also be taken as an interpretive frame that guides our understanding of his novelistic satire and polyphony. This option, then, gives the issue of shared elements in Waugh's African fiction and nonfiction a different context, raising the difficult question of how his African novels relate to the larger political and colonial narrative—the legitimation of colonial rule and economic exploitation—with which the author so clearly aligns himself in his nonfiction. The two options seem to suggest quite incompatible results. On the one

---

21. Waugh's points of comparison are also Arabic or other African cultures such as "the gracious, intricate art of Morocco or the splendour of Benin" or "the dark, instinctive art of the negro" that, for centuries, had "offered Europe successive waves of aesthetic stimulus" (2003, 593).

hand, the reader can decide that the (implied) author of the novels is more uncertain and possibly more democratic—in the sense of entertaining and perhaps even embracing a multitude of voices and viewpoints on issues relating to race, colonialism, and so on—than the author of the travel narratives. On the other hand, we can argue that not all targets of satire and ridicule in the novels are equal. Furthermore, we can surmise that the kind of audience for whom Waugh wrote the novels was aware of the author's stance on colonialism, as outlined in his travel books that were published before the novels, and possibly shared this stance and, subsequently, read or was even expected to read the satiric novels in this light. I do not seek to privilege or exclude one or the other interpretive alternative, but want to underscore that the study of the interplay between fiction and nonfiction can, as Waugh's case makes particularly evident, require us to consider the ideological implications of how that interplay is understood.

A Critique of the African Picturesque in Georges Simenon's Travel Reportages and Novels

IN THE SUMMER of 1932, Georges Simenon (1903–1989) departed for Africa with his wife Tigy and spent four months travelling through Egypt, Sudan, the Belgian Congo, Congo-Brazzaville, Gabon, and Guinea. The prolific young author, who had recently become famous with his Maigret detective series, was able to finance part of the journey by writing travel reportages for magazines. His main assignment was a series of articles for the photo-weekly *Voilà*, entitled "L'heure du nègre" (1932); it was published in six instalments right after the journey and accompanied by photographs taken by the author himself.[1] He also wrote a travel essay entitled "L'Afrique qu'on dit mystérieuse" (1933), which was published in the short-lived magazine *Police et Reportage* under the pseudonym Georges Caraman. Later Simenon returned to his West African travel experiences on various occasions. In his fiction, he used the spaces of his journey as settings in a series of three novels, *Le Coup de lune* (*Tropic Moon*, 1933), *45° à l'ombre* (*Aboard the Aquitaine*, 1936) and *Le Blanc à lunettes* (*Talatala*, 1937) as well as in some short stories. The novels have been published together in English as *African Trio* (1979).[2] Later, Simenon

---

1. The *Voilà* reportages were published from October 6 to November 12 of the same year.
2. Simenon's African novels are often classified together with the author's other fictions in the category of "exotic novels" or "romans du monde" that he published in the 1930s and 1940s, and that were inspired by his travels. Simenon's trip around the world that he made between December 1934 to May 1935 from New York through South America and Oceania to

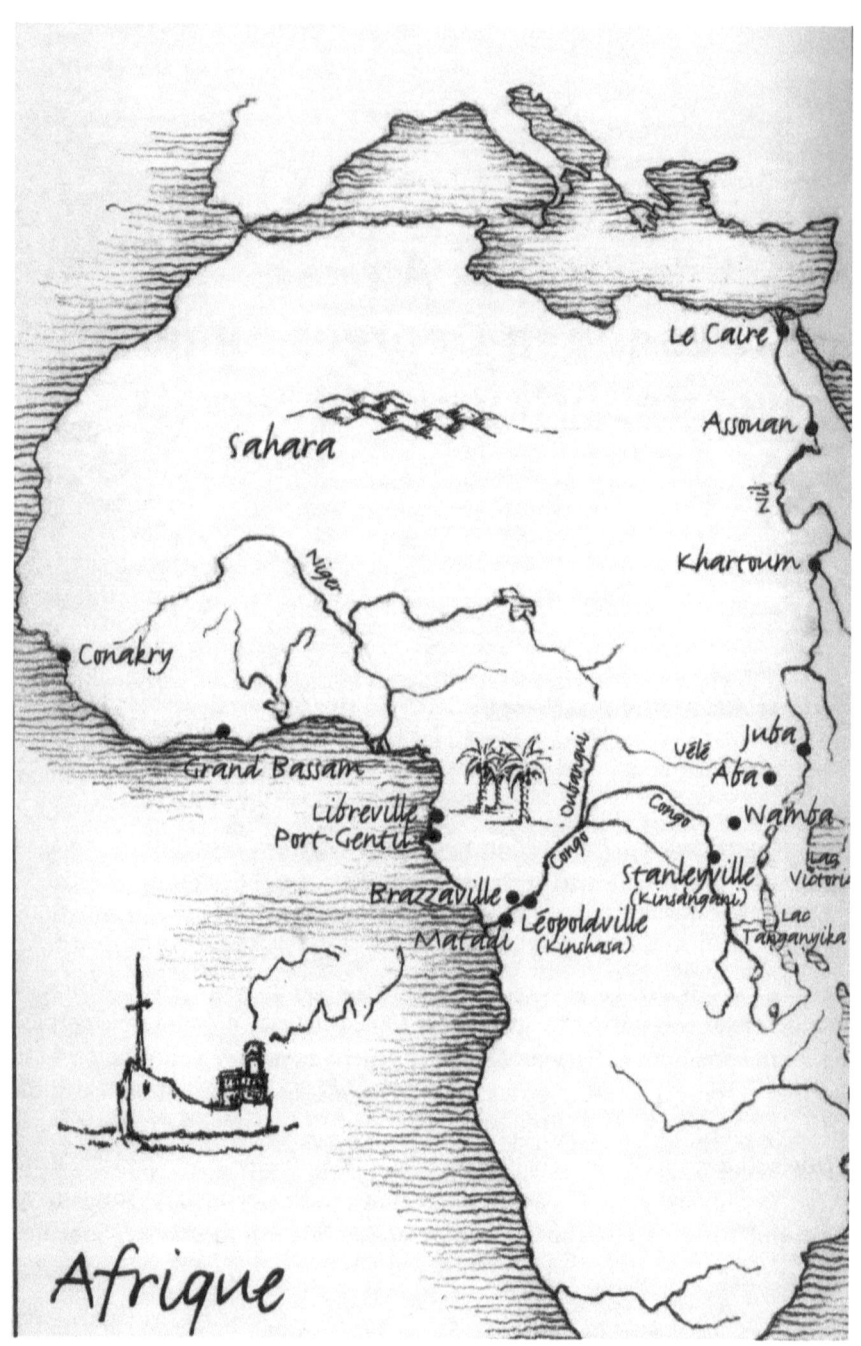

Figure 5. Map of Georges Simenon's travel through Africa in the summer of 1932 (drawn by Julie Scobeltzine) (© John Simenon and Éditions Omnibus).

returned to the travel experience in his memoirs, retelling parts of the journey in *Quand j'étais vieux* (1970) and *Point-virgule* (1979). The spaces in Simenon's three African novels are carefully situated along the writer's African journey as if to underscore the writer's oft-repeated statement that he drew his fiction from memory and experience, not imagination. Simenon claimed that he did not have a good imagination, but instead a good memory, and he claimed to remember places and people that he used as the basis of his fiction particularly well:

> I have no imagination. Everything is taken from life. In the course of my travels, I met so many different types of people, I shared the private lives of so many people, that I need only look for what I need in my memory. Occasionally, I draw my inspiration from an actual occurrence. (1991, 11)[3]

Simenon's claim about not having any imagination should not be taken at face value but, nevertheless, in his African novels, the author drew much from the experiences of his travel. The first and perhaps best known of these fictions, *Le Coup de lune*, is situated in Libreville, the capital of Gabon, which was part of the writer's itinerary in 1932. Many characters and events in the novel are also based on what Simenon saw or heard in Gabon. The novel starts at the harbor of the town, portraying the arrival of the protagonist, a twenty-three-year-old man called Joseph Timar from the French provinces. Unable to find the work that he thought was awaiting him in Libreville, the disillusioned Timar falls in love with Adèle, who is the owner of Hotel Central where he is staying, the only hotel in Libreville and one that Simenon knew himself. Timar then gradually learns that Adèle has had a number of affairs with local men and, moreover, is responsible for the murder of a black servant. Timar also meets a group of white settlers, who have the habit of organizing orgies in the bush with native women. At the end of one such excursion, the men abandon the African women in the forest without transportation.

Le Blanc à lunettes is similarly situated along the author's journey. The novel begins with a description of the main character, Ferdinand Graux, and

---

Egypt and Marseille, repeated the pattern established for the African journey and the following novels set in Africa. The writer made a contract on a series of articles for a weekly illustrated journal (*Marianne*) for a flat fee, publishing articles also in *Paris-Soir*, and later used various places that he visited in his travels as settings in his fiction, including six novels published between 1935 and 1947: *Quartier négre, Long Cours, Ceux de la soif, Touriste de bananes, L'Aîné des Ferchaux,* and *Le Passager clandestin.*

3. Citation translated by Lucille F. Becker in *Georges Simenon: Maigrets and the Romans Durs* (2007).

his voyage from Marseille, through Alexandria, Cairo, Khartoum, Malakal, and Juba, to his home on the tobacco plantations in the Congo. The main events take place there, in northeastern Belgian Congo, within a hundred kilometres from the town of Niangara. The third novel, *45° à l'ombre*, likewise, uses the places of Simenon's African travels as the background and describes a boat trip from Matadi in the Congo to Bordeaux that the author himself took when he returned from Africa in 1932. Even the stopovers described in the novel correspond with the ports along the author's route: Pointe-Noire in Congo-Brazzaville, Port-Gentil in Gabon (which is also the point of departure in the "L'heure du nègre" reportages), Port-Bouët in Ivory Coast, Tabou in Liberia, and then Dakar and Tenerife.

Simenon's African novels, articles, and reportages are closely related in their themes. One key question in this regard is the relation between real and imaginary (or false) notions of colonial black Africa. Simenon's reportages and novels alike make it evident that Western representations of Africa are often romantic and unrealistic, if not altogether misleading. The most common misconception, as the writer argues in his travel reportages, stem from Western fiction and film, and the government campaigns that promoted colonialism. Furthermore, similar misconceived notions were reflected in European tourism and colonial architecture, particularly in colonial administrative towns such as Khartoum, Juba, Stanleyville, Kinshasa, Libreville, or Matadi, and in the illusions of young colonisers, engineers, and tourists whom the writer had met in the colonies and whom he portrays in his reportages and novels.

In the "L'heure du nègre" reportages, Simenon depicts events and encounters in Libreville, Conakry, and elsewhere in West Africa, and poses questions of the colonial administration and mentality. He also describes his personal views and attitudes vis-à-vis colonial Africa, particularly when he had returned home, for instance explaining that he had departed from Africa hating the continent since he had grown tired of the uncomfortable living conditions in that climate. Back in Europe, however, he was soon consumed with nostalgia for Africa, thinking with respect of the white settlers who had made it in Africa and who preferred, to use Simenon's wording, the rough and remorseless qualities of African life to living in the comforts of Europe. The same qualities that Simenon associates with the settlers also characterize his impression of the "real" black Africans of the forest, "naturally sweet, but cruel," just like nature itself (2001, 415). The notion of "real Africans" is clearly exoticizing. This is perhaps surprising, given Simenon's interest, in his reportages and fictions, to question European notions of the picturesque exotic. However, at the same time, the contradiction is yet another example of the way in which early twentieth-century colonial conceptions and discourses were ambiguous.

The essay "L'Afrique qu'on dit mystérieuse," less directly tied to the events of the author's journey than the *Voilà* reportages, focuses explicitly on the question of misconceived notions of Africa. The essay is also more daring in its criticism of such notions than the *Voilà* reportages. In this essay, Simenon ironically presents the likely forms and trajectory of Western understanding of Africa, from the adventure novels read in childhood, or stories of great expeditions, to fictional films, misinformed journalism, and tourists' and safari hunters' overblown stories of the dangerous and exotic "heart of black Africa." Simenon suggests that these legends and fictions reveal the Europeans' desire to construct an image of sub-Saharan Africa as a mysterious world characterized by dangerous animals, cannibals, fierce Pygmies, wild sacred dances, cruel rituals, and nude black people. Simenon argues, moreover, that with regard to the Negros who are used to living naked, their nudity is only an outer difference that does not distinguish their life from the simple living conditions of the poor in Europe. In other words, the poor Africans' lifestyle is not a form of their alleged primitivity, but perfectly justified by the living conditions:

> Cela n'est pittoresque que de loin et surtout quand on se sert, pour le raconter, de mots exotiques. Sinon, c'est tout simple et cela paraît bientôt naturel, que les gens soient nus. (2001, 428)

> This is not picturesque except from a distance and, above all, when one uses exotic words to describe it. Otherwise, it is all simple and seems natural that people would be naked. (my translation)

In his reportages and novels from the 1930s, Simenon mostly uses the term "nègre" for the Black Africans, but sometimes refers to them as blacks, and refers to Europeans in Africa as whites, or sometimes as colonists ("colons").

In this same passage, Simenon suggests that the experience of the picturesque exotic requires a sense of a privileged and fundamentally misconceived distance from the object of observation. Specifically, Simenon's critique of the picturesque involves the necessity to face the multitude of existing African realities, which, consequently, renders the privileged perspective of distance impossible. Furthermore, the author notes that "unfortunately, it is difficult to talk about the Negros in general, since they are different in each region" ("malheuresement, il est difficile de parler des nègres en général, parce que dans chaque région les nègres sont différents"; 2001, 428), and that Africa is immense ("L'Afrique est immense," 2001, 433), not meaning immense in the sense of mysterious or picturesque, but in terms of sheer geographical space and the great variety of lifestyles. Simenon points out that a true image of Africa is simply inconceivable:

> Un tableau vrai de l'Afrique?
> Je n'y prétends pas. Il y a trop d'Afriques. C'est comme si on disait que l'Europe est un pays plat, sillonné de canaux, planté de moulins à vent, parce qu'on débarque en Hollande.
> L'Afrique est multiple. Les conditions de vie changent du tout au tout quand on franchit seulement vingt kilomètres, pour la raison, par exemple, que la route cesse. (2001, 434)

> A real picture of Africa?
> I do not pretend to give that. There are too many Africas. It is like saying that Europe is a flat country, seamed with canals and dotted with windmills, just because one has landed in Holland.
> Africa is varied. The conditions of life change completely within the space of just twenty kilometres, for instance, after the road ends. (my translation)

There is no one truth about Africa but multiple truths. To speak of what is typical to Africa would be comparable to seeing the whole of "Europe" as equal to some of its parts. The same argument is reiterated in "L'heure du nègre," where Simenon explains that he had to give up the idea of drawing a full picture of Africa since there is an infinite variety of Africas, from the Africa of the colonial officials and timber companies to the Africa of the virgin forest, or the Pygmies (2001, 417).

Furthermore, we may infer from the same passage above that to describe Africa's realities truthfully requires not only precision about the particulars of the given place and culture, but also the ability to relativize one's own perspective. In the summer of 1960, when Simenon was following the struggle for independence in the Belgian Congo, he looked up some photographs from his 1932 journey. The event is described in *Quand j'étais vieux*. Here the author again underscores his lack of interest in the picturesque, and his dislike for the distant viewpoint of the passing tourist. Simenon argues that whenever he lives in a new place, he prefers to see a tree as a tree, regardless of whether it might be a kapok tree, flame tree, or an oak. The point is that the particular is not important at the level of mere description, local color, and the picturesque. Rather, the particular is important in itself, as a sign of unique and manifold reality. Furthermore, Simenon emphasizes in his memoirs the ability, gained during any longer sojourn in one place, to see oneself and one's own world from a distance:

> Le pittoresque n'existe que pour ceux qui passent. Et j'ai le tourisme en horreur.
> Je ne cherchais pas le dépaysement. Au contraire. Je cherchais ce qui, partout, chez l'homme, est semblable, les constantes, dirait un scientifique.
> Je cherchais surtout à voir de loin, d'un point de vue diffèrent, le petit monde ou je vivais, à acquérir des points de comparaison, du recul. (1970, 88)

> The picturesque only exists for those who are passing through. And I loathe tourism.
> I am not looking for a change of scenery. On the contrary, I am looking for that which is similar in people everywhere, or the constants, as a scientist would say.
> In particular, I am looking for ways to see from afar, and from a different vantage point, the little world where I was living, to find points of comparison, from some distance. (my translation)

What is important for Simenon is the similar and constant between the cultures, while he also wishes to find points of intercultural comparison that would allow him to better understand the limits of his own world. Distance from home is more valuable than distance from the foreign culture.

From the notion of a heterogeneous multitude of African cultures follows also the possibility that the Africans may gaze back at the Europeans and their respective cultures, possibly entertaining similarly false notions of the West as the Europeans have of Africa. Simenon stresses the Africans' capacity to create their own meanings out of Western institutions and culture that have been imposed on them. Similarly, the Africans both in Simenon's essays and novels have the capacity to talk and look back, and to use the colonial system for their own purposes, despite the fact that Simenon rarely gives voice to Africans (real people or characters in fiction).[4]

---

4. Fraiture (2007, 206) draws our attention to the way in which Simenon's novelistic trilogy set in Africa marks an important passage away from the author's series of novels in the late 1920s that sought to affirm the superiority of the white race and the French nation.

The Archaic Africa

Yet another thematic connection between Simeonon's travel reportages, essays and fictions is the notion of the Archaic Africa, a generalization that escapes the author's outspoken emphasis on the importance of the particular and his critique of the picturesque exotic. What is important from our perspective is also that Simenon associates the notion of the archaic world with the experience of reality. The archaic, in some ways, guarantees the actuality of the real.

Common in both Simenon's African fiction and nonfiction are certain emotional and mental states, forms of sadness (*tristesse*), fatigue, indifference, and madness that evoke for the writer the sense of the ancient Africa. We can see this, for instance, in that the qualities of African climate and landscape, connoting the ancient life forms, have the capacity to become mental states. Simenon argues in "L'heure du nègre" that it is not the other men, who make people commit crimes against each other in the African colonies, but Africa itself ("Ce ne sont pas les hommes qui empoisonnent. C'est l'Afrique!"; 2001, 404). Africa has this "poisonous" effect on people, regardless of their culture and skin color. In these reportages, thus, Africa occasionally becomes an agent, or a name for a kind of remorseless natural force, which may act upon people in unforeseen ways and bring about unprecedented changes in their behavior. This may be caused by the power of the sun, the heat, the moisture, or what Simenon calls the treacherous sweatiness (*moiteurs perfides*), and the monotony and immensity of the landscape. These weapons of African nature, Simenon claims, are also responsible for train line construction deaths in Western Africa, not the whites, the Africans, or the Chinese (2001, 396).

The African indifference and carelessness, or weariness (*lassitude*), and the white settlers' disillusionment, easily deteriorating health, and haunting colonial madness, are recurrent themes in Simenon's travel reportages and fiction alike. These themes are often closely associated with the idea of a forgotten archaic past. While Simenon rejects the African exoticism that is put forward in adventure novels and elsewhere in popular culture or the colonialist rhetoric (the so-called mysteriousness to which the title refers), he retains the mystery of the origins of human culture in a new belated form of exoticism. This means the sense of being the last witness to the archaic age:

> [...] le dernier témoin d'un autre âge que nous avons déjà oublié, un âge où les hommes vivaient sur la terre comme des poux sur la tête d'un clochard, sans s'inquiéter d'autre chose. (2001, 435–436)

[. . .] the last witness of an age that we have already forgotten, an age when the men lived on the land just like the lice in a tramp's hair, without any worries. (my translation)

Just like the lice in a tramp's hair that Simenon imagines here, living simply within the bounds of their own very small world, the Africans' childlike laughter or a sudden fit of anger—to which Simenon refers in the next passage—reveals to the author momentary glimpses of our forgotten origins. Another name given to this sense of the archaic African life in "L'heure du nègre" is the Negro truth: "la vérité, la seule, c'est la vérité nègre" (2001, 412). The Negro truth implies to Simenon that behind the colonial facade of Western beliefs and values, clothing, architecture, technology, and education, there lies the unchanged African setting and the persistent traditional beliefs, a primitive hut made of cut braches, a fire by this hut, and glistening bodies ("le décor africain tel qu'il est resté à travers les siècles: une hutte de branchages, un feu, des corps luisants"; 2001, 412). The striking persistence of this lifestyle motivates Simenon to portray colonial administration and its civilizing mission as a kind of make-believe: Western presence in Africa is not only revealed to be falsely modern and shallow, but also artificially superimposed on a more lasting culture. This falsehood is further confirmed by another form of illusion that interests Simenon in the reportages and that he portrays in the court scene in *Le Coup de lune:* the Africans' penchant for fabrications within the institutions of the colonial rule. Similarly, in the essay "L'heure du nègre," Simenon claims that most of the affairs that the Africans bring to the colonial court are "purely fictional" (2001, 391), concerning endless family disputes of dowry, cheating, cuckoldry, or petty thefts, and intended in part to ridicule the whites and their court.

There is a tendency in both Simenon's fiction and nonfiction also to identify the black Africans, and sometimes also the white settlers, with African nature through their imagined common characteristics. Such characteristics include, for instance, the above-mentioned archaic qualities, including perseverance and spontaneity, cruelty and indifference. It is also indicative of the author's tendency to anthropomorphize African space and nature so that the Africans' ability to talk back belongs both to geographical Africa, or nature, and the people. In "L'heure du nègre," it is Africa in both of these senses of the term that rejects Europe, its values, ideologies and institutions, and does so in a manner that is likely to shock the European listener: "Yes, Africa says shit to us, and right it is" ("Oui! L'Afrique nous dit merde et c'est bien fait"; 2001, 419). This is the last sentence in the *Voilà* reportages and one that Simenon recalls in his memoirs involving the events of 1960, when he was following the Congo's struggle for independence.[5] Yet, it is also important to note that the line was originally a quotation from a skeptical older white settler, not from a black African. The speaker, whom Simenon describes in the reportage as an old white man, who has become "uncivilized" ("un vieux blanc décivilisé"; 2001, 419), spoke to Simenon, among other things, of the Africans' long memory concerning the atrocities committed against them. He, further, evoked the prospect of their likely rebellion, and used the expression as if he were talking of the whole of Africa, not just one place or country.

It must be emphasized, however, that when Simenon refers to the supposedly eternal forces of African nature and lifestyle he does not ever seem to suggest that a Westerner like him could fully escape modernity and to "go native," or attain a more authentic state of self through the African experience. At most, Africa may enable the Western traveller to reflect on what the modern society has forgotten and perhaps minimize the illusions that characterize the civilizing mission and the colonial government. As to the failures and fabrications of the colonial rule, Simenon (in the 1930s) is unable or unwilling to envision any alternatives.

The kinds of problems concerning truthful representation that Simenon raised in the essay "L'Afrique qu'on dit mystèrieuse" and "L'heure du nègre" reportages—the Western misconceived notions of black Africa, the multiple African realities, the relativizing but also haunting quality of the reversed gaze, and the notion of archaic Africa—are investigated by means of fiction in his African novels. In what comes next, I will turn my attention to the ways in which Simenon's novels probe the relation between real circumstances and misconceived notions of Africa and do it similarly to or differently from his travel writing. The question, therefore, is: How do Simenon's African novels present and undermine the notion of African picturesque exotic? Before this question can be properly answered, however, we must consider the narrative situation in these novels, particularly pertaining to the changing distance between the narrator and the characters. Specifically, all general meanings concerning Africa that may be associated with these novels must take into consideration the relation between the narrator and the characters. For instance, what may be seen as real, imaginary, or false from some character's perspective, or what some character openly voices as the truth or falsehood, can be something quite different for another character, let alone for the narrator. Finally, I will return to Simenon's African reportages and

---

5. In the summer of 1960, colonial rule collapsed in the Congo and French Equatorial Africa; both republics soon became fully independent.

ask how fiction is implied in this nonfiction beyond the shared themes and spaces of their description. How does Simenon's nonfiction borrow from his fiction and how does it acknowledge or not acknowledge the borrowing?

Narrative Voice in the African Novels

The narrators in Simenon's African fiction are heterodiegetic, meaning that they narrate in third-person and do not participate in the events of the fictional world. Furthermore, they are not personal characters, that is, they cannot be identified as persons. The narrators do, however, comment on the story indirectly by stylistic means and devices, such as word and perspective choice, or shifts and contrasts between different narrative modes, including contrasts between the predominant impersonal narrative voice and the citation of a character's thoughts in the first person through letters and diary entries. Only very rarely do the narrators voice opinions or make remarks directly. When this happens, it can be particularly significant (as I will show briefly).

With regard to the narrative mode in the novels, a key device in all the novels is the combination of internal focalization (the narrative renders the subjective experience and perception of a character) with the occasional brief presentation of the character's thoughts within the narrator's discourse (so-called free indirect discourse). In free indirect discourse, as it is traditionally defined, character's thoughts or speech is presented in his or her own voice without the quotation marks, tag clauses, or a shift into grammatical first-person discourse, but with the narrator's wording and syntax (Abbott 2008, 234; Prince 2003, 34). While indirect report of the characters' thoughts and emotions is the dominant form of presenting consciousness in these novels, accompanied by the direct discourse of dialogue, the intercepting questions and exclamations in free indirect discourse have an important function as well, for instance as a means of manipulating the distance between the narrative voice and the characters' perspective or mind. The typical function of free indirect discourse in these novels, as in much modern literature, is to render the main characters' states of mind, emotions, and perceptions clearer to the reader, and subtly reveal the limitations of the characters' perspectives. But there are other functions for this narrative mode as well, as we will see.

One significant feature in Simenon's use of free indirect discourse is that it rarely stretches beyond a few sentences at a time. This narrative mode is, however, used constantly and systematically with regard to the main characters thus giving the reader a limited and quite controlled access to their minds.

A good example of how the technique may emphasize distance between the narrator's and the protagonist's voices, is the moment in *Le Coup de lune* when Joseph Timar, infatuated with the hotelkeeper's wife Adèle Renaud, tries to imagine Adèle's and her husband Eugène's life when they arrived in Africa many years ago:

> Il pensait surtout à Adèle qui, alors que lui-même avait sept ans, aidait déjà Renaud à racoler des filles pour l'Amérique du Sud. Elle l'avait suivi au Gabon, à une époque où il n'y avait sur la côte que des bicoques de planches! Ils s'étaient enfoncés dans la forêt et, seuls blancs à des journées et des journées de pirogue, ils avaient entrepris de couper du bois et de lui faire descendre la rivière! (2010a, 25)

> But always his thoughts kept harking back to Adèle, who when he was only seven had already been helping Renaud to recruit young women for South America. She had come with him to French Equatorial Africa in the pioneering days, when there were only log cabins along the coast. After days and days of travel in native canoes they had hacked their way through the bush and set about felling timber and rafting it to the coast. (1979a, 132)

The paragraph starts in indirect discourse revealing the contents of Timar's thoughts. The second and the third sentences, subsequently, shift to a more direct mode, the exclamation points, which are missing in the English translation, marking the potential in the words, and their style, as a manifestation of the character's emotional state. The beginning of the next paragraph, then, further confirms that the thoughts do not belong to the narrator, but to the character whose focal point we share (and as we did already prior to this passage). At the same time, the narrator takes ironic distance from these thoughts:

> Pour Timar, cela se traduisait par des images naïves qui mêlaient aux illustrations de Jules Verne des bribes de réalité. Il suivait la longue route de terre rouge qui longe la mer et il voyait les cocotiers se dessiner moitié sur le ciel, moitié sur le gris plomb des flots. (2010a, 25)

> The picture Timar conjured up was a medley of scraps of reality and illustrations to Jules Verne stories. He was walking along the red laterite road that skirted the bay. The palm trees stood out half against the sky and half against the leaden grayness of the sea. (1979a, 132)

The narrator's evaluation of the character's thoughts as naïve at this moment is quite exceptional in Simenon's African novels. Note that the English translation leaves out the adjective "naïves" (in reference to the mental images that Timar had conjured up) and, furthermore, that the two sentences in the original are broken up into two paragraphs with three sentences. We may, in fact, take the judgement as an important cue for reading that could explain some of the protagonist's consequent reactions and emotions, specifically those concerning his notions and "images of Africa." Timar's naïveté also provides the reader with a context, and an indication of his state of mind which offers us one possible explanation for the gradual disintegration of his mind in the course of the narrative.

The protagonist's misconceived notions of Africa also become apparent in another, brief and subtle application of direct discourse. In the beginning of the fourth chapter, Timar is overtaken by a wave of disorientation as if swept away by a ground swell:

C'est au cimetière que Timar fut envahi à l'improviste par une vague de dépaysement, submergé, imprégné par elle au point d'en rester tout pantelant comme s'il eut perçu le choc d'une lame de fond.

Ce dépaysement, il l'avait cherché dans le pittoresque, dans le panache des cocotiers, la chanson des mots indigènes, le grouillement de corps noirs.

Or, c'était autre chose; la claire et désespérante notion du sens de ces mots:

—Pour quitter la terre d'Afrique, il faut un bateau. Il en passe un tous les mois et il met trois semaines à gagner la France! (2010a, 36)

It was in the graveyard that an immense homesickness descended on Timar, a sense of isolation like a great wave sweeping him off his feet, leaving him faint and gasping. At first he was inclined to attribute it to the strangeness of his surroundings: the feathery, golden-green palms, the surging crowd of blacks, their queer, singsong voices.

Then he realized it was something more; the full meaning of certain words had only just struck home. "There's no escape from Africa except by sea. Only one ship calls each month, and it takes three weeks to reach France." (1979a, 144)

Timar had expected to be disoriented by the African exotic and picturesque but, instead, he becomes conscious of the distance between Libreville and France. Perhaps, since this revelation takes place at a Libreville cemetery, the experience is also associated with the prospect of death and the finality of his separation from home in line with the clichéd image of colonial Africa as the white man's grave. The last two sentences of the passage, which are given to us as a direct quotation, may be something that Timar has heard and that he now remembers. At the same time, the narrator underscores, by giving the quotation, that Timar is thinking of the clear and hopeless meaning of these words (again, the translation is not very accurate). These thoughts may represent something he has heard from Adèle, the men at Adèle's bar, the police officer who checked his papers upon arrival or other settlers, but they are filtered through Timar's consciousness in this scene and for this reason can also be read as something that Timar says or thinks to himself with reflection and concern, realizing their fuller meaning. While there is no sign of the narrator's evaluation of the protagonist's state of mind at this point, it is possible to understand Timar's feeling of immersion, and the unexpected force of the disorienting experience, in light of the narrator's earlier judgement, as another potential reflection of naïveté that, for instance, easily confuses West African reality with illustrations from Jules Verne's novels.

In some important ways, however, the limitations of Timar's mind and perspective, and his sense of the diminishing scope and meaning of France (or Europe), are not unique to him alone. A more general relativization of the European viewpoint becomes evident a few pages later when Timar thinks of the map of France, which had haunted him in his mind in the morning of that day, while looking at the Atlantic Ocean that seemed to him like some flat pond:

> Dehors, dès qu'il revit la mer, plate comme un étang, il retrouva une image qui l'avait hanté le matin, une carte de France, d'une toute petite France assise au bord de l'océan, une carte familière, avec des rivières, des départements dont il connaissait le tracé par cœur, des villes. (2010a, 40)

> The sea was calm as a lake, and as he gazed at it there rose before his eyes a picture that had been haunting him all the morning—or, rather, not a picture but a map: the map of France. A tiny, compact fragment of the continent breasting the Atlantic. How familiar was that map with its towns, rivers, and *départements* whose boundaries he could have reproduced from memory! (1979a, 149)

Seen from this distance and against the flat background of the Atlantic, France appears small and the French settlers as old neighbours from this small country, strangely reunited in Gabon.⁶ Notice that here the translator, unlike in the previous examples, adds an exclamation mark to the last sentence in the quotation and thus gives it an impression of the character's thought. The following exclamation," They were all neighbours!" ("Ils étaient tous voisins!"), is ambivalently positioned between the narrator and the character; it might be possible to attribute these words to both. It also remains ambiguous as to whether the perspective is simply naïve (Timar's confused mind sees the settlers as neighbours in a literal sense) or if it involves a more insightful observation of the implications of the relativizing distance from home, and a process of changing perspectives, which Simenon values in his reportages and memoirs.

In *Le Blanc à lunettes,* free indirect discourse similarly illustrates the protagonist's subjective experience of Africa while shifts between this narrative mode, indirect narratorial report, and dialogue alter the distance between the character and the narrator. However, what makes such shifts in this novel different from those in *Le Coup de lune* is their relation to longer stretches of direct discourse in Ferdinand Graux's diary and letters that are cited in the text from the fourth chapter on. In the novel's beginning, Graux's subjective views of Africa are first revealed directly in conversation with fellow travellers or in free indirect discourse. Upon Graux's return from Europe to his plantation, he sees himself as a villager returning to his true home. Exclamation marks (again missing in the English translation) and italics function once more as markers of the character's diction, thoughts, and subjective feelings:

> Il était chez lui, vraiment, non pas seulement en Afrique, mais dans *son* Afrique! Une Afrique qui ne ressemblait en rien à ces déserts survolés par l'Imperial Airways et qui ne comportait plus d'hôtels ripolinés comme des maisons de santé. (2010b, 21)

> He was really at home here, not merely in Africa, but in *his* Africa. And this Africa of his was very different from the great empty spaces flown over by Imperial Airways. Here were no hotels so white and scrupulously clean as to remind one of hospitals. (1979a, 14)

Graux hands out salt briquettes to the local Africans as, the narrator informs us, one gives candy to children. He meets, by the roadside, Africans whom he

---

6. In another reportage from the same era, "Europe 33" (1933), Simenon refers to "petite Europe" (Simenon 2001, 763).

knows, and also encounters a child that he had taken care of before. The following description of the protagonist's feelings, as he identifies himself as an *African* colonial, creates potential ironic distance between the character and the narrator:

> Il n'était plus Ferdinand Graux, mais Mundele na Talatala, plus sûr de lui que jamais avec ses lunettes, et il accélérait toujours davantage, comme pris de vertige a l'idée de revoir . . .
> Son chez-lui, là-bas, à cent, à soixante, à quarante kilomètres. (2010b, 21)

> No longer Ferdinand Graux, he had become once more Mundele-na-Talatala, bespectacled and self-assured, and he drove faster and faster, thrilled by the joy of nearing home.
> A hundred, sixty, forty kilometers to go . . . . (1979a, 15)

The narratorial distance in the description, and potential irony, remains implied. It is implied, first of all, by the ambiguity in the protagonist's African name, Mundele-na-Talatala, and which means—as has been noted in an earlier conversation between Graux and his fellow travellers—the white man with glasses. This is also an explanation of the novel's title (*Le Blanc à lunettes*). "The white man with the glasses," however, as the reader has also been informed, is not the only nickname Graux has, but the Africans also call him, among themselves, mockingly "the white man who is only a man with his glasses" ("le blanc qui n'est homme qu'avec ses lunettes"). The evolving events, secondly, cast Graux in an ironic light and thus, potentially, recall his second (mocking) African nickname. Graux's affair with Lady Makinson, a diplomat's wife and an adventuress, who has landed at his farm due to a broken propeller on her private airplane, transforms his calm world to the extent that Graux forgets his French fiancée and the development of his plantation.

On his way back to the Congo, Graux had been reading with interest such tedious books as *Statistics for an Economic Survey of the Postwar Decade* ("Statistiques pour servir à l'histoire économique de l'après-guerre") and *Recent Theories of Production and Distribution* ("Réflexions sur l'économie dirigée et sur l'économie en circuit fermé"). Graux's library at the plantation, consisting of books with similar titles, is a reflection of a model colonial settler, who is rational and hard-working but perhaps a bit dull. In the presence of Lady Makinson, Graux finds his whole past life to be unhappy, boring, even disgusting. The excitement and sense of adventure that Graux associates with Lady Makinson are reflected in and accentuated by her choice of reading,

Captain Scott's travels (a likely reference to Robert Falcon Scott's Antarctic expeditions), when she is staying at his farm.

It is then told that Ferdinand Graux has become a stranger to himself in the familiar landscape: "For though at this moment he was walking in familiar surroundings—surroundings that he, to a great extent, had personally created—he felt hopelessly estranged from them, as if some link had snapped between himself and his life's work" (1979a, 45) ("Car voilà qu'il errait dans un paysage familier, un paysage qu'il avait en quelque sorte édifié lui-même et qu'il s'y sentait étranger!"; 2010b, 49). The emotional tie that he had imagined to have been forged between him and his plantation, the environment, and the animals, appears as what it really is: a self-edifying illusion. Again, the exclamation and question marks used in these passages brings us close to the character's mind and emotional state. Graux looks at his favorite hippopotamus, which he has called Potam, in the river and perceives that: "How absurd he has been, idling away whole evenings watching a stupid hippopotamus and making believe they were becoming friends!" (1979a, 45). ("Comment avait-il pu passer des soirées entières à venir regarder un hippopotame et à croire que des liens d'affection se créaient entre eux?"; 2010b, 49). Emilienne had earlier responded in her letter that she was almost jealous of Potam for the way he wrote about the animal.

Both *Le Coup de lune* and *Le Blanc à lunettes* focus, through brief moments of free indirect discourse and accompanying narratorial framing, on the limitations in the protagonists' knowledge, experience, and emotional state, involving their misconceived ideas of African colonial life, or broken expectations. The novel *45° à l'ombre* is different, to a degree, in that the protagonist, Doctor Donadieu, enjoys the privileged position of a more informed perspective. His portrait is also much less ironic. When Donadieu's thoughts punctuate the dialogue in free indirect discourse, they often possess a certain authority, providing the reader with important insight into the events and the other characters' motivations.

Out of the numerous instances of free indirect discourse that include Donadieu's thoughts and speech, let us examine one instance near the beginning of the novel that illustrates the difference. Here the dialogue between Donadieu, the superintendent Neuville, and the ship's main engineer, shifts to Donadieu's mind for a few lines, perhaps just for one short sentence. His thoughts are given in free indirect discourse as he notices the captain and the two lieutenants who, at present, sit in the nearby bar:

Ils étaient assis tous trois à la terrasse du bar, devant des pernods. Donadieu ne les avait pas encore aperçus. Mais ne se ressemblaient-ils pas tous, à tous les voyages? (2010a, 441)

All three happened to be sitting on the bar terrace with glasses of Pernod in front of them. Donadieu had not noticed them before. But didn't everyone look like everyone else on all these trips! (1979a, 236)

It is possible that Donadieu poses the question to himself (the question is transformed into an exclamation in the English translation). The thought is revelatory not only of his experience as a ship's doctor, but also of his ability, of which we will later learn more, to see what is specific in a particular situation. The next paragraph, again in more impersonal narration, gives the reader information about the captain's and the lieutenants' present concerns:

Ils partaient en congé, après trois ans d'Afrique-Equatoriale. Le capitaine, sur sa tunique blanche, portait toutes ses décorations. Il avait l'accent de Bordeaux. Les deux lieutenants n'avaient pas vingt-cinq ans et cherchaient des femmes autour d'eux. (2010a, 441)

They were on furlough after spending three years in Equatorial Africa. The captain was wearing all his medals across the front of his white uniform jacket. He spoke with a Bordeaux accent. The two lieutenants, not yet twenty-five, were staring around looking for women. (1979a, 236)

The observation concerning the Bordeaux accent could belong to Donadieu, but the summary of the captain's and the lieutenants' background is clearly given in indirect discourse that is detached from the character's thoughts. However, it is also quite possible that, even if it is not made explicit in the passage, Donadieu shares the same information as the narrator.

One of Donadieu's traits, which is underscored in the novel and that relates to his particular capacity to know intimate things about other people and figure out what they are thinking, is his compassion for those who are weaker. The frequent references to God in the protagonist's name evoke the same capacity. Donadieu's friend had once told him that "People should call you God the Father!" ("On devrait te surnommer Dieu le Père!"; 2010a, 485). Donadieu, as we are informed, did not find this funny since he recognized in himself the "mania" of being concerned with others, their joys, or catastrophes. His interest in the Huret family, for instance, is also explained through a reference to the connotations of his name, that is, to play God: "Only Donadieu believed he was God the Father" (1979a, 320). ("Il n'y avait que Donadieu à se croire Dieu le Père"; 2010a, 523). The protagonist once introduces himself "Donadieu. As in 'given to God'" (1979a, 291) ("Donadieu. Comme donner à Dieu"; 2010a, 495). Further, it is revealed at the very end of the novel in an impersonal narrative voice that Donadieu lied to Jacques Huret about the severity of his fractured leg since he wanted to continue to play God ("jouer à Dieu le Père"; 2010a, 528).

In his ability to understand the situation of people around him, Donadieu stands out from the other characters. This quality, which also entails the capacity to see the particular in all people, likens him at some level to a narratorial position, or at least makes it difficult for the reader to distinguish between his and the narrator's perspectives and knowledge. Donadieu's interest in the others' physical states or their states of mind is obviously part of his medical profession, but this interest also goes far beyond professional caring. He is, for instance, concerned about Doctor Bassot, who is going to be repatriated because of what is called his derangement of the brain. This concern is partly professional, but Donadieu also entertains the possibility, based on his personal observations and judgement, that Bassot is not as mad as all other people seem to think. As for the complex situation of the members of the Huret family, who are torn by broken illusions of colonial life, financial worries and a very sick child, Donadieu's worries appear profound, specifically when it comes to the father of the family, Jacques Huret. For some reason that he cannot fully explain to himself, Donadieu decides to assist Jacques Huret, despite the suspicions that have been raised about Jacques Huret in the theft of Lachaux's wallet (Lachaux is a rich settler on board the ship). The narrator explains that Donadieu associates with Jacques Huret the same feeling of premonition that he used to have as a child when he felt that someone was haunted by a catastrophe.[7]

In Donadieu's case, thus, and unlike with Timar and Graux, the use of free indirect discourse does not highlight the limitations of the protagonist's mind as much as it foregrounds the capacities of his mind. To some extent also the character's personal history and experience explains why he is capable of having a quite different look on things from the other protagonists in Simenon's African novels: the time spent in the colonies has profoundly changed Donadieu, broken his illusions, but perhaps also given him new insights that Timar and Graux do not have. It is quite possible, furthermore, to associate the Doctor's keen attention to detail, sharp observations, and the

---

7. See Simenon 2010a, 471–72.

flexibility of his mind, to a genius of detection such as that of Simenon's pipe-smoking detective, Commissaire Maigret. These characteristics liken him to the narrator even if there is no full identity between the two.

In all three novels, another important function of free indirect discourse is that it accentuates the effect of realism. André Gide, a longtime correspondent of Simenon's and an admirer and sometimes critic of his work, has made evident this connection. Asserting in his *Journal* that there is a "profound psychological and ethical interest" in all of Simenon's books, Gide explains that:

> Les sujets de Simenon sont souvent d'un intérêt psychologique et éthique profond, mais insuffisamment indiqués, comme s'il ne se rendait pas compte lui-même de leur importance, ou comme s'il s'attendait à être compris à demi-mot. C'est par là qu'il m'attire et me retient. Il écrit pour "le gros public," c'est entendu, mais les délicats et raffinés y trouvent leur compte, dès qu'ils consentent à le prendre au sérieux. Il fait réfléchir; et pour bien peu ce serait le comble de l'art; combien supérieur en ceci à ces romanciers pesants qui ne nous font grâce d'aucun commentaire. Simenon expose un fait particulier, d'intérêt général peut-être; mais se garde de généraliser: c'est affaire au lecteur. (Gide 1954, 321–22)

> Simenon's subjects often have a profound psychological and ethical interest, but insufficiently indicated, as if he were not aware of their importance himself, or as if he expected the reader to catch a hint. This is what attracts and holds me in him. He writes for "the vast public," to be sure, but delicate and refined readers find something for them too as soon as they begin to take him seriously. He makes one reflect; and this is close to being the height of art; how superior he is in this to those heavy novelists who do not spare us a single commentary! Simenon sets forth a particular fact, perhaps of general interest; but he is careful not to generalize; that is up to the reader. (Gide 1951b, 287)

For Gide, the quality in Simenon's work, as in *Le Coup de lune* that Gide claimed was the truest novel about black Africa to date (1979, 116), is the concentration on the particularity of the facts that they describe, the scarcity of direct commentary, and the ability to refrain from generalizations. Even when the particular facts may be generalizable, for instance in references to realities in colonial life in Africa, this is not made explicit.

Simenon's realism of the concrete functions as a kind of antidote to his characters' preconceptions and misconceived notions, including specifically the picturesque and the exotic that shape for instance Timar's experience in colonial Africa. As we have seen, free indirect discourse has an important role in Simenon's African novels in subtly conveying a sense of the particularity of the characters' subjective experience and, consequently, of the interpretation of details, or immersion in the surrounding reality. Appropriately, Jacques Dubois has argued that the observation and tireless search for the detail, and the sense of truth in the instant moment, may take two basic forms in Simenon's realism. These involve interpretation (or interpretive anxiety) and immersion (or adhesion) (2000, 328). First of all, the notion of detail may be a synonym for interpretive anxiety and doubt that is generated by small incidents and particular traces in a layer of banality. Commissaire Maigret is sensitive to details and their particularity, and any suspicious traces and incidents, and he reacts to them as if he were a great collector of the particular (Dubois 2000, 327). From the particular, he infers what may be general, rather than the other way around. Secondly, the notion of detail may have the contrary meaning of immersion when a character, in a tense experience of surrounding reality, abandons himself to the world's indifference and grants the world a kind of floating attention, directed by barely organized impressions, or the world of the others. Donadieu in *45° à l'ombre* incorporates this ambiguity most fully, fluctuating between keen, analytic observations of a scholar-reporter and the self-abandonment and musings of a world-weary drug addict. The sea and the colonial Africa around him, further, connote a particularly tense experience of reality that makes the experience of immersion quite realistic and inviting.

Sometimes it occurs, however, that certain rare objects in Simenon's novels have an overriding symbolic meaning. Ferdinand Graux's eyeglasses function in this way, ambivalently suggesting both his self-certainty and weakness. The glasses are an example of a metonymy, somewhat like Commissaire Maigret's pipe that may be taken as a metonymy for the detective's identity. Beyond identifying the protagonist, Graux's eyeglasses symbolize the man himself and his characteristics, including the most intimate movements of his mind, such as feelings of passion, or shame and insecurity (not wanting to show himself without the glasses). At the end of the novel, when the perspective has shifted to Emilienne, Ferdinand's glasses represent to her the man himself: "it struck her that there was some other change in his appearance; but, until she saw his spectacles on the tablecloth beside his plate, she did not realize why he looked so different" (1979a, 111) ("elle se demanda un instant ce qu'il y avait de changé chez Ferdinand, mais elle comprit, en voyant les lunettes posées sur la nappe, près de son couvert"; 2010b, 109). It is not made explicit to the reader what she has understood, however. It is as if by the mere sight of the glasses she can ascertain the essential, the inner workings of Ferdinand's mind.

Narratives of Gradual Change

Beyond the mediating function of the narrative situation, and the use of free indirect discourse in particular, another important aspect that formally distinguishes Simenon's fiction from his nonfiction is the processual nature of the narrative in the novels, particularly the role given to the gradual change in the protagonist's state of mind and attitude in the course of the narrative. A comparison between Simenon's reportages, essays, and memoirs on the one hand and African fiction on the other allows us to see a significant difference of degree in this respect, that is, the difference between telling stories in nonfiction and developing a character's consciousness and processual experience in the novel.

Nonfiction travelogues certainly may focus on the changes in the traveller's worldview and the perspective, as also occurs in the "L'heure du nègre" reportages. In his travel writing, Simenon frequently refers to his changed perception and mental state, but the novel format allows him to focus on the gradual transformation of a character's mental state. In the novels, the characters' mental and emotional adjustment, changing worldview, and sometimes their mental disintegration, are central elements of the story, and such changes and processes are further emphasized by the means of focalization, including shifts in focalization. For instance, Ferdinand Graux's affair with Lady Makinson takes him through a series of changing mental states and phases of justification and self-definition. The narrator explains, before the affair begins, that any unforeseen event could shatter Graux's peace of mind. The affair with Lady Makinson has just such a shattering effect, perfectly estranging Graux from his former life. When Graux first tries to reflect on his situation more analytically in his journal, he calls it "a moral crisis" and justifies the affair by referring to differences in moral laws and customs among different peoples and cultures. Later, when he realizes that he must give up following Lady Makinson and return to his plantation in the Congo, he sees his sudden passion differently, as a form of self-delusion, blaming his romanticism, and what he calls "the beast within," for what has happened. The affair ends in shameful ridicule: Graux follows Lady Makinson to Istanbul, where she is reunited with her husband and family and no longer wants to have anything to do with him. When Ferdinand returns to his plantation at the end of the novel, his wish to commit himself to his previous life is clearly reflected in his behavior; for instance, he leaves his journal entries on his writing desk on purpose so that Emilienne can understand his regret and learn about the stages he has undergone.

Emilienne, through whom the narrative is focalized upon her arrival in Africa, gradually learns what has happened and what her fiancé has experienced. At the very end of the novel, a final series of shifts between Ferdinand's and Emilienne's perspectives occurs. While it seems that Emilienne now knows the essential facts about Ferdinand's affair and experience, having also observed her fiancé's regret, the novel ends with Emilienne's misguided evaluation of Ferdinand's state of mind, thus possibly pointing to a conflicted future for the two. Here Ferdinand suddenly embraces Emilienne and rests his head on her shoulder after she has asked him whether they should go to the town of Niangara to take care of Georges Bodet's widow, Henriette. Ferdinand, whose glasses have slipped off in the embrace, and who does not want to show his face without them for some reason, says very gravely: "Nous irons à Nyangara . . ." (We will go to Niangara). The seriousness of the reply makes Emilienne laugh: "He said it so gravely that she couldn't help smiling. From his tone one might have thought he was making a profession of faith" (1979a, 116) ("Et il disait cela si gravement qu'elle ne put s'empêcher de rire. On eût pu croire que c'était tout un programme, une profession de foi"; 2010b, 113). Emilienne misreads Ferdinand's mind, however: "And really she did wrong to smile, for that day 'Niangara' meant, above all else, the bearded missionary with the meerschaum" (1979a, 116) ("C'est elle qui avait tort de rire, car, Nyangara, c'était avant tout, ce jour-là, le missionnaire à la pipe!"; 2010b, 113). The reader shares with the narrator the privilege of knowing that this is a misunderstanding and, further, may also realize that the scene, with the fallen glasses, refers ironically to Ferdinand's second African name, Talatala: "the white man who is only a man with his glasses." At the end, the narrative thus moves from Emilienne's subjective perspective to an impersonal viewpoint and a narrative voice that is more informed about Ferdinand's present state of mind and his true intentions in wanting to go to Niangara (to marry Emilienne).

The presentation of gradual changes in the protagonist's mind from various perspectives is similarly crucial in *45° à l'ombre*, where the end of the novel reveals that Donadieu, despite his experience and unique capacities, has not been immune to the "madness" around him. When the boat approaches Tenerife, Donadieu projects his state of mind on the scenery. These sensations are triggered and accentuated by a larger dose of opium. Lying on his bunk, Donadieu perceives himself as being many people at once, living the multiple lives of the whole boat ("Il vivait une autre vie que la sienne. Il vivait dix vies, cent vies, ou plutôt une vie multiple, celle du bateau tour entier"; 2010a, 516). Without rising, he imagines in his mind's eye the Tenerife port and scenery which the liner has entered, attentive to all sounds around him, and thinks of the people who have most often fed his curiosity during the journey: the Bassot, Mme Dassonville, Lachaux, and especially the Hurets. These meditations give him the euphoric feeling of knowing everything and everyone on the boat, even entering the others' minds: "He knew everything! He was incredibly intelligent! For example, he heard the click of the telegraph and knew that the captain was signalling for the ship to be slowed down because he thought he could see the lights of the pilot boat" (1979a, 314). ("Il savait tout! Il avait une intelligence merveilleuse! Il entendait par exemple le déclic du télégraphe, et il savait que c'était le commandant qui ordonnait de ralentir parce qu'il croyait apercevoir les feux de bateau-pilote"; 2010a, 518). As the scene also implies, Donadieu's privileged perspective, like that of Maigret, is only privileged in relation to the other characters. It is never without some potential ambiguity. In Donadieu's case, the irony in the scene is partly due to his drug use, which makes him vulnerable and renders his perceptions potentially unreliable. Further, the sensations of omnipresence in the scene highlight again the ambiguity inscribed in his name: "Donadieu" is a possible reference to self-aggrandizement.

When Donadieu finally gets up and looks out of the porthole, he perceives the scenery in terms of the opposition between African settings and Mediterranean Europe. The Europeanness of the scene is, moreover, associated with the sense of the real:

> Par le hublot, Donadieu apercevait de vrais humains, des gens qui n'étaient ni des nègres, ni des colons, des gens qui habitaient là parce qu'ils y étaient nés et qu'ils y passaient leur vie. (2010a, 520)

> Through the porthole Donadieu saw real human beings, people who were not blacks or colonials, people who lived there because they were born there and were spending their lives there. (1979a, 316)

It is not only that for Donadieu the people in Tenerife have a strong sense of reality and particularity about them, but that he sees, as we are told, real trees, roads and shops and cafés in Tenerife: "This was Tenerife—in other words, this was almost Europe, a mass of colors and sounds reminiscent of Spain or Italy" (1979a, 316). ("C'était Ténériffe, enfin, c'est-à-dire presque l'Europe, un grouillement de couleurs et de sons qui faisaient penser à l'Espagne ou à l'Italie"; 2010a, 520). The reality of the place and the people have to do with their Europeanness, while this quality also confirms, through the opposition between Africa and Europe, that the African colonial reality represents the side of the unreal, the artificial, and, possibly, the undifferentiated. This creates an interesting contrast but also a sense of continuity with the author's travel reportages and essays where Simenon associates the real with the signs of the ancient Africa and the artificial with the colonial presence.

The perceptual position of the scene clearly belongs to Donadieu, but the passage is also given in impersonal, indirect discourse, with very brief lapses in free indirect discourse. If there is a citation of the character's words in the two sentences ("This was Tenerife" and "Donadieu saw real human beings") the narrator's locution remains ambivalent; implied perhaps by the word "enfin" that is not translated into English, if understood as pointing to Donadieu's present thoughts. As to the phrase, "Donadieu saw real human beings," it is even harder to identify the source of the voice. One clear alternative would be to think that the notion of "real people" is the narrator's interpretation of how the protagonist's perception is to be understood, the narrator thus mediating the character's perception. Yet, whether the association between Europeanness and reality is still within the partly delusional sensations that belong to Donadieu, and him only, remains open. The scene portrays Donadieu's capacity for empathy that likens him to a narrator, who can have access to his characters' minds. At the same time, his impression of the Tenerife port appears to be affected by a kind of reversed gaze, representing not only reality to the observer, but also a kind of European picturesque, the port standing for the whole of Europe.

Le Coup de lune, in turn, depicts two interrelated changes in the protagonist Joseph Timar's perception of Africa and Africans. These involve, first of all, the preconceived notion of the African picturesque and, second, of the Africans as part of the same exotic décor, not as real, individual people. Timar's arrival in Gabon and at the scene of the main events, Hotel Central, is conceptually framed by the protagonist's expectation of the picturesque:

> Un bon moment que celui-là, parce qu'il y avait du pittoresque! C'était bien africain! Dans le café, aux murs ornés de masques nègres, où il mettait en marche un phonographe à pavillon tandis que le boy lui versait du whisky. Timar se sentait colon! (2010a, 13)

> How thrilling it had been, this first taste of the tropics, the real thing, an outpost of France placed exactly on the line of the equator! The restaurant, whose walls were hung with African masks, was just as it should be, and as he cranked up a phonograph with a big old-fashioned horn, and the boy handed him his first shot of whisky, Timar felt like a seasoned "coaster"! (1979a, 120)

At first, Timar is, as we are told, "seduced" by the hotel's colonial décor, the Negro masks and other features. The change of his mind in this respect, and the final abandonment of the notion of the African picturesque, is gradual. Here, at the novel's beginning, Timar is the epitome of the kind of hopeful and idealistic newcomer to the colonies, who is ridiculed in Simenon's reportages. Timar wishes to make a fortune, perhaps educate, and "civilize" the Africans, or study everything African, seeking thus, as the young colonial administrators whom Simenon portrays mockingly in "L'heure du nègre," a way to penetrate into the Negro soul ("pénétrer l'âme nègre, le secret de l'Afrique et des rites ancestraux"; 2001, 406).

Simenon associates the sense of the picturesque directly with misconceived notions and naïveté at the beginning of "L'heure du nègre" where he describes a scene at the harbor of Port-Gentil where a group of almost naked black Africans are to be shipped to Libreville as cheap labor. The one hundred or more Africans who were herded there like cattle in the heat of the day, made a scene that, as Simenon claims, one might want to call picturesque. The Africans had worried looks and many of them were wounded. Some of them smoked using tin cans, and none had seen the sea before. Yet, Simenon writes, if this is picturesque, it would make a strange postcard or painting:

> Du pittoresque, n'est-ce pas? Beaucoup de pittoresque, comme on en met dans les livres et même dans les atlas! Pittoresque de l'odeur aussi, âcre, écoeurante! Et de la crasse! Et de la déclaration que me fit un médecin.
>
> « Il y en a quatre-vingt-dix-neuf pour cent de syphilitiques! A l'un il manquait deux doigts de pied, à l'autre, toute une main! » (2001, 380)

> Picturesque, isn't it? So picturesque, just like in the books and even the atlases! Picturesque smells as well, acrid, nauseating! And the filth! And the statement that a doctor made to me.
>
> "Ninety-nine percent of them are syphilitic! One was missing two toes, and another, a whole hand!" (my translation)

If this scene is to be called picturesque, one has to accept, as Simenon suggests, the sharp and nauseating smells, disease, terrible heat, and the exploitation of the people as inseparable elements of the exotic scene. This, however, might make of the picturesque a horrific clichéd image, unacceptable as an aesthetic ideal.

The same dilemma of the temptation of the picturesque is portrayed in various places in Simenon's African fiction. Timar's first attack of unease (*malaise sournois*) occurs on the same night as he arrives at the hotel and tries to come to terms with the strangeness of swarming insects, the need to wash himself in a small bowl and visit the bushes instead of a toilet. Soon, his initial impression of seductive colonial décor gives way to a sense of general hostility toward the environment outside the hotel. Subsequently, it is revealed that Timar becomes strongly attached to the hotel and its décor, no longer in the sense of the picturesque exotic but as the familiar, when the hotel is sold. It is increasingly difficult for Timar to leave Libreville to move to his and Adéle's concession outside town:

> Tout ce décor qui, au début, lui avait été hostile et qu'il avait haï farouchement, il le voyait soudain avec d'autres yeux. Il le connaissait dans ses détails. Des choses futiles lui semblaient émouvantes, comme ce masque blafard façonné par les nègres, qui était accroché au milieu d'un mur gris perle. Le masque était d'un blanc cru, le mur peint à la détrempe et le rapport entre les tons d'une délicatesse rare. (2010a, 57)

> These surroundings, which at first had seemed to him so appalling and which he had loathed with all his heart—he now was seeing them from a different angle. He had grown familiar with all their aspects, and much that had struck him as absurd or ugly now appealed to him in a curious way. The grotesque native mask, for instance, hanging in the middle of a wall. There was a subtle harmony between the tones of the mask and its background, vivid white on silvery-gray distemper. (1979a, 167)

Timar's attachment to the hotel is motivated by a new sense of familiarity that implies a sense of comfort. The polished hotel counter, with its bottles and drinks, gives him the illusion of the security of a French provincial café. Part of what was thus the impression of the picturesque and the reason for the initial attack of unease has now become his comfort zone.

An essential element of Timar's initial notion of the African picturesque is his view of the black Africans as one mass of people. It is only outside the town at the concession that Timar realizes that the Africans are real, three-dimensional people just as the Europeans are. The first time Timar is able to see the Africans as individuals and not as part of the scenery, or as examples of exotic skin art, takes place by a river at the concession. This involves him imagining a reversed gaze, that is, the look of the Africans, who might see him as no more than a schematic white person, a representative of a race or a culture. Timar's wondering about how the Africans may see him—the first phrase in the quotation—is not included in the English translation:

> Timar se demanda s'ils le jugeaient, s'ils se faisaient de lui une idée quelconque autre qu'une idée schématique. Lui, par exemple, c'étaient la première fois qu'il regardait des nègres avec quelque chose de plus qu'une curiosité s'adressant à leur côté pittoresque, aux tatouages ou plutôt aux véritables sculptures de la peau, aux anneaux d'argent que certains portaient dans les oreilles, à la pipe en terre qu'un autre serrait dans ses cheveux crépus. (2010a, 84)

> As for him, this was the first time he was observing blacks otherwise than as decorative figures, tattooed so deeply that the intricate patterns stood out in relief, some wearing big silver earrings or quaint objects fixed in unlikely places—for instance, that boatman with a clay pipe stuck like a flower in his fuzzy hair. (1979a, 196)

In Simenon's fictions as in his reportages the Africans serve as backdrops to the text rather than as individual characters. Yet, while the Africans do not generally have a voice, the author and his characters are able to imagine a situation in which the Africans *would* be able to talk back to the Europeans. In the passage above, as the narrator tells us, the scene with the pirogue, naked and semi-naked rowers, the forest, the river, and Timar in a white colonial suit under a shade in the middle of it, could be very picturesque in a photograph, but the notion is once again discredited. Timar's rejection of this notion is given in free indirect discourse, again marked with the exclamation point that is missing in the English translation:

> Or, ce n'était même pas pittoresque! C'était naturel, apaisant. Timar en oubliait de penser à lui et même de penser. (2010a, 84)

> Actually the impression it produced on Timar was less of picturesqueness than of something natural and restful which soothed his nerves, took his mind off himself and his perplexities. (1979a, 196)

Timar thus finds the situation to be all natural and comforting, distancing himself from the picturesque that, for the duration of this experience, appears as the very opposite of lived reality.

The most powerful effect of the scene for Timar, however, is not the blacks' individuality, but the numbing tranquillity and sadness that seem to infantilize both him and the Africans. For Timar, the Africans are good but naive boys, who shout sharply when the pirogue passes a village or even a single hut, while he himself feels like he is under these rowers' protection, treated as if he were a child who is left in their care. Timar explains that

> Un grand apaisement, voilà vraiment ce qu'il ressentait, mais c'était un apaisement triste, il ignorait pourquoi. Il y avait en lui de la tendresse de reste, sans objet précis, et il lui semblait qu'il était tout près de comprendre cette terre d'Afrique qui jusqu'ici n'avait provoqué en lui qu'une exaltation malsaine. (2010a, 85)

> Above all there had come over him a great calm, though, for some reason he could not fathom, it was tinged with sadness. Yet some capacity for emotion remained, even if it lacked a specific object, and it pleased him to feel that he was on the point of understanding this mysterious continent that until now had brought out only his least healthy instincts. (1979a, 197)

Timar's understanding of Africa and Africans is never free from contradictions. He remains deeply uncertain about his mission and identity as a coloniser, feeling greatly inferior and inadequate with regard to Adèle who has, among her many skills, the ability to speak an indigenous language. To extract revenge from all of Africa, as he says, Timar sleeps with a young virgin from a nearby village. However, the experience makes Timar feel deeply ashamed, especially when he learns that the girl's father may be a man called Amami, who has been wrongly accused of murder. Moreover, we hear Timar lamenting, how he has not been able to act like a true coloniser, that is, to shoot ducks, beat up someone, or prohibit people from going to certain areas. Instead, he had given out all of his cigarettes to Africans. Timar believes he is but a passerby, a visitor, or Adèle's protégé, unable to act like a true colonial settler.

The gradual transformations in Timar's conception of Africa and Africans are intimately tied to another mental process: the slow disintegration of his mind. This process hastens as his suspicions of Adèle's unfaithfulness grow and, especially, when it becomes evident to him that the abovementioned Amami has been sentenced for the murder that Adéle has committed. At the trial, when Timar finds out that Amami is to be sacrificed in a tacit understanding between the white community and Amami's father-in-law who wants to get rid of him, Timar protests deliriously, crying out that Amami has not killed the man, Adèle's aide Thomas, but that Adèle herself is responsible: "It's a lie! It's a damned lie! He is innocent. It was . . . ," and "it was she who killed that boy. And you know it as well as I do!" (1979a, 219).

("Ce n'est pas vrai! Ce n'est pas vrai! Il n'a pas tué! C'est ... C'est elle! Et vous la savez bien!"; 2010a, 106). Timar is then taken down in a struggle and led out of the court.

Later, aboard a boat that is taking him back to Europe, Timar feels more listless than ever before, falling at times into an almost catatonic state, where he seems to ignore all external stimuli. He starts to repeat the words "There is no such thing!" ("Ça n'existe pas!"), sometimes laughingly out loud, sometimes silently to himself (2010a, 106–14). The meaning of these words is ambiguous at first, being possibly a reference to the framing of the man at the trial, Timar's broken illusions, or perhaps his confused thought that he had been taken to the train station in Libreville (which does not exist). Another explanation that soon emerges is that these words reflect the state of his deranged mind where reality, and the West African reality in particular, is in question. Timar is worried that the Doctor may think he is mad, while admitting to himself that he has mad thoughts:

> Il se rendait compte qu'il avait l'air d'un fou, mais il avait conscience de ne pas l'être. Il esquissait des grimaces de fou! Il avait des gestes de fou! Parfois même, dans sa tête, se bousculaient des pensées confuses de fou! (2010a, 109)

> He realized he must look like a madman, yet he knew quite well he wasn't. Of course he made grimaces and, now and then, crazy gestures. Sometimes, too, he found his head buzzing with mad ideas. (1979a, 222)

One of these confused thoughts seems to be the notion in the denial—"There is no such thing!"—that he could make something disappear simply by the force of the words.

The conclusion of *Le Coup de lune* that focuses on Timar's deranged state of mind and manic behavior has the longest section of uninterrupted free indirect discourse in Simenon's three African novels. The passage, consisting of sentences that often end with an exclamation point, follows closely Timar's feverish mind as he goes through memories of Adèle, the young Negro woman he has taken advantage of, and the events in Libreville. These thoughts are accompanied by a sense of increased receptivity and capacity for intelligence. Timar claims to have antennas:

> Et même plus intelligent que lui-même *avant*! Car, maintenant, il avait des antennes! Il devinait des choses trop subtiles pour la plupart des hommes. (2010a, 112)

Cleverer than he himself had been in the past, for now he had developed a sixth—or was it a seventh?—sense. He perceived things that were too subtle for the ordinary run of people. (1979a, 225)

Timar thinks that he can foresee things in the future, such as what will happen when he returns home to his family (getting married to his cousin Blanche and taking the job that would be offered to him). He also predicts how he would not be understood if he told about the beauty of the moment when twelve black rowers jumped in the river simultaneously with their canoes and then turned their eyes to him. Part of his denial of reality, thus, stems from the fact that the African experience would in a sense cease to make any sense once he settles down in France.

The last of his denials Timar repeats for more than a quarter of an hour as he paces up and down the deck: "There's no such place as Africa. No such place" ("L'Afrique, ça n'existe pas! L'Afrique . . ."; 2010a, 114). The reader no longer has access to his mind, however, and thus it is impossible to say whether the protagonist wishes Africa to disappear, laments the likely misunderstanding of his travel stories at home, or whether the words are a reflection of his state of mind, where reality is being erased in a more fundamental sense.

Timar's situation is the most dramatic instance of colonial madness in Simenon's three African novels. The final source of this madness, as in the cases of Georges Bodet and Doctor Bassot, can be located in the African empire of unreason. By this I mean the notion, which is also put forward in Simenon's essays, that Africa in itself is somehow damaging, destructive, and poisonous: "It is not the men who poison you. It is Africa!" ("Ce ne sont pas les hommes qui empoisonnent. C'est l'Afrique!," 2001, 404). Simenon portrays in his reportages the same lethargy, indifference, and madness of Africa that increasingly affects Timar and some of the other characters. But Africa is seen as an empire of unreason in these novels also since the African experience is so consuming and intense for some of the characters and they cannot handle it. Africa marks the men in profound and lasting ways, and in many cases destroys them.[8] As Simenon, in August 1977, comes to the end of his dictated

---

8. Richard C. Keller refers to the Orientalist empire of unreason in *Colonial Madness* (2007, 2), his study of psychiatry in mid-nineteenth-century French North Africa. Bassot's fate recalls Timar's situation on the boat when he is being shipped back home. The mental illness each exhibits is also reflected in their speech: while Timar repeats endlessly that Africa does not exist, Bassot improvises with the sounds of the words. These may transport his mind from Africa to Patagonia in one, broken sentence: "Afrique . . . fric . . . n'en ai pas . . . papa . . . panpan . . . pentagone . . . Pantagonie . . ." (2010a, 483) ("Africa . . . cash . . . don't have any . . . pennies . . . Pentagon . . . Pantagony"; 1979a, 279).

memories concerning his travel over forty years earlier, he again experiences a sudden immersion in the African landscape:

> Tout à l'heure, en terminant ma dictée, j'étais complétement plongé dans l'Afrique telle que je l'ai connue. Je suis resté un bon moment immobile dans mon fauteuil, puis, par la porte-fenêtre, j'ai regardé le paysage presque sans le reconnaître. (1979b, 126)

> Suddenly, having finished my dictation, I was completely immersed in the Africa as I had known it. I had rested in my armchair for some time without moving and then, when I looked out of the French windows, I hardly recognized the landscape. (my translation)

What happens is a form of profound disorientation in Simenon's mind, created by his visual memories of African life and landscape that take over his mind for several minutes. What is noteworthy in this scene, however, given what Simenon repeatedly says of the picturesque in his writings, is that the vivid experience of Africa turns the familiar view into a picturesque image. While he looked out of his window in Montreux, the landscape suddenly transformed into a kind of postcard image, or a label on a can of condensed milk, with a French garden in the foreground, a lake with sails and, in the distance, mountains with snowy peaks. The most familiar view had become suddenly incredible and all too artificial, a form of the picturesque that Simenon so disliked.

We may summarize, then, with the observation that the processual aspect in the presentation of the protagonists' changing worldview and state of mind, mediated through the chosen perspectives and narrative mode, and sometimes also the narrator's evaluation of the characters, is a crucial element in Simenon's novels. The processual aspect of the novelistic narratives is also reflected in the important role of memories of past events and thoughts of possible but unrealized patterns of action. For instance, mental disintegration and self-destruction always haunt the colonial experience in Simenon's African fiction but do not necessarily become a reality. Displacement in the African colony and climate makes total alienation possible, and in Timar's case, his estrangement extends to a wish to reject and negate reality altogether. In *Le Blanc à lunettes,* Ferdinand Graux's and his fiancée Emilienne's life remains shadowed by what has happened, and by the fate of the young Belgian Bodet couple, who accompanied Ferdinand from Egypt to the Congo when he returned to the plantation. Georges Bodet, frustrated by his work in colonial administration, tries to kill his wife and then commits suicide. In *45° à l'ombre*, where all events take place among European settlers and seamen on an ocean liner, the protagonist Donadieu is a witness to the illusions, madness, and greediness of the passengers around him, including the deranged Doctor Bassot. The colonial decadence is further reflected in this novel in Donadieu's opium addiction, similarly to Lady Makinson's opium use in *Le Blanc à lunettes*. Donadieu and Ferdinand Graux are not directly self-destructive, nor are they in any way deranged, but they are compared to others around them who have killed themselves or who suffer from colonial madness. Through these comparisons, self-destruction and madness appear as a virtual reality that could be theirs. For instance, as the narrator underscores in *45° à l'ombre*, Donadieu and his colleague Bassot share many characteristics, such as the same profession and age, explaining further that they would have known each other as students had they studied medicine in the same city. Graux, in turn, compares himself to Georges Bodet and wonders, in his journal, if his fate would be similar to his, if he did not have his instinctive need for equilibrium.

Conclusion: Voices of Fact

Simenon's fiction and nonfiction alike investigate the relation between real and imaginary (or false) notions of Africa, posing similar questions (but in different ways) of misconceived notions of picturesque black Africa, the difficulty of representing African reality, and the experience of immersion in the African landscape. The illusions involved in the colonialist ideology of the civilizing mission, and the naïveté of the new colonisers, are also frequently portrayed across the generic divide. The difficulty, and perhaps also the impossibility, in giving a truthful picture of Africa focuses a number of themes in Simenon's works, such as the question of the relativizing effects of Western traveller's and settler's displacement, the necessity to come to terms with multiple African realities, and the haunting aspect of the reversed gaze, or the possibility of Africans talking back. Furthermore, what one may detect of the narrator's attitude vis-à-vis the characters' voiced opinions in the novels is, to a large extent, in line with the author's outspoken ideas in his nonfiction.

In *Quand j'étais vieux*, Simenon explains that what he wrote in his travel essays enabled him to avoid certain topics in his fiction, such as the picturesque, or certain philosophical and political considerations:

> En définitive, dans ces articles et dans d'autres, je me débarrais d'*avance* de ce que je ne voulais pas mettre dans mes romans, du pittoresque, justement, et aussi des considérations plus ou moins philosophiques ou politiques.
>
> Je ne le faisais pas exprès. C'est instinctivement que j'ai adopté cette règle d'hygiène que je découvre seulement aujourd'hui (1970, 91).

> All said and done, in these articles and in others, I relieved myself in *advance* of all that I did not want put in my novels, the picturesque, precisely, and also all more or less philosophical or political considerations.
>
> I did not do it on purpose. I had adopted instinctively this rule that I have just discovered today. (my translation)

However, it is the dilemma of the picturesque and the problem of how to present African reality that unite the author's travel writing and fiction. The question that I posed earlier about how fiction borrows from nonfiction must also be reformulated in the light of my analyses. Simenon's travel writing does not necessarily give credence to his novels; neither are the novels illustrations of the ideas that are put forward in the reportages. As I have shown above, the difference between the genres that matters lies in the *mode* of narration, specifically with regard to the complexity of the narrative situation and importance given to the gradual development of a character's mind and worldview.

While Simenon's reportages and his fiction are clearly distinct in terms of their modes of narration, there are, however, some passages in his travel reportages, where the text approximates the narrative situation in the novels and seemingly acknowledges the imitation. The question of narrative situation and voice becomes particularly important in the essay "L'Afrique qu'on dit mystérieuse," where the author engages the readers from the beginning in a kind of conversational discourse through an ongoing series of asides. This commentary involves assumptions concerning the readers' views or experiences, and rhetorical questions directed to the audience: "Evidently, you have read" ("Evidemment, vous avez lu"); "Possibly, next, you are curious to know" ("Peut-être, par la suite, avez-vous eu la curiosité"); "After all, not that long ago, you have seen some films" ("Enfin, il n'y a pas bien longtemps, vous avez vu des films"); "Imagine now that we are two old friends" ("Imaginez maintenant que nous sommes de vieux camarades"), etc. Most of the assumptions concern shared notions of Africa and travel in Africa, such as the notion of the picturesque, and kinds of books and films that the writer and the reader supposedly both know. Furthermore, while the author refers to his actual travel experiences between Cairo and Lake Victoria, he also creates for himself a kind of hypothetical narrative voice that could be called pseudofictional.

The pseudonym Georges Caraman that Simenon chose for this text accentuates the distance between the narrative voice and the actual author.[9] Yet, this effect also stems partly from the ambivalent use of the first-person plural form *nous*, with the result that it is not clear who is included in "us." "Us" might involve the writer and his actual companion (Simenon's wife Tigy perhaps), or other travellers, but at times "nous" seems to refer to the author and his potential readers, or the European settlers in general as an imaginary community. At one point in this essay, for example, Simenon writes that "we" look for reasons for the black Africans' strange indifference or childlike laughter. Simultaneously, he further argues, "we" may be using language that is incomprehensible to the Africans:

> Alors, nous cherchons des explications à leur indifférence, ou à leur rire enfantin, ou à leurs colères subites. Nous discutons avec eux et nous ne nous rendons pas compte que c'est nous qui avons tort d'employer un langage incompréhensible. (2001, 436)
>
> So we look for explanations for their indifference, or their childish laughter, or their sudden anger. We have a conversation with them and we do not realise that it is us who have made the mistake of using an incomprehensible language. (my translation)

This "we" indicates as much the general Westerner as any particular travelling companion or reader.

At the same time, as the first-person plural remains ambivalent, the address of the imagined narrative audience becomes increasingly complex in the course of the essay. This is since it is quite possible to imagine an audience that would be willing to distance itself from the addressed reader, since the latter is characterized and caricatured by the misconceived notions of Africa, and rather sides with the author himself. This is to suppose a reader, who is able to share the author's ironic views of the picturesque exotic. The actual reader's wink at the author behind the naïve readers' back becomes possible, for instance, when Simenon invites the reader to imagine the great white hunters of whom we read in the newspapers: "Your imagination is at work. You say that the mister is a famous hunter, and he is not afraid of anything, etc . . . , etc . . ." ("Votre imagination travaille. Vous vous dites que le monsieur est un fameux chasseur, qu'il n'a pas froid aux yeux, etc. . . . , etc. . . ."; 2001, 423). The white hunters' bravery is wholly fabricated, however,

---

9. Simenon used this pseudonym in several articles for the weekly *Police et Reportage* in 1933.

as is soon explained. The reader is, then, invited to reject similar false notions concerning the dangerous animals, primitive people and beliefs, the mysterious Pygmies and other prototypical African legends, or "our" films and literature that abound with such notions. For those who do not have the time to see Africa themselves, Simenon recommends in this essay the next colonial exhibition: "Moreover, if you do not have the time, there will be a colonial exposition in three years" ("Au surplus, si vous n'avez pas le temps, il y aura dans trois ans une exposition coloniale," 2001, 437). It is, however, unlikely that we should take his word at face value and participate in the audience who is thus addressed. After all, we do not want to be like the "bad journalist" or tourist or anyone, who is naïvely looking for impressions of the picturesque exotic or bases his or her views of the colonies on the self-serving presentations of a colonial exhibition.

PART III
Inventions of Life Narrative

7

Virtual Genres in Pierre Loti's and Joseph Conrad's African Travel Diaries and Fiction

THIS CHAPTER focuses on the interrelation between the travel journal and fiction by way of the question of generic potentiality in texts. The examples are drawn from Pierre Loti's (1850–1923) *Journal 1868–1878* and Joseph Conrad's (1857–1924) "Congo Diary" and "Up-river Book," as well as fiction by these writers: notably Loti's novel *Le Roman d'un spahi* (1881; translated as *Between Two Opinions, or the Romance of a Spahi*, 1890, and *A Spahi's Love-Story*, 1907) and Conrad's novella *Heart of Darkness* (1902). My premise is that certain cross-references between travel writing and fiction in these writers' work point to a set of possible directions in the organization of the text, thus exemplifying the logic whereby the narrative is limited by the demands and expectations of the given genre. In particular, I pay attention to the modes of narration and generic framing that could have been adopted to depict the events but that nevertheless remain unrealized projections.

In order to examine such instances within a theoretically consistent framework, I use Gerald Prince's concept of the "disnarrated" and Hilary P. Dannenberg's notion of "narratorial counterfactual" (2008, 123–24) as my points of departure. Prince's concept of "the disnarrated of the told" involves the characters' or the narrator's vision of what could happen or could have happened but has not happened. The "disnarrated of the telling," in contrast, is "everything which, in a narrative, designates the narrating modes that could have been or could be adopted to depict what takes place" (Prince

1992, 33). An example of such virtual narration would be when an author or a narrator explains, "I prefer to use direct instead of reported speech." Dannenberg's related notion of the narrator's counterfactual, in turn, refers to "a hypothetical alteration in a past sequence of events that changes the events in a factual sequence in order to create a different, counterfactual outcome" (2008, 119). The phenomenon and technique that I investigate here has a similar function of creating a reality effect as often happens with the external narrator's counterfactual speculation in nineteenth-century realist fiction (Dannenberg's examples include Trollope, Thackeray, and Austen, among others). However, the kind of counterfactual that I am concerned with does not involve a character's traits or past or future events, which are seen in a new counterfactual light, but the text's hypothetical genre or generic frame. Thus, the chapter identifies a new and hitherto unrecognized dimension of a narrator's counterfactual speculation. Furthermore, as the reading of Loti's novel will demonstrate, such a generic counterfactual can also be voiced by the author or authorial persona, not just the narrator or character.

In the analysis that follows I extend the ideas of the disnarrated and narratorial counterfactual to the question of the text's generic frame, such as its classification as either fiction or nonfiction. This involves, on the one hand, everything in a fictional narrative designating the text as having potential relevance as nonfiction. On the other hand, it refers to everything in nonfiction narratives implying that the story could have been told, or the description could have been written, as fiction but was not. With regard to Loti's and Conrad's travel journals and their fictions, then, the virtual or counterfactual genre of the telling is that which in fiction indicates its potential to have been told and published as a nonfiction travel journal, and that which in the travel journal designates that it could be fiction as well, albeit an unrealized possibility.

The Spahi's Strange Toast

In the middle of Pierre Loti's African novel *Le Roman d'un spahi*, a sudden authorial intervention invites the reader to reflect on its status as fiction. The incident takes place in a passage that describes a dinner party organized by French colonial cavalry troopers, the so-called *spahis*, in the city of St. Louis in Senegal. Here, in the midst of the general tumult of the party, one of the soldiers raises a glass of champagne to propose a toast: "to those who fell at Mecca and Bobdiarah!" (Loti 2005, 166) ("A ceux qui sont tombés à Mecké et à Bobdiarah!"; Loti 1992, 149). The mention of this toast is then followed by the narrator's comment that he has not invented it. Moreover, the narrator stresses that the toast was unforeseen:

> Bien bizarre, ce toast, que l'auteur de ce récit n'a pas inventé; bien imprévue, cette santé portée . . . Hommage de souvenir, ou plaisanterie sacrilège à l'adresse de ceux qui sont morts? . . . Il était très ivre, le spahi qui avait porté ce toast funèbre, et son œil flottant était sombre. (Loti 2006, 149)

> The effect of such a toast,—the author of the present story has not invented the incident,—was strange, startling to a degree! . . . Was it a tribute of remembrance to the dead, or an impious jest? . . . He was very drunk, the Spahi who proposed the ill-sounding toast, and his rolling eye was dark and mournful. (Loti 1907, 157) (anonymous translator)[1]

The unknown *spahi*'s speech act is thus foregrounded not just for its factuality but also for its peculiarity and its ambivalence as a sign of honor. The narrator speculates that, although the toast may well have been a homage to those who had died in colonial campaigns against the legendary Senegalese King Lat-Dior in 1869, it might just as well have been the sacrilegious jest of a drunken, semiconscious soldier.

What makes this intervention stand out in the novel is not so much that it transgresses the impersonal voice of the narrative, which is abandoned in some other passages as well, but that the narrator explicitly refers to himself as the agent of narration, as the author, while simultaneously pointing out a real-life source behind the fiction. Elsewhere the novel relates the events of the story mainly in third-person discourse from the omniscient perspective. It makes frequent use of thought report to describe the main character's internality—the protagonist is a *spahi* called Jean Peyral who at the beginning of the novel had served for three years in French Senegal—with some lapses in free indirect discourse that combine his inner speech with the narrator's perspective.[2]

Thus, something unexpected happens during the scene of the toast: the narrator not only draws attention to himself and speaks in his own name but also refers to himself as the author, who can guarantee the truth value of his narrative. Furthermore, the interruption has no outer, explanatory frame

---

1. I quote here from an unknown translator's version of the novel (Loti 1907) because the line is omitted in M. L. Watkins's 1890 translation.

2. The *Spahis Senegalese*, established in French Africa in 1855, were usually recruited from the inhabitants of Senegal or other parts of French Africa, whereas their officers came from Algerian Spahi regiments. Jean Peyral, however, came from a small village in the Cévennes.

that would indicate a change in perspective. One might ask why, for this brief moment in the narrative, the narrator takes on the author's identity and, moreover, intervenes in the story as the author.

Part of the reason for the intervention certainly lies in its function as a performative gesture, similar to the comments and rhetorical questions the narrator inserts elsewhere in the novel with a view to increasing the sense of mysterious fate around his main character. Yet, what also happens is that the note disclaims the text's fictional status, even if only momentarily. In thus interrupting his narration, the author seems to be claiming something like: "Look. What I am saying here is no longer fiction," or perhaps, because he purports to be citing someone else he has heard, "Look. What I quote here is not my fiction." The intervention, sudden in itself, is thus not an inserted pocket of nonfiction nor is it an autoptic experience of hearing with one's own ears: it is a momentary distortion of the fictional illusion. The quotation points to a process in which real things are brought to light in the fictional world as if it were possible for fiction to undergo a process, for lack of a better word, of "defictionalization." In other words, this is a related phenomenon to what James Phelan has called "mask narration"—that is, the (implied) author's use of a character narrator to express his own thoughts and beliefs (2005, 196)—but in heterodiegetic narration and third-person mode. Loti's novel, for this brief moment, calls into question two main markers of its fictionality: the realist narrator's distance from the scene of narration and his persona as a narrator. The narrator thus suggests that he indeed is the author and capable of freely moving into the realm of the actual world, as if without any substantial modifications. The authorial audience, in turn, is supposed to note his power to do so.

The background of the historical colonial battles in Senegal highlights, as a signpost of factual narrative, the capacity to create a world from fragments of experience. This becomes more obvious if we read Loti's *Journal* along with *Le Roman d'un spahi*. His *Journal* includes a note on the same toast in an entry dated April 1874 in the town of St. Louis, Senegal, during the year (between July 1873 and July 1874) when the author was stationed in Senegal as a midshipman of the French Navy. This time the glass is raised by his acquaintance, a sub-lieutenant called Brémont, in memory of colonial soldiers who had fallen in battles over control of Central and Northern Senegal, specifically concerning the Kingdom of Cayor, which was then ruled by King Lat-Dior. Here, as in his fiction, he calls the toast "funereal" (*funèbre*), but the emphasis is not on its "bizarre" nature, as in the novel, but on the "foolish" (*insensé*): "During the dessert, Brémont raised his glass of champagne and proposed the foolish toast: 'to those who fell at Mecké and Bobdiarah!'" (my translation) ("Au dessert, Brémont levant son verre de champagne, porta ce toast insensé: 'À ceux qui sont tombés à Mecké et à Bobdiarah!'"; Loti 2006, 209). The event inspired Loti to craft a macabre meditation on the destiny of the *spahis*, who operated under the command of sub-lieutenants such as Brémont. These young soldiers, he explains, were vagabonds, adventurers, and bohemians—"sons of Algerian colonials, somewhat Arabic" (2006, 209), and usually without a family of their own. A *spahi*'s fate, as he saw it, was necessarily prone to self-destruction. He further explains that when these troopers died in the line of duty, somewhere in the interior of the "great damned country," they were robbed by "hideous negro women" (2006, 210), their bodies eaten away by hyenas and vultures, and their bones left to whiten in the sands of the desert. These men were remembered by no one and were never even heard of in France.

The toast described in the *Journal*, therefore, is highly suggestive of consequences, a premonition of the death that awaits the toasting colonial soldier and those with him around the table. Brémont's words, with which Loti grimly ends the passage, seemed to have thrown a dark veil over all of them. Later on in March 1875, back in France when he was visiting Joinville-le-Pont, Loti again evoked the same memory, having just heard that Brémont had died during another expedition against King Lat-Dior. Loti's gloomy predictions are thus correct, which again leads him to conclude thus:

> C'est ainsi qu'il devait mourir, il était de cette race d'hommes à part qui ont fait dans leur existence bizarre, leur pays du Sénégal, leur patrie des déserts de sable. Brémont et Faidherbe étaient les deux types les plus singuliers, parmi tous ces hommes qui ne sont pas comme les autres hommes . . . Mon ami Brémont avait 30 ans; il avait quelques dettes à St. Louis; on aura vendu à des mulâtres ses effets, ses armes, son singe et son chien . . . c'est ainsi que finissent les spahis. (2006, 239)

> It was thus that he had to die: he was of a special breed of man who in his bizarre state of existence had made Senegal his country and the desert sands his homeland. Brémont and Faidherbe were the most exceptional of cases among all men who are not like others . . . My friend Brémont was 30 years old; he had some debts in St. Louis; they will have sold his things, his weapons, his monkey, and his dog to mulattos . . . thus die the spahis. (my translation)

Loti highlights the colonial soldiers' estranged and bizarre state of existence, meaning that they sacrificed their lives for the empire with which they had lost contact, or which they had never seen, totally cut off from France both geographically and mentally.

From a close reading of Loti's African novel and his *Journal* it is clear that he used his daily notes, which he made regularly from his adolescence until he was 68 years old, as the laboratory for his fiction. The death of the main character, Jean Peyral, closely resembles the real *spahi* leader's fate as described in the *Journal*.[3] Peyral dies in the desert, robbed by "hideous old negro women" and eaten by vultures, thus realizing Loti's vision of how Brémont must have died to fulfil the prophecy of his toast. Yet the reference to the *Journal* in the novel not only points out its function as a source of fiction, given that so much of what he wrote in his daily notes is more or less directly transposed to his novels, but it also foregrounds ways of creating a world and a character through narrative. Whereas Peyral's story in many ways fleshes out the unknown details of Brémont's true history, the reference to the reality behind the fiction exploits the fictional and literary potential in the *Journal*. What makes the question of virtual genres relevant in relation to Loti's narrator is that he speaks in an assertive yet hypothetical mode, claiming that what he says is not an invention, without exactly stating what the facts are on which the fiction is based and, further, that it transforms.

The narrator–author's self-reference, therefore, makes a claim about the mode of narration that could have been adopted to depict the events. Jean Peyral's story *could* be about a real person and, as such, part of a forgotten colonial history that momentarily surfaces, and Pierre Loti *could* be recalling the event in his *Journal*, directly in his own voice. Yet the gesture remains momentary and partly hidden; the reality behind the fiction cannot be understood from this reference alone. The narrator in *Le Roman d'un spahi* who, no matter how uncertain his distance from the real author, enjoys a position that is not lifelike: he is detached from the scene of the events as their observer, while he also has free access to his main character's mind. With the fiction writer's mandate, Loti fuses Brémont's characteristics with those of his protégé, a real *spahi* called Julien Julia whom he met in Senegal, and lends Brémont's words to a fictional and anonymous colonial soldier. As if to underline the power of fiction to transform the facts, it is not Brémont's alter ego Jean Peyral who repeats his toast but an unnamed *spahi* who is not relevant to the plot development. He is a faceless figure of the real, as the words of his toast

---

3. Jean Peyral shares characteristics with other people besides Brémont, including a *spahi* called Julien Julia whom Loti knew (see Quella-Villéger 1986, 53). Furthermore, Loti mentions a meeting with Brémont's protégé J. Peyral in *Notes of My Youth* (1923, 88–89; 1924, 62–63). This may be a fabrication however. A footnote to this passage explains that the person was the same as in the novel *Le Roman d'un spahi*.

are a fragment of reality, contrasting the reality that the author witnessed with the lifelike representation of it, narrative potential in the incident with a full-blown story. The intervention in the scene of the toast is thus a reminder of how actual events may suggest a potential story and equally how fiction may turn out to be a real story. The reminder is perhaps directed at the author as much as the reader, to whom the reference may remain obscure (without prior knowledge of the author's biography and *Journal*).

There are several localized but less dramatic exceptions to the dominant impersonal mode of narration, elsewhere in *Le Roman d'un spahi*. These include a few letters the main character receives from his relatives in France that are quoted in full in first-person narration, the narrator's lavish impressions of African spaces, in which his voice is more prominent, and a number of rhetorical questions that stress the sense of mysterious in his narrative and in the African landscape. A typical intervention of this kind occurs at the end of the novel when the narrator feigns horror at the protagonist's son's death: "So died the son of Jean Peyral . . . Strange mystery!—What whim of Providence, what capricious God, had launched him into the world, this child of the exiled Spahi? . . ." (Loti 1907, 316) ("Ainsi mourut le fils de Jean Peyral . . .—Mystère!—Quel Dieu l'avait poussé dans la vie, celui-là, l'enfant du spahi?"; Loti 1992, 261). The relationship between the author and the narrator is also ambiguous with regard to the essay on the culture and music of the Griots that is included in the novel, followed by another chapter on female dancers and singers in this society. The essay, which cannot be attributed to any of the characters in the novel, and is only slightly altered from the text that Loti had published in the journal *L'Illustration* in 1875, is evidence in itself that the narrator's voice could at times be identical with that of the author. The title, "Pedantic Digression," however, indicates that the author was aware of the fact that such a change in perspective could be seen as contrived: it warns the reader that he will momentarily slip into a different mode of writing. This involves a shift in focus from third-person extradiegetic narration with figural focalization—meaning that an external narrator tells the story but the events are reflected through a character's consciousness—to a form of journalistic impersonality. The inclusion of the essay in the novel suggests, therefore, that reality and nonfiction—as Loti knew them—inform the fictional narrative, and perhaps even that the fiction has potential factual value.[4]

Two other final paratextual complications concerning the narratorial intervention, which relate to the issue of a hypothetical or counterfactual

---

4. See Mikkonen 2007b for a more detailed analysis of textual ruptures in Loti's novel, including the ambivalence in the narrator's descriptive mode of discourse and the dynamic between the narrator and the main character, Jean Peyral.

genre, must still be noted. First of all, at the time of writing his third novel *Le Roman d'un spahi*, Pierre Loti, alias Julien Viaud (his real name), finally established a new author persona, signing the book for the first time with the nickname of a hero from two of his earlier novels, *Aziyadé* (1879) and *Le mariage de Loti* (1880), which were published anonymously (*Le mariage de Loti* in particular had become tremendously popular).[5] It was under this pseudonym that he went on to publish his journals, memoirs, and auto-portraits. Thus, attribution of authorship of *Le Roman d'un spahi* to "Pierre Loti" could prompt the reader to find potential truth value in Pierre Loti's adventures in the earlier novels. These novels contain fragments from the fictional Loti's journal, for instance, which are not that different from the writer's entries in his actual *Journal*. Curiously enough, the third novel, in which "Pierre Loti" names the author but not the protagonist, contains no excerpts from the character Loti's presumed journal.

Secondly, the mention of the battle at Bobdiarah, which King Lat-Dior won in 1869, is not merely a reference to the writer's *Journal* and a historical event in the colonial war over the control of Senegal and Gambia but is also another evocation of Loti's earlier fiction. Namely, *Le mariage de Loti* includes an entry from the fictional Loti's journal, dated October 1875, written down in the same Bobdiarah (in Sénégambie). However, the "Bobdiarah" referred to in the novel, with no mention of Brémont or other colonial troopers, functions not as a reference to the historical reality but as a generic name for an exotic distant place in Africa. Even more distant from Europe and the known colonies than the Sierra Leone of the previous entry, this accentuates fictional Pierre Loti's isolation and his separation from his lost love. Moreover, in the 1860s and 1870s, the competing French and English colonial powers had plans to unify the region as "Senegambia," which were never realized. The historical status of this colonial region remains to some extent speculative or fictional.

The Found Books

It is known that Joseph Conrad, unlike Pierre Loti who kept a diary for most of his life, did not produce journals. What we have, however, are two short

---

5. Loti's first two novels, *Aziyadé* and *Le mariage de Loti*, weave together material from his personal life, the life of his brother, who was also a sailor, and his friends' experiences. *Le Roman d'un spahi* is not different in this respect. Loti wrote the novel at Toulon in 1880, basing the *Spahi*'s affair with Cora on his affair with the wife of a St. Louis trader in Senegal in the spring of 1874. The importance of his *Journal* in the writing of the novel and his relative disregard for plot and the psychological aspects of his characters led Lucien Duplessy to ask in 1925 whether Loti had even written novels (in his article "Pierre Loti a-t-il fait des romans?" *Grande Revue*, décembre 1925, 219–41).

collections of travel notes from the summer of 1890, which he spent in the Congo, one of which was posthumously called a "diary" by the text's first editor.[6] Scholars investigating the significance of these two texts have typically gone source-hunting in the travel notes for particular passages of *Heart of Darkness*. Conrad's biographer Norman Sherry, for instance, emphasizes the fact that Marlow's and Conrad's journeys were different and recalls how Conrad "crammed into" one paragraph of *Heart of Darkness* all the unpleasant aspects of his 230-mile overland trek in the Congo interior—including his companion's sickness, encountering a corpse by the road, and arguing with carriers (1971, 37–39).[7] Some more recent commentaries, however, consider the relevance of "The Congo Diary," which describes the trek from Matadi to Kinshasa between June 13 and August 1, and the ship's log, "Up-river Book," from another perspective, suggesting how our knowledge of *Heart of Darkness* can retrospectively disclose certain signals of narrativity and literary potential in the travel notes. Jakob Lothe, for instance, illustrates how a specific physical object such as ivory, which made an impression on Conrad in the Congo—writing in the first entry of his "Congo Diary" about the "idiotic employment" of packing ivory in casks (1978, 7)—is transformed into a powerful literary symbol in the novella, symbolizing the colonial exploitation of Africa (Lothe 1998, 45). Lothe's analysis, proceeding from Conrad's fiction to his nonfiction, is well justified in the sense that readers usually come to the "Congo Diary" having already read the novella, perhaps looking for an added sense of authenticity in the fiction (see also Lothe 1998, 48).

However, what I focus on here are the references to travel writing in Conrad's fiction that are worth considering in terms of the potential generic frames they evoke and not only as autobiographical references to the author's trek in the Congo in 1890. In particular, I would like to explore the idea that the references to note-taking and travel writing in his novella suggest to us that fiction can improve upon nonfiction in exploiting the latter's possible or latent narrative structure and imaginative potential. What I therefore

---

6. Loti kept his *Journal* regularly from his adolescence until 1918, and his journal manuscript includes some five thousand large sheets folded in four. The format allowed him to include letters, a dried flower, and an exercise in written Arabic, among other things. Conrad's "Congo Diary," on the other hand, is his only surviving diary and consists only of about ten pages, "Up-river Book" being a short log about navigation along the Congo River.

7. See also Stevens (2002, 69–70), who points out three instances of close correspondence between Conrad's "Congo Diary" and his novella and then goes on to compare the distinctively different narrative styles in Conrad's letters in French to Marguerita Poradowska, the "Up-river Book," and the more personal observations in "The Congo Diary." Richard Curle, in Robert Kimbrough's 1963 edition of *Heart of Darkness*, claims that "the most 'Conradesque' phrase in the diary" is: "Saw another dead body lying by the path in an attitude of meditative repose" (113n16).

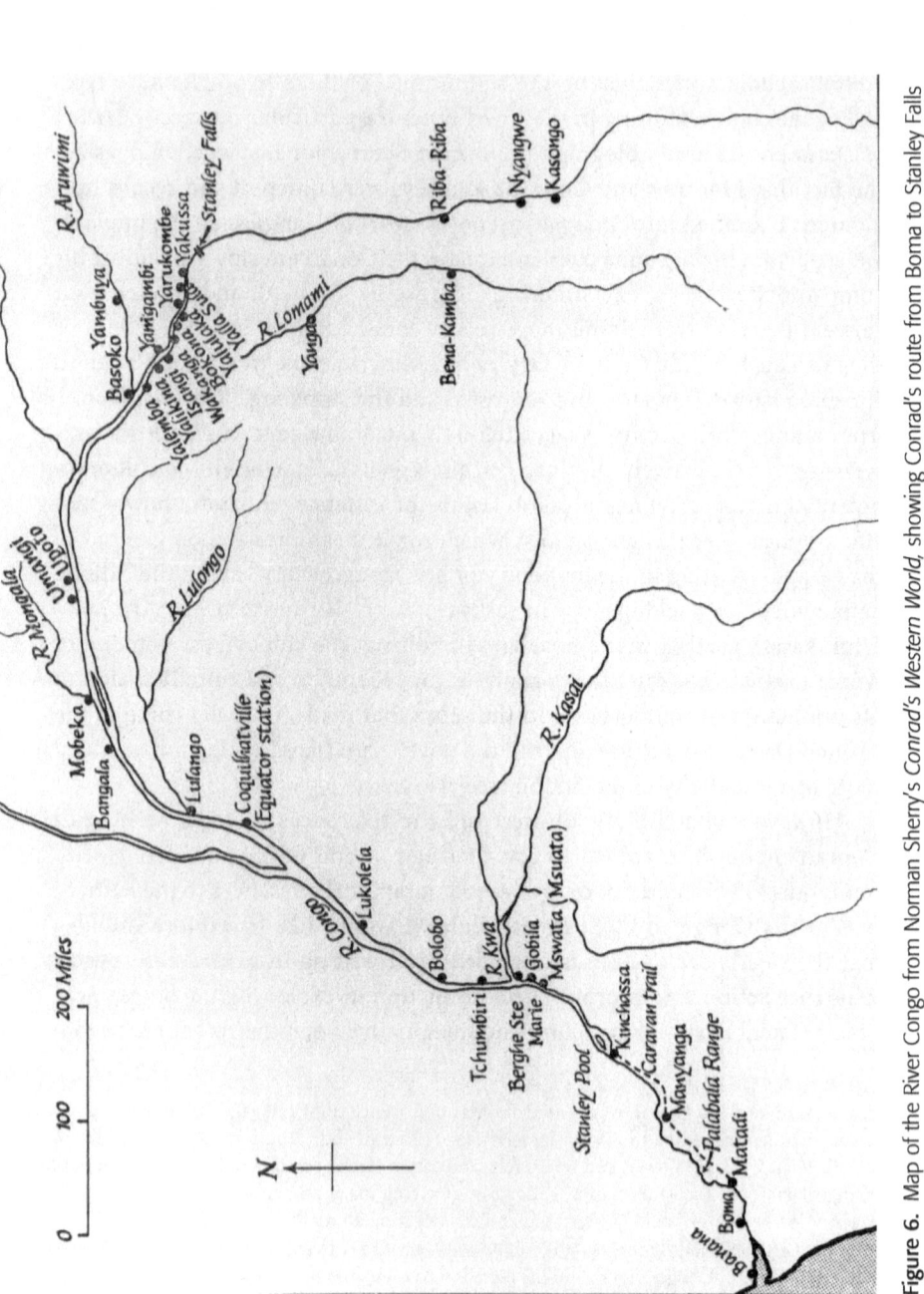

Figure 6. Map of the River Congo from Norman Sherry's *Conrad's Western World*, showing Conrad's route from Boma to Stanley Falls and back between June and December 1890. (© 1971 Cambridge University Press. Reprinted with the permission of Cambridge Uni-

propose is an analysis of the traces of the virtual or counterfactual genre in Conrad's fiction, concerning references to real cases of nonfiction or to "nonfiction" with respect to the fictional world. These traces involve signals of generic potential, narrativity, and style, including the topic of the immersive qualities in nonfiction that raise questions about the choice of mode of narration and genre.

In what follows, I look in detail at the passage in *Heart of Darkness* in which Marlow finds the book *An Inquiry into Some Points of Seamanship* by the Congo River, an episode that has inspired various interpretations among writers ranging from F. R. Leavis to V. S. Naipaul, James Clifford, and Homi K. Bhabha.[8] Here, Marlow, like Kayerts and Carlier in Conrad's earlier short story "An Outpost of Progress" (1896), having lost awareness of his surroundings, comes across a hut made of reeds that quite recently had belonged to some white man. Yet, in contrast to Kayerts and Carlier, who read their deceased predecessor's novels and papers with too much enthusiasm, the scene in the novella evokes the reader's capacity to bring out meanings and narrative potential from the style of writing and mere fragments of text. The book that Marlow finds on the floor is without covers; its pages "had been thumbed into a state of extremely dirty softness" (1994, 54). The author's name is partly illegible; it is perhaps Tower or Towson, "some such name—Master in his Majesty's Navy" (1994, 54).

Marlow's subsequent ruminations raise the question of the authentic narrative voice in Towson's book. At first glance, Marlow considers the sixty-year-old copy "dreary reading enough" and "not a very enthralling book," interspersed as it is with "illustrative diagrams and repulsive tables of figures" (1994, 54). Yet he soon understands the extraordinary nature of his find, which is the writer's "singleness of intention, an honest concern for the right way of going to work" and a sense of humbleness in his voice that made these pages luminous "with another than a professional light" (1994, 54). This discovery of the writer's personal voice and attitude create for Marlow an illusion of reality so strong that it makes him "forget the jungle and the pilgrims in a delicious sensation of having come upon something unmistakably real" (1994, 54). The sensation is further enhanced by the "still more astounding" discovery of notes that are pencilled in the margins of the book, which plainly refer

---

8. Leavis 1993, 204; Naipaul 1980, 215–16; Clifford 1988, 107–9; Bhabha 1994, 104–7. The discovery of the book is also pivotal in Spearey's (2002) reading of the trope of navigation in Conrad's novella. See also Richardson who argues in his investigation of the trope of the book in the jungle, in the works of Conrad, Waugh, Greene, Achebe, Pauline, Melville, and others, that it is "a compact but powerful stage on which the dramas of education, colonialism, interpretation, and resistance continue to be re-enacted" (2011, 12).

to the text but do so in incomprehensible cipher. This reveals for Marlow "an extravagant mystery" in itself. He cannot help but take the book with him.

There are two clear implications to be drawn from this scene in terms of unrealized modes of narration. First, Marlow's discovery reveals that the real interest, and indeed the unrealized potential, in nonfiction can lie in the style of the text—in other words, in what we can detect about the writer's personal voice, such as his intention, honesty, and humility, and not in the factual face value of the genre of writing as evidenced in the diagrams and tables of figures. Furthermore, Marlow's perception of the sympathetic voice coincides with his awareness of the book's particular importance in another individual's life—the reader who had marked the pages, who had read the book many times, and who had made comments in the margins. The merger of these distinctly personal histories, of the writer and the studious reader, constitutes the ultimate mystery for Marlow: "Fancy a man lugging with him a book of that description into this nowhere and studying it—and making notes—in cipher at that! It was an extravagant mystery" (1994, 54).

Second, so many of the signs in this scene that involve fragments of someone's life are only partially recognizable. The unrecognizable shreds of the flag by the hut, a torn curtain of red twill in the doorway, the illegible signature, the partially erased name, and the ciphers in the margins of the book all add to a sense of being cut off from the comprehension of one's surroundings, calling Marlow's attention to a set of possible directions. The various unrecognizable or indecipherable signs in the scene further emphasize the incongruous appearance of the book in the center of an African jungle. In one of the few studies focusing on Conrad's African notebooks, Russell West points out with reference to the same scene from *Heart of Darkness* that the book Marlow finds is a distant relative of the author's travel diary ("Congo Diary") and his travel log ("Up-river Book") with its detailed guidance, for private use, on navigating the river. West claims, more precisely, that *An Inquiry into Some Points of Seamanship* and its accompanying handwritten notes "make up a figure of the novella's own genesis" (1999, 108). What interests me especially in West's argument is the analogy he draws between Tower or Towson's book and Conrad's travel notes, meaning that Marlow's puzzlement upon discovering "this unlikely literary artifact is not unlike that of later generations of critics confronted with what came to be known as the *Congo Diary*" (ibid.). Marlow's response would thus realize the hidden potential in the codified, professional language, perhaps similar to the author's own navigational manual.

Many of Conrad's literary critics associate the book with various real-world models with which he was familiar, including the scientific writer

John Thomas Towson's navigation tables (1848–49), Nicholas Tinmouth's *An Inquiry Relative to Various Important Points of Seamanship* (1845), and A. H. Alston's *Seamanship and Its Associated Duties* (1860).[9] However, whereas these models emphasize the ties between nonfiction and fiction in their own right, another significant detail in the same passage of the novella extends the analogy between the marked copy of *An Inquiry into Some Points of Seamanship* and Conrad's own Congo notes. Before Marlow enters the hut of reeds he stumbles upon another strange fragment of pencilled text. Just outside the hut is a flat piece of board with some faded writing on it, placed on a stack of firewood. He deciphers the text thus: "Wood for you. Hurry up. Approach cautiously." There is an illegible signature which, as Marlow is careful to note does not belong to the man he is looking for, Kurtz, but to someone with a much longer name. Marlow further infers that something is clearly odd about the warning in that it "could not have been meant for the place where it could be only found after approach" (1994, 53). The writing is, therefore, another displaced, grammatically paratactic text comprising juxtaposed clauses without any coordinating conjunctions. The text increases narrativity for Marlow; in other words, it invites him (and perhaps us as readers) to fill in the gaps. The pencilled words, furthermore, give some premonition of what awaits the traveller, anticipating future events: "Something was wrong above. But what—and how much?" (1994, 53). The warning is related to the pencilling in the margins of the book, even if there is no certainty that it belonged to the same hand. The mystery that all these notes evoke about their writer and his situation further raises expectations about what may lie ahead for the narrator.

What these words of warning share with journal writing is an impression of spontaneous style. Marlow dismisses the sentences on the board as some kind of idiotic telegraph: "We commented adversely upon the imbecility of that telegraphic style" (1994, 53). This comment is worth some reflection in its own right. Marlow knows nothing about the context of the message—its time, place, and function, who wrote it and to whom—and therefore would not seem to have any grounds for pointing out its fatuousness. In other respects, the telegraphic style is reminiscent of the travel notes Conrad wrote in a similar pared-down, staccato fashion after the day's journey. The "Congo Diary" includes information on the direction of his march, the camping sites, the conditions en route, the distances covered and the duration, the landscape, the weather, the market places, the missionaries and the government stations, a few comments on his general condition—such as "feel well," "beastly,"

---

9. On the relationship with Tinmouth's book, see Arnold 1976. Eloise Knapp Hay suggests (1963, 144n78) that Alston's book could be a possible source.

"getting jolly well sick of this fun," and "glad to see the end of this stupid tramp"—and a few drawings. His observations on two white men's graves by the road are particularly blunt. He merely mentions the first one in telegraphic style: "a camp—a white man died here—market—govt. post—mount—crocodile pond—Mafiesa" (Saturday, July 26, 1890) (1978, 12). Another entry three days later, in somewhat fuller sentences, gives a few more details about the second one:

> Today did not set tent but put up in Gov[ernmen]t shimbek. Zanzibari in charge—very obliging. Met ripe pineapple for the first time. On the road today passed a skeleton tied up to a post. Also white man's grave—no name. Heap of stones in the form of a cross.
> Health good now. (Tuesday, July 29, 1890) (1978, 13)

The conditions, and perhaps also exhaustion and sickness, did not allow Conrad to write more elaborate notes. All in all, even if they reveal an active mind analysing daily events, the remarks in the "Congo Diary" give very rudimentary information about the traveller's mental state. The much more technical "Up-river Book" reveals even less of his internal thought processes.[10]

As Jakob Lothe argues, the many unresolved tensions in the entries, including the loneliness, frustration, and vulnerability they evoke, differentiate the "Congo Diary" clearly from the contemporary paradigm of travel literature, especially compared with the writings of self-assured travellers such as Livingstone or Stanley (1998, 47–48). Yet, unlike Lothe, I do not think it necessarily "moves towards autobiography" (1998, 47) or could be easily read as a fragment of autobiography.[11] We have, of course, Marlow's example of how one may be able to detect the writer's personality, and perhaps even the story of his life, between the lines of nonfiction without any contextual knowledge about him, not even of his name. However, Conrad's travel notes frustrate the narrative rather than deliver it, unless perhaps we read them in the light of his later fiction. Let us imagine that we did not have the benefit of hindsight and had not read the novella before the "Congo Diary". What kind of voice or mind would these notes evoke? Moreover, given that the diary

---

10. "Up-river Book" was written for a practical purpose: to give technical instructions for navigating the treacherous waters of the immense river in a small steamer.

11. Lothe discusses "Up-river Book," written on a river steamer between August 3 and 19 of 1890, before the "Congo Diary" even if the writing of the "Up-river Book" follows the "Congo Diary" (which was written between June 13 and August 1, 1890). This order reversal apparently strengthens Lothe's claim that the note-taking develops into the "Congo Diary," which as a fragment of an autobiography would complement Conrad's letters from Africa and thus "gives the fiction of *Heart of Darkness* a rare authenticity" (Lothe 1998, 48).

was written before the highly technical "Up-river Book," it is quite possible that when he was in the Congo, Conrad moved away from making more personal observations to noting down technical instructions, and finally fell into silence. We know very little about the last months of his stay in the Congo, beyond a few letters to his aunt and cousin written in late September 1890 that reveal his growing uncertainty and disappointment with his situation.[12]

The passage describing the encounter with the book in *Heart of Darkness*, on the other hand, foregrounds Marlow's mental response, his puzzlement, and his excitement about having the chance to mentally construct a situation, a voice, and a personality, or even two personalities. The contrast between the "imbecilic" pencilled marks on the board and the "extraordinary" pencilled ciphers in the book, and the book's humble style, is another part of the puzzle that calls for more narrative. One of these texts has a relatively clear meaning but an unclear context (the writing on the board), whereas the other has a mysterious meaning although the function is evident (the writing in the margins of the book), and Towson's text implies another subjective voice and experience behind the seemingly objective and somewhat dry style. As Marlow's reactions change within a brief instant from noting the imbecility of the style to a total immersion in reading, the scene thus underlines the potential for narrative meaning and immersion both in Towson's nonfiction and in the handwritten notes.

Later in the novella it is revealed that the words in the margin are, in fact, Russian and were written by Kurtz's Russian assistant and admirer, whose manner of dress resembles a Harlequin. Marlow is thus mistaken not only about the ciphers but also in assuming that the book's owner must be English (Conrad 1994, 55). In generously giving Towson's book to the Harlequin, without knowing that it actually belonged to him, Marlow seems to compromise the English cultural authority of the fragile volume somewhat. The Harlequin, after all, despite Marlow's admiration for his "unreflecting audacity," is something of a comical character due to his strange dress, the rapid shifts in his speech and mood, and his naïve devotion to Kurtz. At the same time, the enthusiasm that these two men share for the same book, and for adventure, functions as a cohesive device in this part of the novella, pointing to the way a narrative, fiction and nonfiction alike, could be constructed so as to maximize its effect on the reader. The Harlequin looks "ecstatically" at the book he thought he had lost. Towson's *Inquiry* thus serves as a narrative relay of sorts: the narrator's immersion in his world of adventure is caught up in the

---

12. Conrad's wife, Jessie, heard from his friends that he nearly died of dysentery while being carried to the coast of the Congo later in the autumn of 1890 (see Jessie Conrad 1935, 13).

inner life of another reader (and a sailor), for whom the book is immensely important. Yet the promised sense of stability and intention is forgotten when Marlow enters Kurtz's estranged world in which, as the Harlequin explains, the mind can become much larger.

As many readers of Conrad's novella have pointed out, the Russian serves the narrative purpose of introducing some aspects of Kurtz's world and emphasizing the mystery of that world to Marlow. The found book has a similar function, and it also suggests a comparison between the means of fiction and nonfiction. The illegibility of the Cyrillic script evidently adds to and is superimposed on the illegibility that Marlow associates with the symbolic heart of Africa. Furthermore, the ambivalent double-perspective of the encounter between Marlow and the Russian, involving both ironic distance and identification between the two figures, suggests another, even if quite undetermined, autobiographical link with the author's life. It is noteworthy, as some Conrad scholars argue, that the Harlequin is *Russian* and not of any other nationality.[13] In other words, we can ask why Marlow meets a Russian, a somewhat incongruous presence, in the middle of the African jungle. One possibility is to draw an analogy with Conrad's native Poland under Russian rule, the nameless Russian representing oppression and European imperialism. Alternatively, the Russian could be a reference to Conrad's past in a more personal sense, a perverse self-image as a Russian subject who had to learn Russian and the Cyrillic script. Be that as it may, the nationality of the Harlequin functions as a point of attention in the text that has inspired biographical readings in Conrad studies.

Finally, what should be taken into consideration in investigating the question of hypothetical genres in this scene is the motif of the found book, in particular the discovery of Western literature in the "heart" of colonial black Africa. Conrad's short story "An Outpost of Progress," for instance, includes a similar find. The main characters, two European agents named Kayerts and Carlier who take charge of a trading post by a river in a remote part of the African jungle, come across some old books and papers, left behind by a deceased predecessor. The books include a few torn novels, such as French classics in the vein of Alexandre Dumas and Balzac:

> Their predecessor had left some torn books. They took up these wrecks of novels, and, as they had never read anything of the kind before, they were surprised and amused. Then during long days there were intermi-

---

13. See Josef Škvorecký, for instance, who refers to the symptomatic importance of the Harlequin's nationality (1984, 259). I would like to thank Laurel Bush for her suggestions and comments in this part of the book.

nable and silly discussions about plots and personages. In the centre of Africa they got acquainted with Richelieu and d'Artagnan, Hawk's Eye and Father Goriot, and many other people. All these imaginary personages became subjects for gossip as if they had been living friends. They discounted their virtues, suspected their motives, decried their successes; were scandalized at their duplicity or were doubtful about their courage. The accounts of crimes filled them with indignation, while tender or pathetic passages moved them deeply. (Conrad 1985, 90)

In Kayerts's and Carlier's imaginations, the courageous heroes of nineteenth-century novels and the ideal colonizers of the Empire, the latter portrayed in colonial literature and propaganda, are clearly linked. The old papers they find with the books appeal to colonialist ideology in their concern with "Our Colonial Expansion," which they promote in "high-flown language" (Conrad 1985, 90), thus affording the men momentary consolation and an opportunity to think highly of their situation. The articles even suggest to them the idea of a glorious posterity, meaning that forthcoming generations will understand their role as pioneers of the civilizing mission. One scene of their novel-reading is interrupted by Carlier, who

> cleared his throat and said in a soldierly voice, "What nonsense!" Kayerts, his round eyes suffused with tears, his fat cheeks quivering, rubbed his bald head, and declared, "This is a splendid book. I had no idea there were such clever fellows in the world." (Conrad 1985, 90)

The two men's isolation from home, the dangerous surroundings, and "contact with pure unmitigated savagery, with primitive nature and primitive man" (Conrad 1985, 86) render their situation profoundly vulnerable. Fiction and colonial literature, then, provide them with the temporary means for coping with the situation, or at least for blotting out its unreality, before the full catastrophe. Moreover, because they are not accustomed to reading such literature, the mimetic illusion of immersing themselves in a storyworld is all the more powerful.

The isolation of the African colonies and the forest and being surrounded by illiterate Africans accentuate the immersion potential of fiction in much early twentieth-century European colonial literature and travel writing. Karen Blixen relates a similar sensation of the enhanced power and effect of fiction at her farm in colonial Kenya in her memoir *Out of Africa*, but does so without the sense of self-delusion that frames Conrad's depiction of Kayerts's and Carlier's readings. In some cases concerning found books in colonial black Africa, however, immersion in reading is not just associated with fictional narratives. The experience of Africa changes the meaning and relevance of fiction for the protagonist Joseph Timar in Georges Simenon's colonial novel *Le coup de lune* for instance. Upon finding three books left behind by some settler in Libreville, Gabon—a Loti, a Maupassant, and a book in chemistry—Joseph Timar finds it impossible to read any fiction. Instead, he is immersed in a treatise on chemistry: "He found the fiction almost unreadable, and yet in Europe he'd devoured it. Here, he wondered why any publisher had thought the pages worth the printer's task" (1979, 182) ("Il fut incapable de lire les romans. En Europe, il les dévorait. Ici, il se demandait pourquoi on s'était donné la peine d'imprimer tant de phrases"; 2010a, 71). Experience of the symbolic heart of Africa thus amounts to a profound personal reevaluation of the meaning of fiction. Evelyn Waugh's story "The Man Who Liked Dickens," first published as a chapter in the novel *A Handful of Dust* (1934), exploits a similar juxtaposition between Western literary classics and the jungle (Amazonian rain forest) as a means of satire. The character Tony Last, held captive in a tribal village by a lonely settler called Mr. Todd, is compelled to read aloud the works of Dickens for the rest of his life. The incongruously placed literature in Waugh's story—as in Simenon's novel, "An Outpost of Progress," *Heart of Darkness,* or in Greene's *Heart of the Matter* where the volumes that Butterworth has left behind are "stained with damp" (Greene 1965, 83)[14]—thus functions as a metonymy for the disintegration of the book owner's mind, in other words as a clichéd image of the colonies as the white man's grave.

Kayerts and Carlier mistake the novels for an authentic experience, just as they mistakenly believe that the narrative of progress directly addresses the reality where they live. Their readings and enthusiasm for books in the African jungle thus foreground the power in narratively creating a world, in a negative sense, as an instance of illusion and ideology. Despite the granting of temporary relief, their strong engagement with fiction and other kinds of narratives finally only postpones the inevitable, preventing them from fully facing the all-too-disturbing situation: their total isolation, the vagueness of their mission, the thinness of their civilization, and the morally suspect exploitation of the Africans in the ivory trade. Kayerts and Carlier are, as the ironic narrator explains, "perfectly insignificant and incapable individuals" (Conrad 1985, 85), and their reading habits during the first months at their colonial trading post further illustrate this sorry state. The men abandon

---

14. In the same novel, Major Scobie reads a missionary book, *A Bishop among the Bantus,* as a detective story to entertain a young sick boy, a survivor from a torpedoes ship, thus transforming nonfiction into fiction by way of his imagination.

reading as they realize that it no longer gives them a sense of control over their reality.

Conclusion

I have looked at two different cases of hypothetical genres in which fiction refers to a potential but unrealized genre of nonfiction. These instances relate to the narrator's vision of the world, foregrounding ways of narratively creating a world and ordering an experience according to a given narrative style, genre, and sense of authority. The generic counterfactual, moreover, serves to question and blur the relationship between the narrator–character, the author, and the reader. In the case of the found book in *Heart of Darkness,* for example, Marlow is likened to the reader who tries to find his or her way through the potential meanings of the narrated events and prepare him- or herself for what lies ahead.[15] In Loti's *Le Roman d'un spahi,* on the other hand, the narrator identifies himself as the author in his intervention on the occasion of the toast.

What Loti's narrator offers in the text is, if we take the words of his authorial counterfactual literally, a momentary disclaimer of fiction rather than just an indication of a hypothetical narrative mode. This could also be conceptualized as the deliberate misrecognition of the fictionality of the story event, implying that the story is steeped in historical and autobiographical reality rather than fiction. It is perhaps only if we read Loti's *Journal* together with his fiction that we may begin to see the fiction as that which still remains potential in the journal, fleshing out a story as it might have happened in reality. As to Conrad, who was known to have enjoyed Loti's fiction, the case of virtual genres does not directly involve the narrator's role and identity.[16] The telling in *Heart of Darkness* underscores the sense of good narrative and the value of its composition by allowing us to follow Marlow's immersion in reading as well as the erroneous suppositions that result from it.

---

15. See also Spearey (2002), who argues that Marlow's discovery of the navigation manual raises questions as to "how any of the story's readers is to navigate through the text, through the reality it posits as well as that which it excludes, through the historical trajectories it posits and through the *topoi* it evokes" (55).

16. On notable parallels with *Le Roman d'un spahi* and *An Outcast of the Islands,* and the proximities between *Mon frère Yves* and the storm in *The Nigger of Narcissus,* see Yves Hervouet's speculation (1990, 29–31, 48–49).

Out of Europe

The African Palimpsest in Michel Leiris's *L'Afrique fantôme*

> Voyage = la joie vague du noyé
> [Voyage = the vague joy of the drowned]
> —Michel Leiris, *Mots sans mémoire*[1]

> Voyage = la joie de voir de ses yeux, voilà—ailleurs—l'enjeu!
> [Voyage = the joy of seeing from one's eyes, there—elsewhere—the stakes!]
> —Michel Leiris, *Langage tangage*[2]

> Écrire un livre de voyage n'est-il pas, il est vrai, une absurde gageure par quelque bout qu'on s'y prenne?
> [To write a travel book, is it not, really, an absurd wager in any way one can see it?]
> —Michel Leiris, *L'Afrique fantôme*

IN HIS TRAVEL JOURNAL classic, *L'Afrique fantôme* (1934), after a year of travel through sub-Saharan Africa on the Mission Dakar-Djibouti, the French writer and ethnographer Michel Leiris listed a group of texts under the simple heading "African Imagery" ("Imagerie africaine"). The list, included in an entry for the June 19, 1932, covers a wide range of heterogeneous names and materials, from events in French colonial history to more or less exoticist European texts such as Giuseppi Verdi's *Aïda*. At this particular moment in

---

1. Michel Leiris, "Glossaire: j'y serre mes gloses, " in *Mots sans mémoire* (1969, 71–116). Unless otherwise indicated, the translations in this chapter are mine.

2. Michel Leiris, "Souple mantique et simples tics de glotte. En supplément," in *Langage tangage* (1985, 7–68).

his journey, Leiris explains that he had "plunged himself" into such a textual atmosphere. He gives no other account for this inscription. The references are presented as separate from the rest of the entry as if they were a fact in themselves, a kind of personal and cultural baggage to be dealt with—but Leiris never explicitly returns to these texts or historical events in the rest of the journal.

> Imagerie africaine:
> *L'Africaine,* l'opéra de Meyerbeer, avec son fameux « unisson » et le grand
>   air de Vasco de Gama;
> la casquette de père Bugeaud et la smalah d'Abd el Kader;
> *Aïda,* que Verdi composa pour les fêtes d'inauguration du
>   Canal de Suez;
> l'histoire du prêtre Jean;
> la mort de Livingstone;
> Fachoda;
> Arthur Rimbaud vendant des armes à Ménélik;
> Savorgnan de Brazza;
> le Prince impérial tué par les Zoulous;
> les massacreurs Voulet-Chanoine;
> les dynamiteurs Gaud-Tocquet;
> l'affaire de la N'Goko Sanga;
> le scandale du Thiès-Kayes;
> le Congo-Océan;
> la bataille des Pyramides;
> le coup d'Agadir;
> la conférence d'Algésiras;
> *Impressions d'Afrique*;
> la reine Ranavalo;
> les amazones de Béhanzin;
> et le sirdar Kitchener, et la guerre du Mahdi, et Samori, etc.
> (Leiris 1981, 365–66)

The aim of this chapter is to examine the indications of Leiris's list, and its framing in the travel journal, as a palimpsest that states itself but also calls into question the writer's knowledge of Africa. More precisely, what I want to do is tease out some finer implications of the specific textual "ambience" to which the author refers by this list and investigate the ways in which the connotations of this list, and Leiris's African travelogue as a whole, are related to the writer's emerging notion of self-writing. By the palimpsestic quality of the list I mean that it foregrounds the fact that writing takes place in the presence of other writings and the contradictory forces of remembering and forgetting. By listing some of his favorite African images, from legends to plays and operas to fictions, with the violent history of French colonialism in Africa, Leiris dramatizes a loss of command of the exotic discourse—thus dissociating himself from some of these images and pointing to the cure of exoticism, or the "mirage exotique," which he later associated with European egocentrism vis-à-vis other cultures, and that he mentions at the journal's end.³

Simultaneously, the inventory suggests an attempt to take hold of a certain textual authority concerning the experience in Africa. The entry from June 1932 thus opens up the question of the use of African imagery in relation to colonialist history and travel experience: How, if at all, can it be legible? The self-conscious taking hold of imagery, together with the potentially ironic juxtaposition of literary myth and colonial reality, contributes to the general tendency of destabilization of the divide between self and other in this travel journal. The inventory contrasts with many earlier and later passages in the travel journal where the writer seeks to affirm notions of the primitive sacred and the authentic exotic.

African Imagery

L'Afrique fantôme is an intimate journal that Michel Leiris (1901–1990) kept during the French government-sponsored ethnographic mission through sub-Saharan Africa from 1931 to 1933. Working as a secretary–archivist of the Mission headed by the ethnographer Marcel Griaule, Leiris passed through thirteen African countries, of which ten were French colonies. This mission contributed more than 3,000 artefacts to the Trocadero exhibitions and research laboratories in Paris, as well as countless photographs and recordings, notations of thirty languages and dialects, and botanical specimens. *L'Afrique fantôme*, likewise, has a vast scope, including 633 entries from 21 months from May 1931 to February 1933. The journal is characterized by a hybrid narrative authority that combines confessional diary entries, travel story, dream journal, self-analysis with ethnographic observations, field notes, and seemingly unmotivated shifts in narration.⁴ After the list of some twenty

---

   3. Towards the end of *L'Afrique fantôme*, Leiris refers to the *mirage exotique*, meaning the desire to 'go to Calcutta' and the desire for 'femmes de couleur,' as an illusion that no longer obsesses him. The same concept is also used in the footnotes (Leiris 1981, 629, 655).

   4. The generic hybridity of *L'Afrique fantôme* reflects a turning point in Leiris's career. Irene Albers has made the important observation that after *L'Afrique fantôme*, Leiris clearly

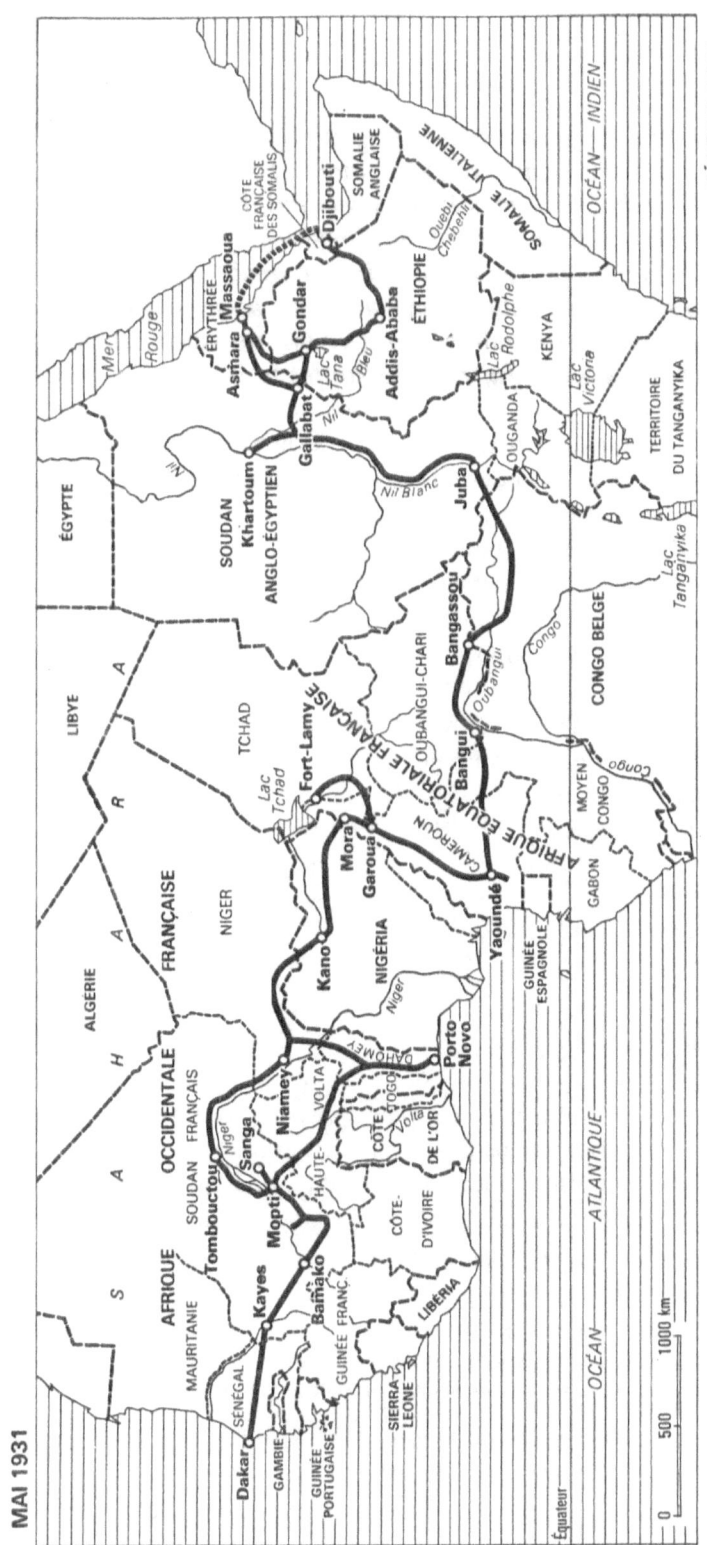

Figure 7. Map of Mission Dakar-Djibouti (May 1931–February 1933) (Michel Leiris. *L'Afrique fantôme*. © Éditions Gallimard).

texts and events that apparently had influenced his vision of Africa, Leiris states briefly that one day he had forgotten himself in the ambience of these texts but then he was interrupted. Leiris never explicates the meanings of the list thereby giving the reader the opportunity to reflect on its contents and implications or to leave it as it is. From the outset, Leiris's African imagery defies the borders of fact and fiction, myth and history—or at least suggests the possibility of their mutual implication. The list opens with one of the great nineteenth-century Orientalist and colonialist operas, Giacomo Meyerbeer's *L'Africaine* (*The African Woman* or *The African Maid*, 1865), about the explorer Vasco da Gama and his slave, the African queen Sélika. *L'Africaine* is accompanied by another reference in the same genre to Verdi's *Aïda* (premiere 1871), an opera about an Ethiopian princess torn between love of her homeland and the man who loves her. The medieval legend of Prester John (Prêtre Jean), who supposedly ruled over a perfect Christian kingdom somewhere in Asia or perhaps in Africa, comes fourth in the list. These references are instances of fanciful images of marvels and the exotic earthly paradise.

The rest of the entries, however, with the important exception of one novel, *Impressions d'Afrique* (1910) by Raymond Roussel, involve names and narratives from the actual history of Africa's colonization with a specific emphasis on French involvement. They make up an anti-colonial palimpsest that exposes the writer's personal memory as interlinked with colonial history and discourse, revealing a mind being colonized by certain imagery. The second entry about the "cap of père Bugeaud" and the Arab leader Abd el Kader, refers to the history of the conquest of Algiers by the French in 1830 and the establishment of their long rule there. Major names connected to African colonization in the list include the Scottish missionary–explorer David Livingstone, along with the Italian-born French explorer Pierre Savorgnan de Brazza who, in competition with Stanley, opened up for the French an entry along the right bank of the Congo. Brazza's endeavours eventually led to the establishment of French colonies in West Africa. Fachoda, where the British-French competition over African colonies culminated in 1898, is on the list as is also the 1879 death of the exiled French imperial Prince in the Anglo-Zulu war in South Africa. The poet Arthur Rimbaud is mentioned in relation to a colonialist scene, selling arms to the Ethiopian emperor

---

subdivided his writing into theoretical texts and autobiographical or literary works. The same tendency may be already observed in the publication of parts of the African travel diary in 1933 and 1934 in roughly two different genres: passages published in the journal *Nouvelle revue française* that conform with the genres of "journal intime" and "journal de voyage" and ethnographic observations published in the June 1933 special issue of the *Minotaure* where the writer supresses his own participation (Albers 2008, 288).

Ménélik. The Rimbaud reference and the story of the death of Livingstone (near Lake Bangweolo in 1873), in their own right, combine colonial history and myth. The fact that Rimbaud left *belles lettres* for action and adventure in East Africa also resonates with Leiris's wish to distance himself from surrealism and Parisian artistic circles. The potential ambiguity with this reference, however, is that there is no genuine break in Leiris's writing activity during the African travel but instead a transition to new forms of (autobiographic) writing through intense documentation, note-taking, and introspection.

These entries are followed by references to the widely covered atrocities committed under French colonial rule. The "Voulet-Chanoine murderers" refers to the bloody mission that in 1898 tried to establish contact with the borders of French Niger and Tchad; the "Gaud-Tocquet dynamite exploders" alludes to French officials in Central Africa who on Independence Day, 1904, exploded a local person named Papka with dynamite in a strange spectacle of public punishment; "N'Goko Sanga affair" points to the colonial company with the same name that exploited a large tract of the French Congo and received much bad publicity from the 1900s to the 1930s; the "Thiès-Kayes scandal" and the "Congo-Océan" refer to the early twentieth-century great railway construction projects that used forced labor recruitment and led to the deaths of thousands of workers. The other references also indicate central events and moments in the French colonial campaigns.[5]

Remembering and Forgetting Africa

The passage has been singled out, although only in passing, by a number of prominent Leiris scholars, including James Clifford and Séan Hand, who mention it as an important instance of self-analysis. Clifford suggests in his analysis of *L'Afrique fantôme* that here "we come across lists of 'imagerie africaine' (to be forgotten)" (1988, 170). Similarly, Séan Hand points out that Leiris notes here a list of European clichés of Africa (2002, 59), and "half-ironically composes an 'imagerie africaine'" (1995, 179).

More could be said about the list's self-analysis or half-irony. The inventory and its framing seem to be marked by a deliberate contrast between an apparent and an intended meaning. Undeniably, some of these entries were clichéd images at the moment when Leiris wrote them down. But it is not simple to justify the claim for the list's potential irony let alone to locate

---

5. These include the Battle of the Pyramids in 1789, the coup of Agadir in 1911, the Algeciras conference in 1906, the exile of Queen Ranavalo of Madagascar, the capture of Samori Ture in 1898, and the 1894 surrender of King Behanzin and his amazons of Dahomey.

irony inside the list. The contrast between the literary imaginations of Roussel, Rimbaud, or romantic opera and stories of colonial violence does not necessarily involve any irony. We know, for instance, that Leiris had much serious interest in Roussel's work even if he also associated Roussel's *Impressions d'Afrique* with a childhood fantasy of "haunting exoticism" that he had outgrown by the time he embarked on the Dakar-Djibouti mission (I will return to Roussel's role in the list later in more detail).[6] Leiris was also a great admirer of opera, such as Verdi, and thought that only opera was able to capture the duration of music in action and space.[7] It is possible, perhaps, to locate irony in the heterogeneity of the list, where fiction, exoticism, and opera are listed alongside actual events, or the way the writer's "revelry"—if "ambience" means that—is suddenly interrupted by a local Ethiopian chief who wanted to talk to Leiris about his good relations with a former French consul in the region. Furthermore, we may argue that the listing implies a certain ironic attitude, which is that the author dissociates himself both from certain popular clichés relating to Africa and the less-than-glorious French colonial history. This seems possible especially if we interpret the listed items as quotations of popular imagery rather than as notes that relate to the writer's self-analysis. More than simply ironic, however, the writer's immersion in the ambience of these references, and the list's strategic placement near the center of the journey, seem to suggest a sense of important personal meaning and weight to be investigated. The references are perhaps something to distance oneself from, but the degree of sincerity, irony (or self-irony), and personal meaning involved remains indeterminate.

On the outset, Leiris's style in this entry is a dry kind of self-irony or Romantic irony; it is certainly not very humorous. As a potential sign of Romantic irony, the writer would thus remind himself (and his reader) with the list, and with this interruption of the travel journal, that it is he who manipulates the description of his world and that this universe is dependent on his knowledge and preconceptions. The potential double meaning in this sense stems from the savvy, self-aware playfulness involved in the inventory

---

6. Leiris starts his 1930 essay "L'œil de l'ethnographe" with a memory of a theater production of Roussel's novel that he saw at the age of eleven (in May 1912). Comparing Roussel's imagery of "Africa" with Helen Bannerman's story "The Little Black Sambo" and André Mouëzy-Eon's play *Malikoko roi nègre*, he points out the distorting Western perspective in such representations while emphasizing the promise in ethnographic research and travel to "dissiper pas mal de ces erreurs et, partant, à ruiner nombre de leurs conséquences, entre autres les préjugés de races, iniquité contre laquelle on ne s'élèvra jamais assez" (Leiris 1930/1992, 33) ("clear up many of these mistakes and, thus, prevent a good number of their consequences, including racial prejudices, and iniquity that we can never fight enough").

7. On Leiris's thoughts on opera, see Leiris 1965/1992, 315–22.

and undermining of personal myths. The meaning of "Africa," so to speak, would thus emphasize the imagination's ability to fuse historical events and struggles with transient, ordering fictions. Perhaps also, as in Romantic self-irony, the emphasis on equivocal voice—between revelry and self-analysis, quotation and self-expression, irony and serious intention—indicates that the experience of a certain time and space must always be other than the memories and literary or other textual models that the experience may evoke.

The inventory, thus, may postulate a double audience, but it is far from evident what the intended meaning of the list is. It also remains uncertain how much weight one should attach to the inventory. The dynamics of the juxtaposition and the framing of the list in the travel journal invite more extended attention, but this attention must necessarily remain open-ended. The idea that the list would involve things to be forgotten is not obvious either. Leiris's African trip evidently led the writer to abandon his juvenile myth of breaking away from the "West," from what he saw as Western rationality, technology, capitalism, and cultural arrogance, through voyage in the exotic. Instead of material to be forgotten, the *explicit* deposition of the textual strata indicates also a sense of self-understanding, revealed to the writer under the pressure of travel. These are mental images that have stayed with him; they are capable of immersing the mind into a specific ambience. The inventory, thus, does not necessarily reveal a desire to forget the imagery, but its function may be to note how much the writer's vision of Africa has been dependent on it.

As Leiris is not explicit about the meanings of the list, there is room to speculate on its various potential implications. Beside the juxtaposition between fictional Africanist imagery and colonialist atrocities within the list, which may invite us to reflect on their potential connection, the entry suggests an important contradiction between mobility and immobility, or between action and revelry that resonates with many other parts of the journal. The heroism of the African myths and histories, implied by the list, stands in ironic contrast to Leiris's present immobile situation on a stop in an Ethiopian village where he had just been offered inedible meat and sour milk. Furthermore, the sense of disparity between an eventful European home and the African immobile abroad is implied through the mentioning, in the beginning of the same day's entry, of the horse races of the Grand Steeple chase taking place in Paris at that particular time. Leiris's capacity suddenly to immerse himself in the ambience of the various African references creates a further contrast with his statements elsewhere where he laments his *inability* to submerge himself in the rituals of the Dogon people of Mali. After all, the religious rituals and the sacred language of the Dogon, which Leiris had investigated in Bandiagara and Sanga, had been for him closest to the kind of authenticity of the noble primitive that he had been looking for.[8] In contrast to this inability to participate, and the immobility from which he suffers, Leiris is able to immerse himself in the images of his mind.

Moreover, still another implication is that the list is a possible early instance of kinds of polysemantic and polymorphous facts that later served as important materials in Leiris's long-lasting autobiographical project. This sustained project included the four volumes grouped under the title *La Règle du jeu* (*The Rules of the Game*) that Leiris wrote from the early 1940s until the mid-1970s, preceded by his memoir *L'Âge d'homme* (*Manhood*, 1939). Leiris had a habit of making notes on events and experiences in his life, which had made an impact on him and seemed to have a multifaceted or ambiguous meaning that required more reflection. These data were included in his *Journal* or an archive of index files to be later worked upon and developed it in his autobiography, *La Règle du jeu* (Hollier 2003, xxxvi; Brée 1980, 197–98). Such events and experiences, Hollier suggests, functioned for instance as a means of foreshadowing, providing the author and his confidante, that is, the reader of *La Règle du jeu*, with clues about where the autobiographic narrative might be going (Hollier 2003, xxxvi). In *Biffures* (1948), the first part of *La Règle du jeu*, Leiris explicitly refers to scenes that, as he says, have laid "dormant" in his *Journal*, preserved in anticipation of his later work. One such occasion is a scene involving a family of street artists dancing on stilts at a town square in Lannion on August 25, 1933, as Leiris was vacationing in Bretagne with his wife, Zette, some six months after his return from Africa. The description of the scene in his *Journal*, which he made the very same day, consists of one detailed paragraph, but the description is rudimentary and gives no insight about the note-taker's experience or reason for writing it down (Leiris 1992a, 230). In contrast, fifteen years later in *Biffures*, the scene is presented much more fully. The description is, further, thematically framed and it re-evokes the writer's state of mind at the time:

> Sur une place de cette petite ville dont je goûte fort le nom (parce qu'il sonne bien campagnard et qu'on croit, l'entendant, voir des paysans aller au marché le bras passé dans l'anse de paniers remplis de volaille, de mottes de beurre ou d'œufs frais) nous vîmes des baladins qui dansaient, montés sur des échasses. Deux adultes et deux enfants; selon toute vraisemblance,

---

8. Before the study of the *zar* cult in Godar, that is. As, for instance, in this "orientalizing" description of the village of Sanga: "Formidable religiosité. Le sacré nage dans tous les coins. Tout semble sage et grave. Image classique de l'Asie" (1981, 122) ("Wonderful religiosity. All corners are filled with a sense of sacred. Everything seems sage and serious. A classical image of Asia."). See also Beaujour 1999, 124.

de la même famille, comprenant outre le père et la mère (qui pouvaient bien avoir l'un comme l'autre une trentaine d'années) un petit garçon et une petite fille; tous quatre, vêtus de couleurs éclatantes et chaussés d'espadrilles. (2003, 146)

In the square of this little town, whose name I relish (because it has a real country ring to it, and when you hear it you seem to see the peasants going to market with their arms through handles in baskets filled with game birds, chunks of butter, or fresh eggs), we saw some mountebanks dancing on stilts. Two adults and two children, in all likelihood from the same family, including, besides the father and mother (who both could have been about thirty) a little boy and a little girl. All four were dressed in dazzling colors with espadrilles on their feet. (1991, 134)

First of all, by placing the scene in a chapter entitled "Il était une fois . . ." ("Once upon a time"), Leiris ties the memory of this scene to the theme of distant past, and the relationship between imagination and the reality he experienced, which is his focus here. The memory is an important instance of the fusion of dream and real experience, as he explains, that the life has offered to him and that he has accepted as such without submitting it "to any poetic maceration" (2003, 134). Second, Leiris also contextualizes the scene in relation to his recent return from Africa and the question of how to perceive unfamiliar or, so to speak, exotic cultures. More precisely, Leiris explains that in the summer of 1933 he was trying to get back in touch with France as if it were a new country that would supply him with a lot of material for "exotic sensations" (2003, 146). It is then not surprising that the street artists appeared to him as a charming "explosion of freshness" in the routine bustle of the town and, as he says, just like a bed of flowers in an old provincial courtyard (2003, 147). Third, through this memory, Leiris recognizes his wish to see the family of artists more as fairy tale characters than real people, as goblins or sylphs in some narrative, living a kind of aerial life far removed from our daily habits. Further, he explains how he deliberately did not want to imagine that the family had any inner discord or everyday problems such as drinking, unfaithfulness, or violence. The mention of all the things Leiris does not want to imagine with regard to this memory is relatively long as if he wanted to underscore how his mind works rather than what was the reality that he witnessed.

This anecdote, and the list in *L'Afrique fantôme*, functions similarly in terms of the kinds of knots of significant but still "dormant" meanings that Leiris uses in his autobiographical project and narrative self-conception.

Leiris's memory of the experience in Lannion, and the inventory in the travel journal, are both woven into a larger autobiographical narrative. As to the scene in Lannion, both its cognitive *and* affective relations are appropriated in the retelling. The list in the travel book, in contrast, stands without clear affective value, but it is framed by the experience of immersion. At the same time, however, it seems somehow simplifying to view these instances as evidence of the way the present may be experienced in the context of a larger life-narrative, or how the past can be relevant with regard to the present processes of narrative self-constitution. What I think needs to be emphasized here is the virtual dimension of the experience, the importance of the memory as having *potentially* meaningful forms before the act of narrativisation. In other words, what seems to come to the fore here is that the meaning potential of past experience is for the first time realized and given form in the retelling, while past consciousness, in terms of its form-finding capacity, also becomes part of the investigation. Thus, what interests the autobiographical author in such "souvenir descriptions" (*objet-témoin*) is that they are subject to reinterpretation as they are placed in a new context. Leiris's rewriting of the scene in Lannion does not only try to re-evoke the past consciousness within the interpretive frame of a life-narrative, so as to restore the state of that mind, but also tries to investigate the multifaceted nature of the experience and the mind that takes hold of that experience before being able to give it a particular narrative, thematic, or other meaning.

Palimpsest, Collage, Found Object

Séan Hand has isolated three intertextual levels in *L'Afrique fantôme*. All of these levels, Hand claims, which vary in their degree of concreteness and intentionality, encourage us to investigate the journal's epistemological groundings and poetic practices. More specifically, Hand argues that the layered textual structure of the journal speaks of the "phantasmic persistence of a general colonial and imperial epistemology within a consciously postimperial and anti-colonial revalorization of native culture" (1995, 178). These textual levels include, first, Leiris's readings that take place in the journal, especially classic and contemporary popular novels, and the writing raised by that reading; second, the writing taking place in and around *L'Afrique* and the reading raised by that writing; and third, the mapping of the culturally other carried out by the French Empire, especially the way Leiris resorts to accounts given by Commandant Gallieni (1849–1916) on his 1879–81 Senegal-Niger campaign.

The list of African imagery activates all these levels in intertextuality. The references are an outcome of Leiris's readings that, in part, have made him write; they also showcase an inventory of persisting European images of the culturally other. It is remarkable how the list functions as an incentive for interpretation in its own right, through association between the materials. This is partly because the entries document the writer's strategic location vis-à-vis Africa and that this documentation is simultaneously meaningful in many respects, in terms of ethnography of the self, surrealist devices, and colonial culture. At this point in his travels, Leiris not only presents to himself and to the reader a kind of chronicle of African colonial myth and history but also *affiliates* himself with other works and histories and thus *takes hold* of a certain textual and narrative authority, the discursive conditions of his knowledge concerning Africa. Africa, therefore, comes forth through this list as a field of knowledge that, further, under the weight of wide travel experience, forces upon the writer an exploration of available sources of reference.

The metaphors of palimpsest and the collage may help us to understand better the heterogeneity of the cultural material in the list. The palimpsest introduces the idea that there can be a fluid relationship between the texts that are written over each other and that the erasure of a textual layer is part of a layering process. In the heterogeneous materials of the list, texts are superimposed to bring about other texts or erasures. The alternating acts of reading and writing during the journey accentuate the effect. Furthermore, we may think here more concretely of Leiris's earlier writings on African imagery such as the 1930 essay "L'œil de l'ethnographe" to which I will return in more detail later. A new erasure creates text; a new text creates erasure.

We can argue that Leiris reworks through his inventory certain unprocessed givens of his memory and his fantasies, to arrange them under a heading—"imagerie africaine"—only to connect them haphazardly according to a taxonomy of personal and cultural memory.[9] The effect of the juxtapositions is an awareness of discursive pressure, of culturally persisting images of the other, and perhaps also, the ideological nature of identity. In this respect, the inventory resembles the juxtapositions of modern art and African sculpture in the periodical *Documents* in which Leiris was engaged prior to his journey. Or, rather, it constitutes an instance of collage and juxtaposition in action. In

---

9. Michel Beaujour has, in fact, claimed, in regard to Leiris's *L'Âge d'homme,* that the literary self-portrait functions as a kind of *objet trouvé* to which "the writer imparts the purpose of self-portrayal in the course of its elaboration" (1991, 4). This means not only the way the self-portrait may not have a clear notion of direction or continuous narrative but also the way the writer's culture may "provide him with the ready-made categories that enable him to classify the fragments of his discourse" (1991, 5).

an intimate chronicle, materials are to be recorded as they present themselves, in their particularity and subjectivity, as Leiris explains in a preface in the middle of the journal:

> Car rien n'est vrai que le concret. C'est en poussant à l'extrême le particulier que, bien souvent, on touche au général; en exhibant le coefficient personnel au grand jour qu'on permet le calcul de l'erreur; en portant la subjectivité à son comble qu'on atteint l'objectivité. (1981, 264)

> Since nothing is real but the concrete. It is very often that in pushing the particular to its extremes, one reaches the general; in exposing the personal coefficient to broad daylight one is able to detect errors; in taking the idea of subjectivity to its farthest limits, one attains objectivity.

Following these principles, the list of African imagery is surrounded by notes on everyday relations with local people. Here, in an ironic instance of a tabulation of quantitative data, or a kind of textual archive of the ethnographer's self, the travel journal turns from describing the African field of perception to the observing subject himself.

One such comprehensive rubric to be undermined was that of the novel. A suspicion towards the novelistic form, and specifically a critique of the conventions of the realist and psychological novel, was a tenet that Leiris shared with the surrealists, even after having distanced himself from the group in 1929.[10] In fact, Leiris saw his first autobiographical narrative *L'Âge d'homme* as a negation of the novel and a conscious move away from conventional narrative structures. In the 1946 preface to the book ("De la literature considérée comme une tauromachie"), Leiris refers to a kind of montage of images where all elements have a rigorous sense of veracity as documents of the writer's life:

> Du point de vue strictement esthétique, il s'agissait pour moi de condenser, à l'état presque brut, un ensemble de faits et d'images que je me refusais à

---

10. On surrealism and the novel, see for instance, Carlos Lynes, 1966, "Surrealism and the Novel: Breton's *Nadja*." *French Studies* XX(4): 366–87, and J. H. Matthews, 1966, *Surrealism and the Novel*. Ann Arbor: University of Michigan Press. In his 1924 "Manifesto of Surrealism," André Breton refers, for instance, to the vacuity in the traditional novelistic descriptions and to the novel in general as an inferior category of literature. In "De la littérature considérée comme une tauromachie" ("The Autobiographer as *Torero*"), Leiris compares *L'Âge d'homme* to a surrealist collage or photo montage that has value as a documentary: "Aucun élément n'y est utilisé qui ne soit d'une véracité rigoureuse ou n'ait valeur de document" (2001, 15–16) ("No element is utilized which is not of strict veracity or of documentary value"; 1992b, 159). Denis Hollier refers to this as Leiris's documentary inspiration (1997, 141).

exploiter en laissant travailler dessus mon imagination; en somme: la négation d'un roman. Rejeter toute affabulation et n'admettre pour matériaux que des faits véridiques (et non pas seulement des faits vraisemblables, comme dans le roman classique), rien que ces faits et tous ces faits, était la règle que je m'étais choisie. (2001, 14–15)

From the strictly aesthetic point of view, it was a question of condensing, in the almost raw state, a group of facts and images which I refused to exploit by letting my imagination work upon them; in other words: the negation of a novel. To reject all fable; to admit as materials only actual facts (and not only probable facts, as in the classical novel), nothing but these facts and all these facts, was the rule that I had imposed on myself. (1992b, 158)

I take "affabulation" here to mean the narrative organization of an imaginary story. The inclusion of Raymond Roussel's experimental novel in the list is important in this respect since it is not devoid of ambiguity. What was important for Leiris in Roussel's novel was the investigation of the limits of the purely imaginary and the possibilities in fictionalizing one's experience, while Leiris also saw that Roussel and Rimbaud believed too strongly in the power of words, or fiction, to change one's life.

It is then telling that toward the end of his African travel, in the entry from December 26, 1932, Leiris appropriates Joseph Conrad's novel *Victory*, planning out a colonial tale that he never completes. This tale, unlike Roussel's wholly imaginary Africa, would borrow its materials from present-day colonial reality in the form of decadent eroticized colonialist writing, based on a Conradian character called Axel Heyst, an unsociable drifter. Leiris lists the assembled materials for the story and sketches an outline that is structured around a *mise en abyme* effect: Heyst's narrative is seen by a second character, a doctor, who pieces the narrative together from Heyst's papers that constitute a kind of intimate journal, but a rather confused one (1981, 617–18). Instead of a heroic adventure, the character's life has something of the ordinary in it that can be reduced to a kind of inventory of the main documents. The protagonist dies during an epidemic and leaves behind a small number of belongings that Leiris goes on to detail in the sketch: a photo of a blonde woman, some books and magazines, and the intimate journal. The journal, in turn, includes Axel Heyst's reflections on suicide, feared impotence, failed relationships and love, work, his tirades against romanticism, and short notes on other matters. Some of Heyst's reactions to black Africans, Leiris explains, reveal that the character's thinking is contaminated by racist prejudice despite his generally open-minded attitude (1981, 654–55). Thus, we find here a list of documents of a fictional personality to be narrated and turned into a story while the fiction, in turn, is firmly grounded in the documents of colonial reality. The act of narrating a life story, and the rules that govern memory, therefore become the subject of travel writing.[11]

But to return to the list of African imagery, the juxtaposition of the various references in this list also poses the question of their separation from their immediate contexts. The early twentieth-century artistic use of "primitive" items as found, hybrid objects meant not only the appropriation of those objects to a modernist primitivizing art discourse but also their appreciation in their own right (Bate 2004, 187, 193). Surrealism, and especially the journal *Documents* to which Leiris actively contributed from 1929 to 1931, broke with the first primitivism of Picasso, Apollinaire, and others. During the Mission Dakar-Djibouti, Leiris became disturbed by the ethnographic plunder of fetish objects for Parisian collections. A crucial moment in this respect is the incident with the sacred *Kono* objects about three and a half months into the expedition. In relation to the appropriation of these ritual objects, Leiris was at the same time excited by the sense of power in his own profanation but also realized the enormity of the ethnographers' responsibility (1981, 105–6). Later, Leiris wrote critically of the European vogue for African art or fetish objects, and the ethnographic appropriation or outright theft of non-European ritual objects, as signs of primitivism wholly cut off from their contexts. In his important 1950 essay "L'ethnographe devant le colonialisme," Leiris discussed the influence of the *l'art nègre* on the development of contemporary Western art and how African art had profoundly modified our very ways of living and our representation of the world (1950/1992, 149). The critical moment in the inventory of the list is that it turns the power of the object of memory, and the whole travel journal entry, into an open form of self-analysis, archaeology of cultural discourses, and personal desires. Perhaps also one is led to think with this list that the exotic phantasmagoria and the Orientalism of romantic opera are somehow tied to the atrocities of the present-day colonial reality.

Zone of Confusion

Leiris's list of African imagery, like the whole journal, is thoroughly marked by an awareness of the fact that self-identity is based on conceptions of a

---

11. For Clifford, in Leiris's sketch of a Conradian novel, the "process of collecting and telling a personal story becomes itself the focus of narration" (1988, 171). For Demeulenaere (2009, 264), Leiris's imagination of writing a fictional story of the experiences of the trek allows him to adopt different identities of the traveller as a character in a novel, no longer the narrator of his travel story.

determinate other, or determinate difference. The motto in the 1950 preface to *L'Afrique fantôme*, a quote from Rousseau's *Confessions*, makes this explicit:

> Moi seul. Je sens mon coeur, et je connais les hommes. Je ne suis fait comme aucun de ceux que j'ai vus: j'ose croire n'être fait comme aucun de ceux qui existent. Si je ne vaux pas mieux, au moins je suis autre. (Leiris 1981, 11)
>
> Myself alone. I feel my heart and I know men. I am not made like any of the ones I have seen; I dare to believe that I am not made like any that exist. If I am worth no more, at least I am different. (Rousseau 1995, 5)

Rousseau emphasized in the beginning of *Confessions* his own uniqueness but in the context of Leiris's travel journal the quotation rather stresses the importance of self-knowledge in relation to a fundamental recognition of otherness in one's self. The self is unique and, as it were, in a unique relationship with itself. But this uniqueness is only possible through a confrontation with the other, meaning either another person or sense of otherness within one's own self.

At the same time, Leiris's writing is affected by the difficulty of presenting the relationship with the other. Despite the persistence of the images of the African, the other in Leiris's inventory, be it within or outside the self, is not very determinate. A radical rupture with the notion of the African exotic other was an important outcome of Leiris's travel. Later, in his 1948 lecture "Message de l'Afrique," Leiris explained how in the course of travel the perception of similarities became more important than finding difference:

> De fil en aiguille et à mesure que je m'accoutumai à ce milieu nouveau, je cessai de regarder les Africains sous l'angle de l'exotisme, finissant par être plus attentif à ce qui les rapprochait des hommes des autres pays qu'aux traits culturels plus ou moins pittoresques qui les différenciaient. (1996, 880)
>
> Little by little and to the extent that I became accustomed to this new environment, I stopped looking at the Africans from the angle of exoticism, becoming more attentive to that which brought them closer to people from other countries than to those more or less picturesque cultural traits that differentiate them.

For Leiris, the African mission contributed to a gradual undermining of the "savage/civilized" pairing and the white/black hierarchy. Leiris explains here how the mythological idea of Africa finally dissipated from his mind and was replaced by a very real Africa (*Afrique bien réelle*). The dilemma includes the need to question the epistemological grounds for representing, describing, and narrating the other, in a dual relation of affirmation and denial of past knowledge on Africa.

The listing, therefore, is not just a sign of self-analysis but a record of a destabilizing moment in the writer's reformation of French colonial, ethnographic, and autobiographic identity. Leiris's teacher at *l'Institut d'Ethnologie*, Marcel Mauss, recommended the keeping of field notebooks. Mauss, however, probably did not have in mind Leiris's type of intimate journal, fuelled in part by psychoanalysis, where the attempt to speak about social reality results mainly in speech about oneself. For Leiris, the concept of national identity was problematic in the first place, but during his journey, as the list so well manifests, there emerges a wish to grasp the foundations of his own exoticizing conception of the other, involving specifically the idea of sub-Saharan cultures as the most distant and different from the European cultures and the desire to live out a myth through the exotic other.[12] The inventory and its heading, therefore, bear the trace of what postcolonial theory has called the "zone of occult instability" (Homi K. Bhabha's term for the geography of imperialism) and the "zone of confusion" in the imperialist space. For instance, Ian Baucom has argued that we should read British imperialism "not simply as the history of England's expansion and contraction but as the history of a cultivated confusion" (1999, 3). This entails that the "empire is less a place where England exerts control than the place where England loses command of its own narrative of identity" (1999, 3). Many entries of *L'Afrique fantôme,* including the entry for the nineteenth of June 1932, suggest an awareness of the loss of exoticism as a master narrative of identity.

Conception of Travel

There is a clear demystifying function to Leiris's list: knowledge of the African space and cultures is based on and presented as images and histories, but these histories are themselves at least partially founded in fiction and legend. Fusing historical events with fiction, and thus levelling between the two, the display of these materials shows how culture has provided the

---

12. By the desire to live out a myth through the other, I refer specifically to Leiris's often ambivalent wish to fully participate in a ritual of spirit possession, that is, to be possessed, during his stay in Gondar, from July to December 1932. On Leiris's ambivalent identification with the practitioners of the *zar* cult, see Albers 2008.

writer with ready-made categories. This interpretation is in line with "L'œil de l'ethnographe" (1930) where Leiris distances himself from exotic fairy tales, vaudeville shows, and *l'art nègre* that represented "Africa" to him in his childhood and youth.

The inventory of the African imagery, therefore, keeps in sight the sense of the loss of exoticism and a dislocation of colonial identity. At the end of this list, Leiris explains how his immersion in this ambience of images was interrupted by a local Ethiopian chief called Asfao who wanted to tell Leiris about his past good relations with the governor of French Somaliland, Léonce Lagarde. Leiris's African memories are thus juxtaposed with other reminiscing. As a result, the writer's revelry is suppressed by the pressure to consider an African's memory and actual colonial relations. But, perhaps more importantly, the composition of the entry thus acts out a dramatic return to the concrete present moment (and we might remember that the sense of the concrete is one aspect that Leiris admires in African societies in his lecture "Message de l'Afrique").

As I already suggested, the list serves to stress how certain narratives, images, and names in memory have the power to triumph over actual observations. From this perspective, it is important that *L'Afrique fantôme* includes, only some weeks later, another list in self-analysis inside an entry for July 7, 1932. The inventory that concerns the theme of travel builds explicitly on the surrealist breach with the restrictions of habit, intelligence, and morality and on a search for the strange and the marvellous within oneself. Like the examples of African imagery, these references are a combination of legendary and imaginary references as well as of historical events in near-contemporary reality. They include references to great mythical journeys in the sky and descents into hell; Oedipus killing his father in the course of his journeying; the revelation of the initiated in a distant place (Moses, Pythagoras, Jesus Christ, etc.); the quest for Sleeping Beauty; the absence of Bluebeard; the apprentice pursuing a tour de France to become a journeyman; the alchemist travellers; and the long distance sports of our day (1981, 389–90). There is little explicit interpretation of the meaning of this list other than Leiris's remark that he still must wait for a revelation—"Je suis bien obligé de constater, quant à moi, que j'attends encore la révélation" (1981, 390)—and that the most important model of a traveller to him is Oedipus. This is the story of a man who, as Leiris specifies, leaves his home and upon returning, being over a hundred years old, does not recognize anyone.

What Leiris underlines in this inventory of great travel is thus the traveller's alienation and misrecognition of identity that is comparable to an ironic occultation in the sense of one's disappearance upon returning—the idea resonates with Rimbaud's "disappearance" in Africa as well as with the occultation of thought demanded by André Breton. The list of great travels is followed, in the same entry, by a note on the numbing effect of travel on one's linguistic capacities. The isolation of the traveller therefore involves both disintegration and redefinition of one's language. In this respect, the inclusion of Rimbaud in the list of African imagery may become somewhat clearer. Rimbaud is obviously a great figure of forgetting and escape, also in terms of writing activity. Yet, for Leiris, who laments the impoverishment of his language, as he has just revised some of his entries in the travel journal, the African journey becomes a means of transition from one form of writing to another. The Rimbaud reference thus does not necessarily stand for the forgetting of poetry in the name of action but for the forgetting of dead expression and an "aestheticizing" mind.

In this second list and also elsewhere in the travel journal, for Leiris journeying through Africa pointed towards a kind of defamiliarization of perception, identity, and language. This equates to the idea of transgressive vagabondage, not wanting to fix oneself to one place or to one point in time. In a later 1935 essay, "L'Abyssinie intime," Leiris holds onto the importance of the idea of travelling to the archaic, not the exotic world, and the importance of forgetting oneself in travel. Leiris explains here how it is still agreeable to travel to Abyssinia:

> Voyager n'était pas une question d'horaire ni même de calendrier, voire d'itinéraire, mais partir simplement à l'aventure, sans trop savoir où l'on arriverait, ni surtout quand l'on arriverait. (1935/1992, 48)
>
> Travelling was not a question of a timetable or a calendar, or even an itinerary, but simply of embarking on an adventure, to not know too much about where one would go and, particularly, not about when one would get there.

In Ethiopia, Leiris no longer had many impressions of the exotic other but rather felt the similarity between the locals and the French, as he was engaged in studying the popular *zar* cult of spiritual possession. In the same 1935 essay, Leiris celebrates travel as an art of forgetting rather than as a means of learning or simple escape: the forgetting of questions of time and aging, skin color, body odor, taste, prejudice, and intellectual habits and means of expression—forgetting even the very meaning of travel (1935/1992, 56). The 1935 essay thus exemplifies the fact that while Leiris had abandoned one kind of exoticist project of escape, as he increasingly had to face a loss of command of the exotic discourse, this did not amount to a complete dissolution of exoticism in his writing practice. The sense of the archaic suggests a potential, residual "denial of coevalness" (in Johannes Fabian's sense of the term)[13] that marks Ethiopia and the Ethiopians as "prehistoric." The contemporary Ethiopia, therefore, functions for Leiris, as for any primitivist, as an access to a mythical past.[14] The "archaic" that Leiris finds in Ethiopia suggests that, while the writer is elsewhere self-reflexively aware of the pitfalls of colonial discourses, his writing practice does not always successfully negotiate through these pitfalls.

Yet, at the same time, the wish to forget oneself in archaic life and ritual is always haunted in Leiris's journal by the sense of the irresistible persistence in identity: the disillusionment in the power of travel to escape oneself or to transform oneself.[15] The ambiguous effect is detectable also in Leiris's mentioning, immediately after the list of great travels, that he is still waiting for a revelation and that, at the end of this entry, his life is becoming more and more "beastly":

> Ma vie est de plus en plus animale. Faute de pain (car je suis parti avec très peu de provisions), je mange de la galette abyssine. Faute d'eau potable, je bois de la bière d'orge. Dégoûté des conserves, je me nourris de lait, d'œufs, de miel et de poulet au berbéri. (1981, 390)
>
> My life is more and more beastly. Having no bread (since I left with very few supplies), I eat Abyssinian flat cake. With no drinking water, I drink barley beer. Disgusted by canned food, I feed myself with milk, eggs, honey, and chicken with barberry.

---

13. Fabian defines a "denial of coevalness" as "a persistent and systematic tendency to place the referent(s) of anthropology in a Time other than the present of the producer of anthropological discourse" (1983, 31). I would like to thank the anonymous reader of *Studies in Travel Writing* for drawing my attention to the problematic nature of the term "archaic" in Leiris's essay.

14. Marie-Denise Shelton argues for the central role of a "primitivist" function of Africa in *L'Afrique fantôme* that would assert "the radical opposition of civilized and primitive" (1995, 336). I find this hypothesis, as well as the references to Leiris's supposed fear of losing a sense of superiority vis-à-vis the colonized Africans, to be unconvincing. While Leiris certainly used Africa and Ethiopia for self-mythologizing purposes throughout his early career, and, as Shelton's essay makes apparent, *L'Afrique fantôme* is deeply involved in a colonialist project at many levels, it is the authority of the observing subject and the "authenticity" of the primitive object that are increasingly called into question in this travel journal. The same anthology where Shelton's article was published (*Prehistories of the Future*, Eds. Elazar Barkan and Ronald Bush) includes an important corrective by Marjorie Perloff to Marianna Torgovnick's critique, in *Gone Primitive* (1990), of Leiris's "exoticism" (1995, 339–54).

15. "Le voyage ne nous change que par moments, la plupart du temps vous restez tristement pareil à ce que vous aviez toujours été" (Leiris 1981, 225) ("Travel changes us only momentarily. Most of the time you remain sadly similar to the person you have always been.").

Leiris's regimen may have become less Western and more local, but it does not seem that beastly. The remark on the animal-like diet contrasts with the interest in journeys of initiation, and other heroic journeys of spiritual or professional growth, which he has just listed. Leiris is still waiting for his revelation, whatever that may be, concerning the meaning of travel and occult rituals. At the same time, the reference to a radical metamorphosis in "animal life" is a potential parody of Leiris's friend Georges Bataille's interest in purification in sacred ritual where one was supposed to strip oneself of all prejudice and instrumental modern knowledge.

Another striking exception to Leiris's emphasis on forgetting and effacement in travel, in *L'Afrique fantôme,* is the dynamic of attraction and repulsion that he reports in his relation with African women. This concerns the Dogon women but especially the Ethiopian woman Emawayish to whom he gradually attributes a true individuality in the travel journal entries during a five-month stay in Gondar.[16] Leiris's incapacity to participate fully in an occult ritual or to start a physical relationship with Emawayish reveals the persistence of Western identity to the writer. In relation to Emawayish it becomes impossible, if it ever was possible, for Leiris to use his African experience as a way to seek one's true, primitive self. Finally, during the stay in Gondar, *L'Afrique fantôme* realizes escapism as illusionary, especially the modernist pattern of "going native" or the wish to possess the exotic land symbolically through the body of the native woman. In this respect, Leiris's earlier European mantra of African images functions as an interim record of the changing relation between an attempt at forgetting himself through the other and a gradual acceptance of the persistence of his old self.

Leiris's Roussel

Raymond Roussel's presence in this list highlights the discrepancy between literary myth and colonial reality. In Roussel's ascetic imagination, the figure of Africa stands for a self-consciously conceived, *phantom* space, or a dream

---

16. While visiting the Dogon, Leiris explains, "Ce qui empêche, à mes yeux, les femmes noires d'être réellement excitantes, c'est qu'elles sont habituellement trop nues et que de faire l'amour avec elles ne mettrait en jeu rien de social" (1981, 148) ("What prevents, in my eyes, the black women from being really exciting is that they are usually too naked, and to make love with them would not bring into play anything social."). Leiris points out Emawayish's charm and beauty despite her "peasant appearance" (1981, 586) and later, in *L'Âge d'homme,* he reinterprets his feelings toward her as love. Vincent Kaufmann argues that Emawayish, since she emerges as a kind of extreme form of simulacra, allows for Leiris to remain European to the end (1989, 150–51). For more on Leiris's ambivalence vis-à-vis Emawayish, see Côté 2005.

space that does not correspond with any real geography or culture, as in a fully imaginary world. What is interesting to Leiris in such a phantom "Africa," however, may not so much be the pure fantasy of Africa but the undermining of the hierarchy between the primitive and the civilized. *Impressions d'Afrique* associates between a wholly imaginary Africa and an image of Europeans in Africa deeply engaged in fantastic phenomena, ritualistic machinery, inventions, and magic that some would, with disdain, call "primitive."[17] It is this levelling of cultures that likens Roussel, even if quite implicitly and within the realm of fiction, to the avant-garde ethnography of Leiris's day, scholars like Maurice Delafosse, who took seriously the proposition that positive knowledge of diverse histories and cultures, not racial theory, was the key for the development of ethnography. With the Roussel reference, Leiris may not be so much distancing himself from this writer and his exoticism than exposing some aspects of colonial discourse of Africa through his favourite reading. Roussel's "Africa," after all, provided Leiris with the possibility of turning the look on the "primitive" back on itself so that the civilized observer starts to look like the primitive. In another strange blend of fantasy and actuality, even if this may not directly relate to the contents of the list, Roussel was also Leiris's sponsor on the Mission Dakar-Djibouti.[18]

Roussel is mentioned in Leiris's essay "L'œil de l'ethnographe" together with the exotic fairy tales, vaudeville shows, and *l'art nègre*. Leiris explains that his first notions of Africa came from Roussel when, at the age of eleven, he attended a theatrical production of *Impressions d'Afrique*. Being inspired by this production, he was able to situate the sense of adventure in actual travel and poetic voyage of the mind at the same level of experience. Poetic travel, however, as Leiris further states, is only more deceptive and much less real, "beaucoup moins réel" (1930/1992, 28). It is both a tempting and a horrifying option for Leiris that imagination could be everything. On the one hand, Roussel's novel, from what we know about Leiris's attachment to this writer's works, including for instance an unfinished biography consecrated to this author, is a figure of revelation, not something to be forgotten. Roussel exem-

---

17. Leiris explains the double interest in Roussel's imaginary vision of Africa: "d'une part une Afrique telle, à peu de chose près, que nous pouvions la concevoir dans notre imagination d'enfants blancs, d'autre part, une Europe de phénomènes et d'inventions abracadabrantes telle que peut-être elle se trouve figurée dans l'esprit de ceux que nous nommons avec dédain des 'primitifs'" (1930/1992, 27) ("on the one hand, almost exactly a kind of Africa that we were able to imagine as white children and, on the other hand, a Europe of ludicrous phenomena and inventions of the kind that can perhaps be imagined to be discovered in the minds of those whom we call, with sneer, the 'primitives'")

18. See "Entretien sur Raymond Roussel" (Leiris 1998a, 268) and Leiris's thank you letter to Roussel signed on February 10, 1931 (Leiris 1998b, 290–91).

plified for Leiris both the perspective of the personal sacred and an interest in breaking mimetic representation (through a rejection of the plot narrative and insistence on the notion of the purely imaginary). Roussel stood for pure poetry for Leiris because he, far from trying to do away with rules in writing so as to make room for the unconscious by automatism, multiplied the rules and constraints of composition. Leiris discusses Roussel's work, in his unfinished "Cahier Raymond Roussel" that he started upon returning from the African mission, especially in terms of a kind of poetics subjected to the demands of a personal imaginary world and myth:

> L'effort de Roussel tend vers la création d'un monde imaginaire, entièrement conçu, qui n'ait plus rien de commun avec la réalité. L'effort est surtout négatif: couper un à un les liens qui retiennent le monde à la réalité. Sorte d'ascèse mystique. (1998c, 122)

> Roussel's efforts tend towards the creation of an imaginary world, entirely construed, which had nothing in common with reality. These efforts are most of all negative: to gradually cut all ties that bind the world to reality. A kind of mystical asceticism.

Leiris refers often in his writings on Roussel to the fact that, despite Roussel's many travels around the world, the exterior reality never seemed to disturb the writer's personal, interior universe. Roussel insisted on the purely linguistic status of his fictional inventions and, like his contemporary Henri Michaux, was a writer of the futility of travel. Instead of learning to know a foreign place, travel made possible for Roussel and Michaux an exploration of ontological and epistemological propositions of the self in relation to the world while being also a means to meet one's own phantasms. Nothing in his works, Roussel claimed, came from outside reality; everything came from inside the text, from the words, their relationships, and their interplay.[19]

There is a Roussel-like levelling of the real with the fantastic in Leiris's list. Roussel employed in his writing hallucinatory imagery and at the same time eschewed the expression of all personality. Yet, while Roussel said nothing

---

19. The experience of foreign places only mattered to Roussel if they corresponded with this particular universe. Upon Roussel's visit to Tahiti, his main interest was to see the tomb of Loti's fictive heroine. In his *Comment j'ai écrit certains de mes livres,* Roussel famously states "Or, de tous ces voyages, je n'ai jamais rien tiré pour mes livres. Il m'a paru que la chose méritait d'être signalée tant elle montre clairement que chez moi l'imagination est tout" (Roussel 1963, 27) ("I have gained nothing from these travels as regards to my books. It is worth pointing this out since it shows clearly how imagination is everything to me."). Roussel was also not interested in hearing about Leiris's experiences in Africa. See Leiris 1998b, 268.

about himself in his texts, and related to the reader very little of his characters' psyche, he nevertheless revealed in his thematic repertoire a consistent psychological content that, in Leiris's interpretation, equalled the content of great myths (Leiris 1998c, 113). Similarly, the title of Leiris's travel journal, suggested to the writer by his editor at Gallimard, André Malraux, points out that what Leiris discovered in Africa was to an important degree an inner experience or a phantasm and part of his personal mythology. His African journey thus made it possible for him to combine living with writing or writing with action as Leiris emphasizes in the preface "The Autobiographer as a Torero" ("De la littérature considérée comme une tauromachie") to his L'Âge d'homme.

On the other hand, the inclusion of Roussel is not devoid of ambiguity. For some child-like fantastic rendering of Africa, like that of Roussel, to triumph over actual observations of colonial reality indicates also the potential terrifying power that all-too-persistent narratives, images, and names can have in memory. In the company of actual instances of colonial violence, or old legends and romantic Orientalist opera, Roussel's imaginary avant-garde version of Africa stands out also as a form of Western belief in the transformative power of words. Leiris saw that Roussel and Rimbaud were similar in having too much confidence in the influence of words in changing the world (1998c, 181). Or as Leiris wrote, Rimbaud and Roussel simply made "foolish and childish demands" on literature to change one's life. It is possible that this exaggerated belief in and near obsession with the power of words and imagination is something that Leiris wanted to forget, together with the whole aestheticizing attitude of Western intellectuals, despite the fact that Roussel remains for him a figure of revelation.[20]

Conclusion

As may have already become evident by my interpretative quest, I believe the juxtaposition and framing of Leiris's African "images," and their ambiva-

---

20. Leiris's writings on Roussel reveal a deep interest in the question of the relation between inspiration and process: how word play and rules of composition could function as sources of writing and as the suspension of the everyday experience. Roussel's emphasis on the opposition between inspiration and process (power of transmutation) attracted but also troubled Leiris. On the one hand, Leiris adhered to Roussel's idea of literature as a process and an act (evidenced, for instance, in Leiris's poetic word play and decomposition of words in his parodic *glossaires*). On the other hand, Leiris's interest in Roussel's *instinct de jeu* and associative play was not surrealist at all—that is, not based on the gratuitous rapprochement between the elements but on the idea of strict rules of composition.

lent status between narrative and non-narrative, to be suggestive in their own right. Let me reiterate three reasons why this would be so. First, the list calls attention to the way meaning is given to the unexpected during the African journey, perhaps even more so since the inventory is (nearly) devoid of commentary. The inventory thus provokes a sense of a dialectic relation between a submission to the travel experience and the projection of desire and memory onto African space and life. Second, the listing indicates awareness, possibly but not necessarily ironic, of the writer's strategic location and of a critical relation to the existing categories for conceiving Africa. The list serves to stress how certain narratives, images, and names in memory are powerful enough to triumph over actual observations. And finally, in its ambivalent mapping of various images of the African other, the list suggests a potentially delirious space where the lines of the guilty colonizer's history and the insubordinate, or the purely fantastic, meet. The effect of such a delirium is accentuated by the interruption of narrative authority at two levels: the inventory of African imagery disrupts the narrative of travel but the "ambience" that these images, which include several narratives, provoke in the note-taker is in turn cancelled by the actuality of the everyday.

However, it is already a kind of interpretation to call this list an inventory. Instead of understanding the title "African imagery" as referring to a detailed, comprehensive list that covers the most significant resources of Africanist discourse from Leiris's perspective, it might serve us better to treat it as a more or less random list of references, the contents of which could vary (the open-ended nature of the list is indicated by the "etc." at the end). The connotations of the terms "ambience" and "imagery" are also manifold, perhaps intentionally so. On the one hand, the textual ambience of the imagery may have the form of revelry, escapism, perhaps memory of childhood sensations of haunting exoticism and horror, or all of these combined. On the other hand, several of these references are not actually "images" as such. They are historical events and situations better known as (traumatic) events and narratives in the culture at large.

For all these reasons, Leiris's African imagery is marked by cultivated confusion. To a considerable degree, the list testifies to a kind of impossibility of transparency, resulting in self-forgetfulness as much as in remembering. The references included in the list may be both signs of the forgotten or the remembered; the missing explanatory frame gives the inscription an unsettling form of inventory and cartography of identity, or artificial memory. The analysis of Leiris's African imagery thus suggests to us that in *L'Afrique fantôme*, "Africa" is not a treatable or manageable entity, as a whole to be transformed into a narrative or a series of notes, neither anything marvellously exotic. The Africa of Leiris's list is rather an excess of experience, analogous perhaps to the unconscious, the personal sacred, or the ceaselessly self-transforming figure of an *objet fantôme*. As David Scott suggests, the travel journal's title "draws implicit attention to the difficulty of grasping the real or the exotic other except as phantom or illusion." For this reason, the notion of Africa is a phantom notion, "an elusive principle as much as a real object, that will be pursued."[21]

Leiris's list of African imagery, however, like his interpretation of Roussel's literary techniques, is not a surrealist celebration of immediate absurdity, even if the list combines the imaginary with colonialist atrocity, romantic opera with the history of railway construction and forced labor. Rather, the inventory transforms the surrealist aesthetic of the object, and its metaphoric *dépaysement,* into ethnography of the self and the colonialism of ethnography. In the process, the self is made strange as an object of description. Here the ethnographic and avant-garde perspectives coalesce but also stay apart as both get tangled up in the textual imagery and the actual space of colonial history.

21. Scott 2005. I am grateful for the author's permission to quote from his unpublished essay.

Africanist Paradoxes of Storytelling in Karen Blixen's *Out of Africa*

KAREN BLIXEN'S (also known as Isak Dinesen, 1885–1962) *Out of Africa* (1937), set in the so-called British East Africa where the writer lived between 1914 and 1931, was an international bestseller. *Out of Africa* has been usually classified as a memoir, but the classification has not been unanimously accepted among critics. In part, this is due to the book's fragmented, episodic form that distinguishes it from traditional memoirs or autobiographies and, in part, to the liberties that Blixen took in her book with some facts of her life in East Africa. Furthermore, Blixen's narrative perspective, which is self-consciously retrospective and nostalgic, draws attention to the idealized reality of the object of description.[1] Blixen points frequently in her memoir to the fact that the people and places that she writes about in her memoir have already disappeared:

> The colony is changing and has already changed since I lived there. When I write down as accurately as possible my experiences on the farm, with the country and with some of the inhabitants of the plains and woods, it may have a sort of historical interest. (1954, 28)

---

1. Susan C. Brantly, among others, points out that Blixen took several liberties with the facts in *Out of Africa*, as Blixen's letters also demonstrate (2002, 75). Brantly refers to *Out of Africa* frequently as a novel.

The Africa that she portrays in *Out of Africa* is a memory recalled through the writing, and the accuracy that she calls upon herself to attain is presumably only of historical interest. In fact, Blixen's Africa was already becoming a place of nostalgia when she lived there: a place that, as she reports, was going to lose its rough qualities because of urban development in the rapidly growing city of Nairobi. Thus, the focus of her description in *Out of Africa* is a lost world,[2] and Blixen's (lost) home is the farm in Africa, to which she attaches herself retrospectively at the moment of narration. In the course of the book, Blixen's farm at the foot of the Ngong Hills becomes a kind of transcendental point of comparison in regard to the present moment and place of narration, which is somewhere in Denmark in the mid-1930s but remains unspecified. In what follows, I will refer to Blixen's work as a memoir, mindful of the complexity of this classification.

Out of Africa is divided thematically into five parts roughly equal in length. Parts one and two describe Blixen's life at her coffee plantation and portray some occupants of her farm, such as a Kikuyu boy named Kamante, who was her medical assistant and helper. She also tells the story of a shooting accident on the farm, in which one native boy shot two others, killing one and seriously injuring the other. In Part three, Blixen writes about the visitors to her farm, who came from other parts of British East Africa, Europe, and Asia and concludes with a description of her aeroplane flights over Kenya, which she calls "the greatest, the most transporting pleasure of my life on the farm" (1954, 204). Part four, entitled "From an Immigrant's Notebook," consists of anecdotes, literary portraits, descriptions of landscape and animals, and some fictional tales. Blixen's expansion of the scope of her memoir in Part four to include fictions will be of particular interest to us in this chapter. The memoir ends with Part five ("Farewell to the Farm"), where Blixen describes her departure from the farm.

My focus in this chapter is the relation between Blixen's notions of Africa and storytelling, particularly in regard to the way in which these notions emerge in Part four of the memoir. I argue that Blixen's "Africa" is to a significant degree a malleable sign, into which the writer projected a personal myth concerning the Africans' innate nobility and their supposed sense of both unity with the environment and the meaning of stories. Blixen's contacts with Africans who listened to her stories, in particular, offered her opportunities for reinvigorating the art of storytelling, beyond the confines of the physical book, private reading of books, and modernist poetics. The investigation

---

2. See also Ekman 2002, 123–24, who argues that paradise before the Fall is the fundamental image of *Out of Africa*.

begins with the story "The Roads of Life," in which Blixen lays down certain principles of storytelling that are important with regard to the organization of her memoir as a whole. These principles are also echoed in a number of Blixen's short stories that raise questions about the functions of narratives and the impact of storytelling.

The Narrative Paradox of the Stork

The fragment "The Roads of Life" enjoys a strategically important position in the beginning of Part four in Blixen's memoir. The fragment starts with a fairy tale about a man who hears a terrible noise at night. The man in the story starts off from his house to find the cause of the noise. After falling into ditches, and taking a wrong turn, he then discovers that there is a big leakage in a nearby dam. He fixes the dam and sleeps peacefully again. The story closes with what seems like an apparition: in the morning, having just woken up, the man is surprised to see a stork in his yard. This is followed by Blixen's interpretation of the story's meaning, to which I will return shortly.

The story foregrounds its narrative design as both a spatially and temporally structured verbal composition. There are repeated geometric patterns within the tale. For instance, the protagonist lives in a *round* house with a *round* window that has a *triangular* garden in front of it. Some of these spatial forms are also made explicit by the storyteller in the tale. The storyteller draws a *plan* of the roads taken by the man in search of the source of the noise, "as upon a map of the movements of an army" (1954, 214). Much of the unfolding of the story takes place in the space of these *roads*, which the listeners supposedly see on a map that is drawn for them. The man runs to-and-fro first to the south, then back to the north, and finally back to the south and the north again. At the very end of the story he sees the stork in his *triangular* yard through the *round* window.

The repeated spatial patterns of the story suggest that the story may be understood as having a spatial and visual form but, at the same time, the relationship between text and image in the story is strained to the point of being almost absurd. Blixen's retelling of the story does not include the map that is mentioned in the story but simple drawings of a stork. These are the only visual images in Blixen's memoir. The drawings are not only divided into parts inside the text, but they are seemingly juxtaposed at random within the story, perhaps reminding us of the way the miraculous bird suddenly appears at the story's end. Moreover, by giving us not just the narrative but also its illustration—an illustration, however, which is fragmented and not merely at

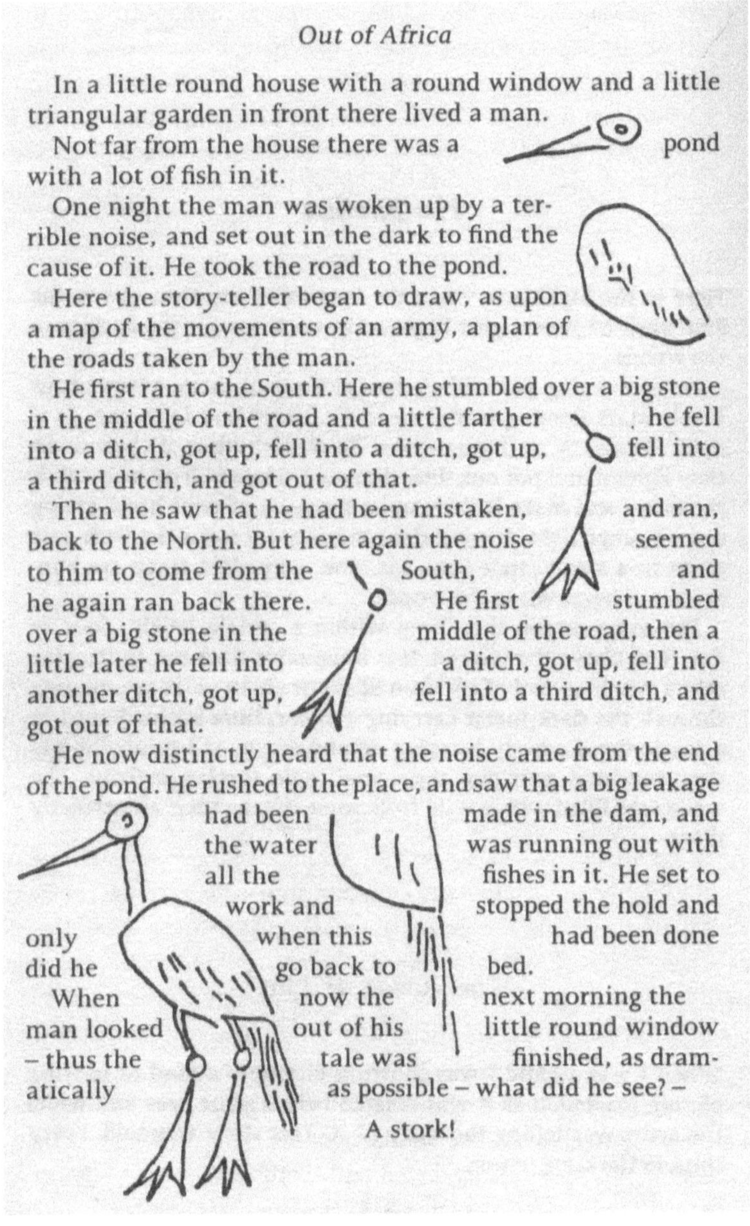

Out of Africa

In a little round house with a round window and a little triangular garden in front there lived a man.

Not far from the house there was a pond with a lot of fish in it.

One night the man was woken up by a terrible noise, and set out in the dark to find the cause of it. He took the road to the pond.

Here the story-teller began to draw, as upon a map of the movements of an army, a plan of the roads taken by the man.

He first ran to the South. Here he stumbled over a big stone in the middle of the road and a little farther he fell into a ditch, got up, fell into a ditch, got up, fell into a third ditch, and got out of that.

Then he saw that he had been mistaken, and ran back to the North. But here again the noise seemed to him to come from the South, and he again ran back there. He first stumbled over a big stone in the middle of the road, then a little later he fell into a ditch, got up, fell into another ditch, got up, fell into a third ditch, and got out of that.

He now distinctly heard that the noise came from the end of the pond. He rushed to the place, and saw that a big leakage had been made in the dam, and the water was running out with all the fishes in it. He set to work and stopped the hold and when this had been done only did he go back to bed.

When the next morning the man looked out of his little round window – thus the tale was finished, as dramatically as possible – what did he see? –

A stork!

Figure 8. The stork figure in the story "The Roads of Life" in Karen Blixen's *Out of Africa* (© Karen Blixen).

the service of the text—the narrative makes the point of storytelling as a performance. The way the fragmented image appears to "cut through" the body of the text on the page points to a question: Where does the sense of the story come from beyond the coextension of the textual and visual parts?

On the one hand, the relation between the text of the story and the image has the potential to undermine the custom of being satisfied with a mere impression of a phenomenon. On the other hand, however, it is possible to find a meaningful correspondence between the visual and the verbal elements in the story. The word and the image "'tell'" the same story in the sense that the narrative closure takes hold of the fleeting image of the stork, just as the image concludes the story. To see a stork first thing in the morning could symbolize, in traditional Western reading at least, a new birth. The stork of the story and the stork of the page might further indicate a fruition of some new idea, implied also by the man's waking up from a dream. Blixen's commentary, which concludes the fragment, affirms this interpretation: the stork is the man's reward after he has completed the task, that is, solved the problem of the source of the noise, after having successfully kept his faith to go forward in his search. The stork, thus, also stands for a continuing belief in life, and in the pattern that one's life has; it may even be, as Blixen suggests in her letters from Africa, "life itself" (1981, 50).

"The Roads of Life" raises important questions of storytelling that involve narrativity (What constitutes a narrative?), narrativisation (How to translate life experience into a narrative? Does one's life have a narrative design?), the composition of narratives (What is required of a well-crafted story?), and the uses of narratives (What are narratives good for?).[3] The complex dynamic between the image and the story both exhibits and generates strong narrativity. But this dynamic also associates narrative with a dream image that is difficult to turn into any simple verbal meaning, as in a narrative. The picture that the storyteller shows is, in Blixen's words, a "kind of moving picture," something that can only be seen as part of the narrative process, and the storyteller's performance that translates the picture into a story. Yet, at the same time, a certain degree of hesitation in interpretation seems to be inscribed into the story and the accompanying pictures. There are, for instance, two images of the same bird or two similar-looking birds on the same page. The first image of a bird is dismembered and doubled. The "dissected" parts of the first bird can be seen in a temporal series so that they gradually become assembled into the second bird, the whole bird that we see in the left-hand

---

3. "Narrativity" is understood here in the sense that Gerald Prince gives the term: "the set of properties characterising narrative and distinguishing it from nonnarrative," and "the formal and contextual features making a narrative more or less narrative, as it were"(2003, 65).

corner of the page. This series reiterates the fact that the listening to or reading of the story must proceed through gaps in information, suggesting thus that the audience processes narrative information gradually. In listening to or reading narratives, we anticipate future events, fill in the gaps and test out hypotheses, and change our inferences when we confront new information, just as the protagonist is first deceived by the direction of the sound but then reorientates towards the true source of the noise. There is always also the option that the reader stumbles over gaps in narrative meaning, just as the man stumbles over a big stone and makes a wrong turn.

The discrepancy in the text-image relation points, moreover, to a more comprehensive design between the various parts of *Out of Africa*. Without being overtly self-reflective, the story explains the way narratives can be told, processed, and experienced and how they can capture their audience by means of suggestion. The narrative of Blixen's African memoir, and in particular the fourth part of the book, is structured around narrative morsels, fragments, anecdotes, juxtapositions, and associative comparisons; it requires that the reader assemble the text from an overall tapestry of the tale.[4] As an analogy and a kind of textual microcosm of Blixen's global narrative, the story "The Roads of Life" thus mirrors in its form the gradually emerging sense of the complex African experience, intimately linked with the question about the meaning and potential effects of storytelling. The sense of renewed perception that Blixen associates with Africa, and that is reflected in the fragmented organization of her memoir, is also echoed in the title of her early poem, which refers to Pliny the Elder's (A.D. 23–79) dictum *Ex Africa semper aliquid novi*, "Always something new out of Africa . . . ," and gives the name to her memoir.

Blixen illustrates the meaning and the personal significance of the tale by way of comparison with the *Aeneid* and the Bible at the end of the fragment. Here she refers to the necessity to tell about unspeakable suffering, as depicted in the second book from Virgil's *Aeneid* that includes Aeneas's line "Infandum regina iubes renovare dolorem" ("You command me, O Queen, to revive unspeakable grief"). This is Aeneas's response to Queen Dido when she insists that Aeneas tell her about the Trojan War. Furthermore, Blixen draws an analogy between the story of the stork and the second article from the Christian Creed of faith, which constitutes a short story in itself, speaking of Christ's state of humiliation and the following exaltation. The protagonists of these three stories, Aeneas, Christ, and the man in the story, just like Blixen

---

4. We may, furthermore, consider the fact that Blixen kept rewriting her African memoir also elsewhere, including her letters, the early poem "Ex Africa" (1915), and *Shadows on the Grass* (1961).

herself, have all faced hardships that appear to be beyond comprehension. Blixen explains that the question for all of them is: "What is to come out of it?" Associating herself with these figures, Blixen further wonders whether she will ever be able to see such a stork: "The tight place, the dark pit in which I am now lying, of what bird is it the talon?" (1954, 215). Her interpretation of "The Roads of Life" develops the personal meaning of the story also by thought report as she imagines what the man in the story must have thought and felt: "He must have thought: 'What ups and downs! 'What a run of bad luck!' He must have wondered what was the idea of his trials: he could not know that it was a stork" (1954, 215). Blixen thus focuses on the man's mental processes. These processes are not explicated in the story itself, however, but only suggested by what is said about the man's actions and behavior. Blixen refrains from making the autobiographical meaning of the story explicit, but it is implied elsewhere in the memoir that the "tight place" and "the dark pit" to which she refers must involve the bankruptcy of her farm that forced her to leave Kenya and the death of her lover Denys Finch Hatton, both of which took place in 1931.

As has already become apparent, the figure of the stork symbolizes a number of related things—perseverance and the final reward (keeping one's purpose in view), the sense of design and completion in one's life—rather than directly pointing to or explaining any one thing. The mystery and suggestiveness of this bird figure repeats a typical trait throughout Blixen's fiction, in *Winter's Tales* (1943) and *Last Tales* (1957), but one which is already evident in *Seven Gothic Tales* (1934), the collection that Blixen started writing in Africa. That is, in response to difficult existential questions, Blixen's characters often explain themselves by telling a story. In one of Blixen's *Last Tales*, "The Cardinal's First Tale," the Cardinal asserts that the best way to answer the question "Who am I?" is to tell a story. In the Cardinal's definition of the ancient art of the divine story, a story is always open to mystery and interpretation, and functions by way of suggestion, instead of giving a definitive answer to the question. In another short story from the same collection, "The Blank Page," the storyteller, an old "coffee-brown, black-veiled woman," explains that it is crucially important to be loyal to the story. This, again, requires telling the story by way of suggestion, rather than by explication: "Where the story-teller is loyal, eternally and unswervingly loyal to the story, there, in the end, silence will speak" (Blixen 1957, 126).

What is also noteworthy in this story and Blixen's framing of it, and the parallel they draw between the man in the fairy tale and the author's own trials, is the technique of embedded narratives so common to Blixen's short stories. More precisely, this involves the use of embedded stories in a way that they forge thematic and structural analogies with the frame story, thus accentuating the given themes. For instance, the inset Orientalist story of a double in "A Consolatory Tale" in *Winter's Tales* illustrates and furthers the theme of duality, and the idea of interdependence between the artist and his audience, which the main characters in the frame narrative have discussed. In the fairy tale included in the fragment "The Roads of Life," the sense of embedding and doubling is mirrored in the fact that there are two storytellers telling the same story: the narrator, who is situated within the tale, and Blixen, who retells the story in her memoir. The Chinese-box structure suggests that there may be a particular design to life that storytelling can make apparent, as in an image. This has further implications in terms of Blixen's entire attempt to retell the story of her African life through various narrative fragments. Therefore, we may take the art of storytelling itself to be one of the possible meanings of the stork figure. Blixen turns "The Roads of Life" into a story of the telling of the story itself, and the stork figure implies how stories can give a certain design to one's life (no matter how fragmented or suggestive).[5] At the same time, the mystery of the bird—in association with Blixen's puzzlement over the question "Of what bird is it the talon?"—points to the difficulty and perhaps impossibility of knowing the full story of one's life. In the same way as Blixen had to leave her farm because of obstacles put in her way, the man in the story cannot assess the consequences of his actions and choices before it is too late to redo them. He can only see the whole picture of his situation (and story) in retrospect, as a chance occurrence, at the moment when he sees the stork.

The embedded structure of "The Roads of Life" thus accentuates the themes of storytelling and narrativisation in Blixen's memoir. These themes are intimately associated, specifically in Part four of her memoir, with Blixen's notion of the African tradition of storytelling. This tradition is, supposedly, less constrained by the chronological organization of time, and more structured around repetition, sound, and suggestion, than modern written literature. The African natives, as Blixen explains in her letters, are like very young children, who find joy in hearing things repeated (1981, 159–60).[6] This sounds condescending, but the emphasis on repetition and oral storytelling also explains some of Blixen's own compositional choices in *Out of Africa*.

---

5. Tone Selboe has referred to the meta-level of meaning in the stork figure as a symbol of art (1996, 17) and underscored the importance of this anecdote in *Out of Africa* and for Blixen's whole oeuvre (1996, 13).

6. See also one of Blixen's last letters from Africa (dated March 17, 1931): "I am one of Africa's favourite children—a great world of poetry has revealed itself to me and taken me to itself here, and I have loved it" (1981, 416).

The themes and structure of the story "Roads of Life" relate to Blixen's wish, as expressed explicitly elsewhere in *Out of Africa,* to return to the origins of storytelling in a simple but well-crafted story and to continue a tradition. Such basic forms of storytelling, further, maintain their interest over time, even if the audience is already familiar with their turning points and denouement. In another fragment in the same part of the book, "Natives and Verse," Blixen relates how the natives, who had no previous knowledge of verse, quickly understood the poetic function of mere patterns of sounds in rhymes and perceived that meaning in poetry was of no consequence. Such narrative comfort with and excitement about a performance with mere sounds of words, subsequently, requires a certain loosening of the distinction between narrative design and lived reality. The Africans' name for rhyming and poetry, the simile "speaking like the rain," associates the sounds of words with the natural phenomenon of rain, thus reaffirming Blixen's notion of authentic storytelling situations that are motivated in part by her views about the sense of unity with the surrounding African nature. Blixen identifies storytelling as a common thread in the European and African relationship, as a form of social interaction that requires engagement from all participants, but in Europe, Blixen laments, the art of telling stories is lost: the white people take in their impressions by the eye and prefer reading to listening.[7] By this Blixen does not mean that she would prefer the Africans' illiteracy to Western book culture, but that viewed over a long historical perspective the practices of writing and reading have undergone certain irrevocable changes in Western societies, changes that Blixen regrets and, in some sense, would like to challenge.

It is important to note how the problem of narrativisation relates to Blixen's notions of African pride, freedom, and the Africans' instinctual relation with nature and God. "The Roads of Life" comes from Blixen's childhood, and she heard it many times as a child; it is not an African tale. The story was familiar to her whole family, as becomes obvious in Blixen's frequent references to the story in her letters to her mother and brother from Kenya,[8] and

---

7. Tamar Yacobi has pointed out Blixen's "deliberate throwback to *oral* storytelling"—for instance, in her preferred techniques of perspective and narration (omniscient storyteller) and her enactment of the process of narration: "So the superhuman frame combines with its insets to bring back (to mind; if possible, to life) the origins of narrative art in 'story': divine, not earthly, vision and management; telling, not writing" (1991, 451).

8. For instance, in a letter to her mother on June 14, 1917: "Just when one feels one is floundering in the deepest despair,—'fall into a ditch, get out again,'—is when one is perfecting the work of art of one's life . . . the greatest moments have been those when I have been able to glimpse the stork" (1981, 49). See also Blixen 1981, 269–70, 288, and 293–94. The story has been later published separately as a picture book and retold by Jette Ahm as *Storken: En berättelse av Karen Blixen* (Copenhagen: Opal, 1978). Another possible form of symbolism in the story is

in Blixen's explanation at the very end of the fragment that "I am glad that I have been told this story and I will remember it in the hour of need" (1954, 215). Yet, at the same time, Blixen gives a new African dimension to this tale by placing it in the memoir with other stories about wild animals that function as a metonymic device for the nobility and pride of the whole of Africa. "The Roads of Life" is preceded, for instance, by a fragment on fireflies, which concludes with an emphasis on "a wild frolicsome life" that fills the woods, and is followed by an anecdote entitled "The Wild Came to the Aid of the Wild" that tells about a young wild ox that could not be domesticated. Before the manager of her farm and her ox-drivers were able to break the animal's will, a leopard managed to eat off one of the bound animal's hind legs and the ox had to be finished off. Part four of the book abounds with such stories of wild and captured animals, and also other birds and storks are mentioned. Blixen explains later in the same part of her memoir, in a fragment entitled "Some African Birds," how storks have quite different habits in Africa than in Europe. By this she refers to the way in which the storks in Africa fly in large flocks, hunting locusts, mice, and snakes, seemingly enjoying their time, unlike in Europe where the bird has to mate and live like a "married" couple, which makes the stork a symbol of domestic happiness there (1954, 243). All these and other fragments on African animals and wildlife develop the same thematic oppositions between the wild versus the tame, and Africa versus Europe, which are important in "The Roads of Life." The intertwined oppositions of traditional oral storytelling versus modern written literature (or mere reading), narrative design in life versus unpredictable and episodic modern life, and unity with one's surroundings versus separation from nature also reemerge in other stories that follow "The Roads of Life." Thus, in order for us to deepen our understanding of Blixen's notion of the nature and power of storytelling, and her conception of the relationship between fiction and her memoir, we must discuss her depiction of African wildlife in more detail.

Metonymies of the Wild

In *Out of Africa*, the wild animals and birds, and the African landscape of her farm and the nearby game reserve, represent for Blixen what she calls the pride of God. The natives, as Blixen saw them, had preserved much of this natural nobility and their instinctual sense of unity with the natural world,

---

the gender of the stork: Blixen frequently described women in bird images in her oeuvre. See Cederborg 1986, 23.

unlike the Europeans. The sense of nobility that she associates with East African landscape becomes apparent right from the book's famous opening. It is worth quoting it in full:

> I had a farm in Africa at the foot of the Ngong Hills. The Equator runs across these highlands, a hundred miles to the north, and the farm lay at an altitude of over six thousand feet. In the day-time you felt that you had got high up, near to the sun, but the early mornings and evenings were limpid and restful, and the nights were cold.
>
> The geographical position and the height of the land combined to create a landscape that had not its like in all the world. There was no fat on it and no luxuriance anywhere; it was Africa distilled up through six thousand feet, like the strong and refined essence of a continent. The colours were dry and burnt, like the colours in pottery. The trees had a light delicate foliage, the structure of which was different from that of the trees in Europe; it did not grow in bows or cupolas, but in horizontal layers, and the formation gave to the tall solitary trees a likeness to the palms, or a heroic and romantic air like full-rigged ships with their sails furled, and to the edge of a wood a strange appearance as if the whole wood were faintly vibrating. Upon the grass of the great plains the crooked bare old thorn-trees were scattered, and the grass was spiced like thyme and bog-myrtles; in some places the scent was so strong that it smarted in the nostrils. All the flowers that you found on the plains, or upon the creepers and liana in the native forest, were diminutive like flowers of the downs—only just in the beginning of the long rains a number of big, massive heavy-scented lilies sprang out on the plains. The views were immensely wide. Everything that you saw made for greatness and freedom, and unequalled nobility. (1954, 13)

Blixen's description of the landscape, the geography, and the flora of and around her farm evokes the themes and features that she associates with Africa throughout her memoir: the sense of vast space and renewed perception, the privileged view from above, the heroism and romanticism of African trees, animals and people, their innate nobility and aristocracy, and freedom, in contrast with European modern civilization. With regard to the traditional Africanist dual evaluations of monstrousness *and* nobility, the latter being for instance evident, as Christopher L. Miller suggests, in Pliny's "newness," Blixen's notion of Africa prioritizes the side of the noble—the demonic that she associates with African nature and the Africans is another manifestation of their nobility and innate aristocracy. The description is in the past tense, which further accentuates the impression of a lost and idealized world.

A similar pantheistic view of the unity between people, animals, their environment, and God can be found in many places in Blixen's memoir, including the fictional story "In the Menagerie" about Count von Schimmelmann, a Danish traveller to Hamburg who visits an itinerant menagerie, in Part four of the book. In this story, the proprietor of a menagerie, who is also called a showman, explains his philosophy about the hyena and the wild animals to Count von Schimmelmann. The Count is driven to the show by some inexplicable inner necessity; the menagerie responds to "something within his own mind" (1954, 259), but he is unable to understand what the proprietor explains to him. The proprietor's speculation about whether the hyena's supposed hermaphroditic nature—"because he unites in himself the complementary qualities of creation" (1954, 259)—doubles the animal's suffering in captivity leads the conversation to the question as to whether life amongst the wild animals is somehow unique. The self-satisfied Count doubts whether it can be said that wild animals like the giraffe see each other at all—that is, whether they are at all conscious of each other as creatures. The proprietor, in contrast, much in line with the views that Blixen voices elsewhere in *Out of Africa*, assumes that the giraffe and the hyena are seen directly by God. To the proprietor, these wild animals are a possible proof of the existence of God and, therefore, to love them is to love God: "The wild animals, your Excellency, are perhaps a proof of the existence of God. But when they go to Hamburg [. . .] the argument becomes problematic" (1954, 260). The showman finds it quite possible to see beauty in snakes as well since, he explains, God will mostly give us those—unlike the Count who believes that an aversion to snakes is a sound human instinct.

The fantastic atmosphere of the story relates closely to the short stories included in Blixen's *Seven Gothic Tales* and, in fact, the character of Count von Schimmelmann is familiar to Blixen's readers from two stories in this collection, "The Roads Round Pisa" and "The Poet." The inclusion of the story "In the Menagerie" in the memoir thus points out how fiction, and the narrative conventions of fiction to present a character's mind, such as the narrator's report of some character's thoughts, may deepen the themes in the memoir—in this case, the themes of suffering in captivity, the captors' greed and insensitivity, and the Westerners' inability to understand the beauty in the wildlife. Count von Schimmelmann's thoughts and mental reactions, which are rendered visible to us by thought report—his absorption in his own thoughts, incapacity to pay attention to others, and the conformism of his thinking—

deepen Blixen's caricature of Western prejudices about wild life and the Africans by showing us a narrow-minded Westerner partly from the inside.

The theme of captured wild animals emerges in several stories in Blixen's memoir around and after "The Roads of Life," including the tales of the captured giraffes, waiting to be sent to a zoo in Hamburg, and of the caged flamingos that are shipped to Marseilles. In the story "The Iguana," Blixen also advises against shooting the iguana, since the lizard loses its beautiful colors at death, recalling a hero's saying in some book that the author had read as a child: "I have conquered them all, but I am standing amongst graves" (1954, 221).[9] What is remarkable in most of these stories is the intimate connection between the Africans and wild animals. The metaphors and similes that Blixen employs in "The Iguana," for instance, make this evident: just like the colourful bracelet that only looks good on the black skin of a native girl—"No sooner had it come upon my own arm that it gave up the ghost" (1954, 220)— the iguana will maintain its beautiful colors only when it is alive and free. The story of the native called Kitosch, similarly, who is flogged and humiliated to death by whites for some slight misdemeanour (riding the mare of his white employer), also embodies for Blixen

> the fugitiveness of the wild things who are, in the hour of need, conscious of a refuge somewhere in existence; who go when they like; of whom we can never get hold. (1954, 243)

Kitosch suffers from similar injustice as the bound, wild oxen in the story "The Wild Came to the Aid of the Wild," in another analogy between African animals and people. However, it is important to note that by including Kitosch's story in her memoir against her English publisher's wishes, Blixen also made a conscious decision to depict violence committed by the settlers against the Africans and, thus, to point out the disgrace of the colonial system that tried to conceal such incidents.[10]

---

9. Blixen's constant praise of African wild nature, and the pride of the wild animals, did not prevent her, however, from hunting the giraffe or the lion and describing her enjoyment of the hunt. In effect, participation in hunting provided her with extraordinary sensations that were sometimes associated with feelings of unconditional love. This is revealed, for instance, when a shot with Denys Finch-Hatton's rifle equals to her "a declaration of love" (1954, 198). Blixen found many other forms of hunting or killing wild animals repulsive, however. For instance, she casts in an ironic light a Swedish scholar who wanted to kill fifteen hundred monkeys for scientific reasons. Blixen's relationship to hunting changed in the last ten years of her stay in Africa to the extent that she started to see all hunting, as she explains in *Shadows on the Grass*, as unreasonable, ugly, and vulgar (1985, 306).

10. See, for instance, Rasmussen 1983.

In another story entitled "The Parrot," which is the last of the fragments included in Part four of the memoir, it is revealed that a certain parrot in Singapore had for many years cited a stanza by Sappho in classic Greek while its owner, an old Chinese woman, had thought that the bird was perhaps speaking some words in Danish, another language that she or her visitors had not understood. The story is told by an old Danish shipowner, who visited the Chinese woman as a young boy and recognized the parrot's lines as Greek. The lyric that the parrot kept citing came from the distant past; it was something that the woman's lost lover had taught the bird: "The moon has sunk and the Pleiads, And midnight is gone, And the hours are passing, passing, And I lie alone" (1954, 272). These lines are a message sent from the lost lover, with the help of the parrot, but the poetry of the lines, which the Chinese woman wants to hear repeated, also suggests that even if the words are finally translated and understood, a sense of mystery still surrounds them (they give voice to the dead). We must also note that the story of "The Parrot" is ambivalently placed between fiction and nonfiction. The man who tells the tale could be Blixen's actual visitor, the old Dane Knudsen, who, as we are told, is fond of telling stories about himself that are partly invented. There is, however, no other indication of the storyteller other than that he is Danish, and there is no certainty either whether the story is fiction or nonfiction. What is certain, however, is that Sappho's stanza is another literary allusion in the memoir that develops Blixen's central themes of loss and natural pride (or wisdom).

In many places in her memoir, Blixen may use animal and bird metaphors to make a distinction between the conduct of various African tribes and nations. For instance, she sometimes portrays the Masai, the Somali, and the Swaheli as birds of prey, in contrast to other native peoples who appear to be more easily subjected to a stronger tribe or nation (1954, 132–35). In this comparison, echoing Victor Hugo's poem "Joie hors du château" that describes ruthless birds of prey feeding on carrion at night ("Tout les tristes oiseaux mangeurs de chair humaine"), the freedom of the wild birds again functions as an ennobling trait. The African domestic animals, in contrast, like the sheep and the cow, with which the Kikuyu are associated, make a different case. Blixen's association between the Kikuyu and domestic animals relates to what she saw as an age-old division of labor in East Africa, that is, the Kikuyu tradition of taking good care of animals. To Blixen, the Somali were the "young illegitimate half-brothers" of the Arabs, whereas the Kikuyus' relationship with the Somali was like that of the sheep to the sheepdog (1954, 132). This hierarchy, however, is to be imagined as having an ancient and mythical foundation that is not based on subordination or unidirectional cultural exchange involving imitation of the stronger but on mutual agreement and conscious role-play.

The inevitable racist undertone in Blixen's associations and comparisons between African people and wildlife has been one of the most hotly debated features in *Out of Africa*. Predominantly, Blixen's use of animal metaphors for the Africans, or for the white settlers for that matter, is descriptive: the comparison that is made between a certain animal and an individual (or in some cases a tribe/nation) is supposed to describe that individual's characteristics. Moreover, while these comparisons between animal species and Africans appear condescending, we must remember that many Westerners are compared to animals in her memoir and that they fare worse than the Africans in this respect. The Kikuyu, unlike the majority of the white men, are "adjusted for the unforeseen and accustomed to the unexpected" since they are, supposedly, at home with their destiny (1954, 29–30). Blixen sees, furthermore, that the Kikuyu, in their own passive way, also resist assimilation. A Kikuyu called Kinanjui, whom Blixen compares to an old ram, had the capacity to transform himself, "in a single movement, into lifeless matter" (1954, 137).

Yet, as Susan C. Brantly, for instance, has remarked, the racially charged context in which Blixen employed these metaphors renders them easily misunderstood (2002, 85). In the fragment "Of Pride," for instance, which includes one of the few direct references that Blixen makes to colonialism, she explains, at the very end of this fragment, that one must love the pride of the conquered nations and let them honor their own father and mother. However, Blixen's description of the pride of the African people, and their supposed love of the destiny that is granted to them, is again motivated in this fragment by Blixen's understanding of the surrounding landscape of the big game reserve and the wild animals that live in it.[11]

Likewise, the portraits of the Kikuyu boy Kamante and the forest antelope Lulu, in Part one of the memoir, are built around subtle associations between the boy and the animal,[12] even if Blixen depicts them as anything but lovely, cute pets. Kamante, who becomes her dog-boy, later a houseboy, a trusted cook, and a medical assistant, who converts to Christianity, still maintains in his manners, as Blixen explains, a certain "demonic" quality that will always

---

11. As yet another example of the way in which the anecdotes and fragments in Blixen's memoir develop each others' themes, the story "Of Pride" makes more apparent something that is only implied in "The Roads of Life,"—that is, the importance of an instinctual understanding of one's fate and the definition of pride as "faith in the idea that God had, when he made us" (1954, 224).

12. As in the beginning of the subchapter on Lulu ("A Gazelle") when Blixen writes: "Lulu came to my house from the woods as Kamante had come to it from the plains" (1954, 63).

remain partially unpredictable and incomprehensible. For Blixen, Kamante was always "a fantastic figure" who was "half of fun and half of diabolism" (1954, 37). As a cook, she claims, Kamante was a genius whose work precluded all classification. Similarly, the bushbuck Lulu that is found as a fawn in the bush "was not really gentle, she had the so-called devil in her" (1954, 69). The young antelope symbolizes for Blixen the sense of unity that she thought the farm and its inhabitants had with the African landscape; she regards her close relation with the animal as a very special "token of friendship from Africa" (1954, 75). At the same time, the story of Lulu is also a tale of loss that relates how a wild animal slowly withdraws from the farm to return to the wilderness. In this sense, Lulu's story shadows Blixen's grand narrative of loss, the nostalgia for her lost farm, and lost contact with Africans like Kamante.[13]

An Ancient Form of Storytelling

Blixen had started writing fiction before her marriage and departure to Africa, but the early stories had not attracted much attention. She first came to wider public attention under the pseudonym Isak Dinesen in 1934 with the publication of her first collection of stories, *Seven Gothic Tales*. As Blixen was unable to find a publisher in England or Denmark, *Seven Gothic Tales* was published by Random House in the United States. It was originally written in English, the language that Blixen had most used at her Kenyan farm, and Blixen then translated the book into Danish. The same pattern was repeated with the publication of *Out of Africa* in that Blixen first wrote the memoir in English and then translated the book into Danish. As Blixen explains in September 1935, in the forward to the Danish edition of her first collection of stories, *Syv fantastiske Fortællinger*, much of the book was "thought of, and some of it written in Africa."[14] All seven stories are set in mid-nineteenth-century Europe and none in Africa.

---

13. In *Out of Africa* and in her letters from her farm, Blixen makes use of Western classical literary tradition, writers such as Virgil, Sappho, Shakespeare, Shelley, and Huxley; fairy tales and fables; and the Bible. Her emphasis in these references is the theme of loss and rise and fall, as in *King Lear* and the Book of Job. The first and the last part of her memoir have mottos from Shelley's "Hymn of Pan" that tells the story, in Pan's voice, of the changed mood of Pan's piping, having been deluded by the nymph Syrinx. The motto of Part five in *Out of Africa*, "Gods and men, we are all deluded thus!" reiterates the theme of loss, as does also the motto of Part three, "Post res perditas" ("After lost things").

14. "En stor Del af 'Syv fantastiske Fortællinger' et tænkt, og noget af den er skrevet, i Afrika, og de Steder i min Bog, der handler om Danmark, maa tages mere som en dansk Emigrants Fantasier over danske Temaer end som noget Forsøg paa Virkelighedsskildring" (Blixen 1958, 5).

Blixen frequently discusses the meaning of literature and stories in *Out of Africa,* for instance, in reference to her favorite books and readings, such as the story of the stork, the Arabian Nights, the Book of Job, or various Western classics. She also writes about listening to her visitors' stories and telling them stories in return. One of these visitors, a blind old Dane called Old Knudsen, often told her about the tragedy of losing his fishing business, but always in the third-person voice (except once in the first person when he had suffered a heart attack) and changing details of the story whenever he retold it. Blixen told Denys Finch-Hutton long stories, since, as she explains, Finch-Hutton preferred hearing stories to reading them.

Moreover, Blixen describes her own habits of writing in *Out of Africa,* explaining that she started to write stories at her African farm in the evenings in her dining room, and later also in the mornings, partly because of her strong sense of work ethic, as she was not able to "acquire the absolute passivity of the Native, as some Europeans will do, who live for many decennaries in Africa" (1954, 47). Another reason for writing fiction was the need to exercise the imagination: "I began in the evenings to write stories, fairy-tales, and romances, that would take my mind a long way off, to other countries and times" (1954, 47). Blixen's houseboys, like Kamante, took an interest in her writing, thinking that it was her last attempt to "save the farm through the hard times" (1954, 48). These African responses to storytelling, Western literature, and poetry play a seminal role in illustrating Blixen's views about the value of storytelling. On one occasion, Blixen relates how her young cook Kamante, who had come to her dining room to see her writing with the typewriter, asked her if she was able to write a book of her own. Kamante was doubtful whether Blixen could ever make a book similar to the copy of the *Odyssey* that was in her library and that Kamante greatly admired for its impressive binding and size. When Blixen answered that she did not know if she was able to write a book, Kamante then inquired what was there inside the books. To this question Blixen responded by telling the story of Odysseus and the Cyclops, Polyphemus, and how Odysseus had called himself Noman. This is yet another instance in Blixen's oeuvre where a storyteller lets a story explain something, such as a difficult existential question, by suggestion and insinuation.

Kamante's reaction to the story of Odysseus is sketched through a series of questions and comments that Blixen summarizes or quotes. In these comments, Kamante tied the story to familiar things in his own life, presupposing that the race of Odysseus's sheep must be the one he personally had seen at a cattle show, or that Polyphemus's fear of Noman was the same fear that the boys on the plain, like him, were familiar with. Kamante also assumes that

Polyphemus was black and Odysseus was of Blixen's own tribe or family. All in all, as Kamante understood it, the story is intimately related to his own life.

At some level in Blixen's depiction of the Africans' reactions to bound books and the typewriter, together with the act of writing, literary culture is made to seem somewhat ridiculous in the African context. The books and writing at her desk are objects of curiosity for the Africans, similar in some sense to the old German cuckoo-clock on Blixen's wall, which attracted the attention of all those who did not understand the clock's purpose. At the same time, however, Blixen's description of the Africans' responses to her stories implies that the Africans had a specific sensitivity to and almost instinctual way of relating to stories. Even if Kamante confuses the time and space of the story with his own time and space, the spontaneity and intensity of his response suggests for Blixen the continuity of an ancient tradition of storytelling. First of all, it appears that the reactions of Blixen's audiences to stories can be curiously literal in nature, in the sense that her listeners are able to live out fictional stories and make their events, situations, and choices directly relevant in their own lives. For them, in other words, the stories relate directly to their daily struggles and thus have inestimable worth. Moreover, Blixen's African audiences respond to her stories in more spontaneous, imaginative, and profound ways than is possible for most Europeans. She explains, for instance, that when the Africans speak of the personality of God, "they speak like the Arabian Nights or like the last chapters of the book of Job; it is the same quality, the infinite power of imagination, with which they are impressed" (1954, 30). The Africans' powerful and imaginative reactions to stories suggest to Blixen, furthermore, their ability to understand the common fate through stories, not just the personal struggle. The Africans, then, are still in touch with the origins of storytelling and the art of listening, similarly to some of Blixen's later fictional characters, including the Cardinal in "The Cardinal's First Tale"[15] and the black storyteller in "The Blank Page" in *Last Tales* and young Ibsen, who is collecting folktales in the Norwegian mountains in the story "The Pearls" in *Winter's Tales*. Secondly, the African responses to literature highlight the importance of immersion in the story and the subtle means of suggestion that make this immersion possible. In other words, the Africans recognize and know how to appreciate a well-crafted narrative and

---

15. Two forms of story are opposed in the Cardinal's and the Lady's conversation: on the one hand, the divine or true story, with ancient roots in the human history and myths, that is still able to depict luminous, heroic characters and, on the other hand, the "new art of narration" that focuses on modern individuals with whom the readers can easily sympathize. Both kinds of story seem to be valued in this tale but for different reasons.

a good performance of a story, as if by instinct, without any knowledge of the conventions of written literature and a literary tradition. All of these qualities are required of the kind of traditional culture of storytelling that Blixen promotes in her memoir: the capacity to engage meaningfully with the story as a listener, to think that the story is in some sense alive, and, equally, to retell and perform the story in a suggestive and attentive manner.

Blixen depicts another African response to a Western story in a fragment entitled "Farah and the Merchant of Venice," where she relates how she told the plot of Shakespeare's *The Merchant of Venice* to her Somali servant Farah, who, "like all people of African blood, liked to hear a story told" (1954, 22). Farah's response was surprising, however, in that he had much sympathy for the Jewish moneylender Shylock, objecting to the man's defeat in the play. Farah wished that the moneylender had found some means to resolve his difficult situation, for instance by having found a way to take little bits of Antonio's flesh, piecemeal as it were (one pound of flesh was the condition that Shylock had given in case Antonio was unable to repay the debt at the specified date). Blixen concludes two things from Farah's reaction. First, she claims that the Africans are first and foremost interested in imaginative, well-made plots: "coloured people do not take sides in a tale, the interest to them lies in the ingeniousness of the plot itself" (1954, 222). Blixen suggests thus that Africans like Farah listen to literature differently from the Europeans since they appear to be able to better submerge themselves in the fictional world, unconditionally as it were or by instinct, and to live out narratives in a fuller sense. Second, Farah also appears to be a natural storyteller himself. At some point when listening to her story, Farah takes on a dramatic and dangerous countenance "as if he were really in the Court of Venice, putting heart into his friend or partner Shylock" (1954, 222). In Europe, by contrast, Blixen believes that such imaginative engagement in stories is lost:

> Fashions have changed, and the art of listening to a narrative has been lost in Europe. The Natives of Africa, who cannot read, have still got it: if you begin to them: 'There was a man who walked out on the plain, and there he met another man,' you have them all with you, their minds running upon the unknown track of the men on the plain. But white people, even if they feel that they ought to, cannot listen to a recital. (1954, 194)

White people, Blixen claims, are accustomed to taking in their impressions by the eye, becoming easily absorbed "in any kind of print handed them" (ibid.). The African response to stories, meanwhile, is not only attentive and imaginative but also engaging at an emotional as well as dramatic level.

Blixen portrays Farah's reaction to the play in terms of his strong dramatic presence.[16]

The reading of Western classics to Africans functions in *Out of Africa* as a kind of testing ground for varieties of literary response and communication. What is essential in these stories about reading and listening, however, is not any "civilizing" imposition of Western classics on illiterate Africans but the capacity of the stories to capture and amuse the audience and, furthermore, the imaginative modifications that the texts undergo in their retelling and the Africans' appropriations of these narratives as their own. The Africans' responses to Homer and Shakespeare, whose stories Blixen transforms into oral narratives, manifest the importance and pleasure of being fully immersed in a story, while the Africans' literary asceticism, that is, the necessity of living with no written literature, seems to further accentuate the effects of these stories. The Africans at Blixen's farm were mostly illiterate and did not have a written literature of their own, a matter of concern to Blixen, who had plans to translate Aesop's fables into Swahili, a lingua franca in the region, but, as she explains in *Out of Africa*, never found the time to do it (1954, 37).

The Africans' responses to stories and poetry, as related to us in the fragments on Kamante and the *Odyssey*, Farah and *The Merchant of Venice*, and "Natives and Verse" seem to suggest to Blixen a kind of adaptive truth: how stories and poetry can help make sense of one's environment and destiny. What she saw as the Africans' instinctive response to and retelling of the story enabled Blixen to redefine the relationship between literature and its material form as well as narrative form and the potential design in one's life (fate). In her description of her own responses to the fictions that she read at the farm, Blixen shows, moreover, how she was herself profoundly affected by these considerations. At the end of her memoir, Blixen explains that her books in a colony, and by this she means works of fiction in particular, played a different role in her existence than they did in Europe or elsewhere in so-called civilized countries. More precisely, Blixen felt she was more affected by literature at her Kenyan farm than ever before, and that her own response to her readings was stronger than ever, according to the quality of a given book, feeling for instance deeply grateful to books, or strongly indignant with them. Fictions became intimately tied to her everyday life at the farm: "there is a whole side of your life which they alone take charge of" (1954, 309). The experience of reading fiction in the Kenyan colony was more intense for

---

16. In *Shadows on the Grass*, Blixen draws a comparison between the Somali, such as Farah, and the Icelanders of the old Nordic Sagas: "I had read the old Nordic Sagas as a child, and now in my intercourse with the Somali I was struck by their likeness to the ancient Icelanders" (1985, 285).

Blixen also in that it came naturally to her in this environment to imagine that fictional characters inhabited her farm: "The fictitious characters in the books run beside your horse on the farm, and walk about in the maizefields. On their own, like intelligent soldiers, they find at once the quarters that suit them" (1954, 309). Blixen thus tells about meeting with Aldous Huxley's, Walter Scott's, and Racine's characters at her farm, as well as Odysseus and his men and Peter Schlemiel. In this sense, Blixen experienced fictions in the same way and with the same intensity and instinct that she thought was typical of the Africans' responses to well-crafted and performed stories.

The Africanist Field of Texts

The popular, early-twentieth-century ideas of Africans as undifferentiated, pre-rational beings, determined by their "primitive mentality," belief in the occult, and lack of individuality, do not resonate well with Blixen's memoir, where she portrays differences between various African cultures and traditions and often focuses on Africans as individuals. Her frequent use of the term "native" is problematic, however, to the extent that it represents one unified nation or people, who functions as a kind of frozen metonymic device for the whole of Africa. JanMohamed has claimed in this respect that the mythical structure of Blixen's narrative is constituted by this radical metonymy: the Natives who "were Africa in flesh and blood" (1983, 53–55). Blixen's occasional sweeping generalizations are revelatory of this tendency, for instance, when she writes that the Natives "have no sense or taste for contrasts; the umbilical cord of nature has, with them, not been quite cut through" (1954, 145). However, while Blixen uses the general term "native" to refer to black East Africans, she also frequently employs the tribal denominations like the Kikuyu, the Somali, and the Masai to point out ethnic and cultural differences.[17] Furthermore, her generalizations are simultaneously contrasted and undermined, both in *Out of Africa* and her later African memoir *Shadows on the Grass*, through her portrayal of various individuals, such as Kamante and Farah, who elude any simple classification, be that their Africanness or their ethnic identity as a Somali or a Kikuyu. It is important to note, moreover, that the many African words and names that are mentioned in her memoir do not function as simple markers of primitivism, exoticism, or Africanism but are also indexes of the Africans' experience, speaking to the effect that the familiar Western lexicon is inadequate to describe this experience.

---

17. It is also worth asking whether there were any less unifying terms than "native" that were available at the time.

Blixen's literary portraits of various African individuals suggest that, as was the case with many French colonialist writers of the 1920s and the 1930s, earlier forms of picturesque exoticism were to her an unreal proposition, detached from real life in the colonies.[18] Absent from Blixen's colonial memoir are clichéd images of the white man's grave, colonial decadence, and the madness-inducing forests. In stark contrast with these images, Blixen's African landscape connotes nobility, innate aristocracy, and natural pride, and the Africans in her descriptions share the same characteristics. The possibility and even the necessity of learning from African nature and the Natives is a theme running throughout *Out of Africa* and one that is underscored already in the book's opening. Things to be learned from Africa also include the ability to accept one's destiny, that is, to not fear the risks in life, which is one of the messages of "The Roads of Life." Furthermore, Blixen thought highly of what she understood as the natives' great skill in the "art of mimicry," which is related to their art of storytelling, listening, and the ability to be immersed in a story. The notion of African "mimicry" does not, however, refer just to the Africans' ability to mislead (especially Europeans) by appearances but to a way of adapting to one's environment, to be one with the surrounding nature in a way that the Europeans have forgotten. This means, equally, a worldview according to which one does not divide God and the Devil into two persons or substances (1954, 26–27).[19] Both the African tradition of storytelling, and the art of mimicry, are related to the ability to experience unity with nature.

In Blixen's version of the exotic, African wildlife has identity-endowing properties precisely because it enables the restatement of identity as the assertion of cultural and creative origin. Such an assertion also involves establishing a system of "othering" whereby the African is invented as a kind of mythological other, that is, an untameable noble savage or a mystery. Blixen emphasizes in her memoir that she never quite understood the Natives even if she regarded them as her friends (1954, 27). A similar sense of Africa and the Africans, which remain to an important extent beyond rational explanation

---

18. Roland Lebel claimed in his *Histoire de la littérature coloniale en France* (1931) that the French colonial literature of the early twentieth century, which sought to describe the colonial experience from within, contributed to the acquisition of a new realism, "colonial consciousness," providing the colonial enterprise and experience with psychological depth. For some of these writers, the rejection of exoticism was also a reaction to the values of literariness in modernism and what was thought to be its excesses of subjectivity, detachment, delinquent aestheticism, and pessimism (see Lebel 1931, 79, 82–83, 140; Moura 1998, 116).

19. "Africa, amongst the continents, will teach it to you: that God and the Devil are one, the majesty coeternal, not two uncreated but one uncreated, and the Natives neither confounded the persons nor divided the surface" (1954, 27).

and language, becomes evident also in Blixen's portrayal of Africa's adorable music and "rhythm": "When you have caught the rhythm of Africa, you find that it is the same in all her music. What I learned from the game of the country was useful to me in my dealings with the native people" (1954, 24). While the African "music" thus makes possible a total experience of life and love, the analogy with music also lets Blixen position herself: as a passive but loyal listener to an (organic) orchestra and its all-encompassing music. Setting out the routine of her daily life "to the orchestra" (1954, 25), this connoisseur of native lifestyle and mentality is also, metaphorically, a conductor of an orchestra of natives, even if she may never fully control them.

In the beginning of *Out of Africa,* Blixen formulates her relationship with the native Africans as a form of unconditional love. She explains that her "discovery of the dark races" led to a "magnificent enlargement" of her world, comparable to someone who, with an inborn sympathy for wild animals, first comes into contact with animals, or a person with an instinctive taste for woods first enters a forest, or someone with an ear for music hears music for the first time (1954, 25). Her affection for the Africans is thus intimately associated with a sense of renewed perception—another central theme in *Out of Africa,* also underscored by the memoir's title. In contrast, modern Europe is often cast as a place of pathology, and most Europeans, such as Count von Schimmelmann, epitomize a closed, narrow-minded worldview. In the story "Fellow-Travellers," for instance, Blixen tells about her encounter with a Belgian and an Englishman on a boat from Europe to Africa. These two Europeans, whose languages Blixen first accidentally mixes up, confusing the verb *travailler* to mean "to travel," are similar types of Western colonizer and traveller, who are reproachable for their condescending attitude towards the Africans and all non-Europeans. The Englishman is a hunter who is travelling to Africa to shoot rare animals and who enjoys telling jokes about the ignorant natives in Mexico. One of his jokes is about an old Spanish woman in the mountains of Mexico who, unable to conceive of the idea of an aeroplane that she has never seen, wonders whether the fact that the man has learned to fly means that the men fly "with their legs drawn up under them, like the sparrows, or stretched out behind them, like the storks" (1954, 262). In Blixen's retelling of the story, the butt of the joke is not the old Spanish woman, however, but the Western teller, who, for his narrow-mindedness, is only able to find ignorance in the Mexicans. The reference to storks, and the insight about different kinds of birds, in the woman's reply may also suggest that there is hidden wisdom in her response, unnoticed by the hunter. The Belgian, in turn, is a fervent believer in the Belgian civilizing mission in the Congo. This meant for him, however, the conscious effort of keeping the Africans ignorant:

to teach the Negro to work honestly and nothing else, *rien de plus*—not, for instance, to build schools.

Blixen's depiction of her relationship with the Africans around her is deeply ambiguous. In relation to her workers, squatters, and neighbors, Blixen casts herself in the role of a doctor, a lawyer, a landowner, and a "superior squatter." The agricultural, nomadic people of the Kikuyu, whose land had been appropriated by the British colonial government to be handed over to British settlers, or other Europeans like Karen Blixen and her husband Baron Bror von Blixen-Finecke, epitomize for Blixen the conquered but proud nation. Some of the Kikuyu, as she describes them, continued to live in the new farms as squatters over whom the owner of the farm exercised power. Blixen acknowledges that she inhabited their land, for instance, by pointing out that many of the Kikuyu of her farm, whose fathers had been born on the farm, "very likely regarded me as a sort of superior squatter of their estates" (1954, 18; see also Brantly 2002, 76–77). Later, after the bankruptcy of her farm, Blixen successfully defended her squatters' right to their own land.[20]

At the same time, the identity-breaking qualities in some of Blixen's stories in *Out of Africa* and *Shadows on the Grass*, where she associates herself with her servants or projects them as inseparable elements of her existence, can be directly linked, as JanMohamed argues, to her experience as a stranger in the colonies.[21] As a woman settler, farmer, and writer, Blixen had to negotiate different constraints and social conventions than most of the Europeans around her. The limitations set by the middle- and upper-class European lifestyle in the colonies dictated, for instance, that women define themselves through family, not work. Blixen's situation was always somewhat precarious for this reason while, moreover, the Empire did not necessarily mean authority, efficiency, and, even less so, national faith in her memoir and letters. What Blixen called her outspoken "pro-nativeness" (1981, 283), which she differen-

---

20. JanMohamed has defined Blixen's paradoxical use of the signs of Africans' alterity as a dynamic of centripetal and centrifugal forces (1983, 63–70). This is based on the observation that Blixen ceaselessly moved between, on the one hand, a sense of absolute ownership, even a God-like role as a kind of doctor–judge of a native village, and, on the other hand, a sense of humility, respect, and absolute responsibility for her workers and squatters, her passionate and unconditional love for the Natives—a relationship that she also likened to her officer father's love for his soldiers at the time of war (Blixen 1954, 25). In *Shadows on the Grass*, Blixen compares her relationship with her servant Farah Aden to the great literary unities of master and servant, such as those between Don Quixote and Sancho Panza, or King Lear and the Fool (1985, 282, 300).

21. JanMohamed argues, more precisely, that "the prevalence of disguised identities and the repeated hints of the absence of a 'true' or 'permanent' self in *Out of Africa* can be linked directly to her experience as a stranger; the subservience of character to plot can be related to her admiration for the African's 'friendliness' with destiny, and so forth" (1983, 74).

tiated from predominant notions among the British settlers, further emphasized her identity as an outsider.

What Mary Louise Pratt has called the "seeing-man" in her analysis of eighteenth- and nineteenth-century travel writing, meaning the main protagonist of the anti-conquest travel narrative,[22] is relevant with regard to certain passages but not the entirety of *Out of Africa*. The "seeing-man" is someone, typically a male traveller, whose "imperial eyes passively look out and possess" (Pratt 1992, 7). The kind of nostalgic storyteller persona whom Blixen constructs for us in her memoir shares certain key characteristics with this passive anti-hero, particularly when she describes her visual experiences of the African landscape from the aeroplane or when she assimilates the Africans to their landscape. The experience of the African visual field as seen from above was something that Blixen always found exciting, but that she could not, as she explains, fully recapture in words. It is as if the Western storyteller were dependent on the encounter with the *absolute* and ultimately untranslatable alterity of the wildlife and the vastness of the landscape, in order to be able to learn how to return to a tradition and compose a story that might endure through difficult times. In the description of the Kenyan mountain landscape in the beginning of her memoir, likewise, Blixen foregrounds the experience of astonishment and awe, while she is still very much in possession of what she sees, by assigning value to what she perceives in terms of her notions of African nobility, pride, and freedom, and her personal sense of exaltation through the mystery of nature. The highland landscape around her farm, Blixen thought, was unique in Africa since it displayed, through some kind of metonymy, what she thought to be the essence of African space: "There was no fat on it and no luxuriance anywhere; it was Africa distilled up through six thousand feet, like the strong and refined essence of a continent" (1954, 13). The panorama of the landscape and its people, and their conversion into a personal memory and a myth—instead of a conversion into natural history as happens with the eighteenth- and nineteenth-century traveller-writers, whose work Pratt has investigated (1992, 51)—forms the narrative and descriptive scaffolding in the opening of *Out of Africa*.

Conclusion

The analysis here has served to demonstrate how Blixen's notion of "African" nobility, pride, and freedom, and the Africans' supposed instinctual response

---

22. For Pratt, the term "anti-conquest" means "the strategies of representation whereby European bourgeois subjects seek to secure their innocence in the same moment as they assert European hegemony" (1992, 7).

to storytelling and inclination to appropriate stories and retell them, is associated with her redefinition of literary norms, concerning in particular the kind of storytelling tradition in which she wanted to join. In Blixen's memoir, thus, "Africa" is a malleable sign that enables the writer to redefine a persisting tradition of storytelling and explore the relationship between a modern memoir and a mythical story. The mythical nature of this tradition can be understood in at least two senses. First of all, Africa suggested to her an *authentic* and instinctual form of storytelling. Blixen's contacts with African audiences and narrative traditions, in particular, offered her models of how stories may help make sense of the environment and one's destiny and, moreover, provided her with opportunities for literary extension, renewal, and reinvigoration. Africa connotes for Blixen the power to renew perception, concerning for instance the sense of unity with nature but also with regard to the way in which the storyteller sees the relationship between narratives and lived experience. The most extensive treatment of this question is given in the story "The Roads of Life" and its frame that recontextualize an old Danish fairy tale. Secondly, as Blixen frequently argues in her memoir, Africa or Africans as such cannot be fully understood but may perhaps best be conceived of in and through stories. The best stories, in turn, work by suggestion, according to the notion of storytelling that emerges in Blixen's memoir and particularly in relation to the important role of anecdotes in Part four of the book. The various anecdotes, memories, and short fictions in this section of her memoir, and the many meaningful continuities and connections between them, accentuate the central themes of the book (loss and renewal, the pride and wisdom of nature). The organization of *Out of Africa* thus acts out the implications of the metonymy of Africa—a metonymy that is enacted both spatially and temporally in Blixen's memoir but that will always remain, to some extent, evasive and untranslatable.

IN CONCLUSION

Fiction, Colonial Travel Narrative, and the Allegorist

IN THE COURSE of this book, I have explored the influences and convergences between travel journal keeping, the memoir, and fiction. The study has identified five main dimensions of interplay between fiction and nonfiction in this body of work: the author's, the narrator's, or the character's mediating mind (the experiential frame of the journey); the conventions of description; the shared references and cultural givens concerning sub-Saharan Africa; the theme of narrativisation; and the issue of virtual genres. These dimensions reveal the important role that travel has played as a frame in Modernist fiction and the way in which fiction has been appropriated in the nonfiction travel narrative and journal during our period.

It seems that travel writing, with its particular traditions, conventions, and expectations concerning, for instance, the centrality of the mediating consciousness or the importance of description, provided many of these writers with a locus for experimenting with new strategies of voice, style, world construction, and perspectival techniques that could be tried out in fiction as well. In some of these cases, it appears that by interlacing different worlds with different reality status—be they real, possible, metaphorical, or fictional—modern writer–travellers thus asserted for their travelling persona and for their writing (and sometimes for the places visited or the people encountered) a kind of "transworld" identity between the actual, the possible, and the fictional world. This effect, or illusion, is in turn reinforced by the sense of displacement and distance between one cultural zone and another. It is further strengthened in many of these texts by the modern topos of sub-Saharan Africa as a free, undetermined space and the imperialist notion of non-European places that supposedly do not have a history. The modernist authors included in this study inherit and affirm but also complicate and, in some cases, seek to undermine these imperialist notions.

The research also goes to show that the African travel writing produced by these writers was an important element in the development of their literary careers. The various findings that the comparison between travel writing, life narrative, and fiction yielded are important for the sometimes conventional interpretation of many of these writers—notably Waugh, Greene, Blixen, and Simenon (who emerged on the literary scene during the 1930s)—as working in the shadow of the great Modernist innovators such as James Joyce, Virginia Woolf, and Marcel Proust. To read these authors' nonfiction side by side with their fiction enables us to see better the full extent of their formal innovation and interest in experimenting with different narrative voices, styles, genres, varieties of realism, as much as the criteria of referentiality. Furthermore, this opens up new strategies for investigating the cross-fertilization and mutual influence between fiction and travel writing, or other forms of nonfiction narrative, in the literatures of early twentieth-century Europe.

The research has sought to highlight the worth of analyzing travel writing and journals in narrative-theoretical terms and studying fiction and nonfiction as intersecting categories, despite the distinct constraints of their narrative situation and generic expectations. These writers' travel writing and journals make apparent how many identifying markers of the modern novel may be employed in nonfiction: the centrality of the mediating consciousness, the importance of detailed scenes and descriptions, the presentation of verbatim speech, shifts between observation and inner reflection, and even interruptions between different narrative levels are all evidenced across genres. Moreover, quotations from or references to fiction and discussions of reading fiction whilst actually travelling can be used in various important ways in nonfiction travel writing: as a guarantee of the reality of experience, to emphasize or to blot out certain experiences, or as a model for presenting those basic sources of autobiography that are not verifiable, such as thoughts and emotions, memories, associations, dreams, and desires. The references to hypothetical genres, furthermore, can draw the reader's attention to generic expectations and their justification and emphasize an affinity between the narrative strategies and conventions or other means of expression across the fiction/nonfiction divide.

Dorrit Cohn's signposts of fiction, listed and discussed in the Introduction, are only partly valid in terms of distinguishing between fiction and nonfiction in these examples. In the nonfiction works included here, the narrative regularly adheres to a bilevel story/discourse model; it focuses on the representation of the author's inner life and experience of space and time, even if it does not (usually) employ narrative situations that open up to inside views of other peoples' minds; and it may, in certain cases, articulate narrative voices that can be detached from their authorial origin (thus creating an impression of a traveller's persona). The latter does not involve, however, a full break with Philippe Lejeune's notion of "autobiographical pact" (i.e., the identity between the author, the narrator, and the character), to which Cohn refers, as may be the case with some contemporary examples of autofiction, literary journalism, or nonfiction novel. Greene's and Waugh's travelling persona, or Simenon's pseudonym Georges Caraman, is a new and stylized version of the author's self, evoked in the travelogue and by the experience of travel, and as such is somewhat detached from the autobiographical self. By contrast, in Gide's and Leiris's cases, their travel journals suggest a clear continuity with the autobiographical self and project.[1]

The interaction between travel writing, journal keeping, and fiction in these writers' works makes evident the porosity of the boundary between nonfiction and fiction, while the analyses also reveal the way in which their distinction constantly reasserts itself, despite the many juxtapositions, borrowings, and boundary crossings (actual or hypothetical) between the genres. The relative stability of their distinction is in part due to, as I argued in the Introduction, certain extratextual generic expectations. The form of the text, such as the narrative voice, style, and perspective that is employed in the text, for instance when fiction makes the reader share in a character's experience of time through free indirect discourse, is likely to have some influence on our classification of a given text's genre. Yet a text's formal and semantic features also invite interpretation in relation to generic expectations, pertaining for instance to the expectation, in nonfiction, of a correspondence between the world of the text and actual reality (in so far as the reality can be known through other descriptions, narratives, and documents). The expectation of

---

1. However, Alex Demeulenaere has convincingly argued that Leiris adopts different narrative identities in his travelogue (adventurer, ethnographer, intimate self-analysis) and, gradually, towards the end of his travel journal, apparently transforms himself from an observing narrator to a character of his own narrative, thus becoming a kind of fascinated spectator of the theater of sacrifice and possession in Gondar (2009, 264, 270). A more profound analysis of Leiris's autobiographical series would allow us to evaluate whether similar instances of identity adaptation take place there.

referentiality in travel writing, at least in the sense of the traveller being true to his or her subjective experience in some given geographical space, affects these writers' and the readers' understanding of the narrated world as well as the usage of devices that are more characteristic of fiction.

Cohn illustrates the meaning of the referential level in the analysis of nonfiction narratives under the issue of plotting versus "emplotting" in a way that is useful for our discussion. She argues that in the process of transforming archival sources into a narrative form, which is necessary both in the making of fictional and nonfictional narratives, fictional narratives are distinct in that they are plotted compositions whereas nonfictional narratives are both plotted and emplotted: "A novel can be said to be plotted, but not *emplotted*: its serial moments do not refer to, and can therefore not be selected from, an ontologically independent and temporally prior data base of disordered, meaningless happenings that it restructures into order and meaning" (1999, 114). Fiction, in other words, creates a world by referring to this world, whereas nonfiction travel writing or a memoir gives narrative form to lived experience. However, Cohn's prototypes for a referential (nonfictional) narrative—a historical narrative (historiography that relates past events in a reliably documented way or a historical autobiography) and a psychoanalytical case study—appear to be, generally speaking, more constrained by the principle of correspondence to reality in their process of emplotting than the modern fiction writers' travel books, journals, and memoirs. In other words, the latter genres, at least in the works that are included here, are more relaxed about the obligations of testimonial evidence or correspondence to the actuality of the narrated events, despite the journalistic motivation and documentary impulse that also characterize some of these writers' African nonfiction.

The assertions that I have made here about the interplay between fiction and nonfiction obviously depend to some extent upon the choice of examples. This research has focused on early twentieth-century European writers who wrote both fiction and nonfiction set in sub-Saharan Africa and, in addition, on works that have certain recurring themes, patterns, and intertexts in common. The selection is artificial, however, in that there are other writers whose work might have been discussed within the same framework. To mention two examples, the French writer Paul Morand's travel book to West Africa *Paris-Tombouctou* (1928) and his novel entitled *Magie noire* from the same year, which is framed as a travel narrative, could have been investigated within this comparative analysis. Similarly, the English aviator and adventurer Beryl Markham's memoir *West with the Night* (1942) and her autobiographical and fictional stories set in Africa from the 1940s (collected posthumously in *The Splendid Outcast*, 1987) would meet the same criteria.

More importantly, however, I believe that the main assertions and the general framework of the study, concerning the issue of cross-fertilization, borrowing, and hypothetical potential between the genres, and the dimensions of interplay between fiction and nonfiction that I have identified, could be tested with regard to other kinds of examples from the same era, involving for instance a different place of departure or travel destination. If I had included American writers in this study, Ernest Hemingway's account of a month-long hunting safari in East Africa in 1933, *Green Hills of Africa* (1935), and his subsequent short stories about African safari-life—"The Short Happy Life of Francis Macomber" (1936) and "The Snows of Kilimanjaro" (1936)—would have provided me with a similar case to the ones that I investigated. For instance, the way in which literary discussions between Hemingway and his companions alternate with hunting scenes in *Green Hills of Africa* is a delicious example of the role that books can take on the voyage. Hemingway also calls the reader's attention to the generic relation between travel writing and fiction in the Foreword to his travel book, declaring that "the writer has attempted to write an absolutely true book to see whether the shape of a country and the pattern of a month's action can, if truly presented, compete with a work of the imagination" (1994, Foreword).

A greater geographical scope would have made it possible to include, for instance, Isabelle Eberhardt's North African travel fiction and nonfiction in my case studies. Eberhardt travelled and lived in Algeria between 1897 and 1904, including a period dressed as an Arab man and calling herself Mahmoud Essadi, Mahmoud Saâdi, or Si Mahmoud. She published essays and articles from Algeria and Tunisia, wrote travel books that were published posthumously, including *Notes de route Maroc, Algérie, Tunisie* (1908), and *Dans l'ombre chaude de l'Islam* (1921), and wrote fiction such as the short story collection *Amours nomades* (posthumous) and the novel *Trimardeur* (1922, finished and published by her Algerian mentor Victor Barrucand). She also kept a diary that was published posthumously (*The Nomad: The Diaries of Isabelle Eberhardt*). The twelve short stories of *Amours nomades*, some of which came out in the journals of Paris and Alger during the author's lifetime, are all set in Arabic-speaking North Africa and draw regularly on the writer's life and travels there.

Other non-European travel destinations would obviously allow a great body of works to be investigated within the same research framework. Early twentieth-century European authors who published fiction and nonfiction travel set in the same places include, for instance, the French writers Paul Claudel, Victor Segalen, Antoine de Saint-Exupéry, and André Malraux and the British writers D. H. Lawrence, E. M. Forster, and George Orwell. The

Swiss writer Annemarie Schwarzenbach, whose travel writing and fiction were rediscovered in the 1980s, travelled to Turkey, Afghanistan, Iran, and elsewhere between the wars and also visited the Belgian Congo in 1941. Her book *Death in Persia* (*Tod in Persien*, published posthumously) would provide an interesting opportunity to test the same theoretical assertions: although it is labelled a novel it also documents the author's four trips to Persia between 1933 and 1939. Likewise, the French writer Henri Michaux's travel books might offer an interesting test bed for these assertions. Michaux poses the question of intercultural translation in terms of a paradox in the motto of his travelogue *Un Barbare en Asie* (*A Barbarian in Asia*, 1945, written in the 1930s). In writing about India he observes, "There is nothing to see—everything to interpret" (1986, 3). In Michaux's *Ecuador* (*Ecuador: A Travel Journal*, 1929), likewise, the pseudo-ethnographic observations during a yearlong journey to Ecuador often become fantastic, or too subjective (where just about everything is seen as a matter for interpretation), whereas his works of travel fiction, including *Voyage en Grande Garabagne* (1936) and *Au Pays de la Magie* (1941), use conventions of ethnographic writing to speak of imaginary people and impossible spaces. For Michaux, to write about travelling involved the exploration of the very notion of travel.

Still another limitation in my corpus is the missing African perspective on travel, relating both to the important role that the Africans played during these European writers' journeys and the African writers' travel accounts of journeys to Europe. Comparisons between European and African travel writers could have provided us an interesting counterweight to the chosen examples and possibly prompted quite different kinds of questions, for instance, about the uses of African imagery or the relation to the legacy of colonialism. To mention some potential candidates for such comparisons, the Senegalese writer Birago Diop's short story "The Humps" ("Les Mamelles," 1947) describes an African storyteller's return from France to Africa. In this story, a fellow female passenger, a European, makes an ironic comment about the famous hills called Humps—"So that's all your famous Humps are?" (1985, 1) ("Ce n'est que ça les Mamelles?"; Diop 1961, 32)—that mark the western-most point of Senegal and, thus, the African continent (the extremity of the Cape Verde Peninsula). As a belated response to the woman's question, the writer-narrator then relates the story of the fantastic origin of the Humps as it has been told to him by Amadou Koumba, the legendary West African storyteller and musician, a *griot*, to whom all Birago Diop's stories are ascribed. According to the story, the Humps belong to a jealous wife who threw herself into the waves, but the sea did not manage to swallow her entirely. The arrival scene on which the story focuses thus portrays an African writer's journey "back" from the European "center" to Africa, contrasting African and European perspectives in the description of the scene, quite unlike in the examples studied in Chapter 1.[2]

The question of African representations of travel also raises the issue as to what this study might contribute to the body of postcolonial studies that has critically examined European colonial travel literature in recent decades. There are three principal ways I would suggest. First of all, the focus on European preconceived notions of Africa and Africans in this body of travel literature is relevant for the postcolonial inquiry about the ways in which travel literature can be imbued with colonial ideology and ethnocentrism. One historical specificity of this corpus, written and published just prior to the anticolonial and independence movements in Africa, is that these works reflect the loss of the great opposition between the civilized and the exotic primitive, whilst maintaining and reaffirming this opposition through reversal, estrangement, or irony. The distance from nineteenth-century heroic and exoticizing travels that is evident in these works makes it possible to modify some of the accepted views of European travel writing—for instance, the ways in which this genre "produced" non-European cultures for our consumption or how it opened up issues of inter-culturality and imperial relationships (for instance, how the colonial periphery helps to define the metropolitan centre). Second, the focus on the modes of functioning in a particular genre of writing (rather than merely on content), including the question of a hypothetical audience that is related to generic expectations, can help us ask more precise questions about narrative voice and authority and the writer's strategic location vis-à-vis a colonized culture. The study of generic conventions, expectations, and cross-generic relations may be highly relevant if we seek to understand how a text grasps and represents another culture and cultural encounter, or wish to make claims about literary genres as ideologically infused categories. Third,

---

2. Compare this with Aimé Césaire's anticolonial poem *Cahier d'un retour au pays natal* (1939, *Notebook of a Return to the Native Land*) that relates the poet's return from France to his native Martinique. An early African travel account of an arrival in Europe is included in the Senegalese infantryman Bakary Diallo's memoir *Force-Bonté* (1926), which is the first African soldier's narrative of the First World War. In his memoir, which is also a vehement apologia for French colonialism in Africa, Diallo describes a warm welcome at a French home when his infantry unit arrives in Sète (Hérault) in 1914. Aedín Ní Loingsigh (2009) focuses on the cultural and historical realities of African textualizations of travel, including generic considerations, within the tradition of French-language travel writing. Loingsigh investigates, for instance, the Senegalese writer Ousmane Diop Socé's *Mirages de Paris* (1937), a semi-autobiographical novel in which the writer incorporates personal experiences of an affair with a French woman in Paris. See also Miller (1998, Chapters 1 and 2). Early twentieth-century African travel stories from England include, amongst others, Ham Mukasa's *Uganda's Katikiro in England* (1904) and A. B. C. Merriman-Labor's *Britons through negro spectacles* (1909).

postcolonial studies and theory do regularly, and sometimes uncritically, argue that the dividing line between fiction and nonfiction travel writing, or other forms of colonial nonfiction, is wholly elusive and, as such, irrelevant. This study specifies the grounds on which the argument about cross-fertilization across the fiction/nonfiction divide can possibly be made, as it analyzes the features that imaginative and real journeys share and identifies the dimensions of their infiltration in this particular body of work. In the light of this approach it might also be possible to reevaluate the grounds for the claim often made in postcolonial studies that Western nonfictional travel writing and fictional narratives conspired to form an ideological apparatus in the service of colonialism.

Finally, in my case studies, a few pertinent traditions of travel literature and *récit de voyage* emerged that can be sketched out briefly here. First of all, most of these travelogues, as well as much of the fiction, refer in one way or another to the traditional storyline of travel into the interior of Africa. This occurs, for instance, by way of references to or recountings of famous expeditions, such as those of Mungo Park, Sir Richard Francis Burton, Stanley, and Livingstone, or the romantic 'disappearance' of Arthur Rimbaud and the fictional travels of Charles Marlow and Kurtz. Conrad's *Heart of Darkness*, as has become obvious during this study, is a common point of reference for all of our texts written after 1902 (with the possible exception of Evelyn Waugh). The readily recognizable storyline increases narrativity both in fiction and nonfiction. At the same time, it can also be argued that there is a difference of degree between the ways in which fictional and nonfictional narratives use this storyline: travel writers then often seem to "emplot" (in Cohn's sense of the term) their travel experiences by borrowing plots from fiction, while in fiction the aspect of emplotting is missing or refers to an imaginary narrative situation.[3]

A story about an adventure into the interior of Africa remains an oft-repeated topos in Western travel narrative and fiction today. The hero of this storyline, typically, is fascinated by the sense of the marvellous and the danger that he or she associates with the unknown interior of Africa that, typically, serves as an allegory for our ancient past, the darkness of our minds, or the powers of natural forces. A similarly allegorical but simultaneously ironic African take on this storyline is the Guinean Camara Laye's novel *The Radiance of the King* (*Le regard du roi*, 1954) that tells the story of Clarence, a wandering white man who has been shipwrecked off the coast of Africa.

---

3. I would like to thank one of the anonymous readers for The Ohio State University Press for this formulation.

Stripped of his belongings and fantasies of superiority over the Africans and abandoned by his compatriots, Clarence goes deeper and deeper on the path of disorientation and humiliation, ending up as a slave in a harem in an unnamed Western African country. Clarence's languishing at the overwhelming scent of African flowers and vegetable molds upon entering a great forest parallels some of the African forest scenes in the European writers' travelogues discussed above.[4]

Contemporary Western travel writers who still follow this storyline are often motivated by an effort to retrace some hero–traveller's route and thus recover the expressive content of the original experience despite the burden of the colonial past. For instance, among the many present-day followers of Mungo Park belong the travel writer Peter Hudson, who pursued Park's route on a moped in 1989, as described in his travelogue *Two Rivers: Travels in West Africa on the Trail of Mungo Park* (1991), and the travel writer Tom Fremantle, who retraced the two journeys that Park made in the years 1795 to 1797 and 1805 in West Africa, as reported in *The Road to Timbuktu: Down the Niger on the Trail of Mungo Park* (2005). Inspired by Park's diary, Fremantle emphasizes in his travelogue that he has set as his objective the investigation of the mystery of Park's personality as much as the famous expeditioner's route, asking himself: "So how would I trace Mungo Park, this man every bit as intriguing as the river he had so doggedly pursued?" (2005, 9).[5] Fremantle thus assumes for himself a position in a long tradition of travel, expeditions, and travel writing, like so many other European writer–travellers in Black Africa in the early twentieth century, including Waugh in Ethiopia, Gide in the Congo, and Greene in Liberia or Paul Theroux, who reads Conrad's novella no fewer than twelve times between Cairo and Cape Town, as explained in his travelogue *Dark Star Safari* (2002),[6] thus beating Gide, who read *Heart of Darkness* four times during his African journey in 1925 and

---

4. See Laye 1981, 94–95. I would like to thank one of the anonymous readers for The Ohio State University Press for drawing this novel to my attention.

5. Fremantle travelled from The Gambia to Nigeria carrying with him a copy of *Travels in the Interior Districts of Africa* (1799) and some other Park-related books. In his rewriting (and re-travel) of Park's journeys into the interior of Africa, Fremantle tells the story of Park's travels in alternating passages with the story of his own journey. The bookish context of the journey also becomes apparent in the writer's numerous references to other famous European travellers in West Africa, including Mary Kingsley, Daniel Houghton (whose route Park followed in the beginning of his journey), Friedrich Hornemann, Captain Gordon Laing, René Caillié, and Richard Lander.

6. Among Theroux's most important literary references in *Dark Star Safari* are Flaubert's travel notes in Egypt, Richard Burton's travels in Ethiopia and East Africa, Waugh's *Tourist in Africa* (while in Tanzania), Nadine Gordimer's works (when Theroux comes to Johannesburg), and Montaigne's "On Cannibals" (during the final train ride to Cape Town).

1926. Some of the writer-travellers who are included in this study have also had their own followers, such as the journalist Tim Butcher, who retraced Graham and Barbara Greene's West African trek in 2009 and published the travelogue *Chasing the Devil: The Search for Africa's Fighting Spirit* (2010) on this experience, thus continuing the same storyline of adventure, to which Greene's travelogue belongs.

Second, many of my early twentieth-century examples of travel writing maintain an ambivalent relation with the Romantic and Orientalist tradition of literary travel, established in the early nineteenth-century travel books by Goethe, Hugo, Lamartime, Gautier, Nerval, and many others. In these European Romantic travelogues, the traveller, better known as an author of fiction or poetry, travels in order to write a book about the experience. During the Romantic period, the genre of travel writing entered the field of literature and was acknowledged as a creative form of self-expression and, thus, a potential contribution to the author's literary works. Typically, the Romantic writer-traveller concentrates on the movements, associations, and various impressions in his mind, as the sole subject of the experience, loosely inspired by the exotic locations of his journey (Turkey, Greece, Egypt, etc.). In the examples that I have examined, sub-Saharan Black Africa still enjoys a similar capacity to collect and exhibit alterity, including the traveller's alterity towards him- or herself. Evidence can still be found in these writings of some remnants of the exoticist discourse of the marvellous,[7] the "incredible" and "empty" heart of Africa, reflected for instance in the threatening "madness" of the surroundings, the decadence of "the white man's grave," or the stupefying vastness of the forest.

However, all the writers featured in this study could be identified as post-exotic writers in the sense that they are self-conscious about the disappearance of unknown worlds yet to be discovered. Exoticism has clearly lost much of its relevance as an attitude or a form of expression in this context, even if it remains imaginatively powerful. In *Journey Without Maps*, Greene refers to his disappointment with Western civilization, and this sense of disillusionment characterizes his own search for a total experience of authentic Africa as well. Many of these writers attempted to undermine and ridicule the West's favorite representations of black Africa, such as when Simenon critiques the picturesque or Gide challenges the preconceived notion of the African "enemy." What emerges with Michel Leiris is the (pseudo)ethnographic traveller who, partly in reaction to the scientific impulse towards ethnographic

---

7. Bongie argues that the underlying project of exoticism was to recover the possibility of "total experience" and "sovereign individuality" (1991, 9).

investigation and partly in response to the demand to treat different cultures and societies on an equal footing, promotes the idea that non-European cultures can be positive sources of knowledge. Critical of earlier proponents of Romantic exoticism and local colour, and the narrative of progress that measured types of society according to their supposed place in the evolution of human culture, this new (pseudo)ethnographic traveller comes to the conclusion that he must refuse to see the world from a European perspective.

However, in this early twentieth-century context of colonial travel writing, it is still impossible to envisage a travelogue in sub-Saharan Africa that could focus on the encounters with the local people and let the Africans speak for themselves. Leiris and Blixen showed great interest in the ways in which their contemporary Africans lived, made a living, told stories, and practiced their religion, but these interests are still far removed from the late twentieth-century or contemporary European travel writing that explicitly focuses on encounters with local people, who themselves may have a travel story to tell. For instance, much of the interest in the recent rewritings of Mungo Park's travels, or in Paul Theroux's account about his journey on land from Cairo to Cape Town, lies in the traveller's encounters with others on the road and his interviews and dialogues with local people. What, in other words, has become important in much contemporary travel writing is the experience of those who live in the places where Europeans travel, the "what it's like" to be an African.

In his *On Human Diversity* (1993), Tzvetan Todorov has proposed an illustrative typology of modern French exoticist travellers, from Jean-Jacques Rousseau to Pierre Loti and Victor Segalen, according to the forms of interaction in which these writer–travellers engaged with others in the course of their journey. By this typology, which includes ten different categories (such as the assimilator, the profiteer, and the tourist), Todorov wanted to draw our attention to the relation of contiguity, or coexistence, in the travelogue. This means posing the question "How does one live with others?" instead of investigating the way in which the traveller represents the others and their cultures. The latter has been a central concern in the study of Orientalism and Africanism, for instance.

In the course of my research it became clear, somewhat to my surprise, that Todorov's typology is not terribly relevant. It was not that the typology was incompatible with my corpus but that most of these writers and their travelogues, with the notable exception of Blixen's African memoir and perhaps Waugh's *Waugh in Abyssinia* (since Waugh was in some sense an *assimilator* due to his open support for Italian imperialism), fall within one type of interaction with the others, or to be more precise, within a similar combination of Todorov's categories. All of these writers were *allegorists* and at the same time also exoticists (*exotes*), who, moreover, had an ambivalent relationship with the *impressionist traveller*. Todorov defines the latter as a highly perfected tourist, as someone who is mainly interested in the impressions that countries or human beings leave him with, not the countries or the people in themselves (1993, 345). Pierre Loti, Todorov argues, was the first to systematize the impressionist attitude of travel. As *allegorists*, all of these writers speak of African places and people in order to discuss something else, such as their own supposed primitivism, the history of humanity, their poetics or the art of storytelling, the disturbing modernity of Europe, Western prejudices, the life of the settlers, problems of colonialism, and so on. Furthermore, as *exotes*, they sought to break the automatism of life at home and, thus, renew perception of the everyday and their literary art.

Blixen's place in this typology is complicated in that she was both an *exote* and *the assimilated*, that is, because she also reached out toward the Africans around her to make herself in some way like them (see 1993, 346). If we discount Blixen's colonial memoir, where the encounter with Africans is the writer's central concern, and Leiris's (ethnographic) interest in the African experience of sacred ritual of which he learns through his informants and translators, or the end of Leiris's travel journal where he gradually attributes a true individuality to Emawayish, the other writers' travelogues do not include many descriptions of encounters with actual Africans, especially not with black Africans. It is, nevertheless, implicit in many of these texts, and as was already the case with Mungo Park's travel journal from West Africa (1799),[8] that the Africans whom they met and portrayed were not simple embodiments of preconceived notions. It is implied, in most of these cases, that the Africans could also speak for themselves, even if they hardly do so within the space of the text. However, the actual focus in these travelogues is neither the dilemma of how to represent other cultures nor how to coexist with them but the processes of self-reflection, self-analysis, and self-fashioning. Their primary interest, in other words, is the traveller's subjective experience (how he or she personally felt in the foreign African setting). This means the way in which the authors *perceived themselves* in Africa and in their travels and, further, how the personal experience of Black Africa in some sense created an identity for the writer–traveller.

---

8. Mary Louise Pratt also points to Mungo Park's interest in "reciprocal vision," that is, how Park "often takes pains to report the Africans' relations to him as well as his to them, and to affirm the commensurability of European and African lifeways, different though they may be" (1992, 83).

REFERENCES

Abbott, H. Porter. 2008. *The Cambridge Introduction to Narrative.* 2nd edition. Cambridge: Cambridge University Press.

Adams, Percy G. 1962. *Travelers and Travel Liars, 1660–1800.* Berkeley: University of California Press.

———. 1983. *Travel Literature and the Evolution of the Novel.* Lexington: University Press of Kentucky.

Albers, Irene. 2008. "Mimesis and Alterity: Michel Leiris's Ethnography and Poetics of Spirit Possession." *French Studies* 62.3: 271–89.

Aldrich, Robert. 2003. *Colonialism and Homosexuality.* London: Routledge.

Appadurai, Arjun. 1988. "Putting Hierarchy in Its Place." *Cultural Anthropology* 3.1 (February): 36–49.

Arnold, A. J. 1976. "The Young Russian's Book in Conrad's *Heart of Darkness*." *Conradiana: A Journal of Joseph Conrad* 8: 121–26.

Auden, W. H. 1991. *Collected Poems.* Ed. Edward Mendelson. London: Faber and Faber.

Bakhtin, Mikhail. 1981. "Forms of Time and of the Chronotope in the Novel." In *The Dialogic Imagination: Four Essays,* 84–258. Trans. Caryl Emerson and Michael Holquist. Austin: University of Texas Press.

Bal, Mieke. 1997. *Narratology: Introduction to the Theory of Narrative.* Toronto: University of Toronto Press.

Barthes, Roland. 1977. "Introduction to the Structural Analysis of Narratives." In *Image—Music—Text,* 79–124. Trans. Stephen Heath. New York: Hill and Wang.

Bate, David. 2004. *Photography and Surrealism: Sexuality, Colonialism and Social Dissent.* London and New York: I. B. Tauris.

Batten, Charles L. 1978. *Pleasurable Instruction: Form and Convention in 18th-Century Travel Literature.* Berkeley: University of California Press.

Baucom, Ian. 1999. *Out of Place: Englishness, Empire, and the Locations of Identity.* Princeton: Princeton University Press.

Baudelaire, Charles. 1954. *The Flowers of Evil.* Trans. William Aggeler. Fresno, CA: Academy Library Guild.

———. 1991. *Les Fleurs du Mal.* Paris: Flammarion.

Beaujour, Michel. 1991. *Poetics of the Literary Self-Portrait.* Trans. Yara Milos. New York: New York University Press.

———. 1999. *Terreur et Rhétorique. Breton, Bataille, Leiris, Paulhan, Barthes & Cie. Autour du surréalisme.* Paris: Jean-Michel Place.

Becker, Lucille F. 2007. *Georges Simenon: Maigrets and the Romans Durs.* London: Haus Publishing Limited Dubois.

Behdad, Ali. 1994. *Belated Travelers: Orientalism in the Age of Colonial Dissolution.* Durham and London: Duke University Press.

Bergonzi, Bernard. 2006. *A Study in Greene: Graham Greene and the Art of the Novel.* Oxford: Oxford University Press.

Bhabha, Homi K. 1994. *The Location of Culture.* London: Routledge.

Blachère, Jean-Claude. 1996. *Les Totems d'André Breton: Surréalisme et primitivisme littéraire.* Paris: L'Harmattan.

Blanton, Casey. 2002. *Travel Writing. The Self and the World.* Routledge: New York.

Blixen, Karen (Isak Dinesen). 1954. *Out of Africa.* London: Penguin Books.

———. 1957. *Last Tales.* London: Putnam.

———. 1958. *Syv fantastiske Fortællinger.* København: Gyldendal.

———. 1981. *Letters from Africa 1914–1931.* Ed. Frans Lasson. Trans. Anne Born. London: Weidenfeld and Nicolson.

———. 1985. *Out of Africa and Shadows on the Grass.* London: Penguin Books.

Bongie, Chris. 1991. *Exotic Memories: Literature, Colonialism, and the Fin de Siècle.* Stanford: Stanford University Press.

Bradburn, Elizabeth. 2011. "1620–1700. Mind on the Move." In *The Emergence of Mind: Representations of Consciousness in Narrative Discourse in English*, 132–58. Ed. David Herman. Lincoln and London: University of Nebraska Press.

Brantlinger, Patrick. 1988. *Rule of Darkness: British Literature and Imperialism, 1830–1914.* Ithaca: Cornell University Press.

Brantly, Susan C. 2002. *Understanding Isak Dinesen.* Columbia: University of South Carolina Press.

Brée, Germaine. 1968. "The Ambiguous Voyage: Mode or Genre." *Genre* 1.2: 87–96.

———. 1980. "Michel Leiris: Mazemaker." In *Autobiography: Essays Theoretical and Critical*, 195–206. Ed. James Olney. Princeton: Princeton University Press.

Brosman, Catharine Savage. 1986. "Gide et le Démon." *Claudel Studies* 13.2: 46–55.

Bruner, Jerome. 1987. "Life as Narrative." *Social Research* 54.1: 11–32.

Butcher, Tim. 2010a. "The Unsung Heroine Who Saved Graham Greene's Life." *Telegraph*, September 5. http://www.telegraph.co.uk/culture/books/7981793/The-unsung-heroine-who-saved-Graham-Greenes-life.html

———. 2010b. "Graham Greene: Our Man in Liberia." *History Today* 60.10 (October). http://www.historytoday.com/tim-butcher/graham-greene-our-man-liberia

Buzard, James. 1990. *The Tourist Gaze*. London: Sage Publications.

Byron, Robert. 1933. *First Russia Then Tibet*. Edinburgh: Macmillan & Co.

———. 2007. *The Road to Oxiana*. Oxford: Oxford University Press.

Campbell, Mary Baine. 2009. "Asia, Africa, Abyssinia. Writing the Land of Prester John." In *Travel Writing, Form, and Empire: the Poetics and Politics of Mobility*, 21–37. Eds. Julia Kuehn and Paul Smethurst. New York: Routledge.

Carens, James E. 1966. *The Satiric Art of Evelyn Waugh*. Seattle: University of Washington Press.

Carpenter, Humphrey. 1989. *The Brideshead Generation: Evelyn Waugh and His Friends*. London: Weidenfield and Nicolson.

Carr, Helen. 2002. "Modernism and Travel (1880–1940)." In *The Cambridge Companion to Travel Writing*, 70–86. Eds. Peter Hulme and Tim Youngs. Cambridge. Cambridge University Press.

Cederborg, Else. 1986. "Introduction: Karen Blixen—Her Life and Writings" In *Karen Blixen: On Modern Marriage and Other Observations*, 1–31. Trans. Anne Born. London: Fourth Estate.

Céline, Louis-Ferdinand. 1952. *Féerie pour une autre fois*. Paris: Gallimard.

———. 1961. *Voyage au bout de la nuit*. Paris: Gallimard.

———. 1978. *Lettres et premiers écrits d'Afrique 1916–1917*. Cahiers Céline 4. Paris: Gallimard.

———. 1983. *Journey to the End of the Night*. Trans. Ralph Manheim. New York: New Directions Book.

Cendrars, Blaise. 1992. *Complete Poems*. Trans. Ron Padgett. Berkeley: University of California Press.

———. 2001. *Du monde entier au cœur du monde*. Poésies complètes. Ed. C. Leroy. Paris: Gallimard.

Certeau, Michel de. 1984. *The Practice of Everyday Life*. Trans. Steven Rendall. Berkeley: University of California Press.

———. 1988. *The Writing of History*. Trans. Tom Conley. New York: Columbia University Press.

Chadourne, Jacqueline. 1968. *André Gide et l'Afrique. Le rôle de l'Afrique dans la vie et l'Œuvre de l'écrivain*. Paris: Nizet.

Chupeau, Jacques. 1977. "Les récits de voyages aux lisières du roman." *Revue d'Histoire littéraire de la France* 3–4: 536–53.

Clifford, James. 1988. *The Predicament of Culture: Twentieth-Century Ethnography, Literature, and Art*. Cambridge: Harvard University Press.

Cogez, Gérard. 2004. *Les écrivains voyageurs au XXe siècle*. Paris: Éditions du Seuil.

Cohn, Dorrit. 1978. *Transparent Minds: Narrative Modes for Presenting Consciousness in Fiction*. Princeton: Princeton University Press.

———. 1999. *The Distinction of Fiction*. Baltimore: Johns Hopkins University Press.

Conrad, Jessie. 1935. *Joseph Conrad and His Circle*. London: Jarrolds.

Conrad, Joseph. 1978. *Congo Dairy and Other Uncollected Pieces*. Ed. Zdzislaw Najder. New York: Doubleday.

———. 1983. *The Collected Letters of Joseph Conrad*. Vol. I, 1861–1897. Cambridge: Cambridge University Press.

———. 1985. "An Outpost of Progress." In *Tales of Unrest*, 83–110. Harmondsworth: Penguin Books.

———. 1994. *Heart of Darkness*. London: Penguin Books.

Côté, Sébastien. 2005. "Michel Leiris et la fuite impossible: Ethnographie, autobiographie et altérité dans L'Afrique fantôme." *MLN* 120.4: 849–87.

Cronin, Michael. 2000. *Across the Lines: Travel, Language, Translation.* Cork: Cork University Press.

Culler, Jonathan. 1975. *Structuralist Poetics: Structuralism, Linguistics and the Study of Literature.* London: Routledge & Kegan Paul.

Cunningham, Valentine. 1989. *British Writers of the Thirties.* Oxford: Oxford University Press.

Damrosch, David. 2009. *How to Read World Literature.* Oxford: Wiley-Blackwell.

Dannenberg, Hilary P. 2008. *Coincidence and Counterfactuality. Plotting Time and Space in Narrative Fiction.* Lincoln and London: University of Nebraska Press.

Demeulenaere, Alex. 2009. *Le récit de voyage français en Afrique noire (1830–1931): Essai de scénographie.* Berlin: LIT Verlag.

Diop, Birago. 1961. *Les Contes d'Amadou Koumba.* Paris: Présence Africaine.

———. 1985. *Tales of Amadou Koumba.* Trans. Dorothy S. Blair. Essex: Longman.

Doležel, Lubomir. 1988. "Mimesis and Possible Worlds." *Poetics Today* 9.3: 475–496.

———. 1999. "Fictional and Historical Narrative: Meeting the Postmodernist Challenge." In *Narratologies: New Perspectives on Narrative Analysis,* 247–73. Ed. David Herman. Columbus: The Ohio State University Press.

Dubois, Jacques. 2000. *Les Romanciers du réel: De Balzac à Simenon.* Paris: Éditions su Seuil.

Dunwoodie, Peter. 1983. "Merveilleux, étrange et fantastique dans les romans de Louis-Ferdinand Céline." *Les Lettres Romanes* 37.1–2: 82–111.

———. 1993. "Voyage au bout de la nuit et 'la poésie des tropiques.'" In *Actes du Colloque international de Paris Louis-Ferdinand Céline. Paris 2–4 juillet, 1992,* 139–155. Tusson: Éditions du Lérot et Société des Études Céliniennes.

Durosay, Daniel. 1993. "L'Afrique des mystères et des misères." *Magazine littéraire* 306 (janvier): 44–48.

Ekman, Hans-Göran. 2002. *Karen Blixens paradoxer: Om Sju romantiska berättelser, Den afrikanska farmen och Vintersagor.* Södertälje: Gidlunds Förlag.

Elsner, Jaś, and Joan-Pau Rubiés. 1999. "Introduction." In *Voyages and Visions: Towards a Cultural History of Travel,* 1–56. London: Reaktion Books.

Fabian, Johannes. 1983. *Time and the Other. How Anthropology Makes Its Object.* New York: Columbia University Press.

Felman, Shoshana. 1985. *Writing and Madness: Literature/Philosophy/Psychoanalysis.* Ithaca: Cornell University Press.

Fludernik, Monika. 1996. *Towards a "Natural" Narratology.* London and New York: Routledge.

———. 2009. *An Introduction to Narratology.* London and New York: Routledge.

Fraiture, Pierre-Philippe. 2007. *La Mesure de l'autre: Afrique subsaharienne et roman ethnographique de Belgique et de France (1918–1940).* Paris: Honoré Champion.

Fremantle, Tom. 2005. *The Road to Timbuktu: Down the Niger on the Trail of Mungo Park.* London: Constable and Robinson.

Fussell, Paul. 1980. *Abroad: British Literary Traveling between the Wars.* New York: Oxford University Press.

Gallagher, Donat (ed.). 1983. *The Essays, Articles and Reviews of Evelyn Waugh.* London: Methuen.

Gannier, Odile. 2001. *La littérature de voyage.* Paris: Ellipses.

Gearhart, Suzanne. 1984. *The Open Boundary of History and Fiction: A Critical Approach to the French Enlightenment.* Princeton: Princeton University Press.

Genette, Gérard. 1972. *Figures III.* Paris: Seuil.

———. 1980. *Narrative Discourse.* Trans. Jane E. Lewin. Oxford: Basil Blackwell.

———. 2004. *Fiction et diction.* Paris: Seuil.

Gibson, Andrew. 1996. *Towards a Postmodern Theory of Narrative.* Edinburgh: Edinburgh University Press.

Gide, André. 1951a. *Journal 1889–1939.* Paris: Gallimard/Pléiade.

———. 1951b. *The Journals of Andre Gide, Volume 4: 1938–1949.* Trans. Justin O'Brien. New York: Knopf.

———. 1952. *Ainsi soit-il ou Les jeux sont faits.* Paris: Gallimard.

———. 1954. *Journal 1939–1949. Souvenirs.* Paris: Gallimard.

———. 1957. *Travels in the Congo.* Trans. Dorothy Bussy. Berkeley: University of California Press.

———. 1960. *So Be It: or, the Chips Are Down.* Trans. Justin O'Brien. London: Chatto & Windus.

———. 1966. *The Counterfeiters.* Trans. Dorothy Bussy. London: Penguin Books.

———. 1967. *Journals 1889–1949.* Trans. Justin O'Brien. Harmondsworth: Penguin.

———. 2002a. *Les Faux-Monnayeurs.* Paris: Gallimard.

———. 2002b. *Voyage au Congo suivi de Le retour du Tchad. Carnets de route.* Paris: Gallimard.

———. 2008. *Le Journal des Faux-Monnayeurs.* Paris: Gallimard.

Godard, Henri. 2006. *Le roman modes d'emploi.* Paris: Gallimard.

Goethe, J. W. 1965. *Die Wahlverwandtschaften. Roman.* Stuttgart: Reclam.

———. 1994. *Elective Affinities.* Trans. David Constantine. Oxford: Oxford University Press.

Gorer, Geoffrey. 2003. *Africa Dances.* London: Eland.

Greene, Graham. 1947. *Nineteen Stories.* London: William Heinemann.

———. 1965. *The Heart of the Matter.* London: Penguin Books.

———. 1968. *In Search of a Character.* London: Penguin Books.

———. 1969. *Collected Essays.* London: The Bodley Head.

———. 1975. *A Burnt-Out Case.* London: Penguin Books.

———. 1980. *Ways of Escape.* London: The Bodley Head.

———. 2002a. *Journey Without Maps.* London: Vintage.

———. 2002b. *The Lawless Roads.* London: Vintage.

Hacking, Ian. 1998. *Mad Travellers: Reflections on the Reality of Transient Illnesses.* Charlottesville: University of Virginia Press.

Hamon, Philippe. 1973. "Un discours constraint." *Poétique* 16: 411–45.

———. 2001. *Imageries. Littérature et image au XIXe siècle.* Paris: Librairie José Corti.

Hand, Seán. 1995. "Phantom of the Opus: Colonialist Traces in Michel Leiris's *L'Afrique fantôme*." *Paragraph* 18.2 (July): 174–93.

———. 2002. *Michel Leiris: Writing the Self.* Cambridge: Cambridge University Press.

Harshaw, Benjamin. 1984. "Fictionality and Fields of Reference: Remarks on a Theoretical Framework." *Poetics Today* 5.2: 227–51.

Hay, Eloise Knapp. 1963. *The Political Novels of Joseph Conrad.* Chicago: University of Chicago Press.

Healey, Kimberley J. 2003. *The Modernist Traveler: French Detours, 1900-1930.* Lincoln: University of Nebraska Press.

Hegel, G. W. F. 1956. *The Philosophy of History.* Trans. J. Jibree. New York: Dover.

Hemingway, Ernest. 1994. *Green Hills of Africa.* London: Arrow Books.

Herman, David. 2009. *Basic Elements of Narrative.* West Sussex: Wiley-Blackwell, John Wiley & Sons Ltd.

Hervouet, Yves. 1990. *The French Face of Joseph Conrad.* Cambridge: Cambridge University Press.

Hollier, Denis. 1997. *Absent Without Leave: French Literature under the Threat of War.* Trans. Catherine Porter. Cambridge: Harvard University Press.

———. 2003. "Préface." In *La Règle du jeu,* ix–xlvii. Ed. Denis Hollier. Paris: Gallimard.

Holmes, Oliver Wendell. 1896. *Life and Letters of Oliver Wendell Holmes.* Vol. 1 of *The Works of Oliver Wendell Holmes: Illustrated with Steel Portraits and Photogravures, In Thirteen Volumes.* Ed. John T. Morse Jr. Boston and New York: The Riverside Press.

Housman, A. E. 1922. *Last Poems.* XL, ll. 1–2. London: Grant Richards Ltd.

Huggan, Graham. 1989. "Voyages Towards an Absent Centre: Landscape Interpretation and Textual Strategy in Joseph Conrad's *Heart of Darkness* and Jules Verne's *Voyage au centre de la terre.*" *Conradian: The Journal of the Joseph Conrad Society* 14:1–2: 19–46.

Jacob, Christian. 1992. *L'Empire des cartes. Approche théorique de la cartographie à travers l'histoire.* Paris: Albin Michel.

Jakobson, Roman. 1987. "The Dominant." In *Language in Literature,* 41–46. Eds. Krystyna Pomorska and Stephen Rudy. Cambridge: The Belknap Press of Harvard University Press.

JanMohamed, Abdul R. 1983. *Manichean Aesthetics: The Politics of Literature in Colonial Africa.* Amherst: The University of Massachusetts Press.

Kaufmann, Vincent. 1989. "Michel Leiris: 'on ne part pas.'" *Revue des Sciences Humaines* 90/214: 145–62.

Keller, Richard C. 2007. *Colonial Madness: Psychiatry in French North Africa.* Chicago: University of Chicago Press.

Kermode, Frank. 1966. *The Sense of an Ending: Studies in the Theory of Fiction.* Oxford: Oxford University Press.

Keyserling, Count Hermann. 1920. *Das Reisetagebuch eines Philosophen.* Darmstadt: Otto Riechl Verlag.

———. 1925. *The Travel Diary of a Philosopher I-II.* Trans. J. Holroydreece. New York: Harcourt, Brace & Company.

Korte, Barbara. 2008. "Chrono-Types: Notes on Forms of Time in the Travelogue." In *Writing Travel: The Poetics and Politics of the Modern Journey,* 25–53. Ed. John Zilcosky. University of Toronto Press.

Lakoff, George, and Mark Turner. 1989. *More than Cool Reason: A Field Guide to Poetic Metaphor.* Chicago: University of Chicago Press.

Laye, Camara. 1981. *The Radiance of the King.* Trans. James Kirkup. Glasgow: Fontana Books.

Leacock. N. K. 2002. "Character, Silence, and the Novel: Walter Benjamin on Goethe's Elective Affinities." *Narrative* 10.3: 277–306.

Leavis, F. R. 1993. *The Great Tradition: George Eliot, Henry James, Joseph Conrad.* London: Penguin Books.

Lebel, Roland. 1931. *Histoire de la littérature coloniale en France.* Paris: Librairie Larose.

References • 311

Leiris, Michel. 1930/1992. "L'œil de l'ethnographe." In *Zébrage*, 26–34. Paris: Gallimard.

———. 1935/1992. "L'Abyssinie intime." In *Zébrage*, 48–56. Paris: Gallimard.

———. 1950/1992. "L'ethnographe devant le colonialisme." In *Brisées*, 141–64. Paris: Gallimard.

———. 1965/1992. "L'opéra, musique en action." In *Brisées*, 315–22. Paris: Gallimard.

———. 1969. *Mots sans mémoire*. Paris: Gallimard.

———. 1981. *L'Afrique fantôme*. Paris: Gallimard.

———. 1985. *Langage tangage*. Paris: Gallimard.

———. 1991. *Rules of the Game: Scratches*. Trans. Lydia Davis. Paragon House.

———. 1992a. *Journal 1922–1989*. Ed. Jean Jamin. Paris: Gallimard.

———. 1992b. "The Autobiographer as a *Torero*." In *Manhood: A Journey from Childhood into the Fierce Order of Virility*, 153–64. Trans. Richard Howard. Chicago: University of Chicago Press.

———. 1996. "Message de l'Afrique." In *Miroir de l'Afrique*, 873–87. Paris: Gallimard.

———. 1998a. "Letter to Raymond Roussel signed on February 10, 1931." In *Roussel & Co*, 290–91. Ed. Jean Jamin. Paris: Fata Morgana/Fayard.

———. 1998b. "Entretien sur Raymond Roussel." In *Roussel & Co.*, 265–70. Ed. Jean Jamin. Paris: Fata Morgana/Fayard.

———. 1998c. "Cahier Raymond Roussel." in *Roussel & Co.*, 65–197. Ed. Jean Jamin. Paris: Fata Morgana/Fayard.

———. 2001. *L'Âge d'homme*. Paris: Gallimard.

———. 2001. "De la littérature considérée comme une tauromachie." In *L'Âge d'homme*, 9–22. Paris: Gallimard.

———. 2003. *La Règle du jeu*. Ed. Denis Hollier. Paris: Gallimard.

Lejeune, Philippe. 1996. *Le pacte autobiographique*. Nouvelle édition augmentée. Paris: Éditions du Seuil.

Leroy, Claude. 1996. *La main de Cendrars*. Villeneuve d'Ascq: Presses Universitaires du Septentrion.

———. 2001. "Notices et notes." In *Du monde entier au cœur du monde*. Poésies complètes, 358–417. Ed. B. Cendrars. Paris: Gallimard.

Lévi-Strauss, Claude. 1973. *Tristes Tropiques*. Trans. John and Doreen Weightmann. New York: Penguin Books.

Lidström, Carina. 2003. "Berättaren på resa: Om persona och berättarhållning i några svenska reseberättelser." In *Berättaren. En gäckande röst i texten*, 227–53. Ed. Lars-Åke Skalin. Örebro: Örebro Studies in Literary History and Criticism.

———. 2005. "All Travellers Are Liars—On Fact and Fiction in the Travellers Tale." In *Fiction and Fact in Narrative: An Interdisciplinary Approach*, 143–66. Ed. Lars-Åke Skalin. Örebro: Örebro University.

Loingsigh, Aedín Ní. 2009. *Postcolonial Eyes: Intercontinental Travel in Francophone African Literature*. Liverpool: Liverpool University Press.

Loomba, Ania. 1998. *Colonialism/Postcolonialism*. London: Routledge.

Lothe, Jakob. 1998. "Conrad and Travel Literature: From Conrad's 'Up-river Book' and 'Congo Diary' (1890) via *Heart of Darkness* (1899) to Redmond O'Hanlon's *Congo Journey* (1996)." In *Journeys, Myths and the Age of Travel: Joseph Conrad's Era*, 36–54. Karlskrona: University of Karlskrona.

Loti, Pierre. 1907. *A Spahi's Love-Story.* London: Charles Carrington.

———. 1923. *Un jeune officier pauvre* (Fragments de journal intime rassemblés par son fils Samuel Viaud). Paris: Calmann-Lévy.

———. 1924. *Notes of My Youth.* Trans. Rose Ellen Stein. New York: Doubleday.

———. 1992. *Le Roman d'un spahi.* Paris: Gallimard.

———. 2005. *Between Two Opinions, or the Romance of a Spahi.* Trans. M. L. Watkins. New York: Cosimo.

———. 2006. *Journal.* Vol. I. 1868–1878. Eds. Alain Quella-Villéger et Bruno Vercier. Paris: Les Indes Savantes.

MacIntyre, Alasdair. 1984. *After Virtue. A Study in Moral Theory.* 2nd ed. Notre Dame: University of Notre Dame Press.

MacKenzie, John M. 1995. *Orientalism: History, Theory and the Arts.* Manchester: Manchester University Press.

Marin, Louis. 1984. *Utopics: Spatial Play.* Trans. Robert A. Vollrath. New Jersey: Humanities Press.

Masson, Pierre. 1983. *André Gide. Voyage et écriture.* Lyon: Presses Universitaires de Lyon.

Michaud, Gabriel. 1961. *Gide et L'Afrique.* Paris: Collection Alternance.

Michaux, Henri. 1968. *Ecuador: Journal de voyage.* Paris: Gallimard.

———. 1986. *A Barbarian in Asia.* Trans. Sylvia Beach. New York: New Directions.

Mikkonen, Kai. 2006. "Can Fiction Become Fact? The Fiction-to-Fact Transition in Recent Theories of Fiction." *Style* 40.4 (Winter): 291–313.

———. 2007a. "The 'Narrative is Travel' Metaphor: Between Spatial Sequence and Open Consequence." *Narrative* 15.3 (October): 286–305.

———. 2007b. "The Modernist Africa as an Imaginary Foil: From Pierre Loti's Implied Ethnologist to the Heterotopian Zone." In *Modernism*, 715–33. Eds. Vivian Liska and Astradur Eysteinsson. Amsterdam/Philadeplhia: Johns Hopkins University Press.

———. 2008. "It is not the fully conscious mind which chooses West Africa in preference to Switzerland": The Rhetoric of the Mad African Forest in Conrad, Céline and Greene." *Comparative Critical Studies* 5.2–3: 301–15.

———. 2009a. "Du corps du voyageur au cœur de l'Afrique: La métaphore corporelle dans *Feuilles de route* de Cendrars." In *Actes de la rencontre intérnationale « Corps et écriture »*, Helsinki, 25–26 septembre 2008. 65–73. Ed. Sabine Kraenker, en collaboration avec Xavier Martin. Helsinki: Publications du Département des Langues Romanes de l'Université de Helsinki 22.

———. 2009b. "Artificial Africa in European Avant-Garde: Marinetti and Tzara." In *Europa! Europa?: The Avant-Garde, Modernism and the Fate of the Continent* (European Avant-Garde and Modernism Studies 1), 391–408. Eds. Bru, Sascha & Baetens, Jan & Hjartarson, Benedikt & Nicholls, Peter & Ørum, Tania & Berg, Hubert van den. Berlin: Walter de Gruyter.

———. 2011. "Out of Europe: The African Palimpsest in Michel Leiris's L'Afrique fantôme." *Studies in Travel Writing* 15.1: 77–92.

———. 2013. "The Enchanted Arrival: Passage into West Africa in the Travelogues of Blaise Cendrars and André Gide." *Neohelicon* 40.2: 489–506.

Miller, Christopher L. 1985. *Blank Darkness. Africanist Discourse in French.* Chicago: University of Chicago Press.

———. 1998. *Nationalists and Nomads: Essays on Francophone African Literature and Culture.* Chicago: University of Chicago Press.

Montalbetti, Christine. 1997. *Le Voyage, le monde et la bibliothèque.* Paris: PUF.

Moretti, Franco. 2004. "Graphs, Maps, Trees. Abstract Models for Literary History—2." *New Left Review* 26 (March–April): 79–103.

Moura, Jean-Marc. 1998. *L'Europe littéraire et l'ailleurs.* Paris: PUF.

Naipaul. V. S. 1980. "Conrad's Darkness." In *The Return of Eva Perón with the Killings in Trinidad*, 207–28. London: André Deutsch.

O'Brien, Justin. 1953. *Portrait of André Gide: A Critical Biography.* New York: Alfred A. Knopf.

Palmer, Alan. 2004. *Fictional Minds.* Lincoln: University of Nebraska Press.

Pasquali, Adrien. 1994. *Le tour des horizons: Critique et récits de voyages.* Paris: Klincksieck.

Perloff, Marjorie. 1995. "Tolerance and Taboo: Modernist Primitivisms and Postmodernist Pieties." In *Prehistories of the Future: The Primitivist Project and the Culture of Modernism*, 339–54. Eds. Elazar Barkan and Ronald Bush. Stanford: Stanford University Press.

Phelan, James. 2005. *Living to Tell about It: A Rhetoric and Ethics of Character Narration.* Ithaca: Cornell University Press.

———. 2009. "The Beginning of *Beloved*: A Rhetorical Approach." In *Narrative Beginnings: Theories and Practices*, 195–212. Ed. Brian Richardson. University of Nebraska Press.

Porter, Dennis. 1994. "Orientalism and Its Problems." In *Colonial Discourse and Post-Colonial Theory. A Reader,* 150–61. Ed. Patrick Williams and Laura Chrisman. New York: Columbia University Press.

Pratt, Mary Louis. 1992. *Imperial Eyes: Travel Writing and Transculturation.* London: Routledge.

Prendergast, Christopher. 2000. *The Triangle of Representation.* New York. Columbia University Press.

Prince, Gerald. 1973. "Lecteurs et lectures dans *Les Faux-Monnayeurs*." *Neophilologus* 57.1 (January): 16–23.

———. 1992. *Narrative as Theme: Studies in French Fiction.* London/Lincoln: University of Nebraska Press.

———. 2003. *Dictionary of Narratology.* Revised Edition. Lincoln & London: University of Nebraska Press.

Putnam, Walter C. 1990. *L'aventure littéraire de Joseph Conrad et d'André Gide.* Stanford: Stanford French and Italian Studies/Anma Libri.

Quella-Villéger, Alain. 1986. *Pierre Loti l'incompris.* Paris: Presses de la Renaissance.

Rabinowitz, Peter. J. 1977. "Truth in Fiction: A Reexamination of Audiences." *Critical Inquiry* 4: 121–41.

———. 1987. *Before Reading: Narrative Conventions and the Politics of Interpretation.* Ithaca: Cornell University Press.

Rasmussen, Tove. 1983. "Karen Blixen og Afrika—endnu engang." *Bogens verden* 65: 411.

Requemora, Sylvie. 2002. "L'espace dans la littérature de voyages." *Études littéraires* 34.1–2: 249–76.

Richardson, Brian. 2011. "The Trope of the Book in the Jungle: Colonial and Postcolonial Avatars." *The Conradian* 36.1 (Spring): 1–13.

Ricoeur, Paul. 1984. *Time and Narrative. Vol I.* Trans. Kathleen McLaughlin and David Pellauer. Chicago: University of Chicago Press.

Ridon, Jean-Xavier. 2002. *Le Voyage en son miroir. Essai sur quelques tentatives de réinvention du voyage au 20e siècle.* Paris: Éditions Kimé.

Rimmon-Kenan, Shlomith. 1983. *Narrative Fiction: Contemporary Poetics.* London: Methuen.

Rousseau, Jean-Jacques. 1995. *Confessions.* In *The Collected Writings of Rousseau,* Vol. 5. Trans. Christopher Kelly. Hanover and London: Dartmouth College.

Roussel, Raymond. *Comment j'ai écrit certains de mes livres.* Paris: Gallimard, 1963.

Ryan, Marie-Laure. 1991. *Possible Worlds, Artificial Intelligence, and Narrative Theory.* Bloomington: Indiana University Press.

———. 2001. *Narrative as Virtual Reality: Immersion and Interactivity in Literature and Electronic Media.* Baltimore: Johns Hopkins University Press.

———. 2002. "Fiction and its Other: How Trespasses Help Defend the Border." *Semiotica* 138-1/4: 351-69.

———. 2003. "Cognitive Maps and the Construction of Narrative Space." In *Narrative Theory and the Cognitive Sciences,* 214-42. Ed. David Herman. Stanford: CSLI Publications.

Sabot, Philippe. 2003. "Primitivisme et surréalisme: Une 'synthèse' impossible?" *Methodos* 3: 113-36.

Said, Edward W. 1978. *Orientalism.* New York: Vintage Books.

Salwen, Michael B. 2001a. "Evelyn Waugh in Ethiopia: The Novelist as War Correspondent and Journalism Critic." *Journalism Studies* 2.1: 5-25.

———. 2001b. "Evelyn Waugh's *Scoop:* The Facts Behind the Fiction." *Journalism and Mass Communication Quarterly* 78: 150-71.

Scott, David. 2004. *Semiologies of Travel: From Gautier to Baudrillard.* Cambridge: Cambridge University Press.

———. 2005. "Writing the Exotic: The Example of Leiris in *Afrique fantôme.*" Paper given at the conference "Pluralism & Equality" at the University of Helsinki, Finland, May 18-21.

Segalen, Victor. 1983. *Équipée. Voyage au pays du Réel.* Paris: Gallimard.

Selboe, Tone. 1996. *Kunst og Erfaring: En Studie i Karen Blixens Författernskap.* Odense: Odense Universitetsförlag.

Shelton, Marie-Denise. 1995. "Primitive Self: Colonial Impulses in Leiris's *L'Afrique Fantôme.*" In *Prehistories of the Future: The Primitivist Project and the Culture of Modernism,* 326-38. Eds. Elazar Barkan and Ronald Bush. Stanford: Stanford University Press.

Sherry, Norman. 1971. *Conrad's Western World.* London: Cambridge University Press.

———. 1989. *The Life of Graham Greene. Volume One: 1904-1939.* London: Jonathan Cape.

Simenon, Georges. 1970. *Quand j'étais vieux.* Tome I. Paris: Presses de la Cité.

———. 1979a. *African Trio. Talatala, Tropic Moon, Aboard the Aquitaine.* Trans. Stuart Gilbert, Paul Auster, and Lydia Davis. New York: Harcourt Brace Jovanovich.

———. 1979b. *Point-virgule.* Paris: Presses de la Cité.

———. 1991. *La drame mystérieux des îles Galapagos.* Bruxelles: Les Amis de Georges Simenon.

———. 2001. *Mes apprentissages. Reportages 1931-1946.* Paris: Omnibus.

———. 2010a. *Romans du monde I. Le Coup de lune, Les Gens d'en face, Les Client d'Avrenos, 45° à l'ombre, Long cours.* Présentés par Jean-Baptiste Baronian. Paris: Omnibus.

———. 2010b. *Romans du monde II. Le Blanc à lunettes, Ceux de la soif, Touriste de bananes, Un crime au Gabon, L'Ainé des Fercheux, Le Passager clandestin.* Présentés par Jean-Baptiste Baronian. Paris: Omnibus.

Škvorecký, Josef. 1984. "Why the Harlequin?" *Cross Currents: A Yearbook of Central European Culture* 3: 259-64.

Spearey, Susan. 2002. "The Readability of Conrad's Legacy: Narrative, Semantic and Ethical Navigations into and out of 'Heart of Darkness.'" In *Conrad in Africa: New Essays on "Heart of Darkness,"* 41–66. Eds. Attie de Lange and Gail Fincham with Wieslaw Krajka. Boulder: Social Science Monographs.

Stanley, Henry M. 1890. *My Kalulu, Prince, King and Slave. A Story of Central Africa.* New York: Charles Scribner's Sons.

Stannard, Martin. 1986. *Evelyn Waugh: The Early Years 1903–1939.* London: J. M. Dent & Sons Ltd.

Stevens, Ray. 2002. "Three Voices in Conrad's Narrative Journey." In *Conrad in Africa: New Essays on "Heart of Darkness,"* 67–84. Eds. Attie de Lange and Gail Fincham with Wieslaw Krajka. Boulder: Social Science Monographs.

Strauss, George. 1985. *La Part du diable dans l'oeuvre d'André Gide.* Paris: Minard.

Strawson, Galen. 2012. "We live beyond any tale that we happen to enact." *Harvard Review of Philosophy* 18: 73–90.

Thacker, Andrew. 2002. "Journey without Maps. Travel Theory, Geography and the Syntax of space." In *Cultural Encounters: European Travel-Writing in the 1930s,* 11–28. Eds. Charles Burdett and Derek Duncan. New York: Berghahn Books.

Theroux, Paul. 2002. *Dark Star Safari: Overland from Cairo to Cape Town.* London: Penguin Books.

Thomas, Bronwen E. 2002. "Multiparty Talk in the Novel: The Distribution of Tea and Talk in a Scene from Evelyn Waugh's Black Mischief." *Poetics Today* 23.4 (Winter): 657–84.

———. 2012. *Fictional Dialogue: Speech and Conversation in the Modern and Postmodern Novel.* Lincoln and London: University of Nebraska Press.

Thompson, Carl. 2011. *Travel Writing.* London: Routledge.

Todorov, Tzvetan. 1981. *Introduction to Poetics.* Trans. Richard Howard. Minneapolis: University of Minnesota Press.

———. 1993. *On Human Diversity: Nationalism, Racism, and Exoticism in French Thought.* Trans. Catherine Porter. Cambridge: Harvard University Press.

Tomashevsky, Boris. 1965. "Thematics." In *Russian Formalist Criticism: Four Essays,* 61–95. Eds. Lee T. Lemon and Marion J. Reis. Lincoln: University of Nebraska Press.

Trachsel, Judith. 1991–1992. "Sous le signe de Fébronio." *Continent Cendrars* 6–7: 54–61.

Tythacott, Louise. 2003. *Surrealism and the Exotic.* London: Routledge, 2003.

Urbain, Jean-Didier. 1998. *Secrets de voyage. Menteurs, imposteurs et autres voyageurs invisibles.* Paris: Éditions Payot & Rivages.

Urry, John. 2002. *The Tourist Gaze.* 2nd edition. London: Sage Publications.

Warehime, Marja. 1995. "Exploring Connections and Rediscovering Difference: Gide *Au Congo.*" *French Review* 68:3 (February): 457–65.

Waugh, Evelyn. 1960. *Black Mischief.* Boston: Little, Brown and Company.

———. 1961. *Put Out More Flags.* Harmondsworth. Penguin Books.

———. 1976. *The Diaries of Evelyn Waugh.* Ed. Michael Davie. London: Weidenfeld and Nicolson.

———. 1980. *The Letters of Evelyn Waugh.* Ed. Mark Amory. New Haven: Ticknor & Fields.

———. 2000a. *Scoop.* London: Penguin Books.

———. 2000b. *The Complete Stories of Evelyn Waugh.* Boston: Little, Brown and Company.

———. 2003. *Waugh Abroad. Collected Travel Writing.* New York: Alfred A Knopf, Everyman's Library.

West, Russell. 1996. *Conrad and Gide: Translation, Transference and Intertextuality.* Amsterdam: Rodopi.

———. 1999. "Space and Language in the Private Diary: Conrad's *Congo Journal.*" In *Marginal Voices, Marginal Forms: Diaries in European Literature and History,* 107–25. Eds. Russell West and Rachel Langford. Amsterdam and Atlanta, GA: Rodopi.

White, John J. 1990. *Literary Futurism: Aspects of the First Avant Garde.* Oxford: Clarendon Press.

Wolf, Werner. 2007. "Description as a Transmedial Mode of Representation: General Features and Possibilities of Realization in Painting, Fiction and Music." In *Description in Literature and Other Media,* 1–87. Eds. Werner Wolf and Walter Bernhart. Amsterdam: Rodopi.

Yacobi, Tamar. 1991. "Plots of Space: World and Story in Isak Dinesen." *Poetics Today* 12.3 (Fall): 447–93.

Young, Robert. 1990. *White Mythologies: Writing History and the West.* London: Routledge.

INDEX

"Abyssinie intime" (Leiris), 258
Adams, Percy G., 2–3, 2n3, 7n7. *See also* *Travel Literature and the Evolution of the Novel*
affabulation, 253
Africa: archaic, 96, 152, 190–92, 258–59; authentic/real, 152, 186, 256, 301; colonial, 19, 73–74, 84, 130, 179, 186, 196, 203; discourses of exhaustion and excess, 31–32; imaginary, 30, 253, 260–63; mythopoetic, 47; picturesque, 30, 36, 180, 186–190, 192, 195, 202, 210, 214–18, 255, 287, 301; and personal mythology, 45, 47, 50–51, 59, 61, 120, 259n14, 263, 279–80, 286, 291; place of wonder and renewed perception, 29–31, 45, 142, 271, 276, 288, 291; place without history, 33–34, 96, 97n10, 180–81; sub-Saharan, 3, 5, 8, 19–20, 24, 29, 31, 33, 42, 82, 161, 187, 240, 242, 256, 292–93, 295, 301–2
Africa Dances: A Book about West African Negroes (Gorer), 31, 63
African imagery, 251–52, 254, 257–58, 264–65, 297, 240, 242, 244
africanism, 25–26, 34n47, 85, 97n10, 247, 264, 276, 286–90, 302
African Trio (Simenon), 183

Afrique fantôme (Leiris), 22, 36, 240–43, 245, 249–50, 255–57, 259n14, 260, 264
Âge d'homme (Leiris), 248, 251n9, 252, 252n10, 260n16, 263
Albers, Irene, 242n4, 256n12
Aldrich, Robert, 120n9
anti-conquest travel narrative, 290
Appadurai, Arjun, 34
Auden, W. H., 101, 101n16. *See also* "O Where Are You Going"
audience, 10–11, 271; authorial, 26, 26n39, 42n1, 224; hypothetical, 5, 7, 26–27, 26n39, 41n1, 298; narrative, 7, 26, 26n39, 217–18
"Autobiographer as a Torero" (Leiris), 252, 252n10, 263
autobiography, 4, 9, 11n13, 13, 15n20, 29–30, 36–38, 90, 97, 98n11, 149, 169, 234, 234n11, 239, 245, 248–50, 252, 252n10, 266, 293–95

Bacon, Sir Francis, 18. *See also* "Of Travel"
Bakhtin, Mikhail, 2n1
Bal, Mieke, 100n15
Barbarian in Asia (Michaux), 297

317

Barthes, Roland, 90–91. See also *Introduction to the Structural Analysis of Narratives*

Batten, Charles L., 7n, 18n24

Baucom, Ian, 25n36, 256

Baudelaire, Charles, 51–54, 57, 59, 62–63, 120–21, 126. See also "Parfum Exotique"; "Invitation au voyage"; "Musique (La)"

Beaujour, Michel, 251n9

beginning (narrative), 12, 41–42, 51, 53–54, 57, 66–68, 91. See also launch

Behdad, Ali, 25n, 31n43

Belgian Congo, 107, 183, 186, 188, 297

Belloc, Hilaire, 32n45, 167

Bhabha, Homi K., 231, 256

Black Mischief (Waugh), 10, 35, 147, 50, 155, 161, 163, 168–72, 174–75, 179, 180n20

Blanc à lunettes (Simenon), 185–86, 197–99, 201, 205, 214

Blanton, Casey, 13n17

Blixen, Karen (Isak Dinesen), 37–38, 237, 266–91, 293, 302–3. See also *Out of Africa*; *Last Tales*; *Letters from Africa*; *Out of Africa*; *Seven Gothic Tales* (*Syv fantastiske Fortællinger*); *Shadows on the Grass*; *Winter's Tales*

Bongie, Chris, 301n7

Brantlinger, Patrick, 70

Brantly, Susan C., 266n1, 280

Brée, Germaine, 15n20

Bruner, Jerome, 98n11

Burnt-Out Case (Greene), 80–81, 83, 83n9, 86–87, 106–7

Burton, Sir Richard Francis, 18n24, 160–61, 299, 300n6. See also *First Footsteps in East Africa or, an Exploration of Harar*

Butcher, Tim, 9n7, 9n8, 301

Buzard, James, 32n44

Byron, Robert, 16–19, 32. See also *First Russia Then Tibet*; *The Road to Oxiana*

"Cahier Raymond Roussel" (Leiris), 262

Canetti, Elias, 7, 12

Caraman, Georges, 183, 217, 294. See also Simenon, Georges

cardinal narrative unit, 91

Carpenter, Humphrey, 170

Carr, Helen, 32n45

causality (in travel narrative), 18, 88–92, 98, 100, 102–3, 109

Céline, Louis-Ferdinand, 3, 21, 26, 30–31, 34–35, 37–38, 69–70, 72–87. See also *Féerie pour une autre fois*; *Journey to the End of the Night* (*Voyage au bout de la nuit*)

Cendrars, Blaise, 3, 35, 41–51, 66–67. See also *Feuilles de route*

Certeau, Michel de, 100. See also *L'invention du quotidien*

Césaire, Aimé, 298n2

"Chance for Mr Lever" (Greene), 83, 107

characters (in fiction): inspired by travel, 103–6, 226–27

Clifford, James, 231, 245, 254n11

Cogez, Gérard, 15, 114

Cohn, Dorrit, 9n9, 11–14, 29, 90n4, 294–95, 299

colonialism, 19–20, 25n36, 29, 33–34, 58, 66, 97n10, 129, 180n20, 181–82, 190, 215, 237, 242, 247, 259n14, 280, 297, 299. See also colonial literature; colonial madness; postcolonialism

colonial literature, 28, 65, 85, 237, 248, 276, 287, 287n18

colonial madness, 70, 190, 213, 213n8, 215

Colonial Madness: Psychiatry in French North Africa (Keller), 213n8

Comment j'ai écrit certains de mes livres (Roussel), 262n9

Complete Poems (Cendrars), 43n3

Confessions (Rousseau), 255

Congo, 19, 23, 34, 54, 57, 80, 86, 106–7, 114, 128–30, 160, 183, 186, 188, 192, 198, 202, 214, 229, 233, 235, 244–45, 288, 297, 300. See also Belgian Congo; French Congo

"Congo Diary" (Conrad), 79, 80, 81n6, 105, 108n19, 228–235

Conradian, 7, 35, 37, 106, 116, 131, 253, 254n11

Conrad, Jessie, 235n12

Conrad, Joseph, 3, 6–7, 11–12, 21, 33–37, 54, 57–87, 115–16, 125. See also "An Outpost

of Progress"; "Congo Diary"; *Heart of Darkness;* "Up-river Book"
Counterfeiters (Gide), 35, 37–38, 61, 113–46
Coup de lune (Simenon), 10, 185, 191, 194–96, 197, 199, 202, 207–14, 238
Cronin, Michael, 32
Culler, Jonathan, 6n6
cultivated confusion, 25n36, 69, 256, 264
Cunningham, Valentine, 15

Dakar, 42–46, 54, 61, 62–63, 65, 66
Damrosch, David, 3n4
Dannenberg, Hilary P., 22, 222
Dark Star Safari: Overland from Cairo to Cape Town (Theroux), 300, 300n6
Demeulenaere, Alex, 254n, 294n
demonic impulses, 60–61, 117–19, 124, 146, 276, 280
description, 5–9, 14, 16, 18–23, 24n33, 32, 153–54; accurate, 7, 9, 18, 21, 27, 128, 160–61, 177; of the black body, 45, 49, 51, 144n29, 145; conflation of landscape and people, 69, 72, 280; conflation of landscape and the traveller's mind, 69, 71–72, 79, 145; of foreign places, 1–3; functions of, 19; of landscape, 22, 57, 72–73, 82–84, 85, 86, 101–2, 266–67, 276–77, 290; language of, 32, 42, 66, 67, 69; literary, 30, 115, 252n10; and narration, 2n2; parody of, 3; and the particular, 23, 188, 201, 202–3, 252; and perspective, 15–16, 135; poetic language in, 42, 51–52; of the reading experience, 135–36; split, 71
Diallo, Bakary, 298n2
diary, 18, 90, 95, 107, 193, 228–35
Diary (Waugh), 154, 167
Diop, Birago, 297, 298n2. See also "The Humps"
direct discourse, 17, 171, 174, 177, 193, 195, 197
disnarrated, 36, 221–22
Doležel, Lubomir, 4n5
Dubois, Jacques, 203
Dunwoodie, Peter, 74–75, 76n5

Eberhardt, Isabelle, 296

Ecuador (Michaux), 297
Ekman, Hans-Göran, 267n2
Elective Affinities (Goethe), 125, 127, 132–34, 140
Elsner, Jaś, and Joan-Pau Rubiés, 18n24
Équipée (Segalen), 22, 22n31
eroticism, 74–75, 77, 81, 120n9, 145, 253
Ethiopia, 7, 34, 36, 147–48, 152–55, 157, 160–61, 65, 67, 178–79, 180–81, 244, 258–60, 300
"Ethnographe devant le colonialism" (Leiris), 254
ethnography, 16, 22, 47, 143, 242, 246n6, 249n4, 251–52, 254, 256, 261, 294n1, 297, 301–2, 303; language of, 32, 42, 66, 67, 69
exhaustion: discourse of, 31–32, 108
exoticism, 23, 28–30, 34, 121, 179–80, 187, 240, 242, 256, 258–59, 287, 298, 301–3; as *art nègre*, 45, 46–47, 254, 257, 261
experientiality (narrative), 1, 5–6, 14n18, 14–15, 21, 90, 92–93, 193, 292–95, 303; as process, 204–15

Fabian, Johannes, 259
Faust (Goethe), 125, 127
Féerie pour une autre fois (Céline), 31, 74
Felman, Shoshana, 69
Feuilles de route (Cendrars), 8, 43–45, 46–51
fictional world, 4n5, 6, 9, 14, 14n19, 19, 26–27, 30, 99n12, 124, 127, 134, 153, 157, 161, 165, 170–78, 224, 231, 284, 292–93
fiction/nonfiction distinction, 4–5, 7–14, 17–18, 24, 26–27, 34–38, 134, 146, 169, 174–77, 215, 293–95, 299
First Footsteps in East Africa or, an Exploration of Harar (Burton), 160–61
First Russia Then Tibet (Byron), 16
Fleming, Peter, 93
Fludernik, Monika, 6n6, 15n19, 92–93
focalization, 15, 170–71, 173, 193, 204–5, 227
45° à l'ombre (Simenon), 34, 186, 199–202, 203, 205–7, 215
found books, 6, 228, 231–39

fractal dimension of travel, 31–32
Fraiture, Pierre-Philippe, 143n28, 189n4
free indirect discourse, 11, 106, 133–34, 171, 174, 193, 197, 199, 201–4, 207, 210, 212, 223, 294
Fremantle, Tom, 300, 300n5. See also *The Road to Timbuktu: Down the Niger on the Trail of Mungo Park*
French Congo, 19, 245
Fussell, Paul, 8n8, 15n20, 31–32, 166n12, 152

Gannier, Odile, 15
Gearhart, Suzanne, 8
Genette, Gérard, 89, 172n16
genre: cross-generic, 4, 8, 298; conventions, 5, 298; generic expectations, 4, 9–10, 25–26, 177, 293–94, 298; generic framing, 36, 174, 176, 221–22, 229; hypothetical, 146, 221–22 (definition), 230–31, 236, 239, 293; virtual, 6–7, 221–22 (definition), 226, 230–31, 239, 292
Gibson, Andrew, 99n12
Gide, André, 19–23, 29–30, 34–38, 41, 61. See also *So Be It: or, the Chips Are Down (Ainsi soit-il ou Les jeux sont faits)*; *Counterfeiters (Les Faux-Monnayeurs)*; *Journal des Faux-Monnayeurs*, *Travels in the Congo (Voyage au Congo)*
Godard, Henri, 134n21
Goethe, J. W., 125, 127, 132–34, 136–37, 140–41, 301. See also *Elective Affinities (Die Wahlverwandtschaften)*; *Faust*
Gorer, Geoffrey, 31, 63. See also *Africa Dances: A Book about West African Negroes*
Green Hills of Africa (Hemingway), 296
Greene, Barbara, 8n8, 62, 93, 95n8, 301
Greene, Graham, 3, 6–10, 13, 19–21, 29, 31, 34–35, 37, 41–42, 62–67, 69–70, 79–87, 90–98, 100–109, 130, 238, 293–94, 300–301. See also *Burnt-Out Case*; "Chance for Mr Lever"; *The Heart of the Matter*; *In Search of a Character*; *Journey Without Maps*; *Lawless Roads*; *Nineteen Stories*; *Ways of Escape*

Hacking, Ian, 78. See also *Mad Travellers: Reflections on the Reality of Transient Illnesses*
Haggard, Sir H. Rider, 29, 70n2, 79, 80. See also *King Salomon's Mines*
Hamon, Philippe, 19
Hand, Seán, 245, 250
Harshaw, Benjamin, 9
Healey, Kimberley J., 30. See also *The Modernist Traveler: French Detours, 1900–1930*
Heart of Darkness (Conrad), 6, 7, 33–35, 38, 57, 70–72, 73, 76, 79–81, 85, 115, 125, 127–30, 139n27, 140, 144, 228–39, 299, 301
Heart of the Matter (Greene), 81, 86, 107, 107n18, 238
Hegel, G. W. F., 33. See also *Lectures on the Philosophy of History (Vorlesungen über die Philosophie der Weltgeschichte)*
Hemingway, Ernest, 296. See also *Green Hills of Africa*
Herman, David, 15n19
hermeneutic pessimism, 29, 31, 76
Heuser, Kurt, 79, 80
Histoire de la Littérature Coloniale en France (Lebel), 287n18
Hollier, Denis, 248, 252n10
Holmes, Oliver Wendell, 97–98, 101
Housman, A. E., 82, 84. See also *Last Poems*
How I Found Livingstone in Central Africa (Stanley), 21
Huggan, Graham, 71
"Humps" (Diop), 29

ideology (imperial), 25, 178–82, 215, 237, 251, 298–99
Imperial Gothic, 70
implied author, 41, 41n1, 182, 222, 224
Impressions d'Afrique (Roussel), 30, 244, 246, 246n6, 261
"Incident in Azania" (Waugh), 157–58, 168, 169
indirect discourse, 123, 194, 200, 207
individuality: lack of, 34, 59–60, 129, 142–43

In Search of a Character (Greene), 105, 107, 130

intertextuality, 24–25, 63, 82–84, 108, 250–51, 295

"Introduction to the Structural Analysis of Narratives" (Barthes), 90

Invention du quotidien (Certeau), 100

"Invitation au voyage" (Baudelaire), 62–63

itinerary, 89, 91, 97–103. *See also* maps

Jakobson, Roman, 1–2

JanMohamed, Abdul R., 286, 289n20

journal (travel journal), 2–4, 6–8, 11, 15, 90, 115, 122–27, 131–40, 221

Journal des Faux-Monnayeurs (Gide), 113–15, 120, 131, 136, 138

Journal 1868–1878 (Loti), 221–7, 239

Journey to the End of the Night (Céline), 31, 35, 38, 69, 72–79, 82

Journey Without Maps (Greene), 6, 10, 35, 42, 62–66, 69, 79–84, 88–109, 301

Kaufmann, Vincent, 260n16

Keller, Richard C., 213n8, See also *Colonial Madness: Psychiatry in French North Africa*

Keyserling, Count Hermann, 165–66, 166n11. See also *The Travel Diary of a Philosopher I-II* (*Das Reisetagebuch eines Philosophen*)

Kingsley, Mary, 96, 300n5

King Solomon's Mines (Haggard), 29, 80

Korte, Barbara, 90n4

Labels: A Mediterranean Journal (Waugh), 149–50, 152, 166, 179

Lansing, Alfred, 89, 90

Last Poems (Housman), 84

Last Tales (Blixen), 272, 283

launch (arrival scene of the journey), 41–42, 51, 53, 62–63, 67–68, 91. *See also* beginning (narrative)

Lawless Roads (Greene), 87n11, 107

Laye, Camara, 299. See also *The Radiance of the King*

Lebel, Roland, 287n18. See also *Histoire de la Littérature Coloniale en France*

Lectures on the Philosophy of History (Hegel), 33

Leiris, Michel, 6, 7, 20–3, 29–30, 34, 37–38, 125, 240–65, 294, 294n1, 301–3. *See also* "L'oeil de l'ethnographe"; "L'Abyssinie intime"; "L'Ethnographe devant le colonialisme"; *L'Afrique fantôme; Rules of the Game: Scratches;* "The Autobiographer as a Torero"; *Message de l'Afrique;* "Cahier Raymond Roussel"; *L'Âge d'homme; Règle du jeu*

Lejeune, Philippe, 11n13, 294

Letters from Africa 1914–1931 (Blixen), 270, 273n6

Lévi-Strauss, Claude, 22, 22n32. See also *Tristes Tropiques*

Lévy-Bruhl, Lucien, 28, 47n5, 143–44

Lidström, Carina, 13, 13n16

literary travel narrative, 14n8; romantic, 301–2

Loingsigh, Aedín Ní, 298n2

Londres, Albert, 20

Lothe, Jakob, 229, 234

Loti, Pierre, 6, 8, 11, 29–30, 30n42, 36, 70, 74, 221–29, 238–39, 262n19, 302–3. See also *Notes of My Youth; Le Mariage de Loti; Le Roman d'un spahi (A Spahi's Love-Story/Between Two Opinions, or the Romance of a Spahi); Journal 1868–1878*

MacIntyre, Alasdair, 98n11

madness, 69–71, 73, 77, 84–86, 98–104, 116–17, 120, 131, 190, 205, 213; colonial, 70, 190, 213, 215; madness-inducing forces of Africa, 70, 190, 205, 213–15

Mad Travellers: Reflections on the Reality of Transient Illnesses (Hacking), 78

Malaparte, Curzio, 20

"Man who Liked Dickens" (Waugh), 238

maps, 33n47, 71, 91–92, 95–103, 106, 163, 164–65, 196, 268. *See also* itinerary

Mariage de Loti, Le (Loti), 228
Marin, Louis, 15, 100
Markham, Beryl, 295
Masson, Pierre, 144n29
Master of Ballantrae (Stevenson), 125, 127, 132
memoir, 6–7, 15n20, 37, 204, 266–268, 271, 273, 275, 277, 284–85, 290–92, 295
Message de l'Afrique (Leiris), 255, 257
metaphors, 42, 79, 85, 97–98, 103, 116, 119, 121, 292: abyss, 121; animal/bird, 278–80, 288; Barsetshire, 175–176; body, 45, 49–50, 49n6; darkness, 73; demon, 118, 131, 118n8; dress/accessories, 45, 278; empty space/forest, 83–84; heart of Africa, 60, 81n7, 125, 125n10, 236, 238, 301; travel as labyrinth or maze, 102; life as travel, 97–98; narrative as travel, 122, 132, 138, 146; road, 2n1; unknown territory, 96, 106; white man's grave, 70, 84, 179, 196, 234, 238, 287, 301; writing as a journey, 116. See also found books; traveller as allegorist.
Michaux, Henri, 30, 262, 297. See also *Barbarian in Asia*; *Ecuador*
Mikado (Gilbert and Sullivan), 162–63
Miller, Christopher L., 25, 33, 34n47, 85, 276
Modernist Traveler: French Detours, 1900–1930 (Healey), 30
Montalbetti, Christine, 24n. See also *Voyage, le monde et la bibliothèque*
Morand, Paul, 295
Moretti, Franco, 100n14
"Musique" (Baudelaire), 120–21
My Kalulu, Prince, King and Slave. A Story of Central Africa (Stanley), 21

Naipaul, V. S., 7, 231
narration: digressive 102; first- vs. third-person, 122–23, 127, 133–35, 137–39, 146, 171, 227; mask, 224; unrealiable, 31, 206. See also unreliable narration; narrator
narrative consequence, 35, 92, 97, 109
narrative organization/order, 6, 35, 41–42, 89, 92, 108, 253

narrativisation, 6, 6n6 (definition), 35, 250, 270, 273, 274
narrativity, 6n6, 89–92, 102, 108–9, 229, 231, 233, 270, 270n3 (definition), 299
narrator, 11–14, 131, 134, 171–72, 192–3, 196–203, 207, 221–24, 226–27, 239, 254n11, 259n11, 292–97; heterodiegetic, 169, 193, 224; ironic, 26, 123, 171, 178, 194, 198, 238
narratorial counterfactual, 36, 221–22
Nineteen Stories (Greene), 107
noble savage, 28, 65, 248, 276, 287. See also primitivism
non-narrative, 89, 264
nonreferentiality, 9n9, 12n14, 13. See also referentiality
Notes of My Youth (Loti), 226n3
Nouvelles Impressions d'Afrique (Roussel), 30
novel: adventure novel, 187, 190; modern novel, 1–3, 11, 14, 18–19, 26, 103, 134, 293; realist novel, 2, 3, 19, 114–15, 119, 127, 138, 202, 293; pure novel, 131, 138–39, 188n25; Russian novel, 2

Odysseus, 99, 282–283, 286
"Oeil de l'ethnographe" (Leiris), 246n6, 251, 257, 261
"Of Travel" (Bacon), 18
On Human Diversity: Nationalism, Racism, and Exoticism in French Thought (Todorov), 302
Orientalism, 24–26, 28n40, 29n41, 74, 79, 213n8, 254, 301–2
Out of Africa (Blixen), 8, 28, 36, 237–38, 266–91
"Outpost of Progress" (Conrad), 23, 238
"O Where Are You Going" (Auden), 101, 101n16

palimpsest, 241, 244, 251
"Parfum Exotique" (Baudelaire), 51, 59
Park, Mungo, 96, 299–300, 303
Pasquali, Adrien, 15n20
Phelan, James, 41, 42n1, 224

plot: travel into the interior of Africa, 80, 86, 299–301
Point-virgule (Simenon), 185
possible world, 4n5, 9n10, 14n18, 26, 148, 161n8, 165–66, 178, 292
postcolonialism, 25, 25n36, 256, 298–99
Pratt, Mary Louis, 290, 303
Prendergast, Christopher, 26n38
primitivism, 27–29, 33, 45–47, 66, 70, 72, 82, 85–86, 118–19, 152, 154–55, 163, 176, 178, 187, 191, 218, 237, 242, 248, 254, 259–61, 298, 303; as mentality, 27, 33, 47n5, 66, 72, 85, 119, 142–44, 286
Prince, Gerald, 123–24, 221, 270n
Put Out More Flags (Waugh), 170, 170n14

Quand j'étais vieux (Simenon), 185, 188, 215–16

Rabinowitz, Peter. J., 26n39
racism, 143, 144n29, 176, 181, 189n4, 253, 280
Radiance of the King (Camara), 299
reading, 6, 10, 14, 18, 27; act of, 108, 116, 122–27, 132–33
realism, 19, 30, 80, 115, 119, 127, 138, 151, 202–3, 287n18, 293
referentiality, 4, 9, 11–13, 16, 24–25, 24n33, 30, 66, 67, 95, 99, 129, 146, 172, 178, 293, 295. *See also* nonreferentiality
Règle du jeu (Leiris), 248
Remote People (Waugh), 19, 147–49, 152–54, 156, 160, 165, 167–68, 169, 170, 175–77, 178–80
representation: difficulty of, 215; mediated 115, 137–38
reversed gaze, 192, 207, 209, 215
Richardson, Brian, 231n8
Rimbaud, Arthur, 140, 154–55, 241, 244–45, 246, 253, 258, 263, 299
Road to Oxiana (Byron), 16–17
Road to Timbuktu: Down the Niger on the Trail of Mungo Park (Fremantle), 300
Roman d'un spahi (Loti), 70n1, 144n29,

221–22, 224, 226–28, 226n3, 228n5, 239, 239n16
Rousseau, Jean-Jacques, 255. *See also Confessions*
Roussel, Raymond, 246, 253, 260–65. *See also Comment j'ai écrit certains de mes livres; Impressions d'Afrique; Nouvelles Impressions d'Afrique*
Rules of the Game: Scratches (Leiris), 248
Ryan, Marie-Laure, 14n18, 14n19

Said, Edward W., 24–26, 29n41
Salwen, Michael B., 149n3
Schwarzenbach, Annemarie, 297
Scoop (Waugh), 135, 147, 150, 155, 157, 165, 167, 169, 171–73, 176, 179
Scott, David, 67, 126–27, 265. *See also Semiologies of Travel: From Gautier to Baudrillard*
Segalen, Victor, 22, 22n31, 302. *See also Équipée*
Selboe, Tone, 273n5
Semiologies of Travel: From Gautier to Baudrillard (Scott), 67
Seven Gothic Tales (Blixen), 272, 277, 281
Shadows on the Grass (Blixen), 271n4, 278n9, 285n16, 286, 289, 289n20
Sharpe, Sir Alfred, 96
Shelton, Marie-Denise, 259n14
Sherry, Norman, 229
Simenon, Georges, 7, 10–11, 19–21, 26, 29–38, 70, 107, 183–93, 195, 197, 201–4, 207–18, 238, 293–4, 301; romans du monde, 38, 183n2. *See also* Caraman, Georges; *African Trio; Blanc à lunettes; Coup de lune; Point-virgule; Quand j'étais vieux; 45° à l'ombre*
So Be It: or, the Chips Are Down (Gide), 61, 145
Socé, Ousmane Diop, 298n2
space: 2, 24, 27, 48, 79, 85, 89–92, 99–100, 102, 105–6, 108, 152, 162, 165, 173, 178, 185, 191, 193, 227, 247, 256, 283, 290, 293–95; of arrival, 42, 44; blank (vast/open/empty)

33n47, 44, 50–51, 57, 61, 71–72, 79, 83, 96, 293, 276; eroticized, 74; forest, 66, 81, 86; imaginary, 29–30, 176; phantom, 260–261, 264–65; possible 36, 148; potential 7; symbolic, 85–86; traversed 14; urban 77, 81; utopian, 100

spatio-temporal order, 1–2, 6, 18, 35, 42, 88–92, 98–100, 102–3, 108–9, 165, 172–73, 268–70, 291, 295

Spearey, Susan, 231n, 239n15

Stanley, Henry M., 21, 234, 244, 299. See also *How I Found Livingstone in Central Africa*; *My Kalulu, Prince, King and Slave. A Story of Central Africa*

Stannard, Martin, 168, 176

Stevens, Ray, 229n7

Stevenson, Robert Louis, 125, 127, 132. See also *The Master of Ballantrae*

Thacker, Andrew, 96–97, 97n10

Theroux, Paul, 300, 300n6, 302

thought report (narratorial report), 11, 133–34, 171, 197, 223, 272, 277

time: of travel, 102, 108; story-time and discourse-time, 12, 90n4, 98–100, 294; of writing, 17, 19, 61, 89, 102–3, 108

Todorov, Tzvetan, 29, 30n42, 88n1, 302–3. See also *On Human Diversity: Nationalism, Racism, and Exoticism in French Thought*

Tomashevsky, Boris, 88

Tourist in Africa (Waugh), 151–52, 300n6

Trachsel, Judith, 46

Travel Diary of a Philosopher I–II (Keyserling), 165

Travel Literature and the Evolution of the Novel (Adams), 2

travel literature: as genre of writing, 1–15, 17–19, 21–22, 24, 28, 30, 32, 41, 44, 51, 67, 88–92, 103–4, 108–9, 135, 137, 169, 178, 221, 254, 290, 292–96, 298–99, 301–2

traveller, 13, 13n16, 15–17; as allegorist, 303; as antitourist, 32n44, 166; as assimilator, 302; belated, 5, 31, 31n43, 150, 152, 190; as (pseudo)ethnographic, 254, 256, 297, 301–2; as exoticist, 302–3; as explorer, 16, 96, 106, 244; as impressionist, 303; as mad, 78; as profiteer, 302; as tourist, 16–17, 32, 32n45, 96, 150, 166–67, 218, 302–3; as travel snob, 32n45, 166–67, 179

travelling persona, 5, 11, 13, 13n16, 27, 292

Travels in the Congo (Gide), 19–20, 35–36, 38, 42, 51–61, 113, 116, 119, 124–25, 131, 135n23, 145

Tristes Tropiques (Lévi-Strauss), 22n32

unreliable narration, 31, 206

"Up-river Book" (Conrad), 228–35

Urbain, Jean-Didier, 103

Urry, John, 167

vicarious experience, 14, 24, 28

voice (narrative), 5, 11–13, 25–26, 95, 124, 178, 193–201, 216–17, 223, 227, 231, 232, 234–35, 293, 294, 298

Voyage, le monde et la bibliothèque (Montalbetti), 24n33

Warehime, Marja, 126n12

Waugh, Evelyn, 14n2, 147–57, 160–82, 238, 393–94, 299–300, 302. See also *Black Mischief*; *Diary*; "Incident in Azania"; *Labels: A Mediterranean Journal*; "Man who Liked Dickens"; *Put Out More Flags*; *Remote People*; *Scoop*; *Tourist in Africa*; *Waugh in Abyssinia*

Waugh in Abyssinia (Waugh), 8, 29, 147–48, 149n3, 152, 156–57, 160–61, 177, 180–81, 302

Ways of Escape (Greene) 93, 95n8, 108

West, Russell, 129, 232

White, John J., 28n40

Winter's Tales (Blixen), 272

Wolf, Werner, 19n26

Yacobi, Tamar, 274n7

Young, Robert, 26n37

THEORY AND INTERPRETATION OF NARRATIVE
James Phelan, Peter J. Rabinowitz, and Robyn Warhol, Series Editors

Because the series editors believe that the most significant work in narrative studies today contributes both to our knowledge of specific narratives and to our understanding of narrative in general, studies in the series typically offer interpretations of individual narratives and address significant theoretical issues underlying those interpretations. The series does not privilege one critical perspective but is open to work from any strong theoretical position.

Narrative Paths: African Travel in Modern Fiction and Nonfiction
KAI MIKKONEN

The Reader as Peeping Tom: Nonreciprocal Gazing in Narrative Fiction and Film
JEREMY HAWTHORN

Thomas Hardy's Brains: Psychology, Neurology, and Hardy's Imagination
SUZANNE KEEN

The Return of the Omniscient Narrator: Authorship and Authority in Twenty-First Century Fiction
PAUL DAWSON

Feminist Narrative Ethics: Tacit Persuasion in Modernist Form
KATHERINE SAUNDERS NASH

Real Mysteries: Narrative and the Unknowable
H. PORTER ABBOTT

A Poetics of Unnatural Narrative
EDITED BY JAN ALBER, HENRIK SKOV NIELSEN, AND BRIAN RICHARDSON

Narrative Discourse: Authors and Narrators in Literature, Film, and Art
PATRICK COLM HOGAN

Literary Identification from Charlotte Brontë to Tsitsi Dangarembga
LAURA GREEN

An Aesthetics of Narrative Performance: Transnational Theater, Literature, and Film in Contemporary Germany
CLAUDIA BREGER

Narrative Theory: Core Concepts and Critical Debates
DAVID HERMAN, JAMES PHELAN AND PETER J. RABINOWITZ, BRIAN RICHARDSON, AND ROBYN WARHOL

After Testimony: The Ethics and Aesthetics of Holocaust Narrative for the Future
EDITED BY JAKOB LOTHE, SUSAN RUBIN SULEIMAN, AND JAMES PHELAN

The Vitality of Allegory: Figural Narrative in Modern and Contemporary Fiction
GARY JOHNSON

Narrative Middles: Navigating the Nineteenth-Century British Novel
EDITED BY CAROLINE LEVINE AND MARIO ORTIZ-ROBLES

Fact, Fiction, and Form: Selected Essays
RALPH W. RADER. EDITED BY JAMES PHELAN AND DAVID H. RICHTER

The Real, the True, and the Told: Postmodern Historical Narrative and the Ethics of Representation
ERIC L. BERLATSKY

Franz Kafka: Narration, Rhetoric, and Reading
EDITED BY JAKOB LOTHE, BEATRICE SANDBERG, AND RONALD SPEIRS

Social Minds in the Novel
ALAN PALMER

Narrative Structures and the Language of the Self
MATTHEW CLARK

Imagining Minds: The Neuro-Aesthetics of Austen, Eliot, and Hardy
KAY YOUNG

Postclassical Narratology: Approaches and Analyses
EDITED BY JAN ALBER AND MONIKA FLUDERNIK

Techniques for Living: Fiction and Theory in the Work of Christine Brooke-Rose
KAREN R. LAWRENCE

Towards the Ethics of Form in Fiction: Narratives of Cultural Remission
LEONA TOKER

Tabloid, Inc.: Crimes, Newspapers, Narratives
V. PENELOPE PELIZZON AND NANCY M. WEST

Narrative Means, Lyric Ends: Temporality in the Nineteenth-Century British Long Poem
MONIQUE R. MORGAN

Joseph Conrad: Voice, Sequence, History, Genre
EDITED BY JAKOB LOTHE, JEREMY HAWTHORN, AND JAMES PHELAN

Understanding Nationalism: On Narrative, Cognitive Science, and Identity
PATRICK COLM HOGAN

The Rhetoric of Fictionality: Narrative Theory and the Idea of Fiction
RICHARD WALSH

Experiencing Fiction: Judgments, Progressions, and the Rhetorical Theory of Narrative
JAMES PHELAN

Unnatural Voices: Extreme Narration in Modern and Contemporary Fiction
BRIAN RICHARDSON

Narrative Causalities
EMMA KAFALENOS

Why We Read Fiction: Theory of Mind and the Novel
LISA ZUNSHINE

I Know That You Know That I Know: Narrating Subjects from Moll Flanders *to* Marnie
GEORGE BUTTE

Bloodscripts: Writing the Violent Subject
ELANA GOMEL

Surprised by Shame: Dostoevsky's Liars and Narrative Exposure
DEBORAH A. MARTINSEN

Having a Good Cry: Effeminate Feelings and Pop-Culture Forms
ROBYN R. WARHOL

Politics, Persuasion, and Pragmatism: A Rhetoric of Feminist Utopian Fiction
ELLEN PEEL

Telling Tales: Gender and Narrative Form in Victorian Literature and Culture
ELIZABETH LANGLAND

Narrative Dynamics: Essays on Time, Plot, Closure, and Frames
EDITED BY BRIAN RICHARDSON

Breaking the Frame: Metalepsis and the Construction of the Subject
DEBRA MALINA

Invisible Author: Last Essays
CHRISTINE BROOKE-ROSE

Ordinary Pleasures: Couples, Conversation, and Comedy
KAY YOUNG

Narratologies: New Perspectives on Narrative Analysis
EDITED BY DAVID HERMAN

Before Reading: Narrative Conventions and the Politics of Interpretation
PETER J. RABINOWITZ

Matters of Fact: Reading Nonfiction over the Edge
DANIEL W. LEHMAN

The Progress of Romance: Literary Historiography and the Gothic Novel
DAVID H. RICHTER

A Glance Beyond Doubt: Narration, Representation, Subjectivity
SHLOMITH RIMMON-KENAN

Narrative as Rhetoric: Technique, Audiences, Ethics, Ideology
JAMES PHELAN

Misreading Jane Eyre: *A Postformalist Paradigm*
JEROME BEATY

Psychological Politics of the American Dream: The Commodification of Subjectivity in Twentieth-Century American Literature
LOIS TYSON

Understanding Narrative
EDITED BY JAMES PHELAN AND PETER J. RABINOWITZ

Framing Anna Karenina: *Tolstoy, the Woman Question, and the Victorian Novel*
AMY MANDELKER

Gendered Interventions: Narrative Discourse in the Victorian Novel
ROBYN R. WARHOL

Reading People, Reading Plots: Character, Progression, and the Interpretation of Narrative
JAMES PHELAN

www.ingramcontent.com/pod-product-compliance
Lightning Source LLC
Chambersburg PA
CBHW030106010526
44116CB00005B/115